Topic relevant selected content from the highest rated entries, typeset, printed and shipped.

Combine the advantages of up-to-date and in-depth knowledge with the convenience of printed books.

A portion of the proceeds of each book will be donated to the Wikimedia Foundation to support their mission: to empower and engage people around the world to collect and develop educational content under a free license or in the public domain, and to disseminate it effectively and globally.

The content within this book was generated collaboratively by volunteers. Please be advised that nothing found here has necessarily been reviewed by people with the expertise required to provide you with complete, accurate or reliable information. Some information in this book maybe misleading or simply wrong. The publisher does not guarantee the validity of the information found here. If you need specific advice (for example, medical, legal, financial, or risk management) please seek a professional who is licensed or knowledgeable in that area.

# Contents


Tablet computer 1
Acer Tablet 13
Archos 101 15
Archos 43 16
Archos 70 17
ASUS Eee 18
ASUS Eee Pad Transformer 21
EnTourage eDGe 23
Pocket eDGe 25
ExoPC 27
History of tablet computers 30
Huawei Ideos Tablet S7 35
iPad 36
iPad 2 53
Magic W3 62
Microsoft Courier 64
Motorola Xoom 67
Pocket computer phone 71
Sakshat 73
T-Mobile G-Slate 76
Toshiba Tablet 77
Comparison of tablet PCs 78
Microsoft Tablet PC 87
Encipher Inye 93
EO Personal Communicator 94
Fujitsu Lifebook T900 95
Gateway C-Series 97
HP Compaq TC1100 98
HP Compaq TC4200 100
HP Compaq TC4400 101
HP Pavilion TX1000 Series Tablet PC 102
HP Slate 500 104
HP TouchSmart 106
HTC Flyer 110
Ink Serialized Format 112
MobileDemand 112

OLPC XO-3 114
Pepper Pad 114
Soft Input Panel 116
Tablet personal computer 117
Tablet PC Input Panel 127
TabletKiosk 129
Ultra-mobile PC 130
Windows Journal 135
Mobile operating system 136
Linaro 149
Maemo 152
MeeGo 166
MotoMagx 170
Palm OS 171
Pilot-link 182
PlayStation Portable system software 183
Series 30 (software platform) 192
Series 40 193
Smarterphone 195
Smeegol Linux 197
Symbian Foundation 198
Symbian 200
webOS 215
Comparison of ARM tablets 223

# References

Article Sources and Contributors 225
Image Sources, Licenses and Contributors 229

# Article Licenses

License 231

# Tablet computer

**Tablet computer**

The Apple iPad

A **tablet computer**, or simply **tablet**, is a complete mobile computer, larger than a mobile phone or personal digital assistant, integrated into a flat touch screen and primarily operated by touching the screen. It often uses an onscreen virtual keyboard or a digital pen rather than a physical keyboard.[1] [2]

The term may also apply to a "convertible" notebook computer whose keyboard is attached to the touchscreen by a swivel joint or slide joint so that the screen may lie with its back upon the keyboard, covering it and exposing only the screen for touch operation.

## Tablet computers and tablet PCs

As of 2010, two distinctly different types of tablet computing devices exist, whose operating systems are of different origin.

Older tablet personal computers are mainly x86 based[3] and are fully functional personal computers employing a slightly modified personal computer OS (such as Windows or Ubuntu Linux) supporting their touch-screen, instead of a traditional display, mouse and keyboard. A typical tablet personal computer needs to be stylus driven, because operating the typical desktop based OS requires a high precision to select GUI widgets, such as a the close window button.

Since mid-2010, new tablet computers with mobile operating systems forgo the Wintel paradigm, have a different interface and have created a new type of computing device.[4] These mobile OS tablet computer devices are normally finger driven and use multi-touch capacitive touch screens, instead of the simple resistive touchscreens of typical stylus driven systems (also a standard external USB keyboard can be used). First of these was the iPad, with Samsung Galaxy Tab and others following. In forgoing the x86 precondition (a requisite of Windows compatibility), the new class of tablet computers use a version of an ARM architecture processor heretofore used in portable equipment (e.g., MP3 players and cell phones) now powerful enough (especially with the introduction of the ARM Cortex family) for tasks such as internet browsing, light production work and gaming.[5]

### Tablets based on IBM-PC architecture

A *tablet personal computer (tablet PC)* is a portable personal computer equipped with a touchscreen as a primary input device, and running a (modified) classic desktop OS.[6] designed to be operated and owned by an individual.[7] The term was made popular as a concept presented by Microsoft in 2000[8] and 2001[9] but tablet PCs now refer to any tablet-sized personal computer regardless of the (desktop) operating system[10]

### Post-PC Tablets

Many tablets do not use a traditional desktop OS or use the Wintel paradigm,[11] nor are x86 based. Most often their OS is a Unix-like OS, such as Darwin, Linux or QNX. The first was the iPad with iOS, and others continue the common trend towards multi-touch and other natural user interface features, as well as flash memory solid-state storage drives, and 2-second warm-boot times. Some use ARM for longer battery life versus battery weight. Some have 3G mobile telephony capabilities.[12]

### Developing programs for tablet computers

A significant trait to define whether a tablet computer can be regarded as a personal computer is the ability for the final user to install arbitrary or self-developed software. The new class of devices heralded by the iPad has spurred the tendency of a walled garden approach where the vendor reserves rights as to what can be installed. The software development kits for these platforms are restricted and the vendor must approve the final application for distribution to users. Proponents of open source software deem that these restrictions on software installation and lack of administrator rights make this category one that, in their view, cannot be properly named *personal computers*.[13] [14] [15] But there are newer mobile operating system based tablet computers that don't use the walled garden concept, and are like personal computers in this regard.

## History

The tablet computer and the associated special operating software is an example of pen computing technology, and thus the development of tablets has deep historical roots. The depth of these roots can be quite surprising to people who are only familiar with current commercial products. For example, the first patent for an electronic tablet used for handwriting was granted in 1888.[16] The first patent for a system that recognized handwritten characters by analyzing the handwriting motion was granted in 1915.[17] The first publicly-demonstrated system using a tablet and handwriting text recognition instead of a keyboard for working with a modern digital computer dates to 1956.[18] Alan Kay attempted to formulate his Dynabook concept as a tablet as early as 1968; to this day, his concept has not yet been fully realized.

In addition to many academic and research systems, there were several companies with commercial products in the 1980s: Pencept, Communications Intelligence Corporation, and Linus were among the best known of a crowded field. Later, GO Corp. brought out the PenPoint OS operating system for a tablet product: one of the patents from GO corporation was the subject of recent infringement lawsuit concerning the Tablet PC operating system.[19]

One early implementation of a Linux tablet was the ProGear by FrontPath. The ProGear used a Transmeta chip and a resistive digitizer. The ProGear initially came with a version of Slackware Linux, but could later be bought with Windows 98.

In 1999, Microsoft attempted to re-institute the by-then decades-old tablet concept by assigning two well-known experts in the field, from Xerox Palo Alto Research Center, to the project.[20]

In 2000 Microsoft coined the term "Microsoft tablet PC" for tablet PCs built to Microsoft's specification, and running a licensed specific tablet enhanced version of its Microsoft Windows OS.[8] [21] Microsoft Tablet PCs were targeted to address business needs mainly as note-taking devices, and as rugged devices for field work.[22] Tablet PCs failed to gain popularity in the consumer space because of unresolved problems.[23]

The tablet computer market was invigorated by Apple through the introduction of the iPad device in 2010.[24] While the iPad places restrictions on the owner to install software[13] [14] [15] thus deviating it from the PC tradition, its attention to detail for the touch interface[25] is considered a milestone in the history of the development of the tablet computer.[23] On May 20, 2010, IDC published a press release defining the term *media tablet* as personal devices with screens from 7 to 12 inches, lightweight operating systems "currently based on ARM processors" which "provide a broad range of applications and connectivity, differentiating them from primarily single-function devices such as ereaders".[26] IDC also predicted a market growth for tablets from 7.6 million units in 2010 to more than 46 million units in 2014. More recent reports show predictions from various analysts in the range from 26 to 64 million units in 2013. [27] On 2nd March 2011 Apple announced that 15 million iPads had been sold in three fiscal quarters of 2010.[28]

At Consumer Electronics Show 2011, over 80 new tablets were announced to compete with the iPad. Companies who announced tablets included: Motorola which released its Xoom tablet (Android 3.0) , Samsung came up with its new Samsung Galaxy Tab (Android 2.2), Research in Motion demonstrated their BlackBerry Playbook, Vizio with the Via Tablet, Toshiba with the Android 3.0 - run Toshiba tablet, and others include Asus, and the startup company Notion Ink. Many of these tablets are set to be running Android 3.0 Honeycomb (except some which are also featuring Android 2.3 or above), Google's mobile operating system for tablets.[29]

In the healthcare sector, tablet computers can be used for data capture - such as registering feedback on the patient experience at the bedside.

## Touch user interface

A key and common component among tablet computers is touch input. This allows the user to navigate easily and intuitively and type with a virtual keyboard on the screen.

Galaxy Tab

A tablet presents a more natural user interface to the user than a command line interface or the traditional mouse driven WIMP interface . The event processing of the operating system must respond to touches rather than clicks of a keyboard or mouse, which allows integrated hand-eye operation, a natural part of the somatosensory system. Although the device implementation differs from more traditional PCs or laptops, tablets are disrupting the current vendor sales by weakening traditional laptop PC sales in favor of the current tablet computers.[30] [31] [32] This is even more true of the "finger driven multi-touch" interface of the more recent tablet computers, which often emulate the way actual objects behave.

## Handwriting recognition

Because tablet personal computers normally use a stylus, they quite often implement handwriting recognition, while other tablet computers with finger driven screens do not. Finger driven screens however are potentially better suited for inputting "variable width stroke based" characters, like Chinese/Japanese/Korean writing, due to their built in capability of "pressure sensing". However at the moment not much of this potential is already used, and as a result even on tablet computers Chinese users often use a (virtual) keyboard for input.[33]

Chinese characters like this one meaning "person" can be written by handwriting recognition (人, Mandarin: *rén*, Korean: *in*, Japanese: *jin*, *nin*; *hito*, Cantonese: jan4). The character has two strokes, the first shown here in dark, and the second in red. The black area represents the starting position of the writing instrument.

## Touchscreen hardware

Touchscreens are usually one of two forms;

- **Resistive**: Resistive touchscreens are passive and can respond to any kind of pressure on the screen. They allow a high level of precision (which may be needed, when the touch screen tries to emulate a mouse for precision pointing, which in Tablet personal computers is common) but may require calibration to be accurate. Because of the high resolution of detection, a stylus is often used for resistive screens. Although some possibility exist for implementing multi-touch on a resistive touch-screen, the possibilities are quite limited. As modern tablet computers tend to heavily lean on the use of multi-touch, this technology has faded out on high-end devices where it has been replaced by capacitive touchscreens.
- **Capacitive**: Capacitive touchscreens tend to be more accurate and responsive than resistive screens. Because they require a conductive material, such as a finger tip, for input, they are not common among (stylus using) Tablet PCs but are more prominent on the smaller scale "tablet computer" devices for ease of use, which generally do not use a stylus, and need multi-touch capabilities.

Other touch technology used in tablets include:

- Palm recognition. It prevents inadvertent palms or other contacts from disrupting the pen's input.
- Multi-touch capabilities, which can recognize multiple simultaneous finger touches, allowing for enhanced manipulation of on-screen objects.[34]

Some professional-grade Tablet PCs use pressure sensitive films that additionally allows pressure sensitivity such as those on graphics tablets.

Concurrently capacitive touch-screens, which use finger tip detection can often detect the size of the touched area, and can make some conclusions to the pressure force used, for a similar result.[35]

## Form factor

Tablet computers come in a range of sizes, currently ranging from tablet PCs to PDAs. Tablet personal computers tend to be as large as laptops and often are the largest usable size for mobile tablet computing while the new generation of tablet computers can be (much) smaller and use a RISC (ARM or MIPS) CPU, and in size can border on PDAs.

### Booklet

Booklet computers are dual-touchscreen tablet computers that fold like a book. Typical booklet computers are equipped with multi-touch screens and pen writing recognition capabilities. They are designed to be used as digital day planners, internet surfing devices, project planners, music players, and displays for video, live TV, and e-reading.

### Slate

Slate computers, which resemble writing slates, are tablet computers without a dedicated keyboard. For text input, users rely on handwriting recognition via an active digitizer, touching an on-screen keyboard using fingertips or a stylus, or using an external keyboard that can usually be attached via a wireless or USB connection.

Slate computers typically incorporate small (8.4–14.1 inches/21–36 centimetres) LCD screens and have been popular in vertical markets such as health care, education, hospitality and field work. Applications for field work often require a tablet computer that has rugged specifications that ensure long life by resisting heat, humidity, and drop/vibration damage. This added focus on mobility and/or ruggedness often leads to elimination of moving parts that could hinder these qualities.

### Convertible

Convertible notebooks have a base body with an attached keyboard. They more closely resemble modern laptops, and are usually heavier and larger than slates.

Typically, the base of a convertible attaches to the display at a single joint called a swivel hinge or rotating hinge. The joint allows the screen to rotate through 180° and fold down on top of the keyboard to provide a flat writing surface. This design, although the most common, creates a physical point of weakness on the notebook.

A Lenovo X61 in slate mode

Some manufacturers have attempted to overcome these weak points. The Panasonic Toughbook 19, for example, is advertised as a more durable convertible notebook. One model by Acer (the TravelMate C210) has a sliding design in which the screen slides up from the slate-like position and locks into place to provide the laptop mode.

Sliding screens were presented at CES 2011. The first product to use it is the Samsung Sliding PC7 Series,[36] a tablet with Intel Atom hardware and a unique sliding screen that allows the product to be used as a laptop or slate tablet when the screen is locked in place covering the whole keyboard. The concept still has to prove its reliability, but is intended to combine the virtues of tablet PCs with those of notebooks. Also presented was the upcoming Inspiron Duo from Dell, which rotates the screen horizontally when opened. Convertibles like that with hardware specs of a netbook are called netvertibles.

### Hybrid

Hybrids, a term coined by users of the HP/Compaq TC1000 and TC1100 series, share the features of the slate and convertible by using a detachable keyboard that operates in a similar fashion to a convertible when attached. Hybrids are not to be confused with slate models with detachable keyboards; detachable keyboards for pure slate models do not rotate to allow the tablet to rest on it like a convertible.

### Desktop

A *tablet personal computer (tablet PC)* is a portable personal computer equipped with a touchscreen as a primary input device, and running a (modified) classic desktop OS.[6] designed to be operated and owned by an individual.[7] The term was made popular as a concept presented by Microsoft in 2000[8] and 2001[9] but tablet PCs now refer to any tablet-sized personal computer regardless of the (desktop) operating system[10]

Older tablet personal computers are mainly x86 based,[3] and are fully functional personal computers employing a slightly modified personal computer OS (Like Windows or Ubuntu Linux) supporting their touch-screen, instead of a traditional display mouse, and keyboard. A typical tablet personal computer needs to be stylus driven, because operating the typical desktop based OS requires a high precision to select GUI widgets, such as a the close window button.

## System architecture

Two major computer architectures compete in the tablet market,[37] x86 and ARM architecture. x86, including x86-64, is popular on tablet PCs due to its use on laptops which can share common software and hardware and which can run a version of Windows. There are also non-PC based x86 tablets like the JooJoo. ARM gained popularity following the success of the iPad.[38] ARM is more power and cost efficient for mobile computing and is gaining popularity for smaller tablets from other manufacturers such as Samsung with the Galaxy Tab which runs on Android.

## Other features

- **Accelerometer**: An accelerometer is a unit that detects the physical movements of the tablet. This allows greater flexibility of use since tablets do not necessarily have a fixed direction of use. The accelerometer can also be used to detect the orientation of the tablet relative to the center of the earth, but can also detect movement of the tablet, both of which can be used as an alternative control interface for a tablet's software.
- **Ambient light and proximity sensors** are additional "senses", that can provide controlling input for the tablet.
- **Storage drive**: Large tablets use storage drives similar to laptops, while smaller ones tend to use drives similar to MP3 Players or have on-board flash memory. They also often have ports for removable storage such as Secure Digital cards. Due to the nature of the use of tablets, solid-state memory is often preferable due to its better resistance to damage during movement.
- **Wireless**: Because tablets by design are mobile computers, wireless connections are less restrictive to motion than wired connections. Wi-Fi connectivity has become ubiquitous among tablets. Bluetooth is commonly used for connecting peripherals and communicating with local devices in place of a wired USB connection.
- **3D**: Following mobile phone, there are also 3D slate tablet with dual lens at the back of the tablet and also provided with blue-red glasses.[39]

## Operating systems and vendors

Tablets, like regular computers, can run a number of operating systems. These come in two classes, namely desktop-based operating systems and mobile-based ("phone-like") operating systems.

For the former class popular OS's are Microsoft Windows, and a range of Linux distributions. HP is developing enterprise-level tablets under Windows and consumer-oriented tablets under webOS. In the latter class the popular variants include Apple iOS, and Google Android. Manufacturers are also testing the market for products with Windows CE, Chrome OS,[40] [41] and so forth.

Boot times for iPads are one-half the boot times for current Windows 7 netbooks, which can take over 50 seconds to display the login prompt.[42] The BIOS initialization for a PC, which has remained unchanged since the invention of the PC, can still take 25 seconds.[43]

### Tablet PC operating systems

#### Microsoft

Following Windows for Pen Computing, Microsoft has been developing support for tablets runnings Windows under the Microsoft Tablet PC name.[44] According to a 2001 Microsoft definition[45] of the term, "Microsoft Tablet PCs" are pen-based, fully functional x86 PCs with handwriting and voice recognition functionality. Tablet PCs use the same hardware as normal laptops but add support for pen input. For specialized support for pen input, Microsoft released Windows XP Tablet PC Edition. Today there is no tablet specific version of Windows but instead support is built in to both Home and Business versions of Windows Vista and Windows 7. Tablets running Windows get the added functionality of using the touchscreen for mouse input, hand writing recognition, and gesture support. Following Tablet PC, Microsoft announced the UMPC initiative in 2006 which brought Windows tablets to a smaller, touch-centric form factor. This was relaunched in 2010 as Slate PC, to promote tablets running Windows 7, ahead of Apple's iPad launch.[46] [47] Slate PCs are expected to benefit from mobile hardware advances derived from the success of the netbooks.

While many tablet manufacturers are moving to the ARM architecture with lighter operating systems, Microsoft has stood firm to Windows.[48] [49] [50] [51] Though Microsoft has Windows CE for ARM support it has kept its target market for the smartphone industry with Windows Mobile and the new Windows CE 6 based Windows Phone 7. Some manufacturers, however, still have shown prototypes of Windows CE-based tablets running a custom shell.[52] To date, the full Windows 7 does not yet support ARM architecture.[53]

#### Linux

One early implementation of a Linux tablet was the ProGear by FrontPath. The ProGear used a Transmeta chip and a resistive digitizer. The ProGear initially came with a version of Slackware Linux, but could later be bought with Windows 98. Because these computers are general purpose IBM PC compatible machines, they can run many different operating systems. However, the device is no longer for sale and FrontPath has ceased operations. It is important to note that many touch screen sub-notebook computers can run any of several Linux distributions with little customization.

X.org now supports screen rotation and tablet input through Wacom drivers, and handwriting recognition software from both the Qt-based Qtopia and GTK+-based Internet Tablet OS provide promising free and open source systems for future development.

Open source note taking software in Linux includes applications such as Xournal (which supports PDF file annotation), Gournal (a Gnome based note taking application), and the Java-based Jarnal (which supports handwriting recognition as a built-in function). Before the advent of the aforementioned software, many users had to rely on on-screen keyboards and alternative text input methods like Dasher. There is a stand alone handwriting recognition program available, CellWriter, which requires users to write letters separately in a grid.

A number of Linux based OS projects are dedicated to tablet PCs. Since all these are open source, they are freely available and can be run or ported to devices that conform to the tablet PC design. Maemo (rebranded MeeGo in 2010), a Debian Linux based graphical user environment, was developed for the Nokia Internet Tablet devices (770, N800, N810 & N900). It is currently in generation 5, and has a vast array of applications available in both official and user supported repositories. The Ubuntu Netbook Remix edition, as well as the Intel sponsored Moblin project, both have touchscreen support integrated into their user interfaces. Canonical has hinted at better supporting tablets with the Unity UI for Ubuntu 10.10.[54]

TabletKiosk currently offers a hybrid digitizer / touch device running openSUSE Linux. It is the first device with this feature to support Linux.

### Intel and Nokia

Nokia entered the tablet space with the Nokia 770 running Maemo, a Debian-based Linux distribution custom-made for their Internet Tablet line. The product line continued with the N900 which is the first to add phone capabilities.

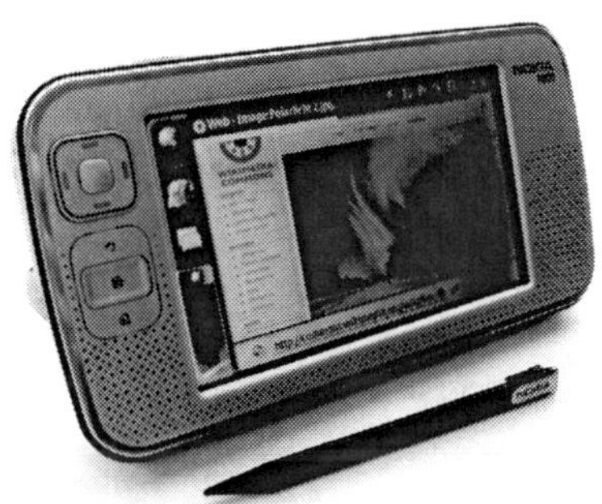

The Nokia N800

Intel, following the launch of the UMPC, started the Mobile Internet Device initiative, which took the same hardware and combined it with a Linux operating system custom-built for portable tablets. Intel co-developed the lightweight Moblin operating system following the successful launch of the Atom CPU series on netbooks. Intel is also setting tablet goals for Atom, going forward from 2010.[55] [56]

### MeeGo

MeeGo is a new Linux-based operating system developed by Intel and Nokia that supports Netbooks, Smartphones and Tablet PCs. In 2010, Nokia and Intel combined the Maemo and Moblin projects to form MeeGo. The first tablet using MeeGo is the Neofonie WeTab launched September 2010 in Germany. The WeTab uses an extended version of the MeeGo operating system called WeTab OS. WeTab OS adds runtimes for Android and Adobe AIR and provides a proprietary user interface optimized for the WeTab device.

## Mobile operating systems

Tablets not following the personal computer tradition use operating systems in the style of those developed for PDAs and smartphones.

### Apple

Apple's tablet product is the iPad, a tablet computer that mainly focuses on media consumption such as web browsing, email, photos, videos, and e-reading. A WiFi-only model of the tablet was released in April 2010, and a WiFi+3G model was introduced about a month later, using a no-contract data plan from AT&T. Since then, the iPad 2 has launched, bringing 3G support from both AT&T and Verizon Wireless.

The iPad in its case

The iPad runs a version of iOS which was first created for the iPhone and iPod Touch. Unlike Windows on Tablet PCs, iOS is built for the ARM architecture. Previous to the iPad's launch, there were long standing rumors of an Apple tablet, though they were often about a product running Mac OS X and being in line with Apple's Macintosh computers.[57] This became partially true when a 3rd party offered customized Macbooks with pen input, known as the Modbook.

Previous to Apple's commercialization of the iPad, Axiotron introduced at Macworld in 2007[58] an aftermarket, heavily modified Apple MacBook called Modbook, a Mac OS X-based tablet personal computer. The Modbook uses Apple's Inkwell for handwriting and gesture recognition, and use digitization hardware from Wacom. To get Mac OS X to talk to the digitizer on the integrated tablet, the Modbook is supplied with a third-party driver called TabletMagic [59]; Wacom does not provide driver support for this device.

### Research in Motion

The BlackBerry PlayBook is a tablet computer announced in September 2010 which runs the BlackBerry Tablet OS.[59] The OS is based on the QNX system that Research in Motion acquired in early 2010. Delivery to developers and enterprise customers is expected in October 2010. The BlackBerry PlayBook was officially released to US and Canadian consumers on April 19th, 2011.

### Google

Google's linux-based Android operating system has been targeted by manufacturers for the tablet space following its success on smartphones due to its open nature and support for low-cost ARM systems much like Apple's iOS. In 2010, there have been numerous announcements of such tablets.[60] However, much of Android's tablet initiative comes from manufacturers as Google primarily focuses its development on smartphones and restricts the App Market from non-phone devices.[61] There is, moreover, talk of tablet support from Google coming to its web-centric Chrome OS.[62] [63] Some vendors such as Motorola[64] and Lenovo[65] are delaying deployment of their tablet computers until 2011, after Android is reworked to include more tablet features.[66]

### HP

**HP's webOS**: Hewlett Packard has announced the TouchPad running webOS 3.0 on a 1.2Ghz Snapdragon CPU will be release in June 2011.

### OLPC

The **OLPC** organization is developing a new version of the OLPC, strongly resembling a tablet computer, called the OLPC XO-3, running its "Sugar" operating system, based on Linux. The new XO-3 will be based on ARM technology from Marvell.[67]

# Comparison with laptop computers

The advantages and disadvantages of tablet computers are highly subjective measures. What appeals to one user may be exactly what disappoints another. The following are commonly cited opinions of tablet computers versus laptops:

## Advantages

- Usage in environments not conducive to a keyboard and mouse such as lying in bed, standing, or handling with a single hand.
- Lighter weight, lower power models can function similarly to dedicated reading devices like the Amazon Kindle.
- Touch environment makes navigation easier than conventional use of keyboard and mouse or touch pad in certain contexts such as image manipulation, musical, or mouse oriented games.
- Digital painting and image editing are more precise and intuitive than painting or sketching with a mouse.
- The ability for easier or faster entry of diagrams, mathematical notations, and symbols.
- Allows, with the proper software, universal input, independent from different keyboard localizations.

- Some users find it more direct and pleasant to use a stylus, pen or finger to point and tap on objects, rather than use a mouse or touchpad, which are not directly connected to the pointer on screen.

### Disadvantages

- Higher price — convertible tablet computers can cost significantly more than non-tablet portable PCs although this premium has been predicted to fall.[68]
- Input speed — handwriting or typing on a virtual keyboard can be significantly slower than typing speed on a conventional keyboard, the latter of which can be as high as 50-150 WPM; however, Slideit, Swype and other technologies are offered in an effort to narrow the gap.
- Ergonomics - a tablet computer, or a folded slate PC, does not provide room for a wrist rest. In addition, the user will need to move their arm constantly while writing.
- Weaker video capabilities - Most tablet computers are equipped with embedded graphics processors instead of discrete graphics cards. In July 2010, the only tablet PC with a discrete graphics card was the HP TouchSmart tm2t, which has the ATI Mobility Radeon HD5450 as an optional extra.
- Business-oriented tablet personal computers have been slow sellers from 2001 to date.[69]
- Screen risk - Tablet computers are handled more than conventional laptops, yet many are built on similar frames; in addition, since their screens also serve as input devices, they run a higher risk of screen damage from impacts and misuse.
- Hinge risk - A convertible tablet computer's screen hinge is often required to rotate around two axes, unlike a normal laptop screen, subsequently increasing the number of possible mechanical and electrical (digitizer and video cables, embedded WiFi antennas, etc.) failure points.

## Tablets in developing countries

OLPC XO-3, a tablet computer concept[70]

The low hardware requirements and easy operation of tablet computers has made it subject to various design studies for use in developing countries. Prototype tablet computers such as the Sakshat have been projected to cost $35, according to researchers in India which shall be soon available for the masses as the cheapest tablet working on Android with full functionality;[71] [72] however the bill of materials currently comes to $47.[73] One laptop per child (OLPC) plans to introduce a tablet computer for $100.[74] Nicholas Negroponte, Chairman of OLPC, has invited the Indian researchers to MIT to begin sharing the OLPC design resources for their tablet computers.[75] OLPC has been awarded a grant for an interim step to their next generation tablet, OLPC XO-3.[76]

# References

[1] Editors PC Magazine. "Definition of: tablet computer" (http://www.pcmag.com/encyclopedia_term/0,2542,t=tablet+computer&i=52520,00.asp). *PC Magazine*. . Retrieved April 17, 2010.

[2] Editors Dictionary.com, "tablet computer - 1 dictionary result" (http://dictionary.reference.com/browse/tablet+computer), *Dictionary.com*, , retrieved April 17, 2010

[3] Are Intel, AMD threatened by tablet growth? Every two to three tablets sold means one lost PC sale, analyst says (http://www.marketwatch.com/story/tablet-growth-may-threaten-pc-chip-makers-2010-10-22?pagenumber=2) accessdate=2010-10-24

[4] Lev Grossman (Thursday, Apr. 01, 2010) " Do We Need the iPad? A TIME Review (http://www.time.com/time/business/article/0,8599,1976932,00.html)", *TIME*

[5] The Coming War: ARM versus x86 (http://vanshardware.com/2010/08/mirror-the-coming-war-arm-versus-x86/) Mirror for: *The Bright Side of News* April 8, 2010

[6] Beck H *et al*, *Business Communication and Technologies in a Changing World*, Macmillan Education Australia, 2009, p 402

[7] Haven, Kendall F. *100 greatest science inventions of all time*, Libraries Unlimited, 2006, p 191

[8] Bill Gates introduces Tablet PC, COMDEX Nov 2000 (http://www.microsoft.com/presspass/features/2000/nov00/11-13comdex.mspx)

[9] Page, M Microsoft Tablet PC Overview (http://www.transmetazone.com/articleview.cfm?articleID=499), TransmetaZone, 2000-12-21

[10] Kuhn, Bradley M. Free software and cellphones (http://www.fsf.org/working-together/next-steps/free-software-phones), Free Software Foundation, 2010

[11] Roger Kay on Intel and Microsoft, as quoted April 29, 2011: "Clearly, each one is looking at a post-PC world..." MarketWatch (http://www.marketwatch.com/story/microsoft-offers-more-muted-view-of-pcs-2011-04-29)

[12] i.e. ZTE V9 Tablet and Samsung Galaxy Tab and some iPads

[13] Brown, Peter iPad is iBad for freedom (http://www.fsf.org/news/ibad_launch), Free Software Foundation, 2010

[14] Cherry, Steven The iPad Is Not a Computer (http://spectrum.ieee.org/consumer-electronics/portable-devices/the-ipad-is-not-a-computer), IEEE Spectrum, 2010

[15] Conlon, Tom The iPad's Closed System: Sometimes I Hate Being Right (http://www.popsci.com/gadgets/article/2010-01/ipadâ s-closed-system-sometimes-i-hate-being-right), Popular Science, 2010

[16] Gray, Elisha (1888-07-31), *Telautograph* (http://www.freepatentsonline.com/386815.pdf), United States Patent 386,815 (full image),

[17] Goldberg, H.E. (1915-12-28), *Controller* (http://www.freepatentsonline.com/1117184.pdf), United States Patent 1,117,184 (full image),

[18] Dimond, Tom (1957-12-01), *Devices for reading handwritten characters* (http://rwservices.no-ip.info:81/pens/biblio70.html#Dimond57), Proceedings of Eastern Joint Computer Conference, pp. 232–237, , retrieved 2008-08-23

[19] Mintz, Jessica (2008-04-04), *Microsoft to Appeal $367M Patent Ruling* (http://www.usatoday.com/tech/products/2008-04-04-2507619152_x.htm), The Associated Press, , retrieved 2008-09-04

[20] John Markoff, *The New York Times*, August 30, 1999, " Microsoft brings in top talent to pursue old goal: the tablet (http://www.nytimes.com/1999/08/30/business/microsoft-brings-in-top-talent-to-pursue-old-goal-the-tablet.html)"

[21] MSDN, *Microsoft Tablet PC* (http://msdn.microsoft.com/en-us/library/ms840465.aspx)

[22] "Tablet PC: Coming to an Office Near You?" (http://itmanagement.earthweb.com/netsys/article.php/1495701/Tablet-PC-Coming-to-an-Office-Near-You.htm). .

[23] Bright, Peter Ballmer (and Microsoft) still doesn't get the iPad (http://arstechnica.com/microsoft/news/2010/07/ballmer-and-microsoft-still-doesnt-get-the-ipad.ars), Ars Technica, 2010

[24] Eaton, Nick The iPad/tablet PC market defined? (http://blog.seattlepi.com/microsoft/archives/199045.asp), Seattle Post-Intelligencer, 2010

[25] Jobs, Steve Thoughts on Flash (http://www.apple.com/hotnews/thoughts-on-flash/), Apple, 2010

[26] IDC Press Release:. "IDC Forecasts 7.6 Million Media Tablets to be Shipped Worldwide in 2010" (http://www.idc.com/about/viewpressrelease.jsp?containerId=prUS22345010§ionId=null&elementId=null&pageType=SYNOPSIS). .

[27] Bright Side Of News. "ZTE Pushes Into US With Light 2 Tablet And Pixel Qi Display" (http://www.brightsideofnews.com/news/2011/2/17/zte-pushes-into-us-with-light-2-tablet-and-pixel-qi-display.aspx). .

[28] 15 Million iPads sold from April 2010 through December 2010, for 9.5 Billion USD in 2010. (http://www.engadget.com/2011/03/02/live-from-apples-ipad-2-event/) Accessdate=2011-3-2

[29] Los Angeles Times Jan 6 2011 (http://articles.latimes.com/2011/jan/06/business/la-fi-ces-tablets-20110106) Tablets at CES

[30] Best Buy: iPad cutting into laptop sales (http://news.cnet.com/8301-13579_3-20016818-37.html)

[31] Notebook sales growth goes negative. Can we blame the iPad yet? (http://tech.fortune.cnn.com/2010/09/17/notebook-sales-growth-goes-negative-can-we-blame-the-ipad-yet/)

[32] Tablets hurt PC sales but not Macs (http://www.marketwatch.com/story/tablets-hurt-pc-sales-but-not-apples-mac-2010-10-13)

[33] China using keyboards versus tablet input (http://webcache.googleusercontent.com/search?q=cache:rX3A5F0UJKQJ:ca.news.yahoo.com/s/afp/100826/technology/lifestyle_hongkong_china_japan_culture_technology+ca.news.yahoo.com/s/afp/100826/technology/lifestyle_hongkong_china_japan_culture_technology&cd=1&hl=nl&ct=clnk&gl=nl)

[34] jkOnTheRun:So what is multi-touch? (http://jkontherun.blogs.com/jkontherun/2007/12/so-what-is-mult.html)

[35] Buxton, Bill. "Multitouch Overview" (http://www.billbuxton.com/multitouchOverview.html)

[36] product presentation and demo Samsung Sliding PC7 Series (http://www.alltouchtablet.com/touchscreen-tablet-news/samsung-sliding-pc-7-is-the-slider-laptoptablet-you-ever-wanted-6343/), AllTouchTablet, 2011
[37] Intel has ARM in its crosshairs (http://news.cnet.com/Intel-has-ARM-in-its-crosshairs---page-2/2100-1006_3-6210033-2.html?tag=mncol)
[38] "Apple iPad Price, Features Say "ARM" All Over" (http://www.bnet.com/blog/mobile-internet/apple-ipad-price-features-say-8220arm-8221-all-over/133). bnet. .
[39] T-Mobile to sell tablet with 3-D cameras, glasses http://news.yahoo.com/s/ap/20110202/ap_on_hi_te/us_tec_techbit3_d_tablet
[40] HP vice-president Todd Bradley projects HP Slates for enterprise-level tablets, webOS for consumer-level tablets accessdate=2010-10-5 (http://www.eweekeurope.co.uk/news/hp-hints-at-business-focused-windows-7-tablet-8704)
[41] HP Slate 500 runs Win 7 Pro (http://www.csmonitor.com/Innovation/Horizons/2010/1023/HP-Slate-500-brings-professional-spin-to-the-tablet-wars), an enterprise-level tablet from HP accessdate=2010-10-23
[42] Boot time comparisons for iPad vs netbook (http://reviews.cnet.com/8301-31747_7-20001653-243.html?tag=mncol;txt)
[43] Getting a Windows PC to boot in under 10 seconds (http://news.cnet.com/8301-13924_3-20018475-64.html#ixzz12lPFj4kf)
[44] Microsoft Tablet PC (http://msdn.microsoft.com/en-us/library/ms840465.aspx)
[45] Tablet PC Brings the Simplicity of Pen and Paper to Computing: In a conversation with PressPass, Tablet PC general manager Alexandra Loeb discusses how the Tablet PC will brin... (http://www.microsoft.com/presspass/features/2000/nov00/11-13tabletpc.mspx)
[46] "Live from Steve Ballmer's CES 2010 keynote" (http://www.engadget.com/2010/01/06/live-from-steve-ballmers-ces-2010-keynote/). Engadget. . Retrieved 4 August 2010.
[47] Initial Windows 7 tablets are slated to appear during holiday 2010 season. (http://news.cnet.com/8301-13860_3-20019267-56.html?tag=mncol;mlt_related) accessdate=2010-10-19
[48] "Ballmer Admits Apple is Beating Microsoft in the Tablet Sector" (http://www.dailytech.com/Ballmer+Admits+Apple+is+Beating+Microsoft+in+the+Tablet+Sector/article19215.htm). DailyTech. . Retrieved 6 August 2010.
[49] Windows 7 is not yet optimized for fingertip events - 2010-09-24 (http://arstechnica.com/gadgets/news/2010/09/hp-slate-video-shows-all-thats-wrong-with-windows-7-on-tablets.ars)
[50] Windows 7 will not be optimized for slates; that will have to wait for Windows 8 (http://www.foxnews.com/scitech/2010/10/05/microsofts-ipad-answer-coming-christmas-holiday/)
[51] Windows 8 will not appear until 2012 (http://mashable.com/2010/10/24/microsoft-windows-8-2012/) accessdate=2010-10-24
[52] "Asus launches Eee Pad tablets and Eee Tablet note-taking thingie" (http://www.liliputing.com/2010/05/asus-launches-two-tablets-the-eee-pad-and-eee-tablet.html). liliputing. . Retrieved 6 August 2010.
[53] No Windows 7 for ARM (http://www.zdnet.com/blog/microsoft/microsoft-no-windows-7-for-arm-based-netbooks-for-now/2953?tag=mantle_skin;content) accessdate=2010-10-17

- Microsoft plans Windows tied to ARM chips (http://www.marketwatch.com/story/microsoft-plans-windows-tied-to-arm-chips-reports-2010-12-22?dist=beforebell) Dec. 22, 2010, 4:19 a.m. EST

[54] "Ubuntu gets multitouch support, Unity netbook UI" (http://www.linuxfordevices.com/c/a/News/Canonical-uTouch-and-Ubuntu-Maverick-Meerkat/). eWeek. .
[55] Intel shows pricing pressures for Atom due to competition from ARM (http://www.theregister.co.uk/2010/10/17/intel_tablets/) accessdate=2010-10-17
[56] Intel launches FPGA-equipped Atom (http://www.thinq.co.uk/2010/11/22/intel-launches-fpga-equipped-atom/) accessdate=2010-11-23 An FPGA, or field programmable gate array can then be custom-programmed by tablet computer vendors who have purchased these integrated circuits from the semiconductor device manufacturers.
[57] "Apple tablet rumors redux: 10.7-inch display, iPhone OS underneath" (http://www.engadget.com/2009/09/29/apple-tablet-rumors-redux-10-7-inch-display-iphone-os-undernea/). Engadget. . Retrieved 6 August 2010.
[58] Tifanny Boggs (2007) "Axiotron and OWC Unveil the ModBook" (http://www.tabletpcreview.com/default.asp?newsID=695)
[59] BlackBerry PlayBook preview (http://www.youtube.com/watch?v=eAaez_4m9mQ)
[60] "9 Upcoming Tablet Alternatives to the Apple iPad" (http://mashable.com/2010/01/27/9-upcoming-tablet-alternatives-to-the-apple-ipad/). Mashable. . Retrieved 7 August 2010.
[61] "Don't bank on KMart's $150 Augen tablet getting Android Market access" (http://www.liliputing.com/2010/08/dont-bank-on-kmarts-150-augen-tablet-getting-android-market-access.html). liliputing. . Retrieved 7 August 2010.
[62] "Forget all these Android tablets, let me at that Chrome OS" (http://www.crunchgear.com/2010/07/20/forget-all-these-android-tablets-let-me-at-that-chrome-os/). CrunchGear. . Retrieved 7 August 2010.
[63] "Google Chrome OS Tablet Brings Ties With Verizon" (http://www.informationweek.com/news/services/data/showArticle.jhtml?articleID=226700487)
[64] Motorola Android tablet in 2011 (http://www.marketwatch.com/video/asset/digits-motorola-plans-tablet-device-2010-09-16/7CC13B36-0A8B-42E0-AD1A-72FF9BF04348)
[65] Lenovo is waiting for Honeycomb (http://www.slashgear.com/tablets-a-prescription-for-confusion-24109978/) accessdate=2010-10-24
[66] The successor to *Gingerbread*, Android project *Honeycomb* is targeted for tablet computers. — Daniel Lyons ( Oct. 11, 2010), *Newsweek* p. 49

- Google demonstrated Android Honeycomb Tablet 12/7/2010 (http://www.pcmag.com/article2/0,2817,2373943,00.asp)

- Andy Rubin's demo of Motorola Honeycomb tablet (http://www.marketwatch.com/video/asset/digits-best-buys-tv-bust-2010-12-14/FD6C213F-D320-4212-BE7C-FECD5B8FEA33?dist=afterbell#!88F98ADB-3F87-49DF-AD08-385D66B0DDE8)

[67] One Laptop Gets $5.6M Grant From Marvell to Develop Next Generation Tablet Computer | Xconomy (http://www.xconomy.com/boston/2010/10/04/one-laptop-gets-5-6m-grant-from-marvell-to-develop-next-generation-tablet-computer/)

[68] Convertibles: The new laptop bling? - CNET News.com (http://news.com.com/Convertibles+The+new+laptop+bling/2100-1044_3-5900655.html)

[69] *PC World* (Nov 18, 2010 12:25 pm)"Why Tablet Computing Hasn't Been Big Business" (http://www.pcworld.com/businesscenter/article/211066/why_tablet_computing_hasnt_been_big_business.html)

[70] XO-3 concept design is here! | One Laptop per Child (http://blog.laptop.org/2009/12/24/xo-3-concept/)

[71] India unveils prototype for $35 touch-screen computer (http://www.bbc.co.uk/news/world-south-asia-10740817) BBC World news-South Asia Retrieved 25 July 2010

[72] India's ($)35 PC is the future of computing (http://www.pcworld.com/businesscenter/article/201769/indias_35_pc_is_the_future_of_computing.html?tk=hp_pop) PCWorld.com

[73] Bill of materials, *Wired* (http://www.wired.com/gadgetlab/2010/07/india-35-tablet/)

[74] http://www.csmonitor.com/From-the-news-wires/2010/0723/35-computer-introduced-in-India $100 OLPC tablet computer

[75] Adam Shah (31 July 2010), IDC, "Negroponte offers OLPC technology for $35 tablet" (http://www.goodgearguide.com.au/article/355270/negroponte_offers_olpc_technology_35_tablet/)

[76] OLPC X03 grant accessdate=2010-10-04 (http://www.xconomy.com/boston/2010/10/04/one-laptop-gets-5-6m-grant-from-marvell-to-develop-next-generation-tablet-computer/)


## External links

- What makes a tablet a tablet? (FAQ) (http://news.cnet.com/8301-31021_3-20006077-260.html?tag=newsLeadStoriesArea.1) CNET.com May 28, 2010

# Acer Tablet

Acer presented its first tablet line during its global press conference in New York on 23 November 2010.

## Acer tablet series

- Iconia Tab A500 - 10.1" Android Tablet
- Iconia Tab W500 - 10.1" Windows Tablet
- Iconia Tab A100 - 7" Android Tablet
- Iconia Smart - 4.8" smartphone/tablet

### Iconia Tab A500

The Iconia Tab A500 tablet runs Android 3.0 Honeycomb operating system. It is equipped with Nvidia's Tegra 2 Processor and is 13.3mm thick with a 1280×800 screen resolution and 1080p HDMI capacity. It supports 3G and Wi-Fi connectivity. Iconia Tab A500 tablet also features a 5 MP rear-facing camera plus an HD front-facing camera, for video chat. The device will be available on sale from April 2011 [1].

### Iconia Tab W500

The Iconia Tab W500 runs Windows operating system. The tablet is complemented by a full-size chicklet docking keyboard and powered by the next-generation of AMD platform and features two 1.3MP cameras [2]. Starting point of the Iconia Tab W500 touch experience is the Acer Ring. It allows to access all features and touch applications pre-loaded. With clear.fi, Acer media sharing system, Iconia Tab W500 can be connected to the home network and can share multimedia contents with other clear.fi enabled devices. The device will be available on sale in April 2011

### Iconia Tab A100

The Iconia Tab A100 tablet is the smallest tablet Pc of the series.It runs Android 3.0 Honeycomb operating system and it has a capacitive touchscreen display with 1024 x 600 pixel of resolution. Iconia supports multiple connectivity options, including Wi-Fi and 3G [3] . The device will be available on sale on 20 th April 2011 on amazon uk [4] .

### Iconia Smart

This is a tablet with the size of a smartphone: 4.8" widescreen with a 21:9 aspect ratio and 1024x480 screen resolution. It runs Android 2.3 Gingerbread operating system and it is equipped with a 8MP camera with LED flash plus a 2MP front camera for video calling.

## Reviews

Initial reactions see those devices as an attempt to challenge Apple's IPad.[5] According to Stuffmideast magazine Acer Inc. foray into the world of touchscreen tablets will overtake the Apple tablet within the next 2–3 years [6] .

## References

[1] Acer Announces New 10.1 Inch Tablet, Not Many Specifications Announced - Dalan Report (http://dalanreport.com/index.php?option=com_weblinks&view=weblink&catid=125:acer-tablets&id=6397:AcerAnnouncesNew10.1InchTablet,NotManySpecificationsAnnounced)
[2] 10.1-inch Acer Windows 7 Tablet Unveiled: Specs, Pics, And Release Date Confirmed – - SoftSailor (http://www.softsailor.com/news/52145-10-1-inch-acer-windows-7-tablet-unveiled-specs-pics-and-release-date-confirmed.html)
[3] 7-inch Android Tablet but battery is very poor by Acer reviews, prices, specs etc (http://www.iccellphone.com/2010/12/04/7-inch-android-tablet-by-acer/)
[4] Acer 7inch Tablet the battery is very poor that is only 1530 mah tures, Specs (http://www.solidblogger.com/acer-7inch-tablet-features-specs/)
[5] News Headlines (http://www.cnbc.com/id/40346365/Acer_Unveils_New_Tablets_to_Compete_with_Apple)
[6] Acer tablets to outsell Apple iPads by 2014 – Stuff Middle East (http://stuffmideast.com/2010/11/29/18732/acer-tablets-to-outsell-apple-ipads-by-2014/)

# Archos 101

### Archos 101 Internet Tablet

| **Developer** | Archos |
|---|---|
| **Type** | Internet Tablet |
| **Release date** | Varies by region |
| **Storage capacity** | 8 GB or 16 GB, as well as microSD slot available |

The **Archos 101** is part of the Archos Generation 8 range, distributed between 2010-11. It is a 10.1 inches (256.5 mm) Internet Tablet running Android.

## External links

- Archos 101 [1]

# Archos 43

### Archos 43 Internet Tablet

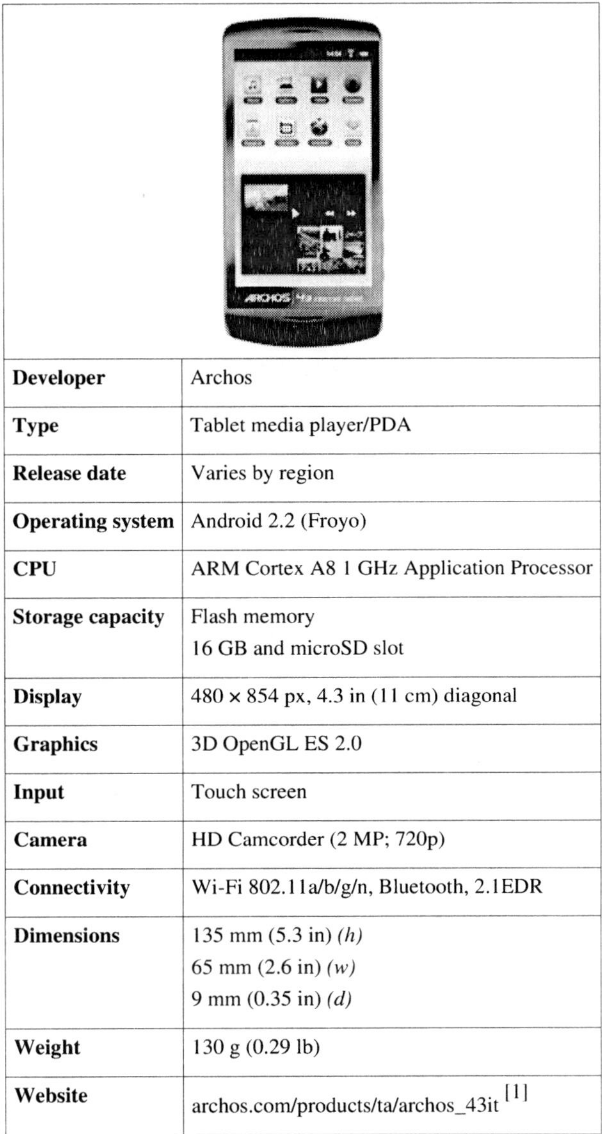

| | |
|---|---|
| **Developer** | Archos |
| **Type** | Tablet media player/PDA |
| **Release date** | Varies by region |
| **Operating system** | Android 2.2 (Froyo) |
| **CPU** | ARM Cortex A8 1 GHz Application Processor |
| **Storage capacity** | Flash memory<br>16 GB and microSD slot |
| **Display** | 480 × 854 px, 4.3 in (11 cm) diagonal |
| **Graphics** | 3D OpenGL ES 2.0 |
| **Input** | Touch screen |
| **Camera** | HD Camcorder (2 MP; 720p) |
| **Connectivity** | Wi-Fi 802.11a/b/g/n, Bluetooth, 2.1EDR |
| **Dimensions** | 135 mm (5.3 in) *(h)*<br>65 mm (2.6 in) *(w)*<br>9 mm (0.35 in) *(d)* |
| **Weight** | 130 g (0.29 lb) |
| **Website** | archos.com/products/ta/archos_43it [1] |

**Archos 43** is a 4.3 inch tablet computer designed and developed by Archos. The Archos 43 runs version 2.2 (Froyo) of the Android operating system. It was released globally in early November 2010.[1] It was met with mixed reviews, with its biggest overall complaint being its resistive touchscreen.[2]

## References


[1] "Archos 43 Internet Tablet Now Available, 101 Tablet Delayed?" (http://phandroid.com/2010/11/02/archos-43-internet-tablet-now-available-101-tablet-delayed/). phandroid.com. 2010-11-02. .

[2] "Customer Reviews: Archos 43 - 16 GB Internet Tablet (Black)" (http://www.amazon.com/Archos-43-Internet-Tablet-Black/product-reviews/B0042RRTOC/ref=dp_top_cm_cr_acr_txt?ie=UTF8&showViewpoints=1). .

# Archos 70

## Archos 70 Internet Tablet

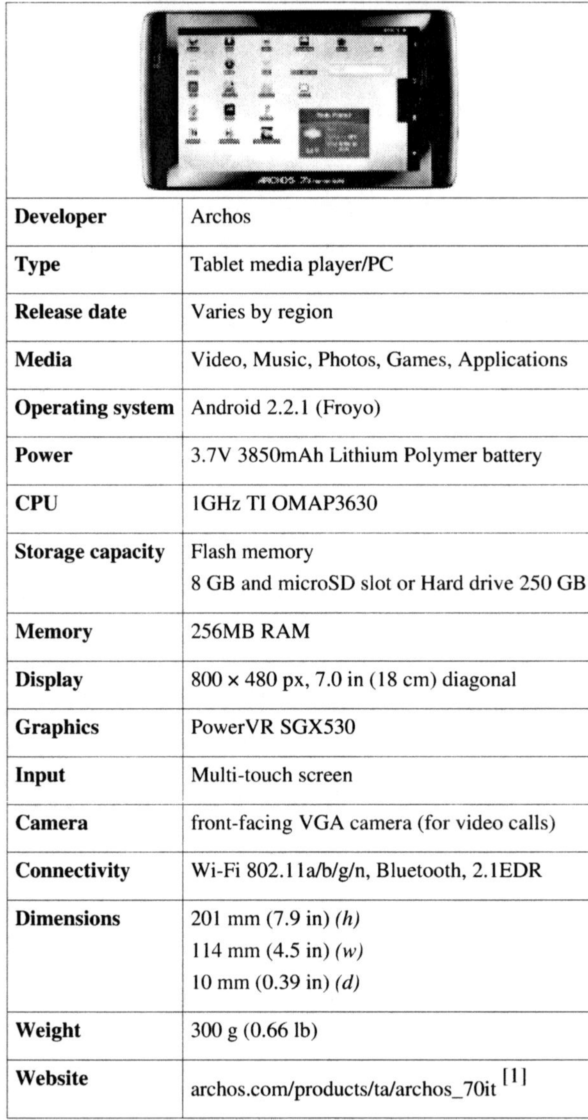

| | |
|---|---|
| **Developer** | Archos |
| **Type** | Tablet media player/PC |
| **Release date** | Varies by region |
| **Media** | Video, Music, Photos, Games, Applications |
| **Operating system** | Android 2.2.1 (Froyo) |
| **Power** | 3.7V 3850mAh Lithium Polymer battery |
| **CPU** | 1GHz TI OMAP3630 |
| **Storage capacity** | Flash memory<br>8 GB and microSD slot or Hard drive 250 GB |
| **Memory** | 256MB RAM |
| **Display** | 800 × 480 px, 7.0 in (18 cm) diagonal |
| **Graphics** | PowerVR SGX530 |
| **Input** | Multi-touch screen |
| **Camera** | front-facing VGA camera (for video calls) |
| **Connectivity** | Wi-Fi 802.11a/b/g/n, Bluetooth, 2.1EDR |
| **Dimensions** | 201 mm (7.9 in) *(h)*<br>114 mm (4.5 in) *(w)*<br>10 mm (0.39 in) *(d)* |
| **Weight** | 300 g (0.66 lb) |
| **Website** | archos.com/products/ta/archos_70it [1] |

The **Archos 70** is part of the Archos Generation 8 range, distributed between 2010-11. It is a 7 inches (18 cm) Internet Tablet running Android.

## References

# ASUS Eee

**ASUS Eee** is a family of products by Asustek. The product family began with the release of the Eee PC subnotebook in 2007; since then, the product family has diversified into a number of PC form factors. According to the company, the name Eee derives from "the three Es," an abbreviation of its advertising slogan for the device: "Easy to learn, Easy to work, Easy to play".[1]

ASUS EeeBox PC white with customized skin

## Eee PC

The ASUS Eee PC is a subnotebook / netbook computer. At the time of its introduction in fall 2007, it was noted for its combination of a light weight, Linux-based operating system, solid-state drive and relatively low cost. Newer models have added the option of the Windows 7 operating system, dual-core Intel Atom CPUs, and traditional hard disk drives, and have also increased in price, though they remain relatively inexpensive as laptops, and notably inexpensive for ultra-small laptops.

ASUS Eee PC

## EeeBox PC

Asus EeeBox PC is a nettop (desktop for the internet) counterpart to the Asus Eee PC netbook (notebook for the internet).[2] Its motherboard employs Splashtop technology called "ExpressGate" by Asus.[3]

## Eee Top

The Asus EEE Top is a touch screen computer designed by ASUS and released in November 2008. Its motherboard employs Splashtop technology (an embedded Linux distribution) called "ExpressGate" by Asus.[4] Both models feature a 1.6 GHz Atom processor, widescreen (16:9) 15.6" display, 1 GB RAM, 160GB HDD, 802.11n Wi-Fi, speakers, SD card reader and a 1.3MP webcam with Windows XP Home modified with Asus' big-icon Easy Mode.

ASUS Eee Top

## Eee Keyboard

**ASUS Eee Keyboard** is a full-size computer keyboard that has a built-in PC motherboard. It has a touchscreen in place of a conventional keypad. ASUS plans to start shipping the device in September 2009.[5]

## Eee Stick

The Eee Stick is an accessory that is expected to be bundled with specific models of the Eee PC and EeeBox PC. These specific models will also come with games that will take advantage of the features of this hardware. This accessory is very similar to the Wii Remote. The device takes two AA batteries in each of the two components (four batteries in total).

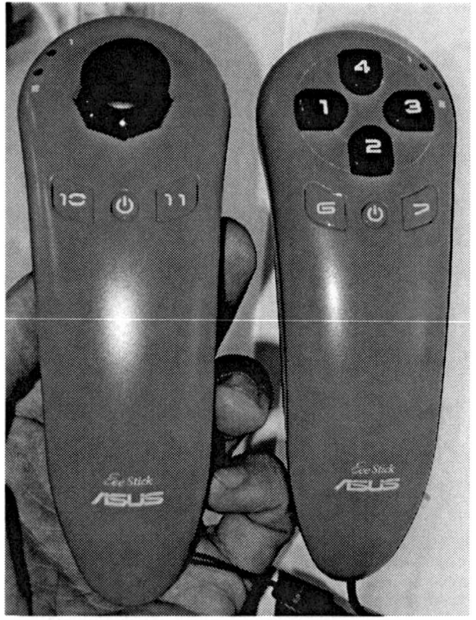


ASUS Eee Stick in red

## Eee PC Media Server

Asus Eee PC Media Server was shown at CES 2009.[6]

## Eee Pad and Eee Reader

Asus showed previews of a dual-touchscreen "Flipbook" notebook at Cebit 2009 in Germany[7] . The company stated that the Flipbook possessed the capability of optionally displaying user interface elements in both screens both horizontally and vertically; the concept design was renamed as the "Eee Reader", rebranded as an e-book reader, and scheduled for launch in Q4 2009[8] , which did not happen as intended. Finally, the Eee Reader was rebranded again as the "Eee Book" and scheduled for launch at the June 2010 Computex in Taipei.

In addition, Asus disclosed to the press in January 2010 that a tablet computer named as "Eee Pad", using an Nvidia Tegra 2 chip, a 3G wireless connection and a 720p or 1080p resolution, would also debut at Computex[9] . It finally materialized in March 2011 as the Eee Pad Transformer (TF101) which has an optional real (hardware) keyboard that can be connected to it.

## References

[1] "ASUS Eee PC" (http://eeepc.asus.com/global/). ASUS. 2008. . Retrieved 2008-04-10.
[2] ASUS Debuts Desktop-Equivalent Eee PC - News and Analysis by PC Magazine (http://www.pcmag.com/article2/0,2817,2316317,00.asp)
[3] AnandTech: ASUS Eee Box Preview & Intel's Atom Benchmarked (http://www.anandtech.com/systems/showdoc.aspx?i=3321&p=3)
[4] 14-Oct-2008 review by CNet (http://crave.cnet.co.uk/desktops/0,39029426,49299331,00.htm)
[5] OSNews preliminary review (http://www.osnews.com/story/20736/Trends_Are_Cyclical_the_Asus_Eee_Keyboard)
[6] http://www.liliputing.com/2009/01/asus-launches-eee-pc-d200-media-server-with-touchscreen.html
[7] *ASUS Flipbook* (http://www.physorg.com/news155476157.html) from physorg.com
[8] *Tech news: For the smarter kind of bookworm* (http://technology.timesonline.co.uk/tol/news/tech_and_web/article6822723.ece)
[9] *Asustek Plans Eee Book E-reader and Tablet PC to Rival IPad* (http://news.yahoo.com/s/pcworld/20100205/tc_pcworld/asustekplanseeebookereaderandtabletpctorivalipad), PC World

# ASUS Eee Pad Transformer

**ASUS Eee Pad Transformer**

| | |
|---|---|
| **Developer** | Asus |
| **Type** | Tablet, media player, PC |
| **Release date** | **2011-03-25:** Taiwan[1]<br>**2011-04-06:** United Kingdom<br>**2011-04-26:** Canada and United States[2]<br>**2011-05-07:** France and Sweden |
| **Operating system** | Android 3.0 Honeycomb[3] |
| **Power** | 9.5 hours; 24.4Wh Li-polymer battery, 16 hours with dock[3] |
| **CPU** | 1 GHz dual-core nVidia Tegra 2[3] |
| **Storage capacity** | Flash memory<br>16 or 32 GB, microSD slot (dock full size SD slot), unlimited ASUS WebStorage[3] [3] |
| **Memory** | 1 GB[3] |
| **Display** | 1280 × 800 px (aspect ratio 16:10), 10.1 in (26 cm) diagonal, 160 PPI[3] |
| **Graphics** | GeForce ULP |
| **Input** | Multi-touch screen, dock keyboard + touchpad, 3-axis accelerometer, compass, GPS receiver, proximity sensor, ambient light sensor, gyroscope |
| **Camera** | 5 MP AF camera with LED flash, 1.3 MP front-facing (for video calls) |
| **Connectivity** | Wi-Fi 802.11b/g/n, Bluetooth 2.1, DLNA[3] 1x mini HDMI 1.3a port, Dock 2x USB 2.0[3] |
| **Dimensions** | 10.6 in (270 mm) H<br>6.9 in (180 mm) W<br>0.51 in (13 mm) D[3] |
| **Weight** | 1.49 lb (680 g)[3] |

The **ASUS Eee Pad Transformer** is an Android 3.0 Honeycomb tablet computer announced at CES 2011 and launched on March 30, 2011.[4]

## Features

The Eee Pad is a tablet computer with an 10.1" IPS multi-touch screen with a resolution of 1280x800 and an Nvidia Tegra 2 system-on-a-chip (SoC). It has a 802.11b/g/n Wi-Fi module, but lacks 3G connectivity, a 3G variant will be available in the coming months.[4] The price at launch of the Eee Pad is £379 (£429 with dock).[4]

### Dock

The dock comes with a full QWERTY keyboard, trackpad, two extra USB 2.0 and one SD card reader as well as an additional battery that increases autonomy from 9.5 hours to 16 hours.[4]

## Software

The Transformer is running a sightly modified version of stock Honeycomb (Android 3.0). The "hard keys" (home, back, menu) have be skinned to resemble the standard Android phone keys. Beyond this small change the experience is almost entirely stock.

Bundled with the tablet are the MyNet, MyLibrary, MyCloud, Press Reader, MyDesktop and Polaris Office 3 for full document editing.

The first software update has now been released from ASUS as of 16th April 2011, this updated the system with extra widgets for MYZINE, which is a desktop 1 stop widget shop, for weather, email, calendar, gallery etc. It also added MYCLOUD, remote desktop, which is splash desktop app, (very smooth, only connection over WIFI though). There are other system improvements and the about screen now shows Android Version 3.0.1

## References


[1] http://vr-zone.com/articles/asus-launches-the-eee-pad-transformer-in-taiwan/11703.html

[2] http://campuslife.asus.com/index/1926/the-eee-pad-transformer-has-arrived/

[3] "Asus EeePad Transformer TF101 10.1 inch Tablet PC (nVidia Tegra2 1GHz, 1Gb, 16Gb eMMC, WLAN, BT, Android 3.0) with docking station" (http://www.amazon.co.uk/Asus-Transformer-Android-docking-station/dp/tech-data/B004TB0EXY/ref=de_a_smtd). Amazon.co.uk. . Retrieved 1 April 2011.

[4] Davies, Chris. "ASUS Eee Pad Transformer first-impressions [Video (http://www.slashgear.com/asus-eee-pad-transformer-first-impressions-video-30143387/)"]. . Retrieved 31 March 2011.


## External links

- Eee Pad Transformer TF101 (http://www.asus.com/product.aspx?P_ID=gHh4q7I8dvWJzhdV) at ASUS.com

# EnTourage eDGe

## enTourage eDGe

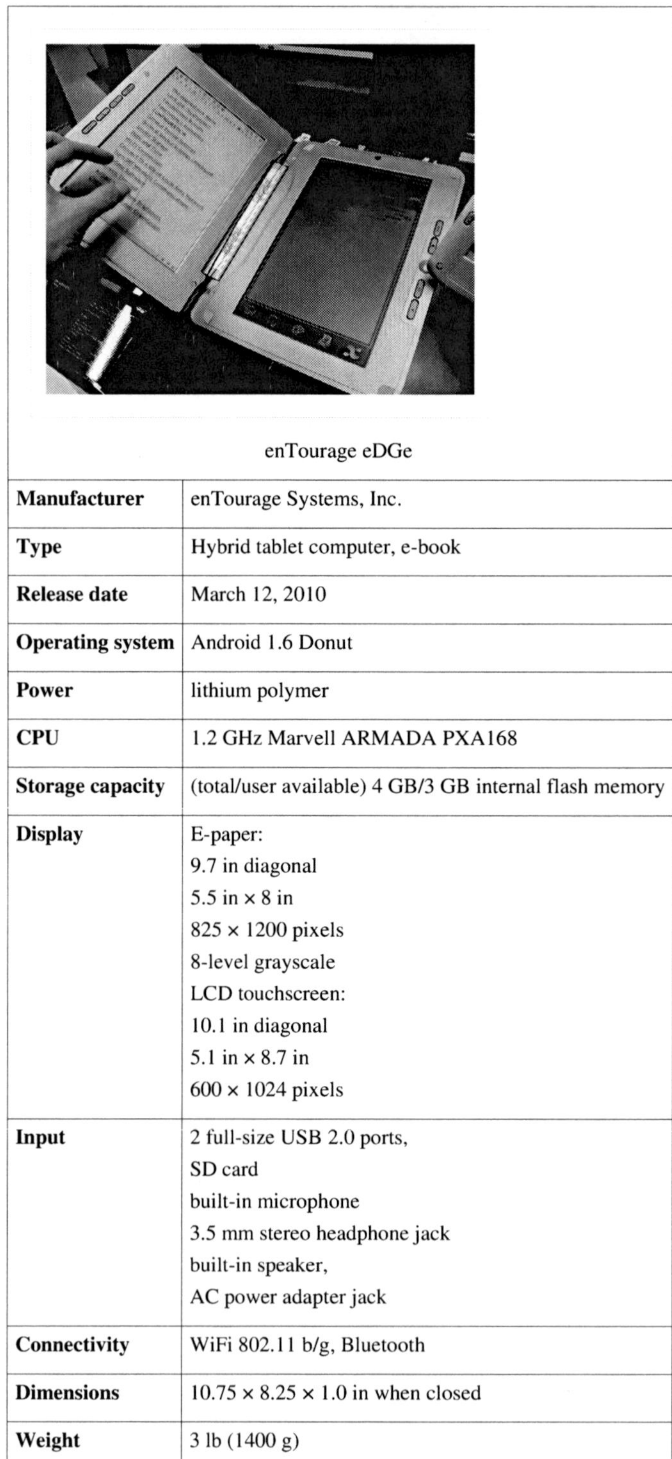

enTourage eDGe

| | |
|---|---|
| **Manufacturer** | enTourage Systems, Inc. |
| **Type** | Hybrid tablet computer, e-book |
| **Release date** | March 12, 2010 |
| **Operating system** | Android 1.6 Donut |
| **Power** | lithium polymer |
| **CPU** | 1.2 GHz Marvell ARMADA PXA168 |
| **Storage capacity** | (total/user available) 4 GB/3 GB internal flash memory |
| **Display** | E-paper:<br>9.7 in diagonal<br>5.5 in × 8 in<br>825 × 1200 pixels<br>8-level grayscale<br>LCD touchscreen:<br>10.1 in diagonal<br>5.1 in × 8.7 in<br>600 × 1024 pixels |
| **Input** | 2 full-size USB 2.0 ports,<br>SD card<br>built-in microphone<br>3.5 mm stereo headphone jack<br>built-in speaker,<br>AC power adapter jack |
| **Connectivity** | WiFi 802.11 b/g, Bluetooth |
| **Dimensions** | 10.75 × 8.25 × 1.0 in when closed |
| **Weight** | 3 lb (1400 g) |

The **enTourage eDGe** is a combined tablet computer and e-book made by enTourage Systems Inc., a small company in McLean, Virginia. It is advertised as "the world's first dualbook". The device runs Google's Android platform, version 1.6 'Donut'.

## Features

The eDGe is a dual-touchscreen device. One screen is a touch-sensitive e-Ink display, while the other screen is a full color 10.1 inch LCD touch screen. The color display side runs Android, but like all non-phone Android devices, the eDGe lacks direct access to Android Market due to Google's internal policy. Both screens are touchscreen, and interact with each other in various ways. For example, if an e-book is downloaded from enTourage's or Google Books' store, the book is added to the library, which can be accessed from the e-Ink side to read it. The enTourage eDGe has a SD card slot for transferring owned e-books or music to the device, a camera located above the LCD screen, and two full-sized USB ports where external flash drives, an external keyboard and other compatible devices may be used. The eDGe includes a stylus pen to write and interact with both screens. The two halves of the device can be folded closed much like a paper book, but can also be turned outwards so the screens are back to back.

## Reception

The enTourage eDGe has received mixed reviews. In a review, Joanna Stern of Engadget stated that "for $499 there are just too many issues with it, including its chunky body, skimpy e-book selection, frustrating touchscreen, poor battery life and lack of Android apps". Ina Fried of CNET was more positive and praised the device's generous assortment of features, but was also disappointed at several bugs with the device. Representatives from enTourage have made several press releases that they are already working on software updates that they hope will correct most of the complaints, including a foreseen upgrade from Android 1.6.

As of April 2011, the device is to be upgraded to Android 2.2 which will enable full flash support, though this has been delayed due to 2.2's poor compatibility with large displays.

## External links

- Official website [1]

# Pocket eDGe

## enTourage pocket eDGe

| | |
|---|---|
| **Manufacturer** | enTourage Systems, Inc. |
| **Type** | Hybrid tablet computer, e-book |
| **Release date** | November 12, 2010 |
| **Operating system** | Android 1.6 Donut |
| **Power** | lithium polymer<br>6 hours on LCD screen,<br>11 hours on e-ink screen |
| **CPU** | 1.2 GHz Marvell ARMADA PXA168 |
| **Storage capacity** | (total/user available) 4 GB/3 GB internal flash memory |
| **Display** | E-paper:<br>6.0 in diagonal<br>800 x 600 pixels<br>8-level grayscale<br>LCD touchscreen:<br>7.0 in diagonal<br>800 x 480 pixels |
| **Input** | 1 full-size USB 2.0 ports,<br>micro-SD card<br>built-in microphone<br>3.5 mm stereo headphone jack<br>built-in speaker,<br>AC power adapter jack |
| **Connectivity** | WiFi 802.11 b/g, Bluetooth |
| **Dimensions** | 7.5 × 5.5 × 1.0 in when closed |
| **Weight** | 1.35 lb (610 g) |

The **enTourage pocket eDGe** is a combined tablet computer and e-book made by enTourage Systems Inc., a small company based out of McLean, Virginia.[1] [2] It is the first follow on to the original EnTourage eDGe released earlier in 2010. The device runs Google's Android platform, version 1.6 'Donut', though there is now a beta version of 2.2 'Froyo'. It is called by the manufacturer as the world's first mini-dualbook".[3]

## Features

The Pocket eDGe is a dual screen device. One screen is a touch-sensitive 6.0 inch E Ink display, while the other screen is a full color 7.0 inch LCD touch screen. The color display side runs Android. Unlike most android devices, entourage pocket edge has its own suite of applications, rather than using the Android Market. Both displays are touchscreens, and the interface of the device provides interaction between the two according to appropriate actions and data formats.

## External links

- Official website [4]

## Reference list

[1] "Entourage Pocket Edge: Specifications, prices and release date" (http://0025.org/entourage-pocket-edge-specifications-prices-and-release-date-tablet-review-for-e-reader/). Gadget Reviews. . Retrieved November 12, 2010.

[2] "Entourage Pocket eDGe Dualbook announced; Specs, Price & Release Date" (http://www.gizmocrave.com/2309-entourage-pocket-edge-dualbook-announced-specs-price-release-date/). Gizmo Crave. . Retrieved November 12, 2010.

[3] "Entourage Pocket Edge 'dualbook' up for $399.99 Amazon pre-order" (http://www.engadget.com/2010/11/01/entourage-pocket-edge-dualbook-up-for-399-99-amazon-pre-order/). Engadget. . Retrieved November 1, 2010.

# ExoPC

## EXOPC Slate[1]

| EXOPC | |
|---|---|
| **Developer** | EXOPC |
| **Manufacturer** | Pegatron |
| **Type** | Tablet |
| **Release date** | October 2010 |
| **Media** | SD/SDHC card-reader (32GB Max) |
| **Operating system** | Microsoft Windows 7 Home Premium, 32-bit Edition |
| **Power** | 4 hour battery [2] |
| **CPU** | Intel Atom Pineview-M N450, 1.66 GHz - 64 bit support |
| **Storage capacity** | 32GB or 64GB SSD Hard Drive |
| **Memory** | 2GB DDR2 SDRAM |
| **Display** | 11.6 inch (diagonal), 1366 x 768 Resolution, 16:9 ratio, 135 PPI (pixels per inch) |
| **Graphics** | Intel GMA 3150 & Broadcom Crystal HD 1080p |
| **Input** | Multi-touch Capacitive dual-touch, Pressure sensitive |
| **Camera** | 1.3 Mega Pixel |
| **Connectivity** | Bluetooth 2.1 + EDR<br>Wireless Wifi 802.11 b/g/n |
| **Online services** | App Store |
| **Dimensions** | 11.6" x 7.7" x 0.55" (295 x 195 x 14.0 mm) |
| **Weight** | 2.09 pounds (950 g) |

The **EXOPC** is a Tablet PC, in slate form, that uses Windows 7 Home Premium as its operating system, and is designed by the company of the same name, based in Quebec, Canada[3] . The EXOPC Slate is manufactured by Pegatron[4] . The first EXOPC slate was launched in October 2010 directly from EXOPC Corp. on their website, and in Canada through the company Hypertechnologie Ciara[5] . Hypertechnologie Ciara markets the slate under the name Ciara Vibe[6] . Probitas markets the EXOPC as Mobi-One in Southern Europe and North Africa.[7] Leader Computers markets the EXOPC in Australia. The EXOPC Slate is also currently available in the United States via the Microsoft Store, both online and in stores.

## Hardware

The architecture is based on an Intel Atom-M Pineview N450 CPU that is clocked at 1.66 GHz, and includes 2GB of DDR2 SDRAM and 32GB of SSD storage in its basic version, with an alternative model having a larger 64GB SSD.

The EXOPC is also equipped with an accelerometer, which lets the display change from a portrait mode to a landscape mode by turning the slate in either direction. Internally it has four mini-PCIe slots of which 3 provide space for full length cards and 1 half length. 3 of these slots are in use and the 4th is available, but intended for a WWAN card. The unit also provides a SIM card slot.

## Display

The EXOPC has a 11.6 inch diagonal, capacitive multi-touch screen. The screen has a resolution of 1366 × 768 pixels (WXGA), a 16:9 ratio, and has 135 pixels per inch. This screen's firmware currently allows detection of two points of simultaneous touch, but is technically capable of up to 10 points of touch.

A light sensor built into the front of the tablet automatically adjusts the display brightness to ambient condition.

It is also possible to use a capacitive stylus for precision work, such as hand drawn art and graphic works.

## Connectivity

The EXOPC offers connectivity equivalent to that of a standard laptop:

- Wi-Fi IEEE 802.11b/IEEE 802.11g / IEEE 802.11n
- Bluetooth 2.1 + EDR
- 2 x USB 2.0 ports
- Audio In/Out SuperJack
- Mini-HDMI for connecting to an external monitor or television, with a maximum output resolution of 1080p
- Proprietary Dock Connector

## External Power Supply

Recharging the battery is done through a standard external power supply:

- Size: 85mm x 33mm x 25mm (3.4" x 1.3" x 1.0")
- Weight: 950 grams (33.51 ozs)
- Input: 100-240V
- Output: 19 V 2.1 Amp
- Recharging can also be done through a dock that is sold as a separate accessory.

## Software Features

### Operating system

The EXOPC use Microsoft Windows 7 as its operating system. The company has developed a GUI interface around the standard Windows 7 GUI, nicknamed by the EXOPC community as the *Connect Four Interface* due to its full screen of interactive circles arranged in a grid pattern[8] . A dedicated button on the touch-screen interface will minimize the EXOPC layer and reveal the Windows 7 desktop, allowing the user to have the EXOPC Slate act as a standard Windows computer when needed.

### Applications

#### Pre-installed Applications

The EXOPC comes with the following pre-installed applications.

- Microsoft Security Essentials
- Microsoft. NET framework 4.0
- Microsoft Silverlight runtime for IE
- Adobe Flash Player 10.2 and Acrobat Reader for reading PDF files
- EXOPC GUI Layer

### Store Specific Applications

An application library, similar to the Apple App Store or the Android Market will be available later for the device..

## Feedback

The tablet captured the attention of several blogs and websites in the Summer of 2010, being heralded as a possible alternative to the iPad[9] . However, early reviews criticized the weight and battery life of the final product[10] , as well of a lot of missing features the interface itself, sluggishness of the internet browser, and difficulties to use the on-screen keyboard[11] .

## References


[1] "EXOPC Slate" (http://www.EXOPC.com/en/EXOPC-slate.php). EXOPC. . Retrieved 2010-08-18.

[2] http://www.EXOPC.com/en/EXOPC-slate.php

[3] http://www.EXOPC.com

[4] "EXOPC slate delayed thanks to Pegatron assembly line issue" (http://www.slipperybrick.com/2010/10/EXOPC-slate-delayed-thanks-to-pegatron-assembly-line-issue/). slipperybrick.com. 2010-10-04. . Retrieved 2010-11-13.

[5] http://www.ciara-tech.com

[6] http://EXOPC.com/forum/viewtopic.php?f=4&t=679

[7] http://www.probitas.pt/detalheProduto.aspx?ido=18101

[8] "EXOPC Slate hands-on" (http://www.engadget.com/2010/05/30/EXOPC-slate-hands-on/). Engadget. 2010-05-30. . Retrieved 2010-11-13.

[9] "EXOPC Slate Hands-On: The Windows 7 Tablet We've Been Waiting For" (http://blog.laptopmag.com/EXOPC-slate-hands-on-the-windows-7-tablet-weve-been-waiting-fo). laptopmag.com. 2010-06-02. . Retrieved 2010-11-13.

[10] "EXOPC Slate Hands-On: The Windows 7 Tablet We've Been Waiting For" (http://www.netbooknews.com/review/EXOPC-windows-7-tablet-review/). netbooknews.com. 2010-11-11. . Retrieved 2010-11-13. "*The biggest draw back of the system so far appears to be battery life and that they are asking you to be patient while they work with their community to built a tablet everyone will love.*"

[11] "EXOPC Slate review" (http://www.engadget.com/2010/10/27/EXOPC-slate-review/). Engadget. 2010-10-57. . Retrieved 2010-11-13. "*Microsoft's lacking consumer touch features, it's not anywhere close to done, and thus requires Windows 7 to fully operate. Yet ultimately, it's Windows 7 -- and the power-hungry parts needed to run it -- that end up crippling the EXOPC the most.(...)With that said, $599 is a lot of money to bet on a platform that isn't ready and a piece of hardware that must be plugged into the wall for the better part of the day*"

# History of tablet computers

The tablet computer and the associated special operating software is an example of pen computing technology, and thus the development of tablets has deep historical roots.

The depth of these roots can be quite surprising to people who are only familiar with current commercial products. For example, the first patent for an electronic tablet used for handwriting was granted in 1888.[1] The first patent for a system that recognized handwritten characters by analyzing the handwriting motion was granted in 1915.[2] The first publicly-demonstrated system using a tablet and handwriting text recognition instead of a keyboard for working with a modern digital computer dates to 1956.[3]

In addition to many academic and research systems, there were several companies with commercial products in the 1980s: Pencept, Communications Intelligence Corporation, and Linus were among the best known of a crowded field. Later, GO Corp. brought out the PenPoint OS operating system for a tablet PC product: one of the patents from GO corporation was the subject of recent infringement lawsuit concerning the Tablet PC operating system.[4]

## Before 1950

- 1888: U.S. Patent granted to Elisha Gray on electrical stylus device for capturing handwriting.[1] [5]
- 1915: U.S. Patent on handwriting recognition user interface with a stylus.[2] [6]
- 1942: U.S. Patent on touchscreen for handwriting input.[7] [8]
- 1945: Vannevar Bush proposes the Memex, a data archiving device including handwriting input, in an essay As We May Think.[9]

## 1950s

- Tom Dimond demonstrates the Styalator electronic tablet with pen for computer input and software for recognition of handwritten text in real-time.[3]

## 1960s

- Early 1960s
  - RAND Tablet invented.[10] [11] The RAND Tablet is better known than the Styalator, but was invented later.
- Late 1960s
  - Alan Kay of Xerox PARC proposed a notebook computer, optionally using pen input, called the Dynabook: however the device is never constructed or implemented with pen input.
- 1966
  - In the science fiction television series Star Trek, crew members carry large, wedge-shaped electronic clipboards, operated through the use of a stylus.
- 1968
  - Filmmaker Stanley Kubrick imagines a flatscreen tablet device wirelessly playing a streaming video broadcast in the movie *2001: A Space Odyssey*.

## 1980s

Wireless tablet device in the movie 2001: A space odyssey

- 1982
  - Pencept of Waltham, Massachusetts markets a general-purpose computer terminal using a tablet and handwriting recognition instead of a keyboard and mouse.[12]
  - Cadre System markets the Inforite point-of-sale terminal using handwriting recognition and a small electronic tablet and pen.[13]
- 1985
  - Pencept[14] and CIC[15] both offer PC computers for the consumer market using a tablet and handwriting recognition instead of a keyboard and mouse. Operating system is MS-DOS.
- 1987
  - The Knowledge Navigator concept piece by Apple Computer.
- 1989
  - The first commercially available tablet-type portable computer was the GRiDPad[16] from GRiD Systems, released in September. Its operating system was based on MS-DOS.
  - Wang Laboratories introduces Freestyle. Freestyle was an application that would do a screen capture from an MS-DOS application, and let the user add voice and handwriting annotations. It was a sophisticated predecessor to later note-taking applications for systems like the Tablet PC.[17] The operating system was MS-DOS
  - In partnership with Fujitsu [18], the Poqet Computer Corporation announced the arrival of the Poqet PC.

## 1990s

- 1991
  - The Momenta Pentop was released.[18]
  - GO Corporation announced a dedicated operating system, called PenPoint OS, featuring control of the operating system desktop via handwritten gesture shapes.[19] [20]
  - NCR released model 3125 pen computer running MS-DOS, Penpoint OS or Pen Windows.[21]
  - The Apple Newton entered development; although it ultimately became a PDA, its original concept (which called for a larger screen and greater sketching capabilities) resembled the hardware of a Tablet PC.
- 1992
  - GO Corporation shipped the PenPoint OS for general availability and IBM announced IBM 2125 pen computer (the first IBM model named "ThinkPad") in April.[22]
  - Microsoft releases Windows for Pen Computing as a response to the PenPoint OS by GO Corporation.
- 1993
  - Fujitsu releases the Poqet PC the first pen tablet to use an integrated wireless LAN[23]
  - Apple Computer announces the Newton PDA, also known as the Apple MessagePad, which includes handwriting recognition with a stylus.
  - The IBM releases the ThinkPad, IBM's first commercialized portable tablet computer product available to the consumer market, as the IBM ThinkPad 750P and 360P[24]
  - BellSouth released the IBM Simon Personal Communicator, an analog cellphone using a touch-screen and display. It did not include handwriting recognition, but did permit users to write messages and send them as

faxes on the analog cellphone network, and included PDA and Email features.
- AT&T introduced the EO Personal Communicator combining PenPoint with wireless communications.
- 1996
  - The Digital Equipment Corporation releases the DEC Lectrice.
- 1999
  - The "QBE" pen computer created by Aqcess Technologies wins Comdex Best of Show.[25]

## 2000s

- 2000
  - PaceBlade [27] develops the first device that meets the Microsoft's Tablet PC standard[26] and received the "Best Hardware" award at VAR Vision 2000
  - The "QBE Vivo" pen computer created by Aqcess Technologies ties for Comdex Best of Show.
- 2001
  - Bill Gates of Microsoft demonstrates the first public prototype of a Tablet PC (defined by Microsoft as a pen-enabled computer conforming to hardware specifications devised by Microsoft and running a licensed copy of the "Windows XP Tablet PC Edition" operating system)[27] at Comdex.
- 2002
  - Microsoft releases the Microsoft Tablet PC.
- 2003
  - PaceBlade [30] receives the "Innovation des Jahres 2002/2003" award for the PaceBook [31] Tablet PC from PC Professionell Magazine at the Cebit
  - Fingerworks[28] develops the touch technology and touch gestures later used in the Apple iPhone.
- 2006
  - Samsung introduces the Samsung Q1 UMPC.
  - Windows Vista released for general availability. Vista included the functionality of the special Tablet PC edition of Windows XP.
  - On Disney Channel Original Movie, *Read It and Weep*, Jamie uses a Tablet PC for her journal.
- 2007
  - Axiotron introduces Modbook, the first (and only) tablet computer based on Mac hardware and Mac OS X at Macworld.[29]
- 2008
  - In April 2008, as part of a larger federal court case, the gesture features of the Windows/Tablet PC operating system and hardware were found to infringe on a patent by GO Corp. concerning user interfaces for pen computer operating systems.[4] Microsoft's acquisition of the technology is the subject of a separate lawsuit.[30][31]
  - HP releases the second Multi-Touch capable tablet: the HP TouchSmart tx2 series.[32]
- 2009
  - Asus announces a tablet netbook, the EEE PC T91 and T91MT, the latter which features a multi-touch screen.
  - Always Innovating announced a new tablet netbook with an ARM CPU.
  - Motion Computing launched the J3400.

## 2010s

- 2010
  - MobileDemand [37] launches the xTablet T7000 Rugged Tablet PC [38] which runs a full Windows OS and includes an integrated numeric keypad.
  - Fusion Garage releases the JooJoo, a Linux-based tablet computer.
  - Apple unveils the iPad, running Apple iOS.
  - Samsung unveils the Galaxy Tab, running Google Android.
  - Neofonie announces the WeTab, a Linux-based slate tablet PC, featuring an 11.6 inch multi-touch screen at 1366x768 pixels resolution.[33] [34]

## References


[1] Gray, Elisha (1888-07-31), *Telautograph* (http://www.freepatentsonline.com/386815.pdf), United States Patent 386,815 (full image),

[2] Goldberg, H.E. (1915-12-28), *Controller* (http://www.freepatentsonline.com/1117184.pdf), United States Patent 1,117,184 (full image),

[3] Dimond, Tom (1957-12-01), *Devices for reading handwritten characters* (http://rwservices.no-ip.info:81/pens/biblio70.html#Dimond57), Proceedings of Eastern Joint Computer Conference, pp. 232–237, , retrieved 2008-08-23

[4] Mintz, Jessica (2008-04-04), *Microsoft to Appeal $367M Patent Ruling* (http://www.usatoday.com/tech/products/2008-04-04-2507619152_x.htm), The Associated Press, , retrieved 2008-09-04

[5] Gray (1888-07-31), *Telautograph* (http://rwservices.no-ip.info:81/pens/biblio70.html#Gray1888b), United States Patent 386,815,

[6] Goldberg, H.E. (1915-12-28), *Controller* (http://users.erols.com/rwservices/pens/biblio70.html#GoldbergHE15), United States Patent 1,117,184,

[7] Moodey, H.C. (1942-12-27), *Telautograph System* (http://users.erols.com/rwservices/pens/biblio70.html#Moodey40), United States Patent 2,269,599,

[8] Moodey, H.C. (1942-12-27), *Telautograph System* (http://www.freepatentsonline.com/2269599.pdf), United States Patent 2,269,599 (full image),

[9] Bush, Vannevar (1945-07-15), *As We May Think* (http://rwservices.no-ip.info:81/pens/biblio70.html#BushV45), The Atlantic Monthly,

[10] *RAND Tablet* (http://users.erols.com/rwservices/pens/biblio70.html#RAND61), 1961-09-01,

[11] *50 Years of Looking Forward* (http://www.rand.org/publications/randreview/issues/rr.fall.98/50.html), RAND Corporation, 1998-09-01,

[12] *Pencept Penpad (TM) 200 Product Literature* (http://rwservices.no-ip.info:81/pens/biblio83.html#Pencept83), Pencept, Inc., 1982-08-15,

[13] *Inforite Hand Character Recognition Terminal* (http://rwservices.no-ip.info:81/pens/biblio83.html#Inforite82), Cadre Systems Limited, England, 1982-08-15,

[14] *Users Manual for Penpad 320* (http://users.erols.com/rwservices/pens/biblio85.html#Pencept84d), Pencept, Inc., 1984-06-15,

[15] *Handwriter (R) GrafText (TM) System Model GT-5000* (http://rwservices.no-ip.info:81/pens/biblio85.html#CIC85), Communication Intelligence Corporation, 1985-01-15,

[16] *The BYTE Awards: GRiD System's GRiDPad* (http://rwservices.no-ip.info:81/pens/biblio90.html#GridPad90a), BYTE Magazine, Vol 15. No 1, 1990-01-12, p. 285,

[17] *WANG Freestyle demo* (http://rwservices.no-ip.info:81/pens/images.html#WangFreestyle), Wang Laboratories, 1989, , retrieved 2008-09-22

[18] Lempesis, Bill (1990-05), *What's New in Laptops and Pen Computing* (http://rwservices.no-ip.info:81/pens/biblio90.html#Momenta90), Flat Panel Display News,

[19] Agulnick, Todd (1994-09-13), *Control of a computer through a position-sensed stylus* (http://users.erols.com/rwservices/pens/biblio95.html#Agulnick94), United States Patent 5,347,295,

[20] Agulnick, Todd (1994-09-13), *Control of a computer through a position-sensed stylus* (http://www.freepatentsonline.com/5347295.pdf), United States Patent 5,347,295 (full image),

[21] *NCR announces pen-based computer press release* (http://web.archive.org/web/20080502135338/http://findarticles.com/p/articles/mi_m0NEW/is_1991_June_24/ai_10957018), FindArticles, archived from the original (http://findarticles.com/p/articles/mi_m0NEW/is_1991_June_24/ai_10957018) on 2008-05-02, , retrieved 2007-04-20

[22] *Penpoint OS shipping press release* (http://web.archive.org/web/20070830050237/http://findarticles.com/p/articles/mi_m0NEW/is_1992_April_17/ai_12165379), FindArticles, archived from the original (http://findarticles.com/p/articles/mi_m0NEW/is_1992_April_17/ai_12165379) on 2007-08-30, , retrieved 2007-04-20

[23] Tablet PCs from Fujitsu and Tablet History (http://solutions.us.fujitsu.com/www/content/products/Tablet-PCS/index.php)

[24] Lenovo - The history of ThinkPad (http://www.pc.ibm.com/us/thinkpad/anniversary/history.html)

[25] *Trends at COMDEX Event 1999* (http://www.guiart.fi/gobr01en.htm), , retrieved 2008-08-11

[26] PaceBlade launches Tablet PC (http://www.allbusiness.com/electronics/computer-equipment-personal-computers/6004956-1.html)

[27] Microsoft (2005), *Windows XP Tablet PC Edition 2005 Hardware Requirements* (http://users.erols.com/rwservices/pens/biblio10.html#Microsoft06i), www.microsoft.com, , retrieved 2009-03-14
[28] Fingerworks, Inc. (2003), *iGesture Game Mode Guide* (http://rwservices.no-ip.info:81/pens/biblio05.html#Fingerworks03), www.fingerworks.com, , retrieved 2009-04-30
[29] Axiotron and OWC Unveil the ModBook (http://www.tabletpcreview.com/default.asp?newsID=695)
[30] http://news.com.com/Go+files+antitrust+suit+against+Microsoft/2100-7343_3-5772534.html
[31] http://www.groklaw.net/article.php?story=20050704045343631
[32] *HP TouchSmart tx2z* (http://www.shopping.hp.com/webapp/shopping/computer_can_series.do?storeName=computer_store&category=notebooks&a1=Category&v1=Mobility&series_name=tx2z_series), HP, , retrieved 2008-11-28
[33] BAETZ, Juergen (April 12, 2010), *German tablet PC sets out to rival Apple's iPad* (http://finance.yahoo.com/news/German-tablet-PC-sets-out-to-apf-890973130.html?x=0&.v=7), Associated Press, , retrieved 2010-04-15
[34] *WeTab specifications* (http://wetab.mobi/files/product_specifications_WeTab_version2.0_100506.pdf), Neofonie, April 12, 2010, , retrieved 2010-04-15

# Huawei Ideos Tablet S7

**Ideos Tablet S7**

| **Manufacturer** | Huawei |
|---|---|
| **Operating system** | Android 2.1 |
| **Display** | 800*480 |
| **Website** | [1] |

The **Huawei Ideos Tablet S7** is an Android 3G tablet/phone with a 7 inch touch-screen that has 800*480 resolution, it runs Android 2.1, can connect via Wifi, has stereo sound and a gravity sensor.[1]

It is sold in Australia by Telstra as the T-Touch Tab.[2] It is the cheapest tablet in Australia, according to PC World "the T-Touch Tab is effectively alone as an affordable, entry-level tablet that doesn't skimp on too many features".[3] It is sold exclusively by Telstra for use on the Telstra Next G network

[1] "Huawei Device Ideos Tablet S7" (http://www.huaweidevice.com/worldwide/productFeatures.do?pinfoId=2586&directoryId=3895&treeId=3290). huaweidevice.com. . Retrieved 2010-11-30.

[2] "Telstra T-Touch tab is a Huawei Ideos Tablet S7" (http://outofoffice.net.au/?p=320). outofoffice.net.au. . Retrieved 2010-11-30.

[3] "Telstra T-Touch Tab Android tablet review" (http://www.pcworld.idg.com.au/review/broadband/telstra/t-touch_tab/365626?pp=2). PC World. . Retrieved 2010-11-30.

# iPad

**iPad**

| iPad<br><br>An iPad showing its home screen | |
|---|---|
| **Developer** | Apple Inc. |
| **Manufacturer** | Foxconn (on contract)[1] |
| **Type** | Tablet media player/PC |
| **Release date** | **Wi-Fi model (U.S.):** April 3, 2010[2] [3]<br>**Wi-Fi + 3G Model (U.S.):** April 30, 2010[4]<br>**International:** May 28, 2010[5]<br>**iPad 2 (U.S.):** March 11, 2011[6]<br>**iPad 2 (international):** March 25, 2011 |
| **Units sold** | 19.48 million (as of 26 March 2011)[7] [8] [9] [10] |
| **Operating system** | iOS 4.3.3 Released May 4, 2011 |
| **Power** | Built-in rechargeable Li-ion battery<br>25 W·h (90 kJ)[11] |
| **CPU** | **1st Generation**<br>1 GHz Apple A4[11] [12]<br>**2nd Generation**<br>1 GHz Apple A5 |
| **Storage capacity** | 16, 32, or 64 GB flash memory[11] |
| **Memory** | **1st Generation**<br>256 MB DDR RAM[13]<br>**2nd generation**<br>512 MB DDR2 RAM[14] |
| **Display** | 1024 × 768 px 132 PPI 4:3 aspect ratio<br>9.7 in (25 cm) diagonal<br>XGA, LED-backlit IPS LCD[11] |
| **Graphics** | **1st generation**<br>PowerVR SGX 535 GPU[15]<br>**2nd generation**<br>PowerVR SGX543MP (cores: 2–4) |

| | |
|---|---|
| **Input** | Multi-touch touch screen, headset controls, proximity and ambient light sensors, 3-axis accelerometer, digital compass<br>**2nd Generation adds:** 3-axis gyro |
| **Camera** | **1st Generation**: None<br>**2nd Generation**: Front-facing and 720p rear-facing |
| **Connectivity** | Wi-Fi (802.11 a/b/g/n)<br>Bluetooth 2.1 + EDR<br>**GSM models also include:**<br>UMTS / HSDPA (850, 1900, 2100 MHz) GSM / EDGE (850, 900, 1800, 1900 MHz)<br>**CDMA model also includes:** CDMA/EV-DO Rev. A (800, 1900 MHz) |
| **Online services** | iTunes Store, App Store, MobileMe, iBookstore |
| **Dimensions** | **1st generation**<br>9.56 in (243 mm) *(h)*<br>7.47 in (190 mm) *(w)*<br>.5 in (13 mm) *(d)*<br>**2nd generation**<br>9.5 in (240 mm) *(h)*<br>7.31 in (186 mm) *(w)*<br>.34 in (8.6 mm) *(d)* |
| **Weight** | **Wi-Fi model:** 1.5 lb (680 g)<br>**Wi-Fi + 3G model:** 1.6 lb (730 g)[11]<br>**2nd Generation:** 1.33 lb (600 g) |
| **Related articles** | iPhone, iPod touch (Comparison) |
| **Website** | apple.com/ipad [16] |

The **iPad** (pronounced /ˈaɪpæd/, *EYE-pad*) is a line of tablet computers designed, developed and marketed by Apple Inc. primarily as a platform for audio-visual media including books, periodicals, movies, music, games, and web content. Its size and weight falls between those of contemporary smartphones and laptop computers. The iPad runs the same operating system as the iPod Touch and iPhone—and can run its own applications as well as iPhone applications. Without modification, and with the exception of websites, it will only run programs approved by Apple and distributed via its online store.

Like iPhone and iPod Touch, the iPad is controlled by a multitouch display—a departure from most previous tablet computers, which used a pressure-triggered stylus—as well as a virtual onscreen keyboard in lieu of a physical keyboard. The iPad uses a Wi-Fi data connection to browse the Internet, load and stream media, and install software. Some models also have a 3G wireless data connection which can connect to HSPA or EV-DO data networks. The device is managed and synced by iTunes on a personal computer via USB cable.

Apple released the first iPad in April 2010, and sold 3 million of the devices in 80 days.[16] During 2010, Apple sold 14.8 million iPads worldwide,[7] [8] [9] representing 75 percent of tablet PC sales at the end of 2010.[17] By the release of the iPad 2 in March 2011, more than 15 million iPads had been sold[18] — more than all other tablet PCs combined. In 2011, it is expected to take 83 percent of the tablet computing market share in the United States.[19]

# History

## Prehistory

Apple's first tablet computer was the Newton MessagePad 100,[20] [21] introduced in 1993, which led to the creation of the ARM6 processor core with Acorn Computers. Apple also developed a prototype PowerBook Duo-based tablet, the PenLite, but decided not to sell it in order to avoid hurting MessagePad sales.[22] Apple released several more Newton-based PDAs; the final one, the MessagePad 2100, was discontinued in 1998.

Apple re-entered the mobile-computing market in 2007 with the iPhone. Smaller than the iPad but featuring a camera and mobile phone, it pioneered the multitouch finger-sensitive touchscreen interface of Apple's iOS mobile operating system. By late 2009, the iPad's release had been rumored for several years. Such speculation mostly talked about "Apple's tablet"; specific names included *iTablet* and *iSlate*.[23] The eventual name is reportedly a homage to the Star Trek PADD, a fictional device very similar in appearance to the iPad. The iPad was announced on January 27, 2010, by Steve Jobs at an Apple press conference at the Yerba Buena Center for the Arts in San Francisco.[24] [25]

Jobs later said Apple began developing the iPad before the iPhone,[26] [27] [28] but temporarily shelved the effort upon realizing that its ideas would work just as well in a mobile phone.[29]

## First generation

Apple began taking pre-orders for the iPad from U.S. customers on March 12, 2010.[3] The only major change to the device between its announcement and being available to pre-order was the change of the behavior of the side switch from sound muting to that of a screen rotation lock.[30] The Wi-Fi version of the iPad went on sale in the United States on April 3, 2010.[3] [31] The Wi-Fi + 3G version was released on April 30.[3] [4] [4] 3G service in the United States is provided by AT&T and was initially sold with two prepaid contract-free data plan options: one for unlimited data and the other for 250 MB per month at half the price.[32] [33] On June 2, 2010, AT&T announced that effective June 7 the unlimited plan would be replaced for new customers with a 2 GB plan at slightly lower cost; existing customers would have the option to keep the unlimited plan.[34] The plans are activated on the iPad itself and can be canceled at any time.[35]

Steve Jobs, Apple CEO, introducing the iPad

The iPad was initially only available online at The Apple Store as well as the company's retail locations. The iPad has since been available for purchase through many retailers including Amazon, Wal-Mart, Best Buy, Verizon, and AT&T. The iPad was launched in Australia, Canada, France, Germany, Italy, Japan, Spain, Switzerland and the United Kingdom on May 28.[5] [36] Online pre-orders in those countries began on May 10.[4] Apple released the iPad in Austria, Belgium, Hong Kong, Ireland, Luxembourg, Mexico, Netherlands, New Zealand and Singapore on July 23, 2010.[37] Israel briefly prohibited importation of the iPad because of concerns that its Wi-Fi might interfere with other devices.[38] On September 17, 2010, the iPad officially launched in China.[39]

The device was initially popular with 300,000 iPads being sold on their first day of availability.[40] By May 3, 2010, Apple had sold a million iPads,[41] this was in half the time it took Apple to sell the same number of original iPhones.[42] During the October 18, 2010, Financial Conference Call, Steve Jobs announced that Apple had sold more iPads than Macs for the Fiscal Quarter.[43] In total, Apple sold more than 15 million first generation iPads prior to the launch of the iPad 2.[18]

### iPad 2

Apple Inc. CEO Steve Jobs unveiled the iPad 2, the second generation of the device, at a March 2, 2011, press conference, despite being on medical leave at the time.[44] [45] About 33% thinner than its predecessor, the iPad 2 has a better processor, a dual core Apple A5 that Apple says is twice as fast as its predecessor for CPU operations and up to nine times as fast for GPU operations. It includes front and back cameras that support FaceTime, as well as a three-axis gyroscope. It retains the original's 10-hour battery life and has a similar pricing scheme. While prices were kept the same in the United States, the iPad 2 sold for less in other countries, such as the United Kingdom.

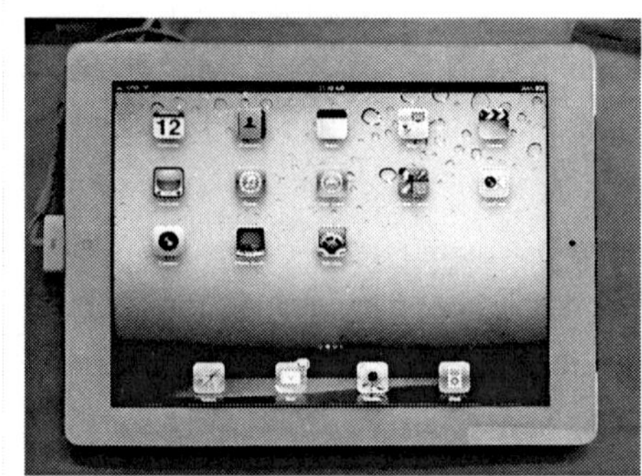

The iPad 2 is thinner and lighter than its predecessor, and is available in black or white (shown).

The iPad 2 has been available for purchase, depending on stock availability, since March 11, 2011, at Apple retail stores in the United States, as well as to United States customers shopping online at Apple's retail website.[46] The iPad 2 was released internationally in 25 other countries on March 25, 2011, including Australia, Canada, France, Germany, Japan, Mexico and the United Kingdom, but not Japan as originally scheduled due to the earthquake and tsunami.[47] iPad owners who bought a first-generation iPad directly from Apple within two weeks before the announcement are eligible for a $100 reimbursement from Apple.[48]

## Hardware

### Screen and input

The iPad's touchscreen display is a 9.7 in (25 cm) liquid crystal display (1024 × 768 pixels) with fingerprint-resistant and scratch-resistant glass. Steve Jobs backed the choice of screen size, saying a 7-inch screen would be "too small to express the software."[49] He said 10 inches was the minimum for a tablet screen.[49] Like the iPhone, the iPad is designed to be controlled by bare fingers; normal gloves and styli that prevent electrical conductivity may not be used,[50] although there are special gloves and capacitive styli designed for this use.[51] [52]

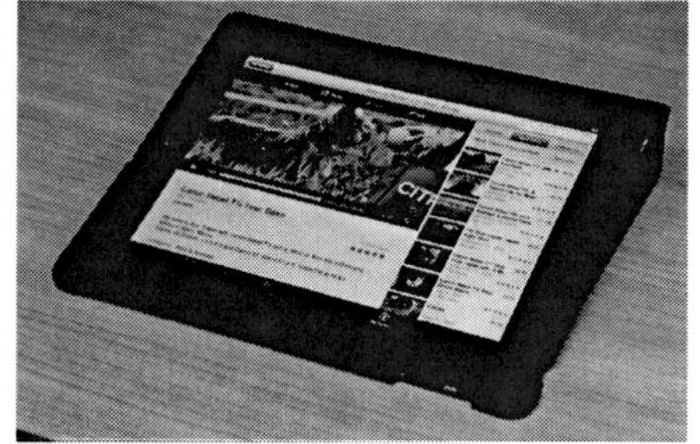

The original iPad in its black case. For the iPad 2, Apple sells a Smart Cover rather than a case.

The display responds to other sensors: an ambient light sensor to adjust screen brightness and a 3-axis accelerometer to sense iPad orientation and switch between portrait and landscape modes. Unlike the iPhone and iPod touch built-in applications, which work in three orientations (portrait, landscape-left and landscape-right), the iPad built-in applications support screen rotation in all four orientations, including upside-down.[53] Consequently, the device has no intrinsic "native" orientation; only the relative position of the home button changes. The iPad 2 added a 3-axis gyroscope that is used only third party apps, usually games.

There are four physical switches on the iPad, including a home button near the display that returns the user to the main menu, and three plastic physical switches on the sides: *wake/sleep* and *volume up/down*, plus a third which, whose function has changed with software updates. Originally, the switch would lock the screen to its current orientation, but the iOS 4.2 changed it to a mute switch, with rotation lock now available in an onscreen menu.[54] In the iOS 4.3 update, released with the iPad 2, a setting was added to allow the user to specify whether the side switch was used for rotation lock or mute.[11]

Apple reduced the size of the iPad 2 by 33% compared to its predecessor by eliminating the stamped sheet metal frame from the display, integrating new thinner glass technology for the touch screen overlay, and slightly reducing the space between the display and battery.[55] The iPad 2's screen is thinner, lighter, and yet stronger than the original iPad's.[56]

The original iPad had no camera. The iPad 2 has front VGA camera and a rear-facing 720p camera, both capable of still images and 30fps video. The rear facing camera has a 5x digital zoom for still images only. Both shoot photo and video in a 4:3 fullscreen aspect ratio, unlike the iPhone 4, which shoots in a 16:9 widescreen aspect ratio. It also lacks the iPhone's tap to focus feature.[57] The cameras allow FaceTime video messaging with iPhone 4, iPod Touch 4, and Snow Leopard Macs.[58]

## Connectivity

The iPad can use Wi-Fi network trilateration from Skyhook Wireless to provide location information to applications such as Google Maps. The 3G model contains A-GPS to allow its position to be calculated with GPS or relative to nearby cellphone towers; it also has a black plastic accent on the back side to improve 3G radio sensitivity.[59]

For wired connectivity, the iPad has only a TRRS headphone jack and a proprietary Apple dock connector; it lacks the Ethernet and USB ports of larger computers.[11]

## Audio and output

the iPad has two internal mono speakers located on the bottom-right of the unit. In the original iPad, the speakers push sound through two small sealed channels leading to the three audio ports carved into the device,[15] while the iPad 2 has its speakers behind a single grill.[14]

A volume switch is on the right side of the unit. A 3.5-mm TRRS connector audio-out jack on the top-left corner of the device provides stereo sound for headphones with or without microphones and/or volume controls. The iPad also contains a microphone that can be used for voice recording.

The built-in Bluetooth 2.1 + EDR interface allows wireless headphones and keyboards to be used with the iPad.[60] However, the iOS does not currently support file transfer via Bluetooth.[61] iPad also features 1024 x 768 VGA video output for limited applications,[62] screen capture,[63] connecting an external display or television through an accessory adapter.

## Power and battery

The iPad uses an internal rechargeable lithium-ion polymer battery (LiPo). The batteries are made in Taiwan by Simplo Technology, which makes 60% of them, and Dynapack International Technology.[64] The iPad is designed to be charged with a high current (2 amperes) using the included 10 W USB power adapter. While it can be charged by a standard USB port from a computer, these are limited to 500 milliamperes (half an amp). As a result, if the iPad is turned on while connected to a normal USB computer port, it may charge much more slowly, or not at all. High-power USB ports found in newer Apple computers and accessories provide full charging capabilities.[65]

The iPad 2 battery is 2.5 mm thick, 59% smaller than the original and has three cells instead of two, allowing the injection-molded plastic support frame to be omitted.[55]

Apple claims that the battery for both generations of iPad can provide up to 10 hours of video, 140 hours of audio playback, or one month on standby. Like any battery technology, the iPad's LiPo battery loses capacity over time, but is not designed to be user-replaceable. In a program similar to the battery-replacement program for the iPod and the original iPhone, Apple will replace an iPad that does not hold an electrical charge with a refurbished iPad for a fee of $99 (plus $6.95 shipping).[66] [67]

## Storage and SIM

The iPad 3G, unlike the Wi-Fi model, has a black plastic piece on the underside which allows cellular signals to pass through it.

The iPad was released with three capacity options for storage: 16, 32, or 64 GB of internal flash memory. All data is stored on the internal flash memory, with no option to expand storage. Apple sells a camera connection kit with an SD card reader, but it can only be used to transfer photos and videos.[68]

The side of the Wi-Fi + 3G model has a micro-SIM slot (not mini-SIM). Unlike the iPhone, which is usually sold locked to specific carriers, the 3G iPad is sold unlocked and can be used with any compatible GSM carrier.[69] Japan is the exception to this, where the iPad 3G is locked to Softbank.[70] In the U.S., data network access via T-Mobile's network is limited to slower EDGE cellular speeds because T-Mobile's 3G Network uses different frequencies.[71] [72] The iPad 2 introducd a third tier of models with CDMA support for Verizon Wireless in the United States, available separately from the AT&T capable version.[73]

## Optional accessories

Apple offers several iPad accessories,[74] most of which are adapters for the proprietary 30-pin dock connector, the iPad's only port besides the headphone jack.[11] A dock holds the iPad upright at an angle, and has a dock connector and audio line out port. Each generation of iPad requires a corresponding dock. A dock that included a physical keyboard is available only for the original iPad,[75] but both generations are compatible with Bluetooth keyboards that also work with Macs and PCs. The iPad can be charged by a standalone power adapter ("wall charger") also used for iPods and iPhones, and a 10W charger is included with the iPad.

Apple sells a camera connection kit that consists of two separate adapters for the dock connector, one to USB Type A, the other an SD card reader, meant to transfer photos and videos. A third party sells an adapter that includes USB, SD, and microSD on a single unit.[76] An adapter to VGA connectors allows the iPad to work with external monitors and projectors. Another adapter mirrors the screen onto HDMI compatible devices in 1080p and works with all apps and rotations. Unlike other adapters, it allows the iPad to charge through another dock connector.[77] While the HDMI adapter was released with and advertised for the iPad 2, it also works with the first generation iPad, the iPhone 4, and the fourth generation iPod Touch.[78]

A Smart Cover can be used as a stand for the iPad 2 while the display is in use.

Smart Covers are screen protectors that magnetically attach and align to the face of the iPad 2. The cover has three folds which allow it to convert into a stand, which is also held together by magnets.[79] While original iPad owners could purchase a black case that included a similarly folding cover, the Smart Cover is meant to be more minimal, easily detachable, and protects only the screen. Smart Covers have a microfiber bottom that cleans the front of the iPad, which wakes up when the cover is removed. There are five different colors of both polyurethane and leather, with leather being more expensive. Smart Covers are not compatible with the original iPad.[80]

## Technical specifications

| Model | | iPad (original) | iPad 2 |
|---|---|---|---|
| Announcement date | | January 27, 2010[24] | March 2, 2011[81] |
| US Release date | | April 3, 2010[3] | March 11, 2011[82] |
| Discontinued date | | March 2, 2011 | In production |
| Display | | 9.7 inches (25 cm) multitouch display at a resolution of 1024 × 768 pixels with LED backlighting and a fingerprint and scratch-resistant coating[11] | |
| Processor | | 1 GHz Apple A4 system-on-a-chip[12] | 1 GHz (dynamically clocked) dual-core Apple A5 system on a chip |
| Memory | | 256 MB DDR RAM built into Apple A4 package[13] | 512 MB DDR2 (1066 Mbps data rate) RAM built into Apple A5 package[14] |
| Storage | | 16, 32, or 64 GB[11] | |
| Wireless | Wi-Fi | Wi-Fi (802.11a/b/g/n), Bluetooth 2.1+EDR[11] | |
| | Wi-Fi+3G | 3G cellular HSDPA, 2G cellular EDGE on 3g models[11] | |
| Geolocation | Wi-Fi | Wi-Fi,[11] Apple location databases[83] | |
| | Wi-Fi+3G | Assisted GPS, Apple databases,[83] Cellular network[11] | |
| Environmental sensors | | Accelerometer, ambient light sensor, magnetometer[11] | Additionally: gyroscope |
| Operating system | | iOS 4.3[84] | |
| Battery | | Built-in lithium-ion polymer battery; (10 hours video,[11] 140 hours audio,[85] 1 month standby[86] ) | |
| Weight | | 1.5 lb (680 g)[11] | 1.33 lb (600 g) |
| Dimensions | | 9.56×7.47×.528 in (243×190×13.4 mm)[11] [87] | 9.5×7.31×.346 in (240×186×8.8 mm)[87] |
| Mechanical keys | | Home, sleep, volume rocker, variable function switch (originally screen rotation lock, mute in iOS 4.2, either in 4.3)[11] | |
| Camera | Back | N/A | 720p HD still and video camera 30fps and 5x digital zoom |
| | Front | N/A | VGA-quality still camera |

## Manufacture

The iPad is assembled by Foxconn, which also manufactures Apple's iPod, iPhone and Mac Mini, in its largest plant in Shenzhen, China.[88] In April 2011 Foxconn announced that it would be moving production of the iPad and other Apple products to Brazil where it could begin production before the end of 2011.[89]

iSuppli estimated that each iPad 16 GB Wi-Fi version costs $259.60 to manufacture, a total that excludes research, development, licensing, royalty and patent costs.[90] Apple does not disclose the makers of iPad components, but teardown reports and analysis from industry insiders indicate that various parts and their suppliers include:

- Apple A4 SoC: Samsung.[11] [91]
- NAND flash RAM chips: Toshiba; except Samsung for the 64 GB model.[92] [93]
- Touch-screen chips: Broadcom.[92]

- IPS Display: LG Display
- Touch panels: Wintek. (Got the job after TPK Touch Solutions was unable to fulfill its orders, delaying the iPad's release from late March to early April.[94] )
- Case: Catcher Technologies.[95]
- LCD drivers: Novatek Microelectronics.[96]
- Batteries: 60% are made in Taiwan by Simplo Technology, 40% by Dynapack International.[64] [97]
- Accelerometer: STMicroelectronics.[98]

## Software

Like the iPhone, with which it shares a development environment (iPhone SDK, or software development kit, version 3.2 onwards),[99] the iPad only runs its own software, software downloaded from Apple's App Store, and software written by developers who have paid for a developer's license on registered devices.[100] The iPad runs almost all third-party iPhone applications, displaying them at iPhone size or enlarging them to fill the iPad's screen.[101] Developers may also create or modify apps to take advantage of the iPad's features.[102] Application developers use iPhone SDK for developing applications for iPad.[103] The iPad has been shipping with a customized iPad-only version of iPhone OS, dubbed v3.2. On September 1, it was announced the iPad would get iOS 4.2 by November 2010.[104] Apple released iOS 4.2.1 to the public on November 22.[105]

### Applications

The iPad comes with several applications, including Safari, Mail, Photos, Video, YouTube, iPod, iTunes, App Store, iBooks, Maps, Notes, Calendar, Contacts, and Spotlight Search.[106] Several are improved versions of applications developed for the iPhone.

The iPad syncs with iTunes on a Mac or Windows PC.[24] Apple ported its iWork suite from the Mac to the iPad, and sells pared down versions of Pages, Numbers, and Keynote apps in the App Store.[107] Although the iPad is not designed to replace a mobile phone, a user can use a wired headset or the built-in speaker and microphone and place phone calls over Wi-Fi or 3G using a VoIP application.[108] The iPad has lots of third party applications available for it; as of September 1, 2010, there were 25,000 iPad specific apps on the App Store.[109] The iPad cannot run the Xcode development suite since it uses iOS.[110]

In December 2010, Reuters reported that iPhone and iPad users have lodged a lawsuit against Apple alleging that some applications were passing their information to third party advertisers without consent.[111]

### Digital Rights Management

The iPad employs Digital Rights Management intended to control certain software—including TV shows, movies, and apps—and prevent its transfer or use outside of Apple's platform. Also, the iPad's development model requires anyone creating an app for the iPad to sign a non-disclosure agreement and pay for a developer subscription. Critics argue Apple's centralized app approval process and control of the platform itself could stifle software innovation. Of particular concern to digital rights advocates is Apple's ability to remotely disable or delete apps, media, or data on any iPad at any time.[112] [113] [114]

Digital rights advocates, including the Free Software Foundation, Electronic Frontier Foundation, and computer engineer and activist Brewster Kahle, have criticized the iPad for its digital rights restrictions. Paul Sweeting, an analyst with GigaOM, is quoted by *National Public Radio* saying, "With the iPad, you have the anti-Internet in your hands. [...] It offers [the major media companies] the opportunity to essentially re-create the old business model, wherein they are pushing content to you on their terms rather than you going out and finding content, or a search engine discovering content for you." But Sweeting also thinks Apple's limitations make its products feel like living in a safe neighborhood, saying, "Apple is offering you a gated community where there's a guard at the gate, and there's probably maid service, too." Laura Sydell, the article's author, concludes, "As more consumers have fears about security on the Internet, viruses and malware, they may be happy to opt for Apple's gated community."[115]

### Jailbreaking

Like other iOS Devices, the iPad can be "jailbroken", allowing applications and programs that are not authorized by Apple to run on the device.[116] [117] Once jailbroken, iPad users are able to download many applications previously unavailable through the App Store via unofficial installers such as Cydia, as well as illegally pirated applications.[117] Apple claims jailbreaking voids the factory warranty on the device in the United States even though jailbreaking is legal.[117] [118]

### Censorship

Apple's App Store, which provides iPhone and iPad applications, imposes censorship of content, which has become an issue for book publishers and magazines seeking to use the platform. *The Guardian* described the role of Apple as analogous to that of the distributor WH Smith, a main distributor which for many years imposed content restrictions on British publishers.[119]

Due to the exclusion of pornography from the App Store, YouPorn and others changed their video format from Flash to H.264 and HTML5 specifically for the iPad.[120] [121] In an e-mail exchange[122] with Ryan Tate from Valleywag, Steve Jobs claimed that the iPad offers "freedom from porn", leading to many upset replies including Adbustings in Berlin by artist Johannes P. Osterhoff[123] and in San Francisco during WWDC10.[124]

## Books, news, and magazine content

The iPad has an optional iBooks application that can be downloaded from the App Store, which displays books and other ePub-format content downloaded from the iBookstore.[125] For the iPad launch on April 3, 2010, the iBookstore is available only in the United States.[3] [24] [106] Several major book publishers including Penguin Books, HarperCollins, Simon & Schuster and Macmillan have committed to publishing books for the iPad.[126] Despite being a direct competitor to both the Amazon Kindle and Barnes & Noble Nook,[127] both Amazon.com and Barnes & Noble have made Kindle & Nook apps available for the iPad.[128] [129]

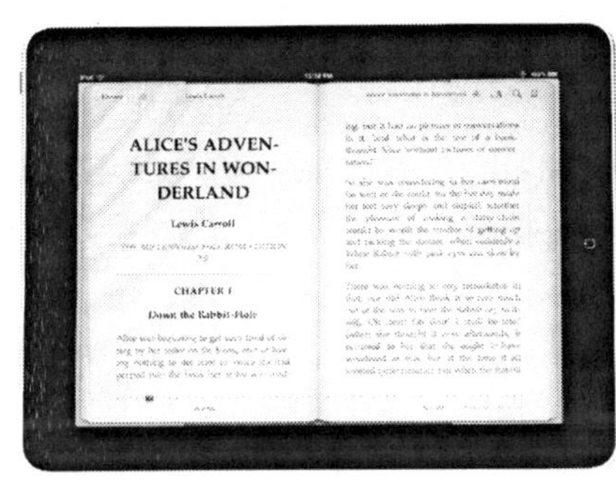


Reading a book on the iPad

In February 2010, Condé Nast Publications said it would sell iPad subscriptions for its *GQ*, *Vanity Fair* and *Wired* magazines by June.[130]

In April 2010, *The New York Times* announced it will begin publishing daily on the iPad.[131] As of October 2010, The New York Times iPad app is ad-supported and available for free without a paid subscription, but will transition to a subscription-based model in 2011.[132] Major news organizations, such as The Wall Street Journal, BBC, and Reuters have released iPad applications, to varying degrees of success.[133]

# Reception

On May 28, 2010, the iPad was released in Australia, Canada, and Japan, as well as several larger European countries. Media reaction to the launch was mixed. The media noted the positive response from fans of the device, with thousands of people queued on the first day of sale in a number of these countries.[134] [135]

## Reaction to the announcement

Media reaction to the iPad announcement was mixed. Walt Mossberg wrote, "It's about the software, stupid", meaning hardware features and build are less important to the iPad's success than software and user interface, his first impressions of which were largely positive. Mossberg also called the price "modest" for a device of its capabilities, and praised the ten-hour battery life.[136] Others, including *PC Advisor* and *The Sydney Morning Herald*, wrote that the iPad would also compete with proliferating netbooks, most of which use Microsoft Windows.[137] [138] The base model's $499 price was lower than pre-release estimates by the tech press, Wall Street analysts, and Apple's competitors, all of whom were expecting a much higher entry price point.[139] [140] [141]

CNET also criticized the iPad for its apparent lack of wireless sync which other portable devices such as Microsoft's Zune have had for a number of years. The built-in iTunes app is able to download from the Internet as well.[142]

## Reviews

Reviews of the iPad have been generally favorable. Walt Mossberg of *The Wall Street Journal* called it a "pretty close" laptop killer.[143] David Pogue of *The New York Times* wrote a "dual" review, one part for technology-minded people, and the other part for non-technology-minded people. In the former section, he notes that a laptop offers more features for a cheaper price than the iPad. In his review for the latter audience, however, he claims that if his readers like the concept of the device and can understand what its intended uses are, then they will enjoy using the device.[144] *PC Magazine*'s Tim Gideon wrote, "you have yourself a winner" that "will undoubtedly be a driving force in shaping the emerging tablet landscape."[145] Michael Arrington of *TechCrunch* said, "the iPad beats even my most optimistic expectations. This is a new category of device. But it also will replace laptops for many people."[146]

*PC World* criticized the iPad's file sharing and printing abilities.[147] and *Ars Technica* said sharing files with a computer is "one of our least favorite parts of the iPad experience."[148]

The media also praised the quantity of applications, as well as the bookstore and other media applications.[149] [150] In contrast they criticized the iPad for being a closed system and mentioned that the iPad faces competition from Android based tablets.[134] However, the Android tablet OS, known as *Honeycomb*, is not open source and has fewer apps available for it than for the iPad.[151] *The Independent* criticized the iPad for not being as readable in bright light as paper but praised it for being able to store large quantities of books.[149] After its UK release the Telegraph said the iPad's lack of Adobe Flash support was "annoying."[152]

## Recognition

The iPad was selected by Time Magazine as one of the 50 Best Inventions of the Year 2010,[153] while Popular Science chose it as the top gadget[154] behind the overall "Best of What's New 2010" winner Groasis Waterboxx.[155]

# Usage

## Business

While the iPad is mostly used by consumers it also has been taken up by business users. Some companies are adopting iPads in their business offices by distributing or making available the iPads to employees. Examples of uses in the workplace include attorneys responding to clients, medical professionals accessing health records during patient exams, and managers approving employee requests.[156] [157] [158]

A survey by Frost & Sullivan shows that iPad usage in office workplaces is linked to the goals of increased employee productivity, reduced paperwork, and increased revenue. The research firm estimates that "The mobile-office application market in North America may reach $6.85 billion in 2015, up from an estimated $1.76 billion [in 2010]."[159]

## Education

The iPad has several uses in the classroom,[160] and has been praised as a valuable tool for homeschooling.[161] [162] Soon after the iPad was released, it was reported that 81% of the top book apps were for children.[163] The iPad has also been called a revolutionary tool to help children with autism learn how to communicate and socialize more easily.[164]

Many colleges and universities have also used the iPad. Youngstown State University in Youngstown, Ohio, began offering three-hour rentals for the iPad for its Fall 2010 semester, in addition to rentals for the Amazon Kindle, laptop computers, and Flip cameras.[165]

## Sports

During the 2010 Major League Baseball free agent season, the agent for the player Carl Crawford was sending iPads to prospective teams interested in Mr. Crawford. These iPads were pre-loaded with video clips highlighting his player, and how it would benefit their team to have him.[166]

Fans attending Super Bowl XLV, the first Super Bowl since the iPad was released, could use an official NFL app to navigate Cowboys Stadium.[167]

## Music

The iPad is able to support many music creation applications in addition to the iTunes music playback software. These include sound samplers, guitar and voice effects processors, sequencers for synthesized sounds and sampled loops, virtual synthesizers and drum machines, theremin-style and other touch responsive instruments, drum pads and many more. Gorillaz's 2010 album, *The Fall*, was created almost exclusively using the iPad by Damon Albarn while on tour with the band.[168]

# References


[1] Wieland Wagner (May 28, 2010). "iPad Factory in the Firing Line: Worker Suicides Have Electronics Maker Uneasy in China" (http://www.spiegel.de/international/business/0,1518,697296,00.html). Spiegel.de. . Retrieved May 31, 2010.

[2] Matt Buchanan (March 5, 2010). "Official: iPad Launching Here April 3, Pre-Orders March 12" (http://gizmodo.com/5486444/official-ipad-launching-here-april-3-pre+orders-march-12). *Gizmodo*. . Retrieved March 4, 2010.

[3] Apple (March 5, 2010). "iPad Available in US on April 3" (http://www.apple.com/pr/library/2010/03/05ipad.html). Press release. . Retrieved March 5, 2010.

[4] Apple (April 20, 2010). "iPad Wi-Fi + 3G Models Available in US on April 30" (http://www.apple.com/pr/library/2010/04/20ipad.html). Press release. . Retrieved April 20, 2010.

[5] Joseph Menn and Tim Bradshaw (May 27, 2010). "Apple in control of iPad's Europe launch" (http://www.ft.com/cms/s/2/62bc6472-69bf-11df-8432-00144feab49a.html?ftcamp=rss). *Financial Times*. . Retrieved May 30, 2010.

[6] "Apple iPad2 website" (http://www.apple.com/ipad). March 2, 2011. . Retrieved March 2, 2011.

[7] "Apple Reports Third Quarter Results" (http://www.apple.com/pr/library/2010/07/20results.html). Apple Inc. July 20, 2010. . Retrieved October 23, 2010.

[8] "Apple Reports Fourth Quarter Results" (http://www.apple.com/pr/library/2010/10/18results.html). Apple Inc. October 18, 2010. . Retrieved October 23, 2010.

[9] "Apple Reports First Quarter Results 2011" (http://www.apple.com/pr/library/2011/01/18results.html). Apple Inc. January 18, 2011. . Retrieved January 18, 2011.

[10] "Apple Reports Second Quarter Results" (http://www.apple.com/pr/library/2011/04/20results.html). Apple. April 20, 2011. . Retrieved April 20, 2011.

[11] "iPad – Technical specifications and accessories for iPad" (http://www.apple.com/ipad/specs/). Apple. January 27, 2010. . Retrieved January 27, 2010.

[12] Brooke Crothers (January 27, 2010). "Inside the iPad: Apple's new 'A4' chip" (http://news.cnet.com/8301-13924_3-10442684-64.html). *CNET*. . Retrieved January 27, 2010.
[13] Miroslav Djuric (April 3, 2010). "teardown of production iPad" (http://www.ifixit.com/Teardown/iPad-Teardown/2183/2). Ifixit.com. p. 2. . Retrieved April 17, 2010.
[14] "iPad 2 Wi-Fi Teardown" (http://www.ifixit.com/Teardown/iPad-2-Wi-Fi-Teardown/5071/1). iFixit. . Retrieved 12 March 2011.
[15] Miroslav Djuric (April 3, 2010). "Apple A4 Teardown" (http://www.ifixit.com/Teardown/iPad-Teardown/2183/3#s11201). *iFixit*. . Retrieved April 17, 2010.
[16] "Apple Sells Three Million iPads in 80 Days" (http://www.apple.com/pr/library/2010/06/22ipad.html). June 22, 2010. . Retrieved June 22, 2010.
[17] "iPad 2 tablet launched by Apple's Steve Jobs" (http://www.bbc.co.uk/news/technology-12620077). BBC. March 2, 2011. . Retrieved March 6, 2011.
[18] "Apple Launches iPad 2" (http://www.apple.com/pr/library/2011/03/02ipad.html). Apple. 2 March 2001. . Retrieved 23 March 2011.
[19] http://www.bloomberg.com/news/2011-03-25/apple-begins-global-sales-of-new-ipad-2-tablet-as-competition-increases.html
[20] John Gruber (January 14, 2010). "The Original Tablet" (http://daringfireball.net/2010/01/the_original_tablet). *Daring Fireball*. . Retrieved March 20, 2010.
[21] Brad Stone (September 28, 2009). "Apple Rehires a Developer of Its Newton Tablet" (http://bits.blogs.nytimes.com/2009/09/28/apple-rehires-newton-and-nike-marketing-whiz/). *The New York Times*. . Retrieved March 20, 2010.
[22] "The Apple Museum: Prototypes" (http://www.theapplemuseum.com/index.php?id=45). *The Apple Museum*. . Retrieved February 23, 2010.
[23] Laura June (January 26, 2010). "The Apple Tablet: a complete history, supposedly" (http://www.engadget.com/2010/01/26/the-apple-tablet-a-complete-history-supposedly/). *Engadget*. . Retrieved January 27, 2010.
[24] Apple (January 27, 2010). "Apple Launches iPad" (http://www.apple.com/pr/library/2010/01/27ipad.html). Press release. . Retrieved January 27, 2010.
[25] "Apple iPad tablet is unveiled at live press conference" (http://www.nj.com/business/index.ssf/2010/01/apple_ipad_tablet_is_unveiled.html). *The Star-Ledger*. January 27, 2010. . Retrieved January 27, 2010.
[26] Cohen, Peter. Macworld Expo Keynote Live Update (http://www.macworld.com/news/2007/01/09/liveupdate/index.php), *Macworld*, (2007-01-09). Retrieved on 2007-02-01.
[27] Block, Ryan. Live from Macworld 2007: Steve Jobs keynote (http://www.engadget.com/2007/01/09/live-from-macworld-2007-steve-jobs-keynote/), *Engadget*, (2007-01-09). Retrieved on 2007-02-01.
[28] Grossman, Lev. The Apple Of Your Ear (http://www.time.com/time/magazine/article/0,9171,1576854,00.html), *Time*, (2007-01-12). Retrieved on 2007-02-01.
[29] "Jobs Says iPad Idea Came Before iPhone" (http://www.foxnews.com/scitech/2010/06/02/jobs-says-ipad-idea-came-iphone/). *Fox News*. June 2, 2010. .
[30] Jacqui Cheng. "Bed readers rejoice: iPad gains last-minute rotation lock" (http://arstechnica.com/apple/news/2010/03/bed-readers-rejoice-ipad-gains-last-minute-rotation-lock.ars). *Ars Technica*. Condé Nast. .
[31] Daniel Lewis (March 5, 2010). "ipad-pre-order-update-march-12" (http://electrobuzz.com/reviews/apple/ipad-pre-order-update-march-12/). *Electrobuzz*. . Retrieved March 5, 2010.
[32] Glenn Fleishman (February 2, 2010). "Can You Get By with 250 MB of Data Per Month?" (http://db.tidbits.com/article/10971). *TidBits*. . Retrieved February 23, 2010.
[33] Roger Cheng (January 27, 2010). "AT&T Gets A Vote Of Confidence From Apple With iPad Win" (http://online.wsj.com/article/BT-CO-20100127-717127.html). *The Wall Street Journal*. Dow Jones Newswires. . Retrieved January 27, 2010.
[34] AT&T (June 2, 2010). "AT&T Announces New Lower-Priced Wireless Data Plans to Make Mobile Internet More Affordable to More People" (http://www.webcitation.org/5qvHxMC1H). Press release. Archived from the original (http://www.att.com/gen/press-room?pid=4800&cdvn=news&newsarticleid=30854) on July 2, 2010. .
[35] "iPad with WiFi + 3G, the best way to stay connected" (http://www.apple.com/ipad/3g/). Apple Inc.. . Retrieved June 10, 2010.
[36] "iPad Available in Nine More Countries on May 28" (http://www.apple.com/pr/library/2010/05/07ipad.html). *Apple Press Release*. Apple. May 7, 2010. . Retrieved May 9, 2010.
[37] "Frustration in NZ over iPad" (http://www.straitstimes.com/BreakingNews/TechandScience/Story/STIStory_556883.html). Straits Times. July 23, 2010. . Retrieved July 27, 2010.
[38] "Israel retira prohibición para importación del iPad | Tecnología" (http://www.el-nacional.com/www/site/p_contenido.php?q=nodo/134548/TecnologÃ-a/Israel retira prohibiciÃ³n para importaciÃ³n del iPad). El Nacional.com. March 23, 2010. . Retrieved May 31, 2010.
[39] "Massive crowds turn out for iPad launch" (http://www.chinadaily.com.cn/photo/2010-09/18/content_11321052.htm). *China Daily*. Xinhua. 18 September 2010. . Retrieved 18 September 2010.
[40] Harvey, Mike (April 6, 2010). "iPad launch marred by technical glitches" (http://technology.timesonline.co.uk/tol/news/tech_and_web/personal_tech/article7088268.ece). *The Times* (London: News Corporation). . Retrieved June 26, 2010.
[41] Jim Goldman (May 3, 2010). "Apple Sells 1 Million iPads" (http://www.cnbc.com/id/36911690). *CNBC*. . Retrieved May 4, 2010.
[42] "iPad sales cross million mark twice as fast as original iPhone" (http://news.yahoo.com/s/ytech_gadg/20100503/tc_ytech_gadg/ytech_gadg_tc1901). Yahoo!. May 3, 2010. . Retrieved June 13, 2010.

[43] "Apple Reports Fourth Quarter Results" (http://www.apple.com/pr/library/2010/10/18results.html). Apple Inc.. October 18, 2010. . Retrieved October 18, 2010.
[44] Miguel Helft (January 17, 2011). "Apple Says Steve Jobs Will Take a New Medical Leave" (http://www.nytimes.com/2011/01/18/technology/18apple.html?_r=1). The New York Times. . Retrieved January 17, 2011.
[45] "IOS 4.3, GarageBand, and IMovie: What You Need to Know" (http://www.pcworld.com/businesscenter/article/221324/ios_43_garageband_and_imovie_what_you_need_to_know.html). PCWorld. . Retrieved 2011-03-04.
[46] "Apple Store: iPad 2" (http://store.apple.com/us/browse/home/shop_ipad/family/ipad/start?mco=MTcyMTgwNjM). Apple Inc.. 2011. . Retrieved 10 March 2011.
[47] John, Paczkowski (15 March 2011). "Apple Postpones iPad 2 Launch in Japan" (http://digitaldaily.allthingsd.com/20110315/apple-postpones-ipad-2-launch-in-japan/). All Things Digital. . Retrieved 4 May 2011.
[48] Satariano, Adam (7 March 2011). "Apple to reimburse recent iPad buyers after new model debut" (http://www.sddt.com/News/article.cfm?SourceCode=20110303faj). San Diego Source – The Daily Transcript. . Retrieved 10 March 2011.
[49] Bosker, Bianca (October 19, 2010). "Apple's 'iPad 2' Won't Be A Smaller, 7-Inch Version, Steve Jobs Suggests" (http://www.huffingtonpost.com/2010/10/19/apples-ipad-2-wont-be-a-s_n_767882.html). The Huffington Post. . Retrieved January 7, 2011.
[50] Pogue, David (January 13, 2007). "Ultimate iPhone FAQs List, Part 2 - Pogue's Posts Blog – NYTimes.com" (http://pogue.blogs.nytimes.com/2007/01/13/ultimate-iphone-faqs-list-part-2/). Pogue.blogs.nytimes.com. . Retrieved May 31, 2010.
[51] "Expo Notes: iPad cases, touch gloves hot items on expo floor | Tablets | MacUser" (http://www.macworld.com/article/146421/2010/02/ipad_accessories.html). Macworld. . Retrieved May 31, 2010.
[52] Broida, Rick (January 28, 2010). "Want to take notes on an iPad? Here's your stylus | iPhone Atlas – CNET Reviews" (http://reviews.cnet.com/8301-19512_7-10443415-233.html). Reviews.cnet.com. . Retrieved May 31, 2010.
[53] "What's Up The Sleeves of the Apple iPad – Apple iPad Specifications | Laptop Reviews UK" (http://www.laptopreviews.org.uk/apple-laptops/sleeves-apple-ipad-apple-ipad-specifications). Laptopreviews.org.uk. . Retrieved May 31, 2010.
[54] "iPad's 'Mute' Switch Replaced With Screen Rotation Lock." (http://www.macrumors.com/2010/03/12/ipads-mute-switch-replaced-with-screen-rotation-lock/). MacRumors. March 12, 2010. . Retrieved March 12, 2010.
[55] Frank Michael Russell (March 19, 2011). "Tech Notebook: Apple's svelte new iPad 2: its weight-loss secrets revealed" (http://www.mercurynews.com/breaking-news/ci_17646727?nclick_check=1). San Jose Mercury News. . Retrieved March 20, 2011.
[56] David Carnoy, cnet.com. " Apple uses stronger glass in iPad 2 (http://news.cnet.com/8301-17938_105-20047098-1.html?part=rss&subj=news&tag=2547-1_3-0-20)." March 25, 2011. Retrieved March 25, 2011.
[57] Ogasawara, Todd (9 March 2011). "iPad 2 Rear Camera Has Tap for Auto Exposure, Not Auto Focus" (http://www.mediabistro.com/thinkmobile/ipad-2-rear-camera-has-tap-for-auto-exposure-not-auto-focus_b11531). Think Mobile. . Retrieved 27 March 2011.
[58] Goldman, David (March 2, 2011). "IPad 2: Thinner, faster, and with a Steve Jobs surprise" (http://money.cnn.com/2011/03/02/technology/ipad_2_announcement/). CNNMoney. . Retrieved 2011-03-02.
[59] Hannah Bouckley (June 1, 2010). "Apple iPad WiFi + 3G review" (http://www.t3.com/reviews/computers/pcs/apple-ipad-wifi-3g-review). T3 Online. . Retrieved June 13, 2010.
[60] "iPad – Design" (http://www.apple.com/ipad/design/). Apple. . Retrieved June 13, 2010.
[61] "iPad's lack of Flash/USB/Bluetooth is all about lock-in (updated)" (http://www.zdnet.com/blog/apple/ipads-lack-of-flashusbbluetooth-is-all-about-lock-in-updated/5922). *ZDNet*. CNet. February 1, 2010. . Retrieved June 19, 2010.
[62] "iPad: About iPad Dock Connector to VGA Adapter compatibility" (http://support.apple.com/kb/ht4108). Apple Inc.. . Retrieved June 11, 2010.
[63] "How to Record Video and Images from iPad" (http://www.epiphan.com/solutions_new/image-capture/how-to-record-streaming-video-and-images-from-ipad/). . Retrieved March 2, 2011.
[64] Huang, Joyce (June 7, 2010). "Best Under a Billion: Batteries Required?" (http://www.forbes.com/global/2010/0607/best-under-billion-10-raymond-sung-simplo-technology-batteries-requried.html?boxes=Homepagetmagazines). Forbes. . Retrieved June 11, 2010.
[65] "iPad: Charging the battery" (http://support.apple.com/kb/HT4060). Apple. . Retrieved December 25, 2010.
[66] Kyle VanHemert (March 13, 2010). "Apple will replace the dead battery of an iPad for $99" (http://gizmodo.com/5492711/apple-will-replace-dead-battery-ipads-for-99). *Gizmodo*. . Retrieved March 15, 2010.
[67] "iPad Battery Replacement Service: Frequently Asked Questions" (http://www.apple.com/support/ipad/service/battery/). Apple. . Retrieved March 14, 2010.
[68] Jeremy Horwitz (April 26, 2010). "Apple iPad Camera Connection Kit" (http://www.ilounge.com/index.php/reviews/entry/apple-ipad-camera-connection-kit/). iLounge. . Retrieved June 19, 2010.
[69] Chris Foresman (April 27, 2010). "iPad WiFi + 3G day is today; here's our data plan primer" (http://arstechnica.com/apple/news/2010/04/ipad-3g-wifi-day-is-today-heres-our-data-plan-primer.ars). *Ars Technica*. Condé Nast. . Retrieved June 11, 2010.
[70] "Sad news for iPad in Japan" (http://lemon.soju.co.uk/2010/05/11/sad-news-for-ipad-in-japan/). .
[71] Kang, Cecilia (January 27, 2010). "Apple's iPad wireless service to be unlocked, partnered with AT&T" (http://voices.washingtonpost.com/posttech/2010/01/from_washington_the_most_inter.html). *Washington Post*. . Retrieved April 26, 2010.
[72] Golijan, Rosa (January 27, 2010). "Unlocked or Not, Your iPad Won't Be Able to Use T-Mobile's 3G Network" (http://gizmodo.com/5458423/unlocked-or-not-your-ipad-wont-be-able-to-use-t+mobiles-3g-network). *Gizmodo*. . Retrieved April 26, 2010.

[73] Baig, Ed (March 2, 2011). "Apple launching iPad 2 on March 11" (http://content.usatoday.com/communities/technologylive/post/2011/03/live-coverage-apple-expected-to-unveil-new-ipad/1). USA Today. . Retrieved 2011-03-02.

[74] "iPad must-haves. And fun-to-haves." (http://www.apple.com/ipad/accessories/). Apple. . Retrieved 22 March 2011.

[75] "Apple iPad Keyboard Dock- English" (http://store.apple.com/us/product/MC533LL/B). Apple Store. . Retrieved 22 March 2011.

[76] Murph, Darren (14 December 2010). "Knockoff 3-in-1 iPad camera connection kit improves Apple's own design" (http://www.engadget.com/2010/12/14/knockoff-3-in-1-ipad-camera-connection-kit-improves-apples-own/). Engadget. . Retrieved 22 March 2011.

[77] Dove, Jackie (2011-03-02). "Smart Cover, Digital AV adapter accompany iPad 2 launch" (http://www.macworld.com/article/158263/2011/03/ipadcovers.html). Macworld.com. . Retrieved 2011-03-02.

[78] "Apple Digital AV Adapter" (http://store.apple.com/us/product/MC953). Apple. . Retrieved 21 March 2011.

[79] "iPad 2 Smart Cover Teardown" (http://www.ifixit.com/Teardown/iPad-2-Smart-Cover-Teardown/5089/1). iFixit. . Retrieved 22 March 2011.

[80] "Apple - Smart Cover" (http://www.apple.com/ipad/smart-cover/). apple.com. 2011-03-02. . Retrieved 2011-03-12.

[81] Apple Launches iPad 2 (Announcement) (http://www.apple.com/pr/library/2011/03/02ipad.html)

[82] [http://www.apple.com/pr/library/2011/03/10ipad.html iPad 2 Arrives Tomorrow

[83] "In April, Apple Ditched Google and Skyhook in Favor of Its Own Location Databases" (http://techcrunch.com/2010/07/29/apple-location/). *TechCrunch*. July 29, 2010. . Retrieved October 14, 2010.

[84] "iPad - iOS 4" (http://www.apple.com/ipad/ios4/). Apple Inc.. March 13, 2011. . Retrieved March 13, 2011.

[85] Christopher Breen (April 6, 2010). "The iPad as iPod" (http://www.macworld.com/article/150427/2010/04/ipad_as_ipod.html). MacWorld.com. . Retrieved June 26, 2010.

[86] Rich Trenholm (January 27, 2010). "Apple iPad launch: The first specs" (http://crave.cnet.co.uk/laptops/0,39029450,49304822,00.htm). CNet. . Retrieved June 26, 2010.

[87] Dockrill, Peter (3 March 2011). "iPad vs iPad 2 back-to-back: what's new, plus all the specs compared" (http://apcmag.com/ipad-vs-ipad-2-back-to-back-whats-new-plus-all-the-newold-specs-compared.htm). *apc*. .

[88] Nick Saint, provided by (March 31, 2010). "Where In The World Is My iPad? (AAPL)" (http://www.sfgate.com/cgi-bin/article.cgi?f=/g/a/2010/03/31/businessinsider-where-in-the-world-is-my-ipad-2010-3.DTL). Sfgate.com. . Retrieved April 17, 2010.

[89] http://www.bbc.co.uk/news/business-13058866

[90] JR Raphael (April 7, 2010). "Apple iPad Costs $260 to build, iSuppli Finds" (http://www.pcworld.com/article/193746/apple_ipad_costs_260_to_build_isuppli_finds.html). PC World. . Retrieved June 11, 2010.

[91] "Chipworks Confirms Apple A4 iPad chip is fabbed by Samsung in their 45-nm process" (http://www.chipworks.com/A4_is_Samsung_45nm.aspx). Chipworks.com. . Retrieved May 27, 2010.

[92] "Inside the iPad: Samsung, Broadcom snag multiple wins" (http://www.eetimes.com/news/design/rss/showArticle.jhtml?articleID=224201247&cid=RSSfeed_eetimes_designRSS). EE Times. . Retrieved April 17, 2010.

[93] Gabriel Madway (April 1, 2010). "Special Report: iPad striptease: It's what's inside that counts" (http://www.reuters.com/article/idUSTRE6300SY20100401). Reuters. .

[94] Sam Oliver (March 26, 2010). "Delays cause Apple to switch iPad touch-panel orders to Wintek" (http://www.appleinsider.com/articles/10/03/26/delays_cause_apple_to_switch_ipad_touch_panel_orders_to_wintek.html). Apple Insider. . Retrieved April 17, 2010.

[95] "Under the Radar; Apple's Asian Suppliers Work Furiously" (http://www.industryweek.com/articles/under_the_radar_apples_asian_suppliers_work_furiously_21483.aspx?ShowAll=1). Industry Week. April 2, 2010. . Retrieved April 26, 2010.

[96] "Inside the Apple iPad" (http://electronicdesign.com/article/embedded/inside_the_ipad.aspx). Electronic Design. April 5, 2010. . Retrieved April 26, 2010.

[97] Harmsen, Peter (April 2, 2010). "Under the radar, Apple's Asian suppliers work furiously" (http://www.google.com/hostednews/afp/article/ALeqM5hpQruUVIlYbsS8gynytmIIUk0vpg). Agence France-Presse. Google. . Retrieved April 17, 2010.

[98] Michelle Maisto (June 10, 2010). "Apple iPhone 4 to Trigger Gyroscope Onslaught: iSuppli" (http://www.eweek.com/c/a/Mobile-and-Wireless/Apple-iPhone-4-to-Trigger-Gyroscope-Onslaught-iSuppli-329651/). eWeek. . Retrieved June 13, 2010.

[99] "iPad SDK" (http://www.apple.com/ipad/sdk/). Apple. January 27, 2010. . Retrieved January 27, 2010.

[100] Adam Ferruci (January 27, 2010). "8 Things That Suck About the iPad" (http://gizmodo.com/5458382/8-things-that-suck-about-the-ipad). *Gizmodo*. . Retrieved February 3, 2010.

[101] Rik Myslewski (January 27, 2010). "Steve Jobs uncloaks the 'iPad': World continues to revolve around sun" (http://www.theregister.co.uk/2010/01/27/ipad/). *The Register*. . Retrieved January 27, 2010.

[102] MG Siegler (January 28, 2010). "The Subplots of the iPad Blockbuster" (http://www.techcrunch.com/2010/01/28/ipad-extras/). *Tech Crunch*. . Retrieved February 1, 2010.

[103] Raghavendra, Nayak (February 2010). "Apple iPad Features" (http://www.latestsets.com/2010/02/apple-ipad-features.html). Latest Sets. . Retrieved May 27, 2010.

[104] "iOS 4.2 available for iPad in November" (http://www.apple.com/ipad/software-update/). .

[105] Snell, Jason (2010-11-22). "Apple releases iOS 4.2.1" (http://news.yahoo.com/s/macworld/20101122/tc_macworld/applereleasesios421). *Yahoo news*. . Retrieved 2010-11-23.

[106] "iPad Features" (http://www.apple.com/ipad/features/). Apple Inc.. January 27, 2010. . Retrieved January 28, 2010.

[107] Jeff Smykil (April 20, 2010). "The keyboardless Office: a review of iWork for iPad" (http://arstechnica.com/apple/reviews/2010/04/iwork-for-ipad-clever-subtitle-goes-here.ars/4). *ArsTechnica*. Condé Nast. . Retrieved May 1, 2010.

[108] David Sarno (January 29, 2010). "Apple confirms 3G VoIP apps on iPad, iPhone, iPod touch; Skype is waiting" (http://latimesblogs.latimes.com/technology/2010/01/apple-confirms-3g-voip-apps-on-ipad-iphone-ipod-touch-skype-is-waiting.html). *Los Angeles Times*. . Retrieved February 7, 2010.

[109] "Apple Event 1st September 2010" (http://events.apple.com.edgesuite.net/1009qpeijrfn/event). September 1, 2010. . Retrieved September 1, 2010.

[110] Dejo. "XCode ON iPad" (http://stackoverflow.com/questions/2150178/run-iphone-sdk-on-ipad).

[111] "IPhone and iPad users sue Apple over privacy issues" (http://www.reuters.com/article/idUSTRE6BR1Y820101228). *Reuters* (Thomson Reuters). 28 December 2010. . Retrieved 28 December 2010.

[112] Bobbie Johnson (February 1, 2010). "Apple iPad will choke innovation, say open internet advocates [sic, apparently meaning '... open-Internet advocates' (http://www.guardian.co.uk/technology/2010/feb/01/apple-ipad-choke-innovation)"]. *The Guardian* (London). . Retrieved February 7, 2010.

[113] "Apple's Trend Away From Tinkering" (http://apple.slashdot.org/story/10/01/31/1657233/Apples-Trend-Away-From-Tinkering). *Slashdot*. January 31, 2010. . Retrieved February 12, 2010.

[114] "All Your Apps Are Belong to Apple: The iPhone Developer Program License Agreement" (http://www.eff.org/deeplinks/2010/03/iphone-developer-program-license-agreement-all). Electronic Frontier Foundation. March 9, 2010. . Retrieved April 17, 2010.

[115] Sydell, Laura (April 5, 2010). "Apple's iPad: The End Of The Internet As We Know It?" (http://www.npr.org/templates/story/story.php?storyId=125561844). *NPR*. . Retrieved April 23, 2010

[116] Charlie Sorrel (May 3, 2010). "iPad Jailbreak Ready for Download" (http://www.wired.com/gadgetlab/2010/05/ipad-jailbreak-ready-for-download/). *Wired*. Condé Nast. . Retrieved May 8, 2010.

[117] John Herrman (May 8, 2010). "How To: Jailbreak Any iPhone, iPod Touch or iPad" (http://gizmodo.com/5533921/how-to-jailbreak-any-iphone-ipod-touch-or-ipad). *Gizmodo*. . Retrieved May 8, 2010.

[118] Daniel Ionescu. "Never Mind Legality, iPhone Jailbreaking Voids Your Warranty" (http://www.pcworld.com/article/201968/never_mind_legality_iphone_jailbreaking_voids_your_warranty.html). *PCWorld*. .

[119] Jack Schofield (May 10, 2010). "Wikipedia's porn purge, and cleaning up for the iPad" (http://www.guardian.co.uk/technology/2010/may/10/ipad-apple). London: The Guardian. .

[120] "NSFW Guide to Watching Porn on your iPad" (http://www.crunchgear.com/2010/04/24/ipad-porn-private/). *GrunchGear*. April 24, 2010. . Retrieved June 28, 2010.

[121] "YouPorn Goes HTML5, Gets on the iPad" (http://newteevee.com/2010/05/18/youporn-goes-html5-gets-on-the-ipad/). *NewTeeVee*. May 18, 2010. . Retrieved June 28, 2010.

[122] "Steve Jobs Offers World 'Freedom From Porn'" (http://gawker.com/5539717/steve-jobs-offers-world-freedom-from-porn). *Gawker*. May 15, 2010. . Retrieved June 20, 2010.

[123] "Apple iPad offers "freedom from porn" – but not in Berlin" (http://eu.techcrunch.com/2010/05/29/apple-ipad-offers-freedom-from-porn-but-not-in-berlin/). *TechCrunch*. May 29, 2010. . Retrieved June 20, 2010.

[124] "Porn again: "Dudes" who like it alter San Francisco iPad ads" (http://www.zdnet.com/blog/btl/porn-again-dudes-who-like-it-alter-san-francisco-ipad-ads/35676). *ZDNet*. CNet. June 9, 2010. . Retrieved October 20, 2010.

[125] Patel, Nilay (January 27, 2010). "The Apple iPad: starting at $499" (http://www.engadget.com/2010/01/27/the-apple-ipad/). *Engadget*. . Retrieved January 27, 2010.

[126] Joshua Topolsky (January 27, 2010). "Live from the Apple 'latest creation' event" (http://www.engadget.com/2010/01/27/live-from-the-apple-tablet-latest-creation-event/). *Engadget*. . Retrieved February 3, 2010.

[127] "Apple tablet due March, to get Kindle-killer book deal?" (http://www.electronista.com/articles/09/12/09/apple.device.at.1m.a.month.70.30.revenue.split/). *Electronista*. December 9, 2009. . Retrieved January 24, 2010.

[128] http://www.amazon.com/gp/feature.html/ref=sa_menu_karl3?ie=UTF8&docId=1000493771

[129] http://www.barnesandnoble.com/u/nook-for-iPad/379002216/

[130] Stephanie Clifford (February 28, 2010). "Condé Nast Is Preparing iPad Versions of Some of Its Top Magazines" (http://www.nytimes.com/2010/03/01/business/media/01conde.html). *The New York Times*. . Retrieved March 2, 2010.

[131] Andy Brett (April 1, 2010). "The New York Times Introduces An iPad App" (http://techcrunch.com/2010/04/01/new-york-times-ipad/). *TechCrunch*. . Retrieved April 1, 2010.

[132] Albanesius, Chloe (October 15, 2010). "New York Times iPad App Gets Overhaul, More Content" (http://www.pcmag.com/article2/0,2817,2370854,00.asp). *PC Magazine*. .

[133] "The 10 Best iPad Applications for News" (http://platform.idiomag.com/2010/06/the-10-best-ipad-applications-for-news/). *idio*. June 14, 2010. . Retrieved July 26, 2010.

[134] "iPad fans mob Apple stores for international launch" (http://news.bbc.co.uk/1/hi/technology/10182143.stm). *BBC News online* (BBC). May 28, 2010. . Retrieved May 31, 2010.

[135] "iPad-mania as thousands queue for global roll-out" (http://www.france24.com/en/20100528-ipad-mania-thousands-queue-global-roll-out-0). *France24*. May 28, 2010. . Retrieved May 31, 2010.

[136] Walter S. Mossberg (January 27, 2010). "First Impressions of the New Apple iPad" (http://mossblog.allthingsd.com/20100127/apple-ipad-impressions/). *All Things Digital*. . Retrieved January 27, 2010.

[137] Eric Lai (January 28, 2010). "Apple iPad versus netbook: features compared: We compare design, functionality and storage" (http://www.pcadvisor.co.uk/news/index.cfm?newsid=3211316). *PC Advisor*. . Retrieved January 28, 2010.

[138] Simon Tsang (February 2, 2010). "iPad vs the Kindle, tablets and netbooks" (http://www.smh.com.au/digital-life/computers/ipad-vs-the-kindle-tablets-and-netbooks-20100202-n9jf.html). *The Sydney Morning Herald*. . Retrieved February 2, 2010.
[139] Eaton, Kit (January 27, 2010). "The iPad's Biggest Innovation: Its $500 Price" (http://www.fastcompany.com/article/apples-tablet-introduced?page=0,0). *Fast Company*. . Retrieved March 7, 2010.
[140] Peers, Martin (January 28, 2010). "Apple's iPad Revolution: Price" (http://online.wsj.com/article/SB10001424052748704094304575029621430370074.html). *The Wall Street Journal*. . Retrieved February 20, 2010.
[141] Stokes, John (January 29, 2010). "Tablet makers rethinking things in wake of iPad's $499 price" (http://arstechnica.com/apple/news/2010/01/tablet-makers-rethinking-things-in-wake-of-ipads-low-price.ars). *Ars Technica*. Condé Nast. . Retrieved February 20, 2010.
[142] Matt Rosoff (January 30, 2010). "How to make the iPad a better music device" (http://news.cnet.com/8301-13526_3-10444796-27.html). *CNET*. . Retrieved March 2, 2010.
[143] Mossberg, Walter S. (March 31, 2010). "Apple iPad Review: Laptop Killer? Pretty Close" (http://ptech.allthingsd.com/20100331/apple-ipad-review/). *All Things Digital*. The Wall Street Journal. . Retrieved March 31, 2010.
[144] Pogue, David (March 31, 2010). "Reviews: Love It or Not? Looking at iPad From 2 Angles" (http://www.nytimes.com/2010/04/01/technology/personaltech/01pogue.html?pagewanted=all&partner=rss&emc=rss). *The New York Times*. . Retrieved March 31, 2010.
[145] Gideon, Tim (March 31, 2010). "Apple iPad (Wi-Fi)" (http://www.pcmag.com/article2/0,2817,2362042,00.asp). *PC Magazine*. . Retrieved April 1, 2010.
[146] Michael Arrington (April 2, 2010). "The Unauthorized TechCrunch iPad Review" (http://techcrunch.com/2010/04/02/the-unauthorized-techcrunch-ipad-review/). *TechCrunch*. . Retrieved April 2, 2010.
[147] Nick Mediati (April 5, 2010). "iPad Struggles at Printing and Sharing Files" (http://www.pcworld.com/businesscenter/article/193520/ipad_struggles_at_printing_and_sharing_files.html). *PC World*. . Retrieved May 1, 2010.
[148] Jacqui Cheng (April 7, 2010). "Ars Technica reviews the iPad" (http://arstechnica.com/apple/reviews/2010/04/ipad-review.ars/4). *Ars Technica*. Condé Nast. p. 4. . Retrieved May 4, 2010.
[149] David Phelan (May 26, 2010). "The iPad: what is it good for?" (http://www.independent.co.uk/life-style/gadgets-and-tech/features/the-ipad-what-is-it-good-for-1982635.html). *The Independent* (London). . Retrieved May 31, 2010.
[150] Kate Bevan (May 31, 2010). "The best iPad media apps" (http://www.guardian.co.uk/media/2010/may/31/best-ipad-media-apps). *The Guardian* (London: Guardian Media Group). . Retrieved June 10, 2010.
[151] http://news.yahoo.com/s/ac/20110505/tc_ac/8424685_android_tablets_will_never_replace_the_ipad
[152] "Lack of Flash support on iPad 'annoying', say consumers" (http://www.telegraph.co.uk/technology/apple/7759268/Lack-of-Flash-support-on-iPad-annoying-say-consumers.html). Daily Telegraph. May 24, 2010. . Retrieved April 14, 2011.
[153] Harry McCracken (2010-11-11). "The 50 Best Inventions of 2010: iPad" (http://www.time.com/time/specials/packages/article/0,28804,2029497_2030652,00.html). Time Magazine. . Retrieved 2010-11-17.
[154] Best of What's New 2010: Gadgets (http://www.popsci.com/bown/2010/category/gadgets) *Popular Science*. Accessed: 5 December 2010.
[155] Jannot, Mark. Best of What's New 2010: Our 100 Innovations of the Year (http://www.popsci.com/announcements/article/2010-11/best-whats-new-2010-our-100-innovations-year) *Popular Science*, 16 December 2010. Accessed: 5 November 2010.
[156] "iPad creeping into business offices" (http://www.computerworld.com/s/article/351462/iPad_Creeping_Into_Business_Offices). *Computer World*. September 13, 2010. .
[157] Sperling, Ed (September 13, 2010). "Rise Of The Tablet Computer" (http://www.forbes.com/2010/09/10/ipad-apple-blackberry-technology-cio-network-tablets.html). *Forbes*. .
[158] Worthen, Ben (August 24, 2010). "Businesses Add iPads to Their Briefcases" (http://online.wsj.com/article/SB10001424052748703846604575447531699309858.html?mod=WSJ_hps_MIDDLESixthNews). *The Wall Street Journal*. .
[159] "MicroStrategy's Corporate Apps Boost Productivity" (http://www.businessweek.com/technology/content/nov2010/tc20101111_549315.htm). *Bloomberg Businessweek*. November 1, 2010. . "About 42 percent of respondents in the survey, which was released in August, sought an increase in user productivity, followed by reduced paperwork (39 percent), and increased revenue (37 percent). The mobile-office application market in North America may reach $6.85 billion in 2015, up from an estimated $1.76 billion this year, Frost & Sullivan estimates."
[160] Teleread.com: Teaching with the iPad (http://www.teleread.com/ipad/teaching-with-the-ipad-first-days). Retrieved October 1, 2010.
[161] Spotty Banana: iPad in the Homeschool. (http://spottybanana.com/2010/04/13/ipad-in-the-homeschool). Retrieved October 1, 2010.
[162] How Will the Apple iPad Change Our Kids' Lives? (http://www.wired.com/geekdad/2010/01/how-will-the-apple-tablet-change-our-kids-lives), Wired.com (http://www.wired.com). Retrieved October 1, 2010.
[163] 81 Percent of Top Book Apps Are Kids Titles (http://www.aolnews.com/tech/article/for-ipad-81-percent-of-top-book-apps-are-kids-titles/19455766), AOL News. Retrieved October 1, 2010.
[164] iHelp for Autism (http://www.sfweekly.com/2010-08-11/news/ihelp-for-autism/), San Francisco Weekly (http://ww.sfweekly.com). Retrieved October 1, 2010.
[165] Shelly Xiaoli Zhu, Library Webmaster (2010-09-01). "blogs in Library" (http://www.maag.ysu.edu/about/ipadkindle.html). Maag.ysu.edu. . Retrieved 2010-11-11.
[166] Mark Topkin, Staff Writer (2010-11-28). "Rays Rumblings" (http://www.tampabay.com/sports/baseball/rays/arbitration-nontender-decisions-to-come-this-week-for-tampa-bay-rays/1136877). tampabay.com. . Retrieved 2010-12-07.

[167] Malinowski, Erik (1 February 2011). "Cowboys Stadium Techs Up for Super Bowl Close-Up" (http://www.wired.com/playbook/2011/02/super-bowl-nerve-center/). Wired. . Retrieved 4 May 2011.
[168] "Gorillaz are to release a free album on Christmas Day" (http://www.bbc.co.uk/newsbeat/11968925). *BBC Newsbeat*. BBC. December 10, 2010. . Retrieved December 25, 2010.

# External links

- iPad official site (http://www.apple.com/ipad/)
- Apple Special Event January 2010 (http://www.apple.com/quicktime/qtv/specialevent0110/) Apple Inc. January 27, 2010
- iMac to iPad: 12 years of big-time Apple innovations (http://www.networkworld.com/slideshows/2010/012610-apple-innovations.html#slide1)
- Nielsen's iPad usability research findings (http://www.nngroup.com/reports/mobile/ipad/ipad-usability.pdf)
- "Why We Prize That Magical Mystery Pad" (http://online.wsj.com/article/SB10001424052748704758904576188511633084364.html), essay by Virginia Postrel at WSJ, Mar 12, 2011.

# iPad 2

## iPad 2

| iPad 2 | |
|---|---|
| 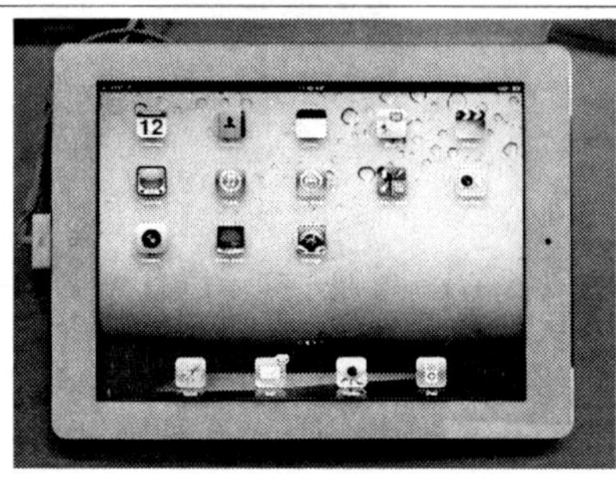 iPad 2 (white) | |
| **Developer** | Apple Inc. |
| **Manufacturer** | Foxconn (contract-basis with Apple) |
| **Product family** | iPad |
| **Type** | Tablet, media player |
| **Generation** | 2nd |
| **Release date** | **2011-03-11:** United States<br>**2011-03-25:** Australia, Austria, Belgium, Canada, Czech Republic, Denmark, Finland, France, Germany, Greece, Iceland, Italy, Ireland, Hungary, Luxembourg, Mexico, Netherlands, New Zealand, Norway, Poland, Portugal, Spain, Sweden, Switzerland, United Kingdom<br>**2011-04-28:** Japan<br>**2011-04-29:** Hong Kong, India, Israel, Macau, Malaysia, Philippines, Singapore, South Africa, South Korea, Turkey, United Arab Emirates<br>**2011-05-06:** China, Estonia, Latvia, Lithuania, Thailand |
| **Operating system** | iOS 4.3.3 |
| **Power** | Internal rechargeable non-removable 25 W·h (90 kJ) lithium-polymer battery |
| **CPU** | 1 GHz dual-core (up to 1GHz) Apple A5 |
| **Storage capacity** | Flash memory<br>16 GB, 32 GB, or 64 GB[1] |
| **Memory** | 512 MB DDR2 (1066 Mbit/s) RAM[2] |
| **Display** | 9.7 inches (250 mm) 4:3 aspect ratio **Resolution:** 1024x768 px (XGA) (1080p – video out via Apple Digital AV Adapter; support simultaneous charging)[3] |
| **Graphics** | PowerVR SGX543MP2[4]<br>67 MPolygon/s<br>2 GPixel/s fill rate |
| **Input** | Multi-touch touch screen, headset controls, proximity and ambient light sensors, 3-axis gyroscope, microphone, magnetometer, accelerometer, Assisted GPS + Cellular (3G Model only), Micro-SIM Card tray (3G-GSM Model only) |
| **Camera** | **Front:** Video recording, VGA up to 30 fps with audio, VGA-quality still camera, 0.3 megapixels.[1]<br>**Back:** Video recording, 960x720 up to 30 fps with audio, 960x720 still camera with 5x digital zoom, 0.7 megapixels.[5] |
| **Touchpad** | Capacitive touchscreen[6] |

| | |
|---|---|
| **Connectivity** | Wi-Fi (802.11 a/b/g/n)<br>Bluetooth 2.1 + EDR<br>**Wi-Fi + 3G GSM model also includes:** UMTS / HSDPA (Quad band–850, 900, 1900, 2100 MHz)<br>GSM / EDGE (Quad band–850, 900, 1800, 1900 MHz)<br>**Wi-Fi + 3G CDMA model also includes:** CDMA EV-DO Rev. A (800, 1900 MHz) |
| **Online services** | iTunes Store, App Store, MobileMe, iBookstore, Safari, Game Center, Photo Booth* |
| **Dimensions** | 9.50 in (241 mm) *(height)*<br>7.31 in (186 mm) *(width)*<br>0.346 in (8.8 mm) *(depth)* |
| **Weight** | **Wi-Fi model:** 1.33 lb (600 g)<br>**Wi-Fi + 3G model (GSM):** 1.35 lb (610 g)<br>**Wi-Fi + 3G model (CDMA):** 1.34 lb (610 g) |
| **Predecessor** | Original iPad |
| **Related articles** | iPad, iPhone, iPod touch (Comparison) |
| **Website** | www.apple.com/ipad [16] |

The **iPad 2** is the second generation of the iPad, a tablet computer designed, developed and marketed by Apple Inc. It serves primarily as a platform for audio-visual media including books, periodicals, movies, music, games and web content, and is available in black or white. The Foxconn-manufactured iPad 2 has a lithium-polymer battery that lasts up to 10 hours, a new dual core Apple A5 processor and VGA front-facing and 720p rear-facing cameras designed for FaceTime video calling.

Apple unveiled the device on March 2, 2011,[7] began selling it by website and retail stores on March 11,[8] and released it in 25 other countries on March 25, including Australia, Britain and Canada.[9] Apple announced that the iPad 2 will be released in Hong Kong, South Korea, Singapore and other countries on April 29, 2011.[10]

## History

Much speculation preceded the iPad's unveiling. More or less typical was a November 2010 piece by *Economic News Daily*, reporting that the iPad 2 would have a better display, a USB port, and front- and back-facing camera — only the last of which was correct.[11] Chinese authorities arrested three Foxconn employees on December 26 for allegedly leaking the metrics of the iPad 2 to case designers.[12]

Apple sent invitations to journalists on February 23, 2011, for a media event on March 2.[13] Apple Inc. CEO Steve Jobs revealed the device at the Yerba Buena Center for the Arts on March 2, 2011, despite being on medical leave.[7]

Apple began selling the iPad 2 on its website on March 11,[8] and in its U.S. retail stores at 5 p.m. local time on that date. Many stores in major cities, such as New York, sold out within hours.[14] Online shipping delays had increased to three to four weeks on Sunday and four to five weeks by Tuesday.[15] [16] One analyst predicted that Apple would sell 35 million iPad 2s in 2011, noting that the iPad is more advanced yet cheaper than most other tablets.[17]

The iPad 2 was released internationally in 25 other countries on March 25, 2011. The countries included Australia, Austria, Belgium, Canada, Czech Republic, Denmark, Finland, France, Germany, Greece, Iceland, Italy, Ireland, Hungary, Luxembourg, Mexico, Netherlands, New Zealand, Norway, Poland, Portugal, Spain, Sweden, Switzerland and the United Kingdom.[9] Apple announced that the iPad 2 will be released in Hong Kong, South Korea, Singapore and other countries in April 2011.[10]

The March 25 release date for Japan has been postponed due to the earthquake and tsunami which struck the nation on 11 March 2011. The iPads may be delayed due to the NAND flash storage chip used in the iPads being created by Toshiba, which has been affected by the earthquake and tsunami and has closed indefinitely.[18] The slowdown caused analysts to downgrade Apple's stock.[19]

## Software

The iPad 2 is currently supplied with iOS 4.3.1, a similar system to previous iOS versions. The 4.3.1 system fixed bug with the graphics on the iPod touch, bugs related to activating and connecting to some cellular networks, authenticating with some enterprise web services.[20] A newer version, 4.3.3 is available for online download once an account is created with the iStore.

## Hardware

The iPad 2 includes a new A5 processor, front and rear cameras plus a 3 axis gyroscope. Several components were made smaller to fit the new iPad.

### Audio

The speaker of the iPad 2.

The iPad can play audio in mono using its built in speaker. Its frequency response ranges from 20 Hz to 20,000 Hz. If attached to the Apple Digital AV Adapter, it can output Dolby Digital stereo or even 5.1 surround sound.

### Screen and input

There are four physical switches on the iPad 2 (same as 1st generation iPad), including a home button near the display that returns the user to the main menu, and three plastic physical switches on the sides: wake/sleep and volume up/down, plus a third which, for either screen rotation lock or mute. Business Insider states that the home button on the iPad 2 is "easier to double tap" than the previous generation of the iPad.[21]

Apple has reduced the size of the iPad by eliminating the stamped sheet metal frame from the display, integrating new thinner glass technology for the touch screen overlay, and slightly reducing the space between the display and battery.[22] The iPad 2's screen is thinner, lighter, and yet stronger than the original iPad's.[23]

### Power

The iPad has a 25 watt-hour rechargeable lithium-polymer battery[24] that lasts 10 hours, like the original iPad. It is charged via USB or included 10-watt, 2-amp power adapter. The battery is 2.5 mm thick, 59% smaller than the original and has three cells instead of two. The improvements allowed the injection-molded plastic support frame to be omitted.[22] The iPad 2 ships with a 10W USB power adapter which provides 4x the power of a conventional USB port.[1]

### Cameras

The revised tablet adds front- and rear-facing cameras, which allow FaceTime video calls with the iPhone 4, fourth-generation iPod Touch and Macintosh computers (running Mac OS X 10.6.6 or later with a webcam).[25] The 0.3MP front camera shoots VGA-quality 30 fps video and VGA-quality still photos.[26] The 0.7MP back camera can shoot 720p HD video at 30 fps[27] and has a 5x digital zoom. Both shoot photo and video in a 4:3 fullscreen aspect ratio, unlike the iPhone 4, which shoots in a 16:9 widescreen aspect ratio.

## Apple A5 processor

The iPad 2 added a dual core Apple A5 processor that Apple claims doubles processing speed and has graphics processing that is up to nine times faster than the previous iPad.[28]

## iPad with 3G

3G versions of the iPad 2 offer CDMA2000 support for customers using the device on a CDMA network (e.g. Verizon Wireless in the United States) or GSM/UMTS support for customers using the device on a GSM/UMTS network.[29]

## Size and weight

The device is 33% thinner than the original iPad, is thinner than the iPhone 4 by 0.5mm,[30] and is 15% lighter than the original iPad.
The Wi-Fi version is 1.33 lb (600 g). Both the GSM and CDMA versions (known respectively as the AT&T and Verizon versions in the US) differ in weight slightly due to the mass difference between the GSM and CDMA cellular radios, with the GSM model at 1.35 lb (612 g) and the CDMA model at 1.34 lb (608 g). The size of the iPad 2 is also less than the original iPad at only 9.5×7.31×.346 in (240×186×8.8 mm),[31] compared to the original iPad's size at 9.56×7.47×.528 in (243×190×13.4 mm).

## Technical specifications

| Model | | Original iPad | iPad 2 |
|---|---|---|---|
| Announcement date | | January 27, 2010[32] | March 2, 2011[33] |
| US Release date | | April 3, 2010[34] | March 11, 2011[35] |
| Discontinued date | | March 11, 2011[36] | In production |
| Display | | 9.7 inches (25 cm) multitouch display at a resolution of 1024 × 768 px (XGA) with LED backlighting and a fingerprint and scratch-resistant oleophobic coating[1] | |
| Processor | | 1 GHz Apple A4 System on a chip[37] | 1 GHz (dynamically clocked) dual-core Apple A5 system on a chip |
| Memory | | 256 MB DDR RAM built into Apple A4 package[38] | 512 MB DDR2 RAM built into Apple A5 package[39] |
| Storage | | Fixed capacity of 16, 32, or 64 GB[1] | |
| Wireless | Wi-Fi | Wi-Fi (802.11a/b/g/n), Bluetooth 2.1+EDR[1] | |
| | Wi-Fi + 3G | 3G cellular HSDPA, 2G cellular EDGE[1] | |
| Geolocation | Wi-Fi | Wi-Fi/Apple location databases[40] | |
| | Wi-Fi + 3G | Assisted GPS, Apple databases,[40] Cellular network[1] | |
| Environmental sensors | | Accelerometer, ambient light sensor, magnetometer[1] | In addition to previous, Gyroscope |
| Operating system | | iOS 4.3 [41] | |
| Battery | | Built-in lithium-ion polymer battery; (10 hours video,[1] 140 hours audio,[42] 1 month standby[43] ) | |
| Weight | | 1.5 lb (680 g)[1] | 1.33 lb (601 g)-1.35 lb (613 g) |
| Dimensions | | 9.56×7.47×.528 in (243×190×13.4 mm)[1] [31] | 9.5×7.31×.346 in (240×186×8.8 mm)[31] |

| Mechanical keys | | Home, sleep, volume rocker, variable function switch (originally screen rotation lock, mute in iOS 4.2, either in 4.3)[1] | |
|---|---|---|---|
| Camera [44] | Back | N/A | 720p HD still camera with up to 30fps and 5x digital zoom |
| | Front | N/A | VGA-quality still camera. |

# Accessories

## Smart Cover

The **Smart Cover** is an accessory just for the iPad 2 tablet computer, and was unveiled at the iPad 2 event by Apple Inc. CEO Steve Jobs.[25] [29] [45] [46] It attaches magnetically to the side of the device and covers the front. The Smart Cover has three folds, dividing the case into four portions, so it can be maneuvered to create a stand for the tablet. This can be either used to prop the iPad up in a position suitable for typing, or in an upright position for watching video and video calling over FaceTime. To expose the rear facing HD video camera on the iPad 2, the cover can also be folded in half.[46] The cover aligns with the front screen of the iPad and is designed to add very little thickness to the overall profile of the device. Additionally, when the Smart Cover is lifted off the face of the iPad 2, it automatically turns the device on from standby, meaning the on/off button on the top right of the device does not need to be pressed when the user wishes to use it.

A Smart Cover being used by an iPad 2.

The Smart Cover also has microfiber on its underside (the side in contact with the screen), which is designed to clean the iPad's screen during everyday usage, and the topside comes in either polyurethane or leather .[47] According to Apple, the cover will be available in ten colors. The polyurethane cases come in pink, orange, blue, green and grey; the leather is available in cream, tan, black, navy blue, and red. As with other Apple products, a portion of the red color's proceeds will be donated to Product Red.[48]

Steve Jobs said during the keynote:

> “This isn’t a case anymore. It’s a cover for the screen. The micro-fiber screen cleans the screen every time you close it, and it’s incredibly minimal.”[47]

## Other accessories

Apple introduced the new **Apple Digital AV Adapter** that mirrors video output. This adapter allows the user to mirror anything on the iPad 2's screen to a HDTV or any other HDMI-compatible display, in up to 1080p, so that whatever the iPad's user does is viewable to the audience watching on the larger HDMI-compatible display. The Apple Digital AV Adapter connects to the iPad or iPad Dock via the 30-pin dock connector, whilst the other end has two connections; one is a 30-pin dock connector to charge/power the device whilst being used, the other is a HDMI-out for connecting to any HDMI-compatible display using an HDMI cable.[46] [49] It is also compatible with the 4th generation iterations of the iPhone and iPod Touch.

The **Apple Composite AV Cable** allows the iPad or iPad 2 to be connected to any TV or home cinema system to allow Movies and other videos to be watched in stereo sound only on a TV from the iPad or iPad 2. This is achieved by plugging the wires into the composite video and audio plugs in a TV or home cinema system and into the 30-pin connector on the iPad or iPad 2.[50]

The **Apple Component AV Cable** allows the iPad or iPad 2 to be connected to any TV or home cinema system to allow Movies and other videos to be watched in stereo sound only on a TV from the iPad or iPad 2. This is achieved by plugging the wires into the component video and audio plugs in a TV or home cinema system and into the 30-pin connector on the iPad or iPad 2.[50]

The **iPad VGA Adapter** is designed to allow an iPad or iPad 2 user to connect their iPad to a TV, monitor or any other display that is capable of input using a VGA cable.[51]

The **iPad Camera Connection kit** is a kit of 2 adapters. One USB, and one for SD Cards. They copy the images from an external camera and import them to the iPad. This accessory is compatible with both the iPad and iPad 2.

The **iPad 2 Dock** is the same as the original iPad dock, however it is formatted specially for the design changes of the iPad 2.

The **iPad Power Cord** is a 1.8 metres (5.9 ft) power cord that can be used to allow an iPad or iPad 2 to be used whilst on charge as the power cord supplied is too short for this to be easy to possible in most circumstances.[52]

The **Apple In-Ear Headphones with Remote and Mic** are designed to allow the wearer to use comfortable ear buds whilst listening to music. These headphones also come with a remote and microphone on the cord for use with iPad and iPad 2.[53]

The **Apple Earphones with Remote and Mic** are the standard earphones made by Apple for their devices. They are fully compatible with the iPad and iPad 2 with the use of the remote and microphone on the cord, this is used to control music and use facetime and voice control (on iOS devices) [54]

The **Apple Wireless Keyboard** allows the user to type and input text onto various iPad applications. It uses bluetooth technology to connect to the iPad or iPad 2.[55]

# Applications

The iPad 2 comes with several applications, including Safari, Mail, Photos, Video, YouTube, iPod, iTunes, App Store, iBooks, Maps, Notes, Calendar, Contacts, Camera, Photo Booth, and Spotlight Search.[56] Several are improved versions of applications developed for the iPhone, or of applications for the Mac.

The iPad 2 syncs with iTunes on a Mac or Windows PC.[57] Apple ported its iWork suite from the Mac to the iPad, and sells pared down versions of Pages, Numbers, and Keynote apps in the App Store.[58] Apple also ported Photo Booth, and two iLife applications, iMovie and Garageband. Although the iPad 2 is not designed to replace a mobile phone, a user can use a wired headset or the built-in speaker and microphone and place phone calls over Wi-Fi or 3G using a VoIP application.[59] The iPad has lots of third party applications available for it; as of March 2, 2011, there were 65,000 iPad specific apps on the App Store.[60]

# Reception

One day after its release, retailers internationally reported they were already sold out of the device and were waiting for the next stock.[61]

# Timeline

*Source: Apple press release library*[62]

# References

[1] "iPad – Technical specifications and accessories for iPad" (http://www.apple.com/ipad/specs/). Apple. January 27, 2010. . Retrieved January 27, 2010.

[2] Siegler, MG. "TechCrunch Review — The iPad 2: Yeah, You're Gonna Want One" (http://techcrunch.com/2011/03/09/ipad-2-review/). Tech Crunch. . Retrieved 10 March 2011.

[3] Johnston, Casey (2011). "iPad 2: Faster, thinner, lighter; same battery, display resolution" (http://arstechnica.com/apple/news/2011/03/ipad-2-faster-thinner-lighter-same-battery-display-resolution.ars). Ars Technica. . Retrieved 10 March 2011.

[4] "Apple iPad 2 GPU Performance Explored: PowerVR SGX543MP2 Benchmarked - AnandTech :: Your Source for Hardware Analysis and News" (http://www.anandtech.com/show/4216/apple-ipad-2-gpu-performance-explored-powervr-sgx543mp2-benchmarked). AnandTech. . Retrieved 2011-03-21.

[5] Gruener, Wolfgang (8 March 2008). "5 Reasons Why You Should Not Buy The iPad 2" (http://www.tomsguide.com/us/ipad-ipad2-tablet-ios,news-10393.html). Tom's Guide. . Retrieved 10 March 2011.

[6] Touchscreen (http://www.intomobile.com/2008/12/15/abi-research-capacitive-touchscreens-not-the-wave-of-the-future-for-most-mobile-phones/)

[7] Miguel Helft (January 17, 2011). "Apple Says Steve Jobs Will Take a New Medical Leave" (http://www.nytimes.com/2011/01/18/technology/18apple.html?_r=1). The New York Times. . Retrieved January 17, 2011. Jobs announced that the iOS 4.3 operating system would be available March 9, 2011.

[8] "Apple Store: iPad 2" (http://store.apple.com/us/browse/home/shop_ipad/family/ipad/start?mco=MTcyMTgwNjM). Apple Inc.. 2011. . Retrieved 10 March 2011.

[9] Chiara Marie Trinidad. "The iPad 2" (http://www.noypi.ph/index.php/technology/3211-ipad2-better-than-competitors.html). Noypi.ph. . Retrieved 20011-03-04.

[10] "Apple to sell iPad 2 in 25 more countries at 5 p.m. local time on Friday" (http://www.appleinsider.com/articles/11/03/22/apple_to_sell_ipad_2_in_25_more_countries_at_5_p_m_local_time_on_friday.html). Appleinsider. 22 March 2011. . Retrieved March 22, 2011.

[11] Matthew Shaer (08). "Apple iPad 2 will ship by February: report" (http://www.csmonitor.com/Innovation/Horizons/2010/1208/Apple-iPad-2-will-ship-by-February-report). The Christian Science Monitor. . Retrieved 11 December 2010.

[12] Marcus Yam (2). "Foxconn Workers Arrested for Leaking iPad 2" (http://www.tomsguide.com/us/ipad-2-leaking-secrets-prototype-design,news-11012.html#). BestofMedia. . Retrieved 2 May 2011.

[13] Hitesh Raj Bhagat, ET Bureau (26). "Apple iPad 2 to be unveiled on March 2" (http://articles.economictimes.indiatimes.com/2011-02-26/news/28636008_1_ipad-galaxy-tab-front-facing-camera). Bennett, Coleman & Co.. . Retrieved 20 March 2010.

[14] The Most Expensive time to buy an iPad 2 (http://www.huffingtonpost.com/2011/03/17/ipad-2-sales_n_837204.html#s254687&title=Outside_The_Fifth)

[15] YUKARI IWATANI KANE And DON CLARK (13 March 2011). "Apple's iPad 2 Chalks Up Strong Sales in Weekend Debut" (http://online.wsj.com/article/SB10001424052748704027504576198832667732862.html). Dow Jones & Company, Inc.. . Retrieved March 13, 2011.

[16] Cromwell Schubarth, Silicon Valley/San Jose Business Journal (15 March 2011). "Apple's iPad 2 Chalks Up Strong Sales in Weekend Debut" (http://assets.bizjournals.com/triad/news/2011/03/15/apple-ups-ipad-2-wait-time-to-4-5-weeks.html). American City Business Journals, Inc.. . Retrieved March 20, 2011.

[17] Adam Satariano (11 March 2011). "Apple Poised to Sell 600,000 IPad 2s in Its Debut, Outpacing First Model" (http://www.bloomberg.com/news/2011-03-11/apple-poised-to-sell-600-000-ipad-2s-in-its-debut-outpacing-first-model.html). BLOOMBERG L.P.. . Retrieved March 14, 2011.

[18] Emily Banks (15 March 2011). "Apple Delays iPad 2 Launch in Japan" (http://mashable.com/2011/03/15/ipad-2-launch-japan/). Mashable. . Retrieved March 15, 2011.

[19] TheStreet staff. "Apple shares fall as iPad 2 delayed in Japan" (http://money.msn.com/market-news/post.aspx?post=a8d14fd5-8d5a-49d5-9c1c-8da9331d65a0). Microsoft. . Retrieved 20011-03-20.

[20] "iOS 4.3.1 Software Update" (http://support.apple.com/kb/DL1358). Apple Inc.. 25 March 2011. . Retrieved 8 April 2011.

[21] Dan frommer (March 21, 2011). "Here's Why I'm Waiting For The iPad 3" (http://www.businessinsider.com/ipad-3-upgrade-2011-3). Business Insider, Inc.. . Retrieved March 21, 2011.

[22] Frank Michael Russell (March 19, 2011). "Tech Notebook: Apple's svelte new iPad 2: its weight-loss secrets revealed" (http://www.mercurynews.com/breaking-news/ci_17646727?nclick_check=1). San Jose Mercury News. . Retrieved March 20, 2011.

[23] David Carnoy, cnet.com. " Apple uses stronger glass in iPad 2 (http://news.cnet.com/8301-17938_105-20047098-1.html?part=rss&subj=news&tag=2547-1_3-0-20)." March 25, 2011. Retrieved March 25, 2011.

[24] iPad specs (http://www.apple.com/ipad/specs/)

[25] Goldman, David (March 2, 2011). "IPad 2: Thinner, faster, and with a Steve Jobs surprise" (http://money.cnn.com/2011/03/02/technology/ipad_2_announcement/). CNNMoney. . Retrieved 2011-03-02.

[26] http://en.wikipedia.org/wiki/IPad_2#cite_note-AppleIPadSpecs-0

[27] http://en.wikipedia.org/wiki/IPad_2#cite_note-4

[28] John Biggs (March 2, 2011). "Apple Announces The iPad 2: A5 Processor, Front And Back Cameras, Available March 11" (http://www.crunchgear.com/2011/03/02/apple-ipad-2-announcement/). . Retrieved 2011-03-12.
[29] Baig, Ed (March 2, 2011). "Apple launching iPad 2 on March 11" (http://content.usatoday.com/communities/technologylive/post/2011/03/live-coverage-apple-expected-to-unveil-new-ipad/1). USA Today. . Retrieved 2011-03-02.
[30] Wayne T. Price and USA TODAY (2011-03-03). "Apple CEO Steve Jobs unveils iPad 2. The iPad 2 comes with a new app, from the mac series, [[Photo Booth (http://www.tallahassee.com/article/A9/20110303/BUSINESS/103030308/1003)]. To distort and edit pictures using the built-in cameras."]. . Retrieved 2011-03-09.
[31] Dockrill, Peter (3 March 2011). "iPad vs iPad 2 back-to-back: what's new, plus all the specs compared" (http://apcmag.com/ipad-vs-ipad-2-back-to-back-whats-new-plus-all-the-newold-specs-compared.htm). *apc*. .
[32] Announcement of iPad (http://www.apple.com/pr/library/2010/01/27ipad.html)
[33] Announcement of iPad 2 (http://www.apple.com/pr/library/2011/03/02ipad.html)
[34] Release of iPad (http://www.apple.com/pr/library/2010/03/05ipad.html)
[35] Release of iPad 2 (http://www.apple.com/pr/library/2011/03/10ipad.html)
[36] Specs (http://www.everyipod.com/ipad-specs/apple-ipad-original-specs.html)
[37] Brooke Crothers (January 27, 2010). "Inside the iPad: Apple's new 'A4' chip" (http://news.cnet.com/8301-13924_3-10442684-64.html). *CNET*. . Retrieved January 27, 2010.
[38] Miroslav Djuric (April 3, 2010). "teardown of production iPad" (http://www.ifixit.com/Teardown/iPad-Teardown/2183/2). Ifixit.com. p. 2. . Retrieved April 17, 2010.
[39] "iPad 2 Wi-Fi Teardown" (http://www.ifixit.com/Teardown/iPad-2-Wi-Fi-Teardown/5071/1). iFixit. . Retrieved 12 March 2011.
[40] "In April, Apple Ditched Google And Skyhook In Favor Of Its Own Location Databases" (http://techcrunch.com/2010/07/29/apple-location/). *TechCrunch*. July 29, 2010. . Retrieved October 14, 2010.
[41] "iPad - iOS 4" (http://www.apple.com/ipad/ios4/). Apple Inc.. March 13, 2011. . Retrieved March 13, 2011.
[42] Christopher Breen (April 6, 2010). "The iPad as iPod" (http://www.macworld.com/article/150427/2010/04/ipad_as_ipod.html). MacWorld.com. . Retrieved June 26, 2010.
[43] Rich Trenholm (January 27, 2010). "Apple iPad launch: The first specs" (http://crave.cnet.co.uk/laptops/0,39029450,49304822,00.htm). CNet. . Retrieved June 26, 2010.
[44] iPad technical specifications (http://www.apple.com/ipad/specs/)
[45] Albanesius, Chloe (2011-03-14). "iPad 2 Smart Cover Teardown: Magnets Galore" (http://www.pcmag.com/article2/0,2817,2381927,00.asp). PC Magazine. . Retrieved 2011-03-18.
[46] Dove, Jackie (2011-03-02). "Smart Cover, Digital AV adapter accompany iPad 2 launch" (http://www.macworld.com/article/158263/2011/03/ipadcovers.html). Macworld.com. . Retrieved 2011-03-02.
[47] Schonfeld, Erick (2011-03-02). "The iPad Gets A Magical, Magnetic, Self-Cleaning Cover" (http://techcrunch.com/2011/03/02/ipad-cover). TechCrunch. . Retrieved 2011-03-02.
[48] "Apple - Smart Cover" (http://www.apple.com/ipad/smart-cover/). Apple Inc.. . Retrieved 8 April 2011.
[49] "Video Mirroring" (http://www.apple.com/uk/ipad/features/mirroring.html). Apple Inc.. 15 March 2011. . Retrieved 22 March 2011.
[50] http://www.apple.com/ipad/accessories/
[51] "iPad VGA Adapter." (http://www.apple.com/ipad/accessories/). Apple Inc.. 15 March 2011. . Retrieved 22 March 2011.
[52] "iPad 10W USB Power Adapter" (http://www.apple.com/ipad/accessories/). Apple Inc.. 15 March 2011. . Retrieved 22 March 2011.
[53] "Apple In-Ear Headphones with Remote and Mic" (http://www.apple.com/ipad/accessories/). Apple Inc.. 15 March 2011. . Retrieved 22 March 2011.
[54] "Apple Earphones with Remote and Mic" (http://www.apple.com/ipad/accessories/). Apple Inc.. 15 March 2011. . Retrieved 22 March 2011.
[55] "Apple Wireless Keyboard" (http://www.apple.com/ipad/accessories/). Apple Inc.. 15 March 2011. . Retrieved 22 March 2011.
[56] "iPad Features" (http://www.apple.com/ipad/features/). Apple Inc.. January 27, 2010. . Retrieved January 28, 2010.
[57] iTunes features (http://www.apple.com/itunes/features/)
[58] Jeff Smykil (April 20, 2010). "The keyboardless Office: a review of iWork for iPad" (http://arstechnica.com/apple/reviews/2010/04/iwork-for-ipad-clever-subtitle-goes-here.ars/4). *ArsTechnica*. Condé Nast. . Retrieved May 1, 2010.
[59] David Sarno (January 29, 2010). "Apple confirms 3G VoIP apps on iPad, iPhone, iPod touch; Skype is waiting" (http://latimesblogs.latimes.com/technology/2010/01/apple-confirms-3g-voip-apps-on-ipad-iphone-ipod-touch-skype-is-waiting.html). *Los Angeles Times*. . Retrieved February 7, 2010.
[60] "Apple (United Kingdom) - iPad - From the App Store" (http://www.apple.com/uk/ipad/from-the-app-store/). March 2, 2011. . Retrieved March 19, 2011.
[61] Whitney, Lance (March 28, 2011). "iPad 2 sells out internationally" (http://news.cnet.com/8301-13579_3-20047858-37.html). *CNET News*. .
[62] Apple Inc. (2010-2011). Press Release Library (http://www.apple.com/pr/library/). Retrieved April 03, 2011.

## External links

- iPad (http://www.apple.com/ipad/) subsite at Apple
- Smart Cover (http://www.apple.com/ipad/smart-cover) subsite at Apple
- iPad 2 launch event (http://events.apple.com.edgesuite.net/1103pijanbdvaaj/event/index.html)
- iPad 2 tech specs (http://www.apple.com/ipad/specs/)
- iPad 2 on Apple Wiki (http://www.apple.wikia.com/wiki/IPad_2)

# Magic W3

## Magic W3

| Manufacturer | Advance Tech Communications |
|---|---|
| Release date | June 2011 |
| Operating system | Windows 7 |

The **Magic W3** is a 4.8" Windows®7 full OS **Pocket Tablet Computer Smartphone** integrated with voice call functionality. The Magic W3 provides true windowed multitasking, multimedia entertainment, social network connectivity such as Renren and Facebook, navigation capability, voice telephony, and the full internet experience. The device is assembled in Malaysia and is expected to be available in June, 2011 in China and Hong Kong, with plans underway to distribute it in other regions.[1]

## Specifications

Processor Intel Atom Z530 1.6 GHz

**Operating System** Windows 7 Home Premium

**Display** Touch Screen Size 4.8" Resolution 800 x 480 WVGA native 800 x 600/1024 x 600 W/SVGA interpolated

**RAM** 1GB DDR2

**Capacity** 32 GB SSD

**Network** GSM Quad Band 3.5G HSPA

**Radio Connectivity** Wi-Fi b/g Bluetooth 2.0 + EDR GPS Transceiver

**Dimensions / Weight** 141 x 81.5 x 22 mm / 260 g

**Battery** 3200 mAh 3.7V

**1.3 MP Camera (Video Conferencing) Accelerometer Vibrate Alert**

**Peripheral Connectivity**

- Mini HDMI
- Mini USB
- Micro SD
- SIM Card Slot
- Charging & Docking I/O
- 3.5mm Jack Connector

**Audio**

- Dual Mics
- Receiver
- Stereo Speakers

**Hardware Interface**

- Volume Control +/- buttons
- Call Key
- End Key
- Power Switch - Sleep/Standby, Screen/Key Lock

## Applications (Apps)

- MAGIC Telephony Touch UI
- Phone Dialer
- Messaging
- Call History
- Contacts
- Microsoft Windows Live Essentials
- Microsoft Office Starter

**Other Applications Not Supplied**

- Adobe Flash
- Netflix
- iTunes
- PhotoShop
- Windows Media Center
- WinAmp
- World of Warcraft
- Millions of other Windows applications

## References

[1] Magic W3 Release Schedule, June, 2011 (http://mmail.com.my/content/64645-its-magic-your-hands)

## External links

- Magic W3 official site (http://www.advancetc.com/)
- Magic W3 review - Worlds First... (http://mmail.com.my/content/64645-its-magic-your-hands)
- Magic W3 review - Engadget (http://www.engadget.com/2011/02/28/advancetcs-4-8-inch-tabletphone-runs-windows-7-on-a-1-6ghz-atom/)
- Magic W3 review - Slashgear video demos (http://www.slashgear.com/magic-w3-win7-smartphone-video-demos-hd-playback-photoshop-more-15139971/)
- Magic W3 distributors in China and Hong Kong - China Media Group Corporation(Public, OTC:CHMD) (http://www.chinamediagroup.net/index.php?action=default&type=20)
- Magic W3 review - enterprise market (http://www.liveatpc.com/microsoft-fights-back)

# Microsoft Courier

***Microsoft Courier*** was the codename for a rumored Booklet PC from Microsoft. The unit would have contained dual-touchscreens that faced each other in a booklet form factor, and would have utilized a stylus and finger touch for input. Microsoft has announced it did work on the product, but will not release the device.[1] The device would have been hinged like a book, with the seven-inch screens facing each other when the "book" was closed. A 3-megapixel digital camera with 4x zoom was integrated into the prototype system,[2] and the final model might have contained an inductive charging pad for charging batteries wirelessly.[3] Reports had indicated that the system was largely developed outside of the normal development channels, and existence of the project was only known by a few key engineers.[4] The project was considered to be a successor of *Codex* and *InkSeine*, two earlier Microsoft Research efforts.[5]

Microsoft had previously classified the project as in "incubation", which is further along than a "research" project but is not yet in the commercial pipeline.[6]

## Design

The tablet was reported to have two seven-inch screens with a flexible hinge to allow closure like a book. The outside of the hinge would have contained wireless signal and battery strength indicators, and a home button to interact with the system while the booklet was closed. Courier would have relied entirely on touch input and handwriting recognition, as no external keyboard would have been available.[7] Reports indicated that it would have been powered by NVIDIA's Tegra 250 processor and would have weighed a little over a pound.[8]

## Usage

The system's main purpose would have been to function as a personal notebook and day planner to track contacts, tasks, and appointments. Courier would have included applications such as Microsoft Paint and notepad to help users create and organize original content, as well as web and photo browsers, email applications, and possibly an e-reader.[7]

### Core operating system

The core operating system of the Courier was reportedly a specialized version of Microsoft Windows CE,[8] however the Courier would not have allowed installation of native Windows applications onto the system. All Courier applications would have had to have been designed specifically for the Courier's booklet form factor.[6] In addition, some reports had indicated that the Courier would incorporate a front-side video camera for live video conferencing (via Microsoft Messenger) on the left side of the notebook so that users could have edited documents or taken notes on the right side.[6]

### Infinite Journal

The primary interface of the Courier would have been the Infinite Journal, an electronic journal with an unlimited number of pages upon which users could have taken notes, dragged photos, sketched drawings, and stored "web clippings." Each page would have been stamped with the current time and location when each page was entered. These concepts are similar to the existing Windows Journal, which has been included in every version of Windows since XP. The mechanism for the location geotagging function might have come through an internal GPS, geolocation through IP connectivity through wireless access points, or through manual entry. Users might also have been able to highlight an infinite number of keywords to tag and index for future searching.[7] The journal (in whole or in part) would have been able to be published online in several formats, including PDF and Microsoft PowerPoint documents.[6]

The Infinite Journal concept reportedly originated from a desire to build Microsoft OneNote from scratch with the dual-screen booklet form factor in mind. This idea spawned from the popularity of the Franklin Covey planner products, which utilize the booklet design.[6]

### Smart Agenda

The "Smart Agenda" would have been a condensed summary of the Infinite Journal, in which hyperlinked content would bring the user to the appropriate pages of the Infinite Journal. The smart agenda would have coordinated daily activities, appointments, and tasks, as well as coordinating email and messaging.[7]

### Clip, Tuck, and Paste

An innovative feature of the Microsoft Courier would have been users' ability to "clip" content from web sites or emails, to "tuck" the clipping underneath the physical hinge of the journal, and then to flip the virtual pages until the clipping was pasted into the appropriate page.[7] This differs from a traditional clipboard, in which copied items are not visible while on the clipboard, and are usually manipulated one at a time.

### Touch

The Courier would have featured multi-touch and stylus operation. The stylus would have operated in several different modes, allowing users to easily toggle between writing, painting, and sketching. Additionally, the physical stylus would have been able to access some new editing functions. It would have contained two quick-access buttons: one would have switched between a writing pen and a marker-style input, the other would have served as a quick "undo" function. Twisting the stylus would have engaged Courier's drawing functionality, and flipping the stylus over (like a pencil) would have caused the stylus to erase content on the virtual page.[7]

## End of Courier

On April 29, 2010, Microsoft confirmed that they will no longer support this project. The official statement was:[1]

> *At any given time, across any of our business groups, there are new ideas being investigated, tested, and incubated. It's in Microsoft's DNA to continually develop and incubate new technologies to foster productivity and creativity. The "Courier" project is an example of this type of effort and its technologies will be evaluated for use in future Microsoft offerings, but we have no plans to build such a device at this time.*

On The Official Microsoft Blog, Frank Shaw, the Microsoft VP who made the statement, referenced the articles published about the cancellation of the project as "speculation" and re-quoted himself, leaving out the "but we have no plans to build such a device at this time" part.[9]

On June 30, 2010, Network World revived hopes by posting that Microsoft received a patent on June 29, which might be for the 'Courier', "patent number D618683 for a 'dual display device'."[10]

## References

[1] "Microsoft Cancels Innovative Courier Tablet Project" (http://gizmodo.com/5527442/microsoft-cancels-innovative-courier-tablet-project). Gizmodo. 2010-04-29. . Retrieved 2010-04-29.

[2] "Courier: First Details of Microsoft's Secret Tablet" (http://gizmodo.com/5365299/courier-first-details-of-microsofts-secret-tablet). Gizmodo. 2009-09-22. . Retrieved 2009-09-22.

[3] "Microsoft's dual-screen Courier booklet emerges, isn't near production" (http://www.engadget.com/2009/09/22/microsofts-courier-booklet-emerges-said-to-be-in-late-prototy/). Gizmodo. 2009-09-23. . Retrieved 2009-09-28.

[4] "Microsoft readying Courier touch-screen tablet" (http://www.telegraph.co.uk/technology/microsoft/6222172/Microsoft-readying-Courier-touch-screen-tablet.html). The Daily Telegraph. 2009-09-23. . Retrieved 2009-09-23.

[5] "Codex and InkSeine -- the roots of Microsoft's Courier?" (http://www.engadget.com/2009/09/23/codex-and-inkseine-the-roots-of-microsofts-courier/). endgadget. 2009-09-24. . Retrieved 2009-09-25.

[6] Foley, Mary Jo (2009-09-29). "Microsoft's Courier tablet: A Franklin Covey planner on steroids?" (http://blogs.zdnet.com/microsoft/?p=4103). ZDNet. . Retrieved 27 November 2009.

[7] Paul, Ian (2009-11-05). "Microsoft Courier: A Feature Breakdown" (http://www.pcworld.com/article/181487/microsoft_courier_a_feature_breakdown.html). *PC World*. . Retrieved 25 November 2009.

[8] Patel, Nilay (2010-03-05). "Microsoft's Courier 'digital journal': exclusive pictures and details" (http://www.engadget.com/2010/03/05/microsofts-courier-digital-journal-exclusive-pictures-and-de/). *Engadget*. . Retrieved 5 March 2010.

[9] "Speculation About the "Courier" Project" (http://blogs.technet.com/microsoft_blog/archive/2010/04/29/speculation-about-the-courier-project.aspx). The official Microsoft Blog. 2010-04-29. . Retrieved 2010-05-02.

[10] "Has Microsoft Courier come back to life?" (http://www.networkworld.com/community/node/63103). Network World. 2010-06-30. . Retrieved 2010-07-01.

# Motorola Xoom

## Motorola Xoom

| | |
|---|---|
| **Manufacturer** | Motorola Mobility |
| **Type** | Tablet media player/PC |
| **Release date** | February 24, 2011 |
| **Introductory price** | $799 GSM & CDMA<br>$599 Wi-Fi only |
| **Operating system** | Android 3.0 Honeycomb |
| **Power** | 6500 mAh[1] |
| **CPU** | Nvidia Tegra 2: 1 GHz dual-core processor[2] |
| **Storage capacity** | Flash memory: 32 GB, external slot: microSD card after SW update |
| **Memory** | 1 GB DDR2 SDRAM |
| **Display** | 1280×800 px (aspect ratio 16:10), 10.1 in (26 cm) diagonal, appr. 46 $in^2$ (300 $cm^2$) at 150 PPI |
| **Input** | Multi-touch capacitive touchscreen display<br>3-axis accelerometer<br>Compass<br>Proximity sensor<br>Ambient light sensor<br>Gyroscope<br>Barometer |
| **Camera** | 5.0 megapixel rear-facing with 4× digital zoom, autofocus 720 p video capture, 30 fps, dual LED flash<br>2.0 megapixel front-facing camera |
| **Connectivity** | Wi-Fi a/b/g/n<br>Bluetooth 2.1 + EDR<br>**CDMA Version**<br>EVDO Rev. A<br>**GSM Version**<br>GSM/EDGE Class 12<br>UMTS/HSDPA[3] |
| **Dimensions** | 9.8 in (250 mm) H<br>6.6 in (170 mm) W<br>0.5 in (13 mm) D |
| **Weight** | 1.6 lb (730 g) |
| **Website** | /xoom [4] |

The **Motorola Xoom** is an Android-based tablet computer by Motorola, introduced at CES 2011 on January 5, 2011. It is the first tablet to run Android 3.0 Honeycomb. It was released on February 24, 2011. It was launched with three other products: the Motorola Atrix, the Motorola Droid Bionic, and the Motorola Cliq 2.[4]

CNET.com named it the "Best of the CES" 2011.[5]

## Features

The Xoom supports up to 720p video playback.[6] It features a 2 MP front-facing camera for video chatting over Wi-Fi or cellular Internet and a rear-facing 5 MP camera that records 720p video. The Xoom has a 1280×800 widescreen, 10.1-inch display and 3D graphics acceleration, as well as HDMI-out. It features a variety of sensors, including a gyroscope, magnetometer, accelerometer, and a barometer. The Xoom uses Nvidia Tegra 2 SoC. In January it was reported that the Xoom will come in a Wi-Fi only model as well as a 3G model through Verizon Wireless.[7]

### Video

The Motorola Xoom has support for the following video (H.263, H.264, MPEG4, VP8), and audio (AAC, AAC+, AMR NB, AMRWB, MP3, XMF) formats.[8]

### Software

The Xoom runs Google's Android 3.0 Honeycomb, whose new features include a redesigned, tablet-optimized user interface, a 3D desktop purportedly taken from BumpTop (which Google acquired in April 2010), improved multitasking, a newly redesigned notification system, Google Maps 5 in 3D and browser enhancements including tabs, form auto-fill and bookmark syncing.[9]

On February 23 Motorola Mobility announced that the Motorola Xoom would break its policy of locking down its devices by providing the gadget with an "unlockable/relockable bootloader that will enable developers to access hardware for development."[10]

### Accessories

The Motorola Xoom supports docking stations for charging and as a stand for viewing video. It also features Bluetooth keyboard support.

Available accessories include: Motorola Xoom portfolio case, dock, HD stereo dock, wireless keyboard.

### Features announced but not initially present

At first release, support for Adobe Flash and a microSD slot was not included. Adobe announced on 11 March that Flash would be available for Android 3.0 devices on 18 March and a predicted future software update will enable the microSD slot.[11] On 12th April it was reported[12] that the developers at the XDA-developers forum have made the microSD slot functional on the Xoom tablet even before the next update.[13] Motorola Xoom tablet did not support Flash on Day 1 of its release in US on February 22, 2011. Before release, no official statement has said whether the microSD slot will support SDHC or SDXC card families.

## Super Bowl commercial

Motorola aired a television spot during Super Bowl XLV in 2011 that was designed as a satire of Apple's landmark Super Bowl ad "1984". It depicted a dystopia in which all of humanity wears white hoodies and are plugged into iPods (iSheep), a jibe at how Apple products had achieved cult-like status and practically ubiquitous market penetration.[14]

The following week, a minor controversy erupted when Los Angeles filmmaker Mike Sarrow claimed that he had, in fact, originated the commercial's idea first. In 2009, he shot a short film portraying a dystopian world where everyone is plugged into iPods to the point that all human conversation has ceased. The controversy was reported on numerous tech news websites, including CNET and Engadget, though no concrete evidence of intellectual property was presented, merely some suspicious similarities, including a nearly identical ending shot. However, the filmmaker has chosen not to pursue Motorola legally, only using the similarity as publicity for his work.[15] [16] [17] [18]

## Reviews

The device's hardware received praise from reviewers; Engadget, PC World and CNET all said that the Xoom's performance was as good as or superior to competing products.[19] [20] [21] The user experience with the installed software was mixed. Android 3.0 was praised for "com[ing] together in a far more cohesive manner than any previous iteration of the software,"[19] according to Engadget, and being "the most polished Google software effort to date,"[21] according to PC World. CNET said that in some areas the software seemed overly complex,[20] and Engadget said that "a lot of the new software feels like it isn't quite out of beta."[20] The device's pricing also attracted criticism; both Engadget and PC World cited the price as a drawback,[19] [21] and CNET said that with the launch pricing, "the Xoom's appeal will be limited to early adopters and Android loyalists."[20]

## Sales

Xoom was estimated by Deutsche Bank analysts to have sold about 100,000 units during the first 6 weeks of availability versus first-day sales of the iPad of 300,000 units.[22] On April 28, 2011, Motorola announced during Q1 2011 earnings conference calls that over 250,000 units of Xoom were shipped to retail channel during the quarter. The company did not reveal its estimate of number of units actually sold to consumers. [23]

## References

[1] "Xoom has only 3250 mAH battery?" (https://supportforums.motorola.com/message/329406#329406). *Motorola Owners' Forum*. February 24, 2011. . Retrieved 2011-02-25.

[2] "Motorola Xoom Fact Sheet" (http://mediacenter.motorola.com/Fact-Sheets/Motorola-XOOM-Fact-Sheet-3537.aspx). Motorola Mobility, Inc. January 5, 2011. . Retrieved 2011-02-07.

[3] "Motorola Xoom Specifications Table" (http://developer.motorola.com/products/xoom-mz601/). Motorola Mobility, Inc. February 16, 2011. . Retrieved 2011-02-16.

[4] "International CES 2011 Press Kit" (http://mediacenter.motorola.com/Press-Kits/International-CES-2011-Press-Kit-351a.aspx). Motorola Mobility, Inc. January 5, 2011. . Retrieved 2011-02-07.

[5] McCullagh, Declan (January 5, 2011). "CES: Motorola reveals iPad-rival Xoom tablet" (http://ces.cnet.com/8301-32254_1-20027500-283.html). *CNET.com*. .

[6] http://www.motorola.com/Consumers/US-EN/Consumer-Product-and-Services/Tablets/ci.MOTOROLA-XOOM-US-EN.alt

[7] Miller, Ross (January 8, 2011). "Motorola Xoom WiFi-only version confirmed by Motorola Latin American exec" (http://www.engadget.com/2011/01/08/motorola-xoom-wifi-only-version-confirmed-by-motorola-latin-amer/). Engadget. . Retrieved 2011-02-07.

[8] "Android Supported Media Formats" (http://developer.android.com/guide/appendix/media-formats.html). *Android Developers*. . Retrieved 2011-02-23.

[9] "Android 3.0 Highlights - User Features" (http://developer.android.com/sdk/android-3.0-highlights.html#UserFeatures). Android Developers. . Retrieved 2011-02-25.

[10] "Motorola Mobility PR Twitter Account" (http://twitter.com/Motorola/status/40166376467341312). Motorola Mobility, Inc. February 23, 2011. . Retrieved February 25, 2011.

[11] [http://latimesblogs.latimes.com/technology/2011/02/motorola-xoom-tablet-arrives-thursday-for-799-or-599-with-a-2-year-data-plan.html
[12] http://www.motorola-xoom.co.uk/xoom-xda-working-sd-card-slot/
[13] http://forum.xda-developers.com/showthread.php?t=978013
[14] "Motorola takes swipe at Apple with ad for Xoom - TechUnicorn" (http://www.techunicorn.co.uk/2011/02/motorola-takes-swipe-at-apple-with-ad-for-xoom-3499). TechUnicorn.co.uk. . Retrieved 2011-02-22.
[15] "Filmmaker says Motorola's Super Bowl ad bears some striking similarities to his short film" (http://www.engadget.com/2011/02/14/filmmaker-says-motorolas-super-bowl-ad-bears-some-striking-simi/). .
[16] Matyszczyk, Chris (2011-02-12). "Filmmaker: Motorola anti-Apple ad looks like my film | Technically Incorrect - CNET News" (http://news.cnet.com/8301-17852_3-20031643-71.html). News.cnet.com. . Retrieved 2011-02-22.
[17] "Filmmaker says Motorola may have plagiarized Super Bowl ad" (http://www.electronista.com/articles/11/02/12/tv.commercials.said.to.match.indy.film.concept/). Electronista. 2011-02-12. . Retrieved 2011-02-22.
[18] Dennis. "Filmmaker says Motorola may have plagiarized Super Bowl ad | Latest electronics" (http://www.latestelectronics-dennis.com/?p=20207). Latestelectronics-dennis.com. . Retrieved 2011-02-22.
[19] "Motorola Xoom review" (http://www.webcitation.org/5xnoujaAT). Engadget. 23 February 2011. Archived from the original (http://www.engadget.com/2011/02/23/motorola-xoom-review/) on 8 April 2011. . Retrieved 8 April 2011.
[20] "Motorola Xoom" (http://www.webcitation.org/5xnp1Gv7f). CNET. 24 February 2011. Archived from the original (http://reviews.cnet.com/motorola-xoom/#reviewPage1) on 8 April 2011. . Retrieved 8 April 2011.
[21] "Motorola Xoom (Wi-Fi + 3G)" (http://www.webcitation.org/5xnp6ie1p). PC World. 23 February 2011. Archived from the original (http://www.pcworld.com/article/220522/motorola_xoom_first_android_30_tablet_impresses_but_drawbacks_remain.html) on 8 April 2011. . Retrieved 8 April 2011.
[22] "Motorola Xoom, Atrix Too Pricey for the Public" (http://www.webcitation.org/5xo0JqoSj). Wired Magazine. 6 April 2011. Archived from the original (http://www.wired.com/gadgetlab/2011/04/motorola-xoom-atrix-price/) on 8 April 2011. . Retrieved 9 April 2011.
[23] http://investors.motorola.com/

# External links

- Official website (http://www.motorola.com/staticfiles/Consumers/US-EN/XOOM)
- Xoom developer page comparing models (http://developer.motorola.com/products/compare/?items=17987,17982,17869)
- Motorola Xoom ES (http://www.xoom.com.es/)

# Pocket computer phone

The **Pocket Computer Phone** is a category in hand held technology. What was once a multiple component, large footprint on the top of a desk can now fit into a pocket or purse. It is powered by a full desktop or laptop OS and all the applications available to that OS. While running a full OS it is also still a phone that is small enough to fit in a pocket.

A Pocket Computer Phone is dock-able to peripherals using technology such as Bluetooth® and HDMI output. This hand held technology then becomes the basis of workplace and personal home computing power. A setup at work may be a 27" flat screen accepting HDMI input and a Bluetooth keyboard and mouse. A similar setup could be used with the same Pocket Computer Phone at home but modified to a 55" flat screen and surround sound system to enjoy HD movies streaming from Netflix®.

Special software can allow multitasked phone functionality making the hand held Pocket Computer a phone. Syncing contact information to a desktop workstation is no longer required as a Pocket Computer Phone is a pocket sized workstation. Having a web based teleconference such as a WebEx® initiated conference from Firefox® running on a Pocket Computer Phone could be possible with a Bluetooth® headset and a wireless service provider.

**Linux Devices**

The N900 designed by Nokia is powered by the open source, Linux-based Maemo software and delivers a PC-like experience on a handset-sized device.

**Windows 7 Devices**

The Magic W3 designed by Advanced Tech Communications is powered by Windows 7 Home Premium OS. The Magic W3 has 4.8" screen and is integrated with voice call functionality that fits in a pocket. It provides users with true windowed multitasking, multimedia entertainment, social connectivity, navigation capability, voice telephony, and the full internet experience.[1]

Applications such as desktop publishing with Microsoft Word®, HD movie viewing with Windows Media Center, and photo editing with Photoshop® can be used while mobile or attached to a screen via HDMI out.

The Fujitsu LOOX F-07C is Windows 7 phone which will dual-boot to Symbian. Fujitsu and DoCoMo are teaming up to unleash a dual-boot device this year that can go from Windows 7 (the desktop OS, not WP7) to Symbian at the flip of a switch.[2]

**Mac OS Devices**

## References

[1] Magic W3 Specifications (http://www.advancetc.com/)
[2] Fujitsu LOOX F-07C info (http://www.engadget.com/2011/04/12/fujitsu-and-docomos-new-dual-boot-handset-windows-7-and-symbia/ )

## External links

- N900 official site (http://maemo.nokia.com/n900/)
- Nokia N900 review - Engadget (http://www.engadget.com/2010/01/19/nokia-n900-review/)
- Nokia N900 - Slashgear video demos (http://www.slashgear.com/ nokia-n900-big-screen-gaming-gets-video-demo-1456253/)
- Magic W3 official site (http://www.advancetc.com/)
- Magic W3 review - Engadget (http://www.engadget.com/2011/02/28/ advancetcs-4-8-inch-tabletphone-runs-windows-7-on-a-1-6ghz-atom/)

- Magic W3 review - Slashgear video demos (http://www.slashgear.com/magic-w3-win7-smartphone-video-demos-hd-playback-photoshop-more-15139971/)
- Magic W3 distributors in China and Hong Kong - China Media Group (http://www.chinamediagroup.net/index.php?action=default&type=20)
- Fujitsu LOOX F-07C review - Engadget (http://www.engadget.com/2011/04/12/fujitsu-and-docomos-new-dual-boot-handset-windows-7-and-symbia/)

# Sakshat

**Sakshat**

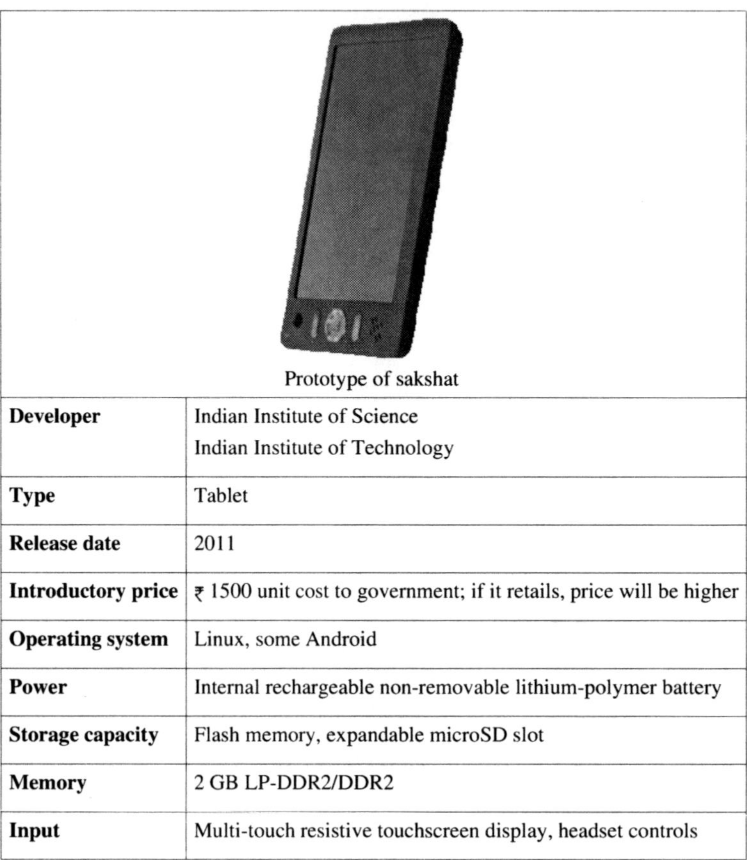

Prototype of sakshat

| | |
|---|---|
| **Developer** | Indian Institute of Science<br>Indian Institute of Technology |
| **Type** | Tablet |
| **Release date** | 2011 |
| **Introductory price** | ₹ 1500 unit cost to government; if it retails, price will be higher |
| **Operating system** | Linux, some Android |
| **Power** | Internal rechargeable non-removable lithium-polymer battery |
| **Storage capacity** | Flash memory, expandable microSD slot |
| **Memory** | 2 GB LP-DDR2/DDR2 |
| **Input** | Multi-touch resistive touchscreen display, headset controls |

**Sakshat** (Sanskrit: साक्षात् "Embodiment") is a tablet computer designed in India as a low cost but full functioning device in order to attempt to bridge the digital divide. The original prototype unveiled in 2009 for $10 was a failure.[1] However, the new prototype, at $35 unveiled in 2010 has been met with enthusiasm. The device has been developed as part of the National Mission on Education through Information and Communication Technology that aims to link 25,000 colleges and 400 universities on the subcontinent in an e-learning program via an existing Sakshat portal.[2]

## History

While it was once projected as a laptop computer, it is actually a tablet computing device. At the inauguration of the national Mission on Education Programme organized by the Union HRD Ministry in 2009, joint secretary N. K. Sinha had said that the computing device is 10 inches (which is around 25.5cm) long and 5 inches (12.5cm) wide and priced at around $30. However, he refused to comment as to why was it being projected as a laptop when it was not.[1] [3]

India's Human Resource Development Minister, Kapil Sibal unveiled a prototype on July 22, 2010. The price of the device exhibited was projected to be around $35 per piece, gradually dropping down to $20 and ultimately to $10 each.[2] [4] [5] After the new device was unveiled, OLPC Chairman Nicholas Negroponte offered full access to OLPC technology, cost free to the Indian team.[6]

Doubts about the tablet being vaporware were dismissed in a television program "Gadget Guru" aired on NDTV in August 2010.[7] The device was demonstrated running the Android operating system and shown to be able to deliver videos, Wi-Fi, 3G, 2 GB RAM among other capabilities.

## Design

### Minimum functionality

As per the Invitation to Innovate published by MHRD,[8] Government of India, the specifications and minimum functionalities of such devices are stated as:

Support for video web conferencing facility; multimedia content viewer for example .pdf, .docx, .ods, .adp, .doc, .xls, .jpeg, .gif, .png, .bmp, .odt, .zip, AVI, AC3, etc.; searchable PDF reader; unzip tool to unzip zip files; possibility to install suitable firmware upgrades; computing abilities such as Open Office, SciLab, cups (for printing support); media player able to play streamed and stored media files; Internet browsing, JavaScript, PDF plug-in Java; wireless communication for audio/video I/O; cloud computing option; remote device management ability; rendering YouTube and other online video services (open source Flash players, e.g., gnash or swfdec).

#### Other preferable

- Playback: AVCHD
- Multimedia I/O interfaces: DTV, IPTv, DTH
- Internet browsing: Flash player (Adobe)

### Specifications

Suitable motherboard; system-on-a-chip to provide the above mentioned functions; QWERTY keyboard, mouse and a minimum display of 7" colour LCD/TFT (touchscreen optional) or suitable all-in one projection system; minimum of 2 USB 2.0 ports and USB hosts; RF certification- all "CE certificate" (FCC guidelines); three hours or more uninterrupted operation via battery or batteryless device; battery charger with adapter or hybrid super capacitor quick charger; SD card slot (supports minimum of 8GB); RGB; support to connect LCD projector; support for external hard disk drive (minimum 32 GB); suitable Ethernet port; WLAN card (IEEE 802.11 a, b , g, n) desirable; alternative battery support through solar cell, or hybrid capacitor is desirable; webcam (embedded desirable); adequate RAM and hard disk drive or NAND flash to meet all desired functions; shock resistant casing of suitable form factor for the device, environmental shield desirable; operating temperature 0 to 48 degrees Celsius. Max humidity 80% shock resistant = 2g; ROHS compliant.

#### Other preferable

- HDMI port

### Hardware

- Rugged casing with a rubberized feel
- Wi-Fi enabled
- Fixed Ethernet ability
- Mini and full USB
- miniSD card slot
- Subscriber Identity Module (SIM card) slot
- Video out
- Headphone jack
- 2 GB of memory using memory card[2] [9]
- 2 Watts of power consumption with solar charging option[9]

### Software

- Android operating system[7]
- Educational software developed at Indian Institute of Technology[7]
- Web browsing, video conferencing and word processing software[2]

## Release

Kapil Sibal has stated that a million devices would be made available to students in 2011. The devices will be manufactured at a cost of ₹ 1500 (23 Euro) each, half of which will be paid by the government and half by the institutions that would use it.[7] [10]

## Contract with initial vendor cancelled

In January 2011, the company initially chosen to build the Sakshat, **HCL Infosystems**, failed to provide evidence that they had at least Rs 60 million in bank guaranteed funds, as required by the Indian government, which has allocated $6.5 million to the project. As a result, the government has put the project out for bidding again.[11]

## References


[1] $10-laptop proves to be a damp squib (http://timesofindia.indiatimes.com/Hyderabad/10-laptop_proves_to_be_a_damp_squib/articleshow/4072417.cms), *The Times of India*, February 4, 2009

[2] India unveils prototype for $35 touch-screen computer (http://www.bbc.co.uk/news/world-south-asia-10740817) BBC World news-South Asia Retrieved 25 July 2010

[3] India to unveil the £7 laptop (http://www.guardian.co.uk/world/2009/feb/02/india-computer-cheapest), *The Guardian*, Febryary 2, 2009

[4] "Why India's $35 computer joke isn't funny" (http://economictimes.indiatimes.com/Hardware/articleshow/6214029.cms). *The Economic Times* (New Dehli). 25 July 2010. . Retrieved 25 July 2010.

[5] PIB Press Release (http://pib.nic.in/release/release.asp?relid=63417) PIB Retrieved 26 July 2010

[6] "OLPC's Negroponte supports India's $35 tablet concept" (http://www.siliconindia.com/shownews/OLPCs_Negroponte_supports_Indias_35_tablet_concept-nid-70313.html). 9 August 2010. . Retrieved 14 August 2010.

[7] NDTV Gadget Guru (http://www.ndtv.com/news/videos/video_player.php?id=157534) Gadget Guru exclusive: $35 laptop is here. Retrieved 13 August 2010

[8] Expression of Interest for Low-Cost Access Device (http://www.education.nic.in/TechnicalEdu/EOI-LCAD.pdf) Expression of Interest by Government of India, Ministry of Human Resource Development

[9] India unveils cheapest laptop (http://www.guardian.co.uk/world/2010/jul/23/india-unveils-cheapest-laptop), The Guardian, Retrieved 25 July 2010

[10] Guardin-India untiels cheapest laptop (http://www.guardian.co.uk/world/2010/jul/23/india-unveils-cheapest-laptop) Retrieved 25 July 2010

[11] (http://economictimes.indiatimes.com/tech/hardware/tender-for-35-laptop-project-cancelled/articleshow/7316466.cms) news clipping by Pragadeesh Sekar on public interest

# T-Mobile G-Slate

## T-Mobile G-Slate

| Manufacturer | LG Electronics |
|---|---|
| Type | Tablet media player |
| Release date | March 2011 |
| Operating system | Android 3.0 (Honeycomb) |
| Power | 6400 mAh |
| CPU | 1GHz Nvidia Tegra 2 AP20H dual-core processor |
| Storage capacity | Flash memory: 32 GB |
| Display | 8.9 in (23 cm) 1280×768 px at 168 ppi |
| Input | Multi-touch capacitive touchscreen display<br>3-axis gyroscope<br>3-axis accelerometer<br>Digital compass<br>Ambient light sensor |
| Camera | 5.0 megapixel rear-facing 3D camera with LED Flash and 1080p video capture<br>2.0 megapixel front-facing camera |
| Dimensions | 243 mm (9.6 in) *(h)*<br>149.4 mm (5.88 in) *(w)*<br>12.8 mm (0.50 in) *(d)* |
| Weight | 630 g (22 oz) [1] |

The **T-Mobile G-Slate** is a tablet computer from T-Mobile USA developed by LG Electronics[2] and scheduled to be released in the US in March 2011.[3] It will be LG's first device running Android 3.0 ("Honeycomb") and is scheduled to appear at the Mobile World Congress in February 2011.[3]

## References

[1] "LG Optimus Pad - Product Information" (http://www.lgnewsroom.com/mwc2011/product_view.php?category=47&product_code=68&product_type=32&post_index=902). *LG News Room*. . Retrieved 2011-02-11.

[2] Trask, Alexandra (2 February 2011). "T-Mobile and LG Mobile Phones Unveil the T-Mobile G-Slate With Google, Delivering a Premium Mobile HD Entertainment Experience on a Tablet" (http://press.t-mobile.com/articles/TMobileGSlate). *T-Mobile USA*. . Retrieved 2011-02-04.

[3] Kremp, Matthias (2 February 2011). "Google attackiert das iPad mit Honigwaben" (http://www.spiegel.de/netzwelt/gadgets/0,1518,743234-2,00.html). Spiegel Online. . Retrieved 4 February 2011.

# Toshiba Tablet

## Toshiba Tablet

| Toshiba Tablet | |
|---|---|
|  Toshiba Tablet | |
| **Developer** | Toshiba |
| **Type** | Tablet, media player |
| **Generation** | 1st |
| **Release date** | **mid 2011** |
| **Operating system** | Android 3.0 Honeycomb |
| **Power** | 23 W-hr Prismatic Lithium Ion User-replaceable |
| **CPU** | 1 GHz dual-core NVIDIA TegraTM 2 |
| **Storage capacity** | Flash memory<br>8 GB, 16 GB, or 32 GB |
| **Memory** | 1GB LP-DDR2 RAM |
| **Display** | 10.1 inches (260 mm) 16:10 aspect ratio **Resolution:** WXGA (1280x800), HD 720p Wide-Viewing Angle 16:10 Toshiba Adaptive Display Technology Resolution+® Video Upconvert Technology |
| **Graphics** | NVIDIA GeForce® Graphics |
| **Input** | Gyroscope, Accelerometer, Ambient Light Sensor, GPS, E-Compass, USB 2.0, Mini USB, Docking Connector, DC Input, Microphone & SD card reader |
| **Camera** | **Front:** 2MP Webcam with Integrated Microphone **Back:** 5MP Camera with Auto Focus and Digital Zoom [1] |
| **Connectivity** | Wi-Fi (802.11/b/g/n)<br>Bluetooth |
| **Online services** | Android Market |
| **Dimensions** | 10.75 in (273 mm) *(height)*<br>6.97 in (177 mm) *(width)*<br>0.62 in (16 mm) *(depth)* |
| **Weight** | 1.6lbs |
| **Related articles** | Xoom, Eee Pad Transformer, Galaxy Tab, iPad 2, T-Mobile G-Slate, Comparison of tablet PCs |
| **Website** | www.thetoshibatablet.com [2] |

The **Toshiba Tablet** is a 10.1" tablet computer running Android 3.0 honeycomb.

## External links

- ToshibaTablet.com [3]
- www.thetoshibatablet.com/pdf/Toshiba%20PDF_V2.pdf [4]
- reviews.cnet.com/tablets/toshiba-tablet [5]
- www.android.com/ [6]
- [7]

## References

[1] www.thetoshibatablet.com/pdf/Toshiba%20PDF_V2.pdf (http://www.thetoshibatablet.com/pdf/Toshiba PDF_V2.pdf)

# Comparison of tablet PCs

Below is a list of presently available and upcoming tablet PCs grouped by intended audience and form factor.

## Media tablets

(Multi-)Media tablets designed for entertainment are compared in the following tables.

### 8" screen and larger

This table compares 8" and larger screen (multi-)media tablets released in **2010** and later.

| Manufacturer | Weight | Display size | Display resolution | Display technology | Input technology | Operating system | CPU model | CPU architecture | CPU frequency (GHz) | CPU cores | Wi-Fi | Cellular | Bluetooth | GPS | Storage type | Storage capacity (GiB) | Storage expansion | RAM (GiB) | Battery life (h) | Battery type | Thickness mm | Release date |
|---|---|---|---|---|---|---|---|---|---|---|---|---|---|---|---|---|---|---|---|---|---|---|
| Acer | 0.73 kg (1.6 lb) | 10.1 in (26 cm) | 1280 x 800 | LCD | Capacitive multi-touch | Android 3.0 Honeycomb | Nvidia Tegra 250 | ARM | 1.0 | 2 | 802.11b/g/n | ✓ UMTS, HSDPA, LTE | ✓ 2.1+EDR | ✓ A-GPS | SSD | 16, 32 | microSD, up to 32 GB | 1 | 10 | lithium-polymer | 13.3 mm (0.52 in) | April 2011 end of month [2] |
| Notion Ink | 0.73 kg (1.6 lb) | 10.1 in (26 cm) | 1024 x 600 | Pixel Qi LCD or TFT LCD | Capacitive multi-touch | Android 2.2 Froyo | Nvidia Tegra 250 | ARM | 1.0 | 2 | 802.11b/g/n | ✓ UTMS, HSPA | ✓ 2.1+EDR | ✓ | SSD | 8 | microSD | 1 | 6 [4] | lithium-polymer | 14.0 mm (0.55 in) | January 21, 2011 |
| Advent | 0.700 kg (1.54 lb) | 10.1 in (26 cm) | 1024 x 600 | TFT LCD | Capacitive 4 fingers Multi-touch | Android 2.2 Froyo | Nvidia Tegra | ARM | 1.0 | 2 | 802.11b/g | ✗ | ✓ | ✗ | SSD | 0.512 | microSD | 0.5 | 6.5 | lithium-polymer | 13.6 mm (0.54 in) | November 14, 2010 |
| Apple Inc. | 0.68 kg (1.5 lb) (Wi-Fi) 0.73 kg (1.6 lb) (Wi-Fi+3G) | 9.7 in (25 cm) | 1024 x 768 | IPS LCD | Capacitive multi-touch | iOS 4 | Apple A4 | ARM | 1.0 | 1 | 802.11a/b/g/n | ✓ Optional 3G (UMTS/HSDPA & GSM/EDGE) | ✓ 2.1+EDR | ✓ 3G version only | SSD | 16, 32, 64 | ✗ | 0.25 | 10 | lithium-polymer | 13.0 mm (0.51 in) | April 2010 |
| Apple Inc. | 0.60 kg (1.3 lb) (Wi-Fi) 0.61 kg (1.3 lb) (Wi-Fi+3G) | 9.7 in (25 cm) | 1024 x 768 | IPS LCD | Capacitive multi-touch | iOS 4 | Apple A5 | ARM | 1.0 [6] | 2 | 802.11a/b/g/n | ✓ Optional 3G (UMTS/HSDPA & GSM/EDGE) | ✓ 2.1+EDR | ✓ 3G version only | SSD | 16, 32, 64 | ✗ | 0.5 | 10 | lithium-polymer | 8.8 mm (0.35 in) | March 11, 2011 |
| Archos | 0.48 kg (1.1 lb) | 10.1 in (26 cm) | 1024 x 600 | TFT LCD | Capacitive multi-touch | Android 2.2 Froyo | TI OMAP 3630 | ARM | 1.0 | 1 | 802.11b/g/n | ✗ | ✓ 2.1+EDR | ✗ | SSD | 8 or 16 | microSD, SDHC | 0.25 | 7 | lithium-polymer | 12.0 mm (0.47 in) | November 2010 |

| | | | | | | | | | | | | | | | | | | | | | | |
|---|---|---|---|---|---|---|---|---|---|---|---|---|---|---|---|---|---|---|---|---|---|---|
| **ASUS Eee Pad Transformer (TF101)** | Asus | 0.68 kg (1.5 lb) | 10.1 in (26 cm) | 1280 x 800 | IPS LCD | Capacitive multi-touch | Android 3.0 Honeycomb | Nvidia Tegra 250 | ARM | 1.0 | 2 | 802.11b/g/n | ✗ | ✓ 2.1+EDR | ✓ | SSD | 16, 32, 64 | SD(SDHC) | 0.5 or 1 | 9.5 (16 with dock) | lithium-polymer | 12.9 (0.5 |
| **Asus Eee Slider (EP102)** | Asus | 0.886 kg (1.95 lb) | 10.1 in (26 cm) | 1280 x 800 | IPS LCD | Capacitive multi-touch, slide out keyboard | Android 3.0 Honeycomb | Nvidia Tegra 250 | ARM | 1.0 | 2 | 802.11n | ✓ Optional 3G | ✓ 2.1 | ? | SSD | 16, 32, 64 | ? | 0.5 or 1 | 8 | lithium-polymer | 17.7 (0.7 |
| **Asus Eee Slate [9] (EP121)** | Asus | 1.16 kg (2.6 lb) | 12.1 in (31 cm) | 1280 x 800 | IPS LCD | Capacitive multi-touch, Wacom Digitizer | Windows 7 Home Premium | Intel Core i5-470UM | x86-64 | 1.33, 1.86 turbo boost | 2 | 802.11b/g/n | ✗ | ✓ 3.0 | ✗ | SSD | 32 or 64 | MMC/SD [10] (SDXC, SDHC) | 2 or 4 | 4.5 | lithium-polymer | 17.0 (0.67 |
| **bModo 12 [12]** | bModo | 0.99 kg (2.2 lb) | 11.6 in (29 cm) | 1366 x 768 | TFT LCD | Capacitive multi-touch | Windows 7 | Intel Atom N450 | x86-64 | 1.66 | 1 | 802.11b/g/n | ✓ GSM, GPRS, EDGE & HSPA, HSUPA, WCDMA | ✓ 2.1+EDR | ✓ | SSD | 32 or 64 | SDHC | 1 or 2 | 5 | lithium-polymer | 14.0 (0.5 |
| **ExoPC [13]** | ExoPC | 0.95 kg (2.1 lb) | 11.6 in (29 cm) | 1366 x 768 | LCD | Capacitive dual-touch | Windows 7 Home Premium | Intel Atom N450 | x86-64 | 1.66 | 1 | 802.11b/g/n | ✗ | ✓ 2.1+EDR | ✗ | SSD | 32 or 64 | SD/SDHC 32 GB max | 2 | 4 | lithium-polymer | 14.0 (0.5 |
| **EviGroup [14] Paddle [15]** | Evigroup | 0.99 kg (2.2 lb) | 10.6 in (27 cm) | 1024 x 600 | LCD | Capacitive multi-touch | Windows 7 | Intel Atom N450 | x86-64 | 1.66 | 1 | 802.11a/b/g | ✓ Optional (WCDMA/TD-SCDMA/CDMA2000) | ✗ | ✗ | SSD | 32 | SD(HC), MMC, MS | 1 | ? | lithium-polymer | 22 (0.8 |
| **HCL ME [16] AP10-A1** | HCL | 0.75 kg (1.7 lb) | 10 in (25 cm) | 1024 x 600 | LCD | Capacitive multi-touch | Android 2.2 Froyo | Cortex A9 | ARM | 1.0 | 2 | 802.11b/g/n | ✓ HSDPA/HSUPA | ✓ 2.1 + EDR | ✓ | iNAND | 16 | microSD, up to 32 GB | 1 | ? | lithium-polymer | 14. (0.5 |
| **HP Slate [17] 500** | HP | 0.68 kg (1.5 lb) | 8.9 in (23 cm) | 1024 x 600 | TFT LCD | Capacitive multi-touch, HP Slate Digital Pen | Windows 7 Professional | Intel Atom Z540 | x86 | 1.86 | 1 | 802.11b/g/n | ✗ | ✓ 3.0 + HS | ✗ | SSD | 64 | SD (SDHC, SDXC) | 2 | 5 | lithium-polymer | 14. (0.5 |
| **HP [18] Touchpad** | HP | 0.74 kg (1.6 lb) | 9.7 in (25 cm) | 1024 x 768 | LCD | Capacitive multi-touch | webOS 3.0 | Qualcomm Snapdragon APQ8060 | ARM | 1.2 | 2 | 802.11b/g/n | ✓ Optional 3g & 4g (later) | ✓ 2.1+EDR | ✓ 3g models only | SSD | 16, 32 | ✗ | 1 | 8 | lithium-ion | 13. (0.5 |
| **Motorola [19] Xoom** | Motorola | 0.73 kg (1.6 lb) | 10.1 in (26 cm) | 1280 x 800 | TFT LCD | Capacitive touch screen | Android 3.0 Honeycomb | Nvidia Tegra 250 | ARM | 1.0 | 2 | 802.11a/b/g/n | ✓ CDMA, LTE | ✓ 2.1+EDR | ✓ | SSD | 32 | microSD | 1 | 10 | lithium-ion | 12.9 (0.5 |
| **MultiPad [20] PMP7100C** | Prestigio | 0.48 kg (1.1 lb) | 10.1 in (26 cm) | 1024 x 600 | TFT LCD | Capacitive multi-touch | Android 2.2 Froyo | TI OMAP 3630 | ARM | 1.0 | 1 | 802.11b/g/n | ✗ | ✓ 2.1+EDR | ✗ | SSD | 8 | microSD, SDHC | 0.25 | 7 | lithium-polymer | 13.8 (0.5 |
| **Optimus Pad [21] (G-Slate) [22]** | LG | 0.654 kg (1.44 lb) | 8.9 in (23 cm) | 1280 x 768 | TFT LCD | Capacitive multi-touch | Android 3.0 Honeycomb | Nvidia Tegra 250 | ARM | 1.0 | 2 | 802.11b/g/n | ✓ UTMS, HSPA+, HSUPA | ✓ 2.1+EDR | ✓ A-GPS | SSD | 32 | microSD, up to 32 GB | 1 | 9 | lithium-ion | 13.( (0.5 |
| **POV Mobii [24] Tegra** | Point of View | 0.73 kg (1.6 lb) | 10.1 in (26 cm) | 1024 x 600 | LCD | Capacitive touch screen | Android 2.2 Froyo | Nvidia Tegra 250 | ARM | 1.0 | 2 | 802.11b/g | ✓ Optional | ✗ | ✗ | SSD | 0.512 | microSD | 0.5 | ? | lithium-ion | |
| **Samsung Galaxy [25] Tab 8.9** | Samsung | 0.47 kg (1.0 lb) | 8.9 in (23 cm) | 1280 x 800 | PLS LCD | Capacitive multi-touch | Android 3.0 Honeycomb | Nvidia Tegra 250 | ARM | 1.0 | 2 | 802.11a/b/g/n | ✓ Optional 3g(HSDPA, HSUPA) | ✓ 3.0 | ✓ A-GPS | SSD | 16, 32, 64 | microSD, up to 32 GB | 1 | 10 | lithium-polymer | 8.6 (0.34 |
| **Samsung Galaxy [26] Tab 10.1** | Samsung | 0.595 kg (1.31 lb) | 10.1 in (26 cm) | 1280 x 800 | PLS LCD | Capacitive multi-touch | Android 3.0 Honeycomb | Nvidia Tegra 250 | ARM | 1.0 | 2 | 802.11a/b/g/n | ✓ Optional 3g & 4g (HSPA+, LTE, WiMAX) | ✓ 2.1+EDR | ✓ | SSD | 16, 32, 64 | microSD, up to 32 GB | 1 | 10 | lithium-polymer | 8.6 (0.34 |
| **Samsung Galaxy [28] Tab 10.1v** | Samsung | 0.599 kg (1.32 lb) | 10.1 in (26 cm) | 1280 x 800 | TFT LCD | Capacitive multi-touch | Android 3.0 Honeycomb | Nvidia Tegra 250 | ARM | 1.0 | 2 | 802.11a/b/g/n | ✓ 3g(HSPA+) | ✓ 2.1+EDR | ✓ | SSD | 16 | ✗ | 1 | 10 | lithium-polymer | 10.9 (0.43 |

| | | | | | | | | | | | | | | | | | | | | | | |
|---|---|---|---|---|---|---|---|---|---|---|---|---|---|---|---|---|---|---|---|---|---|---|
| Toshiba | 0.760 kg (1.68 lb) | 10.1 in (26 cm) | 1024 x 600 | TFT LCD | Capacitive 4-finger Multi-touch | Android 2.2 Froyo | Nvidia Tegra 250 | ARM | 1.0 | 2 | 802.11b/g/n | ✓ Optional 3G | ✓ 2.1+EDR | ✗ | SSD | 16 | SD, SDHC, MMC | 0.5 | 7 | lithium-ion | 14 mm (0.55 in) | December 2010 |
| Toshiba | 0.771 kg (1.70 lb) | 10.1 in (26 cm) | 1280 x 800 | LCD | Capacitive multi-touch | Android 3.0 Honeycomb | Nvidia Tegra 250 | ARM | 1.0 | 2 | 802.11n | ✓ | ✓ | ✓ | SSD | 16 | SD | 1 | 7 | lithium-ion | 15.0 mm (0.59 in) | June 2011 (Mid June)[2] |
| ViewSonic | 0.70 kg (1.5 lb) | 10.1 in (26 cm) | 1024 x 600 | TFT LCD | Capacitive multi-touch | Android 2.2 Froyo | Nvidia Tegra 250 | ARM | 1.0 | 2 | 802.11b/g/n | ✗ | ✓ 2.1+EDR | ✗ | SSD | 16 | Micro SD | 0.5 | 8-10 | lithium-polymer | 13.7 mm (0.54 in) | December 2010 |
| ViewSonic | 0.875 kg (1.93 lb) | 10.1 in (26 cm) | 1024 x 600 | TFT LCD | Capacitive multi-touch | Android 1.6, Windows 7 | Intel Atom N455 | x86-64 | 1.6 | 1 | 802.11b/g/n | ✗ | ✓ 2.1+EDR | ✗ | SSD | 16 | Micro SD | 1 | 4 | lithium-ion | 16.5 mm (0.65 in) | March 2011 |
| MSI | 0.74 kg (1.6 lb) | 10.1 in (26 cm) | 1280 x 800 | IPS LCD | Capacitive multi-touch | Android 3.0 Honeycomb | nvidia Tegra 250 | ARM | 1.0 | 2 | 802.11b/g/n | ✓ Optional 3G | ✓ | ✓ A-GPS | SSD | 32 | micro-SD | 1 | 8-10 | lithium-ion | 14.0 mm (0.55 in) | June 1, 2011[37] |
| MSI | 0.800 kg (1.76 lb) | 10.1 in (26 cm) | 1024 x 600 | TFT LCD | Capacitive multi-touch | Windows 7 Starter | Intel Atom Z530 | x86 | 1.6 | 1 | 802.11b/g/n | ✓ Optional 3G | ✓ 2.1 | ✗ | SSD | 32 | SD, MMC | 2 | 5 | lithium-ion | 18.5 mm (0.73 in) | January 2011 |

## 5"-7" screen

This table compares 5"-7" screen (multi-)media tablets released in **2010** and later.

| Manufacturer | Weight (kg) | Display size (in) | Display resolution | Display technology | Input technology | Operating system | CPU model | CPU architecture | CPU frequency (GHz) | CPU cores | Wi-Fi | Cellular | Bluetooth | GPS | Storage type | Storage capacity (GiB) | Storage expansion | RAM (GiB) | Battery life (h) | Battery type | Thickness mm | Release date |
|---|---|---|---|---|---|---|---|---|---|---|---|---|---|---|---|---|---|---|---|---|---|---|
| RIM | 0.425 kg (0.94 lb) | 7.0 in (18 cm) | 1024 x 600 | LCD | Capacitive multi-touch | BlackBerry Tablet OS | TI OMAP 4430 | ARM | 1.0 | 2 | 802.11a/b/g/n | ✓ Optional LTE, HSPA+, WiMAX | ✓ 2.1+EDR | ✗ | SSD | 16, 32, 64 | ✗ | 1 | 10h | lithium-polymer | 10.0 mm (0.39 in) | April 2011(Mid April)[2] |
| Dell | 0.22 kg (0.49 lb) | 5 in (13 cm) | 800 x 480 | TFT LCD | Capacitive multi-touch | Android 2.2 | Qualcomm Snapdragon QSD8250 | ARM | 1.0 | 1 | 802.11b/g | ✓ UMTS, EDGE, HSDPA, HSUPA | ✓ 2.0 | ✓ A-GPS | SSD | 16 | Micro SD | 0.512 | 10h | lithium-ion | 10.0 mm (0.39 in) | June 4, 2010 |
| Dell | 0.45 kg (0.99 lb) | 7 in (18 cm) | 800 x 480 | TFT LCD, Gorilla Glass | Capacitive multi-touch | Android 2.2 | Nvidia Tegra 250 | ARM | 1.0 | 2 | 802.11b/g/n | ✓ HSPA+ | ✓ 2.1+EDR | ✓ | SSD | 16 | SD (SDHC), up to 32 GB | 0.256 | 4 | lithium-ion | 12.4 mm (0.49 in) | April 2011 (Mid April)[2] |
| Huawei | 0.5 kg (1.1 lb) | 7 in (18 cm) | 800 x 480 | TFT LCD | Resistive touch screen | Android 2.1 | Qualcomm Snapdragon | ARM | 1.0 | 1 | 802.11b/g/n | ✓ HSDPA, HSUPA | ✓ 2.1 | ✗ | SSD | 0.512 | microSD | 0.256 | 2.5h (video), 140h (standby) | lithium-ion | 15.5 mm (0.61 in) | January 2010 |
| Huawei | 0.44 kg (0.97 lb) | 7 in (18 cm) | 800 x 480 | TFT LCD | Capacitive multi-touch | Android 2.2 | Qualcomm Snapdragon | ARM | 1.0 | 1 | 802.11b/g/n | ✓ HSDPA, HSUPA | ✓ 2.1 | ✓ | SSD | 0.512 | microSD | 0.256 | ? | lithium-ion | 12.5 mm (0.49 in) | April 2011 |
| Barnes & Noble | 0.45 kg (0.99 lb) | 7 in (18 cm) | 1024 x 600 | IPS LCD | Capacitive multi-touch | Android 2.1 | TI OMAP 3621 | ARM | 0.8 | 1 | 802.11b/g/n | ✗ | ✗ | ✗ | SSD | 8 | microSD, SDHC | 0.512 | 8h | lithium-ion | 12.0 mm (0.47 in) | October 26, 2010 |
| Olive Telecom | 0.375 kg (0.83 lb) | 7 in (18 cm) | 800 x 400 | TFT LCD | Capacitive multi-touch | Android 2.2 | Qualcomm MSM7227 | ARM | 0.6 | 1 | 802.11b/g | ✓ | ✓ 2.0 + EDR | ✓ | NAND Flash | 0.512 | microSD, up to 32 GB | 0.512 | ? | lithium-polymer | 11.5 mm (0.45 in) | October 2010 |

| | | | | | | | | | | | | | | | | | | | | | | |
|---|---|---|---|---|---|---|---|---|---|---|---|---|---|---|---|---|---|---|---|---|---|---|
| Samsung Galaxy Tab [46] | Samsung | 0.38 kg (0.84 lb) | 7.0 in (18 cm) | 1024 x 600 | TFT LCD | Capacitive multi-touch | Android 2.2 Froyo | Cortex A8 Hummingbird | ARM | 1.0 | 1 | 802.11a/b/g/n | ✓ GSM/GPRS/EDGE, HSUPA, HSDPA, CDMA | ✓ 3.0 | ✓ A-GPS | SSD | 16, 32 | microSD | 0.512 | 7h video, 10h talktime | lithium-polymer | 11.98 mm (0.472 in) |
| ViewPad 7 [47] | ViewSonic | 0.38 kg (0.84 lb) | 7 in (18 cm) | 800 x 480 | TFT LCD | Capacitive multi-touch | Android 2.2 Froyo | Qualcomm MSM7227 | ARM | 0.6 | 1 | 802.11b/g | ✓ GSM/UTMS | ✓ 2.1+EDR | ✓ | SSD | 0.512 | Micro SD | 0.512 | 4-6 | lithium-polymer | 11.43 mm (0.450 in) |

## Older

This table compares (multi-)media tablets released in **2009** and earlier.

| Model | Manufacturer | Weight (kg) | Display size (in) | Display resolution | Display technology | Input technology | Operating system | CPU model | CPU architecture | CPU frequency (GHz) | CPU cores | Wi-Fi | Cellular | Bluetooth | GPS | Storage type | Storage capacity (GiB) | Storage expansion | RAM (GiB) | Battery life (h) | Battery type | Thickness mm |
|---|---|---|---|---|---|---|---|---|---|---|---|---|---|---|---|---|---|---|---|---|---|---|
| Asus R2H [48] [49] | Asus | 0.83 kg (1.8 lb) | 7 inches (18 cm) | 800 x 480 | TFT LCD | Stylus, joystick, 4-way navigation | Windows XP | Intel Celeron | x86 | 0.9 | 1 | 802.11b/g | ✗ | ✓ 2.0+EDR | ✓ | HDD | 60 | SD | 0.768 | 3h | lithium-polymer | 28 mm (1.1 in) |
| Asus R50A [50] [51] | Asus | 0.52 kg (1.1 lb) | 5.6 in (14 cm) | 1024 × 600 | TFT LCD | Stylus, joystick, 4-way navigation | Windows Vista | Intel Atom Z520 | x86 | 1.33 | 1 | 802.11b/g | ✓ UTMS, HSDPA | ✓ 2.0 | ✓ | SSD | 32 | MicroSD | 1 | 3h | lithium-polymer | 29 mm (1.1 in) |
| Asus R70A [53] [54] | Asus | 0.73 kg (1.6 lb) | 7 in (18 cm) | 1024 × 600 | TFT LCD | Stylus, joystick, 4-way navigation | Windows Vista | Intel Atom | x86 | 1.6 | 1 | 802.11b/g | ✓ UTMS, HSDPA | ✓ 2.0 | ✓ | HDD | 120 | SD | 1 | 3h | ? | 24 mm (0.94 in) |
| Axiotron Modbook | Axiotron | 5.3 kg (12 lb) | 13.3 in (34 cm) | 1280 x 800 | TFT LCD | Wacom digitizer | Mac OS X v10.5 | Intel Core 2 Duo | x86 | 2.1-2.4 | 2 | 802.11a/b/g/n | ✗ | ✓ 2.0+EDR | ✗ | HDD | 60-250 GB | ✗ | 1-4 | 3-5h | lithium-polymer | 29.5 mm (1.16 in) |
| Cowon Q5W [55] [56] | Cowon | 0.38 kg (0.84 lb) | 5 in (13 cm) | 800 x 480 | TFT LCD | Touch | Windows CE 5.0 | Alchemy Au1250 | MIPS | 0.6 | 1 | 802.11b | ✗ | ✓ | ✗ | HDD | 40-80 | ✗ | 0.128 | 7h | lithium-polymer | 20 mm (0.79 in) |
| Fujitsu Stylistic ST6012 | Fujitsu | 1.6 kg (3.5 lb) | 12.1 in (31 cm) | 1280 x 800 | TFT LCD | Wacom digitizer | Windows 7 | Intel Core 2 Duo | x86 | 1.4 | 2 | 802.11b/g | ✓ Optional 3G | ✓ 2.1 | ✗ | SSD or HDD | 128-320 | SD | 1-2 | 6-9h | lithium-ion | 23.8 mm (0.94 in) |
| Nokia N810 | Nokia | 0.226 kg (0.50 lb) | 4.13 in (10.5 cm) | 800 × 480 | TFT LCD | Physical keyboard, touchscreen | Maemo Linux | TI OMAP 2420 | ARM6 | 0.4 | 1 | 802.11b/g | ✗ | ✓ 2.0 | ✓ | SSD | 0.256 | SD(HC) | 0.128 | 4h | lithium-ion | 14 mm (0.55 in) |
| Samsung Q1 Ultra | Samsung | 0.70 kg (1.5 lb) | 7 in (18 cm) | 1024 × 600 | TFT LCD | Resistive touchscreen | Windows XP | Intel A110 | x86 | 0.8 | 1 | 802.11b/g | ✓ UTMS, HSDPA | ✓ 2.0 | ✗ | HDD | 60 | SD | 1 | 3h | ? (4-cell) | 24 mm (0.94 in) |
| Wibrain i1 [57] | Wibrain | 0.499 kg (1.10 lb) | 4.8 in (12 cm) | 1024 × 600 | LCD | Soft (Finger) Touch | Windows XP or Linux | Intel Atom | x86 | 1.3 | 1 | 802.11b/g | ✗ | ✓ 2.0 | ✗ | SSD or HDD | 16, 32 (SSD) 30, 60 (HDD) | SD | 1 | 6h | ? (29-Wh) | 82 mm (3.2 in) |

# Industrial tablets

This table compares tablet PCs designed to be used by professionals in various harsh environmental conditions. Most of them are rugged. Some are meant to be mounted in vehicles or used as terminals.

| odel | Manufacturer | Weight (kg) | Display size (in) | Display resolution | Display technology | Input technology | Operating system | CPU model | CPU architecture | CPU frequency (GHz) | CPU cores | Wi-Fi | Cellular | Bluetooth | GPS | Storage type | Storage capacity (GiB) | Storage expansion | RAM (GiB) | Temp range (°C) | Battery life (h) | Battery type | Thickness mm | Release date |
|---|---|---|---|---|---|---|---|---|---|---|---|---|---|---|---|---|---|---|---|---|---|---|---|---|
| ARS-3100S | Advantech | 2.1 kg (4.6 lb) | 10.4 in (26 cm) | 800 x 600 | TFT LCD | ? | Windows XP Embedded | ? | ? | 0.5 | 1 | ? | ? | ? | ? | HDD | 4 | CF | 0.512 | | ? | ? | ? | ? |
| | American Industrial Systems | 4.8 kg (11 lb) | 10.4 in (26 cm) | 800 x 600 | ? | ? | Windows XP Embedded | Intel Atom | x86 | 1.6 | ? | ? | ? | ? | ? | HDD | 80 | ? | 0.512 | −20 to 60 | ? | ? | ? | ? |
| P | Catcher | 2.6 kg (5.7 lb) | 6.4 in (16 cm) | 640 x 480 | ? | ? | Windows XP Professional | ? | ? | 1.4 | ? | ? | ? | ? | ? | SSD, HDD | 40 | ? | 2 | | ? | ? | ? | ? |
| 8300 | Data Ltd | 1.7 kg (3.7 lb) | 8.4 in (21 cm) | 640 x 480, 800 x 600 | ? | ? | Windows XP Pro, Embed, Tablet, Debian GNOME | ? | x86 | 1.1/1.4 | ? | ? | ? | ? | ? | HDD | 40, 60 | CF | 0.512/1.0 | | ? | ? | ? | ? |
| | DLoG | 2.5 kg (5.5 lb) | 7 in (18 cm) | 480 x 272 | TFT LCD | ? | Windows CE 5.0, Linux (on request) | ? | ? | 0.52 | 1 | ? | ? | ? | ? | SSD | 0.512 | ? | 0.064 | | ? | ? | ? | ? |
| Hammerhead, UCC | DRS Technologies | ? | ? | ? | ? | ? | Windows XP [58] | ? | ? | ? | ? | ? | ? | ? | ? | SSD, HDD | ? | ? | ? | | ? | ? | ? | ? |
| WebDT 310 | DT Research | ? | ? | ? | ? | ? | Windows XP [59] | ? | ? | ? | ? | ? | ? | ? | ? | SSD, HDD | ? | ? | ? | 0...40 | ? | ? | ? | ? |
| nd xTablet ed Tablet PC | MobileDemand [37] | 2.5 kg (5.5 lb) | 7 in (18 cm) | 1024 x 600, 1024 x 768 | ? | ? | Windows 7 Professional, Windows XP Tablet PC Edition | Intel Atom Z530P | x86 | 1.6 | ? | ? | ? | ? | ? | SSD, HDD | 32-128+ | ? | 2 | | ? | ? | ? | ? |
| nd xTablet ed Tablet PC | MobileDemand [62] | 4.6 kg (10 lb) | 8.4 in (21 cm) | 800 x 600 / 800 x 480 | ? | ? | Windows 7 Professional, Windows XP Tablet PC Edition | Intel Core Duo ULV U2500 | x86 | 1.2 | ? | ? | ? | ? | ? | SSD, HDD | 64-160 | ? | 2 | | ? | ? | ? | ? |
| ughbook 08, | Panasonic | ? | 5.6 in (14 cm) | 640 x 480 | ? | ? | ? | ? | ? | ? | ? | ? | ? | ? | ? | SSD, HDD | ? | ? | ? | | ? | ? | ? | ? |
| 27] SlimBook 3] | PaceBlade [30] | 1.48 kg (3.3 lb) | 12.1 in (31 cm) | 640 x 480 | TFT LCD | ? | Windows XP Tablet Edition/Professional, Windows Vista Business/Ultimate, [Windows 7] Business/Ultimate | Intel Atom N270 | x86 | 1.6 | 1 | ? | ? | ? | ? | SATA, SSD | 80, 160, 250 | ? | 1-2 DDR2 | -30 to +70 | ? | ? | ? | ? |
| 60] | Quaduro Systems | 1.19 kg (2.6 lb) | 8.4 in (21 cm) | 800x600 | TFT LCD | Resistive touch screen | Windows XP, Windows Vista or openSUSE | VIA C7-M | x86 | 1.2 | 1 | 802.11b/g | ✓ 3G | ✓ | ✓ | HDD | 80 | ✗ | 1 | +1 to +47 | 3h | lithium-ion | 42 mm (1.7 in) | 2007 |

| | | | | | | | | | | | | | | | | | | | | | | | |
|---|---|---|---|---|---|---|---|---|---|---|---|---|---|---|---|---|---|---|---|---|---|---|---|
| **TabletKiosk Sahara eo TufTab v71112XT** [61] | TabletKiosk | 0.895 kg (1.97 lb) | 7 in (18 cm) | 1024 x 768 | TFT LCD | Resistive touch screen | Windows XP, Windows Vista, openSUSE Linux | VIA C7-M ULV | x86 | 1.2 | 1 | 802.11b/g | ✗ | ✓ 2.0+EDR | ✗ | HDD | 40, 80 | ? | 2 | | ? | ? | 31 m… (1.2 in… |
| **TabletKiosk Sahara i310, i400,** | TabletKiosk | 1.6 kg (3.5 lb) | 12.1 in (31 cm) | 640 x 480 | ? | ? | Windows XP/Vista, openSUSE Linux | ? | ? | ? | ? | ? | ? | ? | ? | HDD | 80 | ? | 2 | | ? | ? | ? |
| **Secure RPS Lynx, Orion** | Secure RPS | ? | ? | ? | ? | ? | Windows XP/Vista | ? | ? | ? | | ? | ? | ? | ? | HDD | 80 | | 1 | ? | ? | ? | ? |
| **Talla-Tech Tacter-31M** [62] | Talla-Tech | ? | 6.4-10.4 | 1024 x 768 / 1280 x 800 | ? | ? | ? | ? | ? | ? | ? | ? | ? | ? | ? | HDD | 80 | ? | 2 | | ? | ? | ? |
| **Xplore Technologies ix104ix104C2/ix104C3** [63] | Xplore Technologies | ? | 10.4 in (26 cm) | 640 x 480 | ? | ? | ? | ? | ? | ? | ? | ? | ? | ? | ? | SSD, HDD | ? | ? | ? | | ? | ? | ? |

# Convertible

| Model | Manufacturer | Weight (kg) | Display size (in) | Display resolution, type | Input technology | Windows | Linux | CPU model | CPU frequency (GHz) +32 or 64-bit? | Storage type | Storage capacity (GiB) | RAM (GiB) | Battery life (h) | Thickne… inch |
|---|---|---|---|---|---|---|---|---|---|---|---|---|---|---|
| Acer TravelMate C100, C300, C310 | Acer | ? | ? | ? | ? | ? | ? | ? | ? | ? | ? / ? | ? | ?h (?-cell), ?h (?-cell) | ? |
| Asus R1F, R1E | Asus | ? | 14.1 | 1280 x 800 | ? | Windows Vista Business | ? | Intel Core2 Duo T8300 | 2.4+64 | HDD | 250 | 3 | ?h (?-cell), ?h (?-cell) | ? |
| Averatec C3500 Series | Averatec | 2.5 | 12.1 | 1024 x 768 | ? | Windows XP Professional | ✗ | AMD Athlon XP-M 2200+ | 1.67+32 | HDD | 60 | .5 | 2h (6-cell) | 1.2 |
| Dialogue Flybook V5 | Dialogue | ? | ? | ? | ? | ? | ? | ? | ? | ? | ? | ? | ?h (?-cell), ?h (?-cell) | ? |
| Dell Latitude XT | Dell | ? | 12.1 | ? | Capacitive touch,N-Trig Pen | ? | ? | ? | ? | SDD | ? | ? | ?h (?-cell), ?h (?-cell) | ? |
| Fujitsu LifeBook Series P1610, T4020, T4220, T5010, T2010, U2010 | Fujitsu | ? | ? | ? | ? | ? | ? | ? | ? | ? | ? | ? | ?h (?-cell), ?h (?-cell) | ? |

| | | | | | | | | | | | | | | |
|---|---|---|---|---|---|---|---|---|---|---|---|---|---|---|
| jitsu feBook 4410 Tablet | Fujitsu | 1.8 | | 1280 x 800 | Capacitive multi-touch | Windows 7, Windows XP Tablet PC Edition | ? | Intel Core 2 Duo T6570, P8700 | 2.1, 2.53 + 64 | HDD, SSD | 160-250, 80-120 | 2-8 | 6h (6-cell), 9h (6-cell + 4-cell) | 1.04-1.31 |
| ateway -140X, -120X | Gateway | ? | ? | ? | ? | ? | ? | ? | ? | ? | ? | ? | ?h (?-cell), ?h (?-cell) | ? |
| P Compaq C4200[64] | HP | 2.08 | 12.1 | 1024 x 768 | ? | Windows XP Tablet PC Edition | Certified for Novell Linux Desktop 9 | Intel Pentium M 740, 750, 760 | 1.73, 1.86, 2.0 +32 | HDD | 40, 60, 80 | .25, .5, 1 (max 2) | 5.75h (6-cell) | 1.35 |
| P Compaq C4400[65] | HP | 2.08 | 12.1 | 1024 x 768 | ? | Windows XP Tablet PC Edition | Certified for SUSE Linux Enterprise Desktop 10 and Novell Linux Desktop 9 SP3 | Intel Core Duo T2300E, T2400, T2500, T2600 / Intel Core 2 Duo T5600, T7200, T7400 | 1.66-2.13 +32, 64 | HDD | 60-120 | .5, 1, 2 (max 4) | 5.5h (6-cell) | 1.35 |
| P Compaq 710p[66] | HP | 1.68 | 12.1 | 1280 x 800 | Wacom Sensor, keyboard, Synaptics TouchStyk | Windows XP Tablet PC Edition | Certified for SuSE Linux Enterprise Desktop 10 | Intel Core 2 Duo ULV U7600, U7700 | 1.2, 1.33 +64 | HDD, SSD | 80-120, 64 | 1, 2, 4 (max 4) | 5.5h (6-cell) | 1.11 |
| P Pavilion 1000 | HP | ? | 12.1 | 1280 x 800 | ? | Windows Vista | ? | AMD Turion X2 | 1.8+64 | HDD | 250 | 3,072 | 3h (6-cell), ?h (?-cell) | ? |
| P Pavilion 2000, 2500z | HP | ? | 12.1 | 1280 x 800 dual-touch (WACOM compl) | ? | Windows Vista | ? | AMD Turion X2 Ultra RM-7x / ZM-8x | 2-2.6 +64 | HDD | 320 | 3 (max 4) | 3h (6-cell), ?h (?-cell) | ? |
| ontron evolution | Kontron | ? | ? | ? | ? | ? | ? | ? | ? | ? | ? | ? | ?h(?-cell), ?h (?-cell) | ? |
| enovo hinkPad 41 Tablet, 60 Tablet, 61 Tablet | Lenovo | 1.71, 1.93 | 12.1 | 1400 x 1050 (X60/X61), 1024 x 768 MultiTouch | Wacom Active Digitizer, Multitouch (optional) | Windows Vista Business | ✗ | Intel Core 2 Duo L7500, L7300 | 1.6, 1.4 | HDD | 60-250 | 1-3 | 3h (4-cell), 7h (8-cell) | 1.1"-1.3" |

| | | | | | | | | | | | | | | |
|---|---|---|---|---|---|---|---|---|---|---|---|---|---|---|
| Lenovo ThinkPad X201 Tablet | Lenovo | 3.57 | 12.1 | 1280 x 800 | Wacom Active Digitizer, Multitouch (optional) | Windows 7 | ✗ | Intel Core i5, i7 | ? | HDD, SSD | 250-500, 80-128 | 1-8 | 3.5h (4-cell), 7.9 (8-cell) | 1.04-1.3 |
| LG Electronics C1 Express Dual[67] | LG Electronics | 1.3 | 10.6 in (27 cm) | 1280 x 768 | resistive touchscreen, keyboard | windows vista/xp | ✗ | intel core duo | 1.2 | HDD | 80 | 1 | 2.5h | 1.06 |
| Panasonic Toughbook 19 | Panasonic | 2.31 | 10.4 | 1024 x 768 | ? | ? | ? | ? | ? | ? | ? | ? | ?h (?-cell), ?h (?-cell) | ? |
| Toshiba Portégé 3500, 3505, M200, M400, 405, 700, R400, R405 | Toshiba | ? | ? | 1400 x 1050 | ? | ? | ? | ? | ? | ? | ? | ? | ?h (?-cell), ?h (?-cell) | ? |
| Toshiba Tecra M4/M7 | Toshiba | ? | ? | ? | ? | ? | ? | ? | ? | ? | ? | ? | ?h (?-cell), ?h (?-cell) | ? |
| Toshiba Satellite R10, R15, R20, R25 | Toshiba | 2.7 | 14.1 | 1440 x 900 | ? | Windows XP Tablet PC Edition | ✗ | Intel Core Duo T2050 | 1.6+32 | HDD | 100 | 1 | 4h (6-cell) | 1.6 |

# Hybrid

| Model | Manufacturer | Weight (kg) | Display size (in) | Display resolution, type | Input technology | Operating system | CPU | Storage type | Storage capacity (GiB) | RAM (GiB) |
|---|---|---|---|---|---|---|---|---|---|---|
| Compaq TC1000 | Compaq | ? | ? | ? | ? | ? | ? | SSD, HDD | ? | ? |
| HP Compaq TC1100 | HP | ? | ? | ? | ? | ? | ? | SSD, HDD | ? | ? |
| **ASUS Eee Pad Transformer (TF101)** | Asus | 0.68 kg (1.5 lb) | 10.1 in (26 cm) | 1280 x 800 | Capacitive multi-touch | Android 3.0 Honeycomb | Nvidia Tegra 250 | SSD | 16, 32, 64 | 1 |
| Tatung Tangy | Tatung | ? | ? | ? | ? | ? | ? | SSD, HDD | ? | ? |
| Lenovo U1 | Lenovo | ? | ? | ? | ? | Windows 7 (notebook), Android (slate) | x86 (notebook), 1 Snapdragon (slate) | SSD, HDD | ? | ? |

# References


[1] http://www.91mobiles.com/mobile/Acer+Mobile/Iconia+Tab+A500/9176.html#specificationpart
[2] http://www.engadget.com/2011/03/22/staples-ad-reveals-april-june-ship-dates-for-acer-iconia-tab/
[3] http://www.notionink.com/techspecs.php
[4] http://www.engadget.com/2011/04/27/notion-ink-adam-review/
[5] http://androidcommunity.com/advent-vega-specs-revealed-hdmi-sim-slot-more-video-20101012
[6] "iPad - View the technical specifications for iPad" (http://www.apple.com/ipad/specs/). Apple. . Retrieved April 7, 2011.
[7] http://www.archos.com/products/ta/archos_101it/specs.html?country=us&lang=en
[8] http://pdadb.net/index.php?m=specs&id=2594&c=archos_101_internet_tablet_8gb
[9] http://www.asus.com/Eee/Eee_Pad/Eee_Slate_EP121/
[10] http://ces2011.asus.com/archives/ces-2011/asus-tablet-computers-providing-choice-through-innovation-at-ces-2011/
[11] http://news.softpedia.com/news/Official-Release-Date-for-ASUS-Eee-Slate-EP121-Provided-190740.shtml
[12] http://www.bmodo.com/bmodo12_specs.html
[13] http://www.exopc.com/en/exopc-slate.php
[14] http://www.engadget.com/2010/06/18/evigroup-paddle-gets-specced-and-splayed-now-available-from-59/
[15] http://hypranet.org/nrnet/seline/blog/index.php?2010/06/14/756-paddle-disponible-multitouch-multi-usages
[16] http://www.hclstore.in/hcl_me_tablet_ap10_a1
[17] http://h10010.www1.hp.com/wwpc/us/en/sm/WF06a/321957-321957-64295-3841267-3955550-4332585.html
[18] http://www.palm.com/us/products/pads/touchpad/index.html
[19] Motorola Xoom (http://www.motorola.com/staticfiles/Consumers/US-EN/XOOM/index.html)
[20] http://www.prestigio.com/products/personal-computers/Tablet_PC/MultiPad_PMP7100C
[21] LG G-Slate (http://www.engadget.com/2011/02/02/lg-g-slate-fully-detailed-by-t-mobile-3d-viewing-and-recording/)
[22] http://vschart.com/compare/lg-optimus-pad
[23] http://www.knowyourmobile.com/blog/816830/tmobile_confirms_lg_optimus_pad_release_date_for_april.html
[24] http://www.pointofview-online.com/showroom.php?shop_mode=product_detail&product_id=188
[25] http://www.gsmarena.com/samsung_galaxy_tab_8_9_3g-3891.php
[26] http://www.gsmarena.com/samsung_galaxy_tab_10_1_3g-3892.php
[27] http://www.androidtabletworld.com/android-news/samsung-galaxy-tab-10-1-to-launch-june-8th-for-499-and-up
[28] http://vodafone.com.au/personal/android/tablets/android-tablet-new/index.htm
[29] http://www.toshiba-multimedia.com/eu/media-tablet/folio100/
[30] http://pdadb.net/index.php?m=specs&id=2577&c=toshiba_folio_100
[31] http://www.eurodroid.com/2010/11/toshiba-folio-100-android-tablet-now-on-sale-in-the-uk-for-329-99/
[32] http://www.thetoshibatablet.com/
[33] http://inventorspot.com/articles/toshiba_regza_at300
[34] (http://www.viewsonic.com/gtablet/)
[35] (http://www.viewsonic.com/products/vpad10.htm)
[36] http://www.h-online.com/priceinsight/eu/a620432.html
[37] http://www.phonearena.com/news/MSI-WindPad-100A-is-an-Android-Honeycomb-tablet-coming-June-1st_id17052
[38] http://www.msi.com/product/nb/WindPad-100W.html#/?div=Specification
[39] http://us.blackberry.com/playbook-tablet/
[40] http://www.gsmarena.com/dell_streak-3353.php
[41] http://www.dell.com/us/p/mobile-streak-7/pd
[42] http://www.mobilityfeeds.com/mobility-feed/2011/02/huawei-ideos-s7-slim-android-tablet-launch-video-mwc-google.html
[43] http://www.androidtablets.net/forum/nook-color-technical/3483-nookcolor-full-specifications.html
[44] http://www.barnesandnoble.com/nookcolor/features/techspecs/index.asp
[45] http://www.olivetelecom.in/laptop/olivepad/tech-specs.html
[46] http://www.samsung.com/us/mobile/galaxy-tab/SCH-I800BKAVZW-features
[47] http://www.viewsonic.com/products/vpad7.htm
[48] http://www.asus.com/Product.aspx?P_ID=AYgvN10WR0fczlpn
[49] http://reviews.cnet.com/tablets/asus-r2h-ultramobile-pc/4507-3126_7-32143090.html
[50] http://www.umpcportal.com/products/ASUS/R50A/R50A
[51] http://www.umpcportal.com/2008/12/asus-r50a-full-review/
[52] http://www.cnet.com.au/asus-r50a-yet-another-umpc-339284999.htm
[53] http://www.umpcportal.com/products/ASUS/R70a/
[54] http://www.umpcportal.com/2008/03/1287/
[55] http://www.cowonglobal.com/product_wide/product_Q5W_spec.php
[56] http://pdadb.net/index.php?m=specs&id=1322&view=1&c=cowon_q5w_60gb
[57] http://www.umpcportal.com/products/Wibrain/i1/

[58] DRS Armor (http://www.ruggedpcreview.com/3_slates_drs_armor_x10.html)
[59] DT Research WebDT 310 (http://www.ruggedpcreview.com/3_slates_dtresearch_webdt310.html)
[60] Quaduro systems (http://www.quaduro.com/en/gb/products/src.php?id=2)
[61] http://www.tabletkiosk.com/tkstore/pc/viewPrd.asp?idcategory=35&idproduct=218
[62] Talla-tech Tacter (http://www.ruggedpcreview.com/3_handhelds_tallatech_tacter-31m.html)
[63] Xplore technologies ix104 (http://www.ruggedpcreview.com/3_slates_xplore_ix104.html)
[64] "HP Compaq TC4200 North America QuickSpec" (http://h18000.www1.hp.com/products/quickspecs/12138_na/12138_na.HTML). . Retrieved 2010-07-10.
[65] "HP Compaq TC4400 North America QuickSpec" (http://h18000.www1.hp.com/products/quickspecs/12443_na/12443_na.HTML). . Retrieved 2010-07-10.
[66] "HP Compaq 2710p North America QuickSpec" (http://h18000.www1.hp.com/products/quickspecs/12718_na/12718_na.html). . Retrieved 2010-07-10.
[67] "C1 Tablet PC" (http://ca.lge.com/en/c1express/c1express.htm) (SWF). LG Canada. 2006-11-24. . Retrieved 2010-05-16.

# Microsoft Tablet PC

A **Microsoft Tablet PC** is a term coined by Microsoft for tablet computers conforming to a set of specifications announced in 2001 by Microsoft, for a pen-enabled personal computer, conforming to hardware specifications devised by Microsoft and running a licensed copy of Windows XP Tablet PC Edition operating system or a derivative thereof.[1]

Hundreds of such tablet personal computers have come onto the market since then.[2]

HP Compaq tablet PC with rotating/removable keyboard

## History

In 2002, original equipment manufacturers' released the first tablet PCs designed to the Microsoft Tablet PC specification. This generation of Microsoft Tablet PCs were designed to run Windows XP Tablet PC Edition, the Tablet PC version of Windows XP.[3] This version of Microsoft Windows superseded Microsoft's earlier pen computing operating environment, Windows for Pen Computing 2.0. After releasing Windows XP Tablet PC Edition, Microsoft designed the successive desktop computer versions of Windows, Windows Vista and Windows 7, to support pen computing intrinsically.

## Form variations of Tablet PCs

### Booklets

Booklet PCs are dual screen tablet computers that fold like a book. Typical booklet PCs are equipped with multi-touch screens and pen writing recognition abilities. They are designed to be used as digital day planners, internet surfing devices, project planners, music players, and displays for video, live TV, and e-reading.

### Slates

Slate computers, which resemble writing slates, are tablet PCs without a dedicated keyboard. For text input, users rely on handwriting recognition via an active digitizer, touching an on-screen keyboard using fingertips or a stylus, or using an external keyboard that can usually be attached via a wireless or USB connection.

Tablet PCs typically incorporate small (8.4–14.1 inches/21–36 centimetres) LCD screens and have been popular in vertical markets such as health care, education, hospitality and field work. Applications for field work often need a tablet PC that has rugged specifications that ensure long life by resisting heat, humidity, and drop/vibration damage. This added focus on mobility and/or ruggedness often leads to eliminating moving parts that could raise vulnerability.

### Convertibles

Convertible notebooks have a base body with an attached keyboard. They more closely resemble modern laptops, and are usually heavier and larger than slates.

A Lenovo X61 in slate mode

Typically, the base of a convertible attaches to the display at one joint called a swivel hinge or rotating hinge. The joint allows the screen to rotate through 180° and fold down on top of the keyboard to provide a flat writing surface. This design, although the most common, creates a physical point of weakness on the notebook.

Some manufacturers have attempted to overcome these weak points. The Panasonic Toughbook 19, for example, is advertised as a more durable convertible notebook. One model by Acer (the TravelMate C210) has a sliding design in which the screen slides up from the slate-like position and locks into place to provide the laptop mode.

Convertibles are by far the most popular form factor of tablet PCs, because they still offer the keyboard and pointing device (usually a trackpad) of older notebooks, for users who do not use the touchscreen display as the primary input method.

### Hybrids

Hybrids, coined by users of the HP/Compaq TC1000 and TC1100 series, share the features of the slate and convertible by using a detachable keyboard that operates similarly to a convertible when attached. Hybrids are not the same as slate models with detachable keyboards. Detachable keyboards for pure slate models do not rotate to allow the tablet to rest on it like a convertible.

## System software

Windows 7 touch ability is similar to Microsoft Surface technologies. This is a gesture and touch-centric UI enhancement that works with most current touch computers. Windows has a history of tablet technology including Windows XP Tablet PC Edition.[4] [5] Tablet PC Edition is a superset of Windows XP Professional, the difference being tablet functionality, including alternate text input (Tablet PC Input Panel) and basic drivers for support of tablet PC specific hardware. Requirements to install Tablet PC Edition include a tablet digitizer or touchscreen device, and hardware control buttons including a Ctrl-Alt-Delete shortcut button, scrolling buttons, and at least one user-configurable application button.

A few select high schools in the US use tablet PCs for every student.

Service Pack 2 for Windows XP includes Tablet PC Edition 2005 and is a free upgrade. This version brought improved handwriting recognition and improved the Input Panel, allowing it to be used in almost every application. The Input Panel was also revised to extend speech recognition services (input and correction) to other applications.

With the succession of Windows Vista, the Tablet PC functionality no longer needed a separate edition. Tablet PC support is built into all editions of Windows Vista with the exception of Home Basic and Starter editions. This extends the handwriting recognition, ink collection,[6] and additional input methods to any computer running Vista even if the input device is an external digitizer, a touch screen, or even a regular mouse. Vista also supports multi-touch functions and gestures (originally developed for the Microsoft Surface version of Vista) and is now usable by the public with the release of multi-touch tablets. Windows Vista also significantly improved handwriting recognition functionality with the introduction a handwriting recognition personalization tool as well as an automatic handwriting learning tool.

Tablet functionality is available in all editions of Windows 7 except the Starter edition. It introduces a new Math Input Panel that recognizes handwritten math expressions and formulas, and integrates with other programs. Windows 7 also significantly improved pen input and handwriting recognition by becoming faster, more accurate, and supportive of more languages, including East Asian writing systems. Personalized custom dictionaries help with the recognition of specialized vocabulary (like medical and technical terms), and text prediction speeds up the input process to make note-taking faster. Multi-touch technology is also available on some Tablet PCs, enabling more advanced interaction using touch gestures with your fingers the same way a mouse is used.[7] Despite such advances, problems may arise with tablet functions of the OS, when, for instance, touch screen drivers are recognized as PS/2 mouse input rather than a touch input device. In such instances tablet functions may be unavailable or severely restricted in functionality.

## Windows applications

Applications developed for the tablet PC cater to the form factor and functionality available on the platform. Many forms of applications incorporate a pen-friendly user interface and/or the ability to hand write directly in the document or interface.

A brief description of the applications included follows:

Experience Pack

- Ink Desktop: an Active Desktop control designed to run in the background and allow the user to write directly on the desktop.
- Snipping Tool: a screen capture application which allows the tablet pen to be used to select a portion of the screen and then annotate it and save as a file or send in an email.
- Ink Art: a painting application developed by Ambient Design originally as ArtRage, licensed to Microsoft for release to Tablet PC users.
- Ink Crossword: a crossword application developed to mirror the experience of a paper crossword puzzle on a tablet PC.
- Media Transfer: a synchronization utility designed to download music, pictures, and videos from computers in the same network.

Education Pack

- Ink Flash Cards [8]: an application designed to assist memorization by using a flash card approach, enabling the user to hand write their own flash cards and display them back in a slide show.
- Equation Writer [9]: a recognition tool specializing in converting handwritten mathematical equations to a computer-generated image for pasting into other documents.
- GoBinder Lite [10]: an organization and note-taking application developed by Agilix Labs.
- Hexic Deluxe [11]: a game with a tablet PC specific gesture enabled for easier use with the tablet and better.

Touch Pack

The Touch Pack [12] for Windows 7 is a free package of games and programs optimized for touch input.

- Microsoft Blackboard [13]
- Microsoft Garden Pond [14]
- Microsoft Rebound [15]

- Microsoft Surface Globe [16]
- Microsoft Surface Collage [17]
- Microsoft Surface Lagoon [18]

## Tablet PCs vs. traditional notebooks

The advantages and disadvantages of tablet PCs are highly subjective measures. What appeals to one user may be exactly what disappoints another. The following are commonly cited opinions of the tablet PC platform:

### Advantages

- Use in environments not conducive to a keyboard and mouse such as lying in bed, standing, or handling with one hand.
- Lighter weight, lower power models can function similarly to dedicated reading devices like the Amazon Kindle.
- Touch environment makes navigation easier than conventional use of keyboard and mouse or touch pad in certain contexts such as image manipulation, or mouse oriented games.
- Digital painting and image editing is enhanced and more realistic than painting or sketching with a mouse.
- The ability for easier or faster entering of diagrams, mathematical notations, and symbols.
- Allows, with the proper software, universal input, independent from different keyboard localizations.
- Some users find it more natural and fun to use a stylus to click on objects rather than a mouse or touchpad, which are not directly connected to the pointer on screen.

### Disadvantages

- Higher cost — convertible tablet PCs can cost significantly more than their non-tablet counterparts although this premium has been predicted to fall.[8]
- Input speed — handwriting can be significantly slower than typing speeds, the latter of which can be as high as 50-150 WPM; however, Slideit, Swype and other technologies are able to provide alternate, speedier methods of input.
- Screen and hinge damage risk - Tablet PCs are handled more than conventional laptops, yet are built on similar frames; in addition, since their screens also serve as input devices, they run a higher risk of screen damage via impacts and misuse. A convertible tablet PC's screen hinge often must rotate around two axes, unlike a normal laptop screen, subsequently increasing the number of possible mechanical and electrical (digitizer and video cables, embedded Wi-Fi antennas, etc.) failure points.
- Ergonomics - a tablet PC does not provide room for a wrist rest while the screen is folded into slate mode. In addition, the user will need to move their arm constantly while writing.
- Weaker video abilities - Most tablet PCs are equipped with embedded graphics processors instead of discrete graphics cards. In July 2010, the only tablet PC with a discrete graphics card was the HP TouchSmart tm2t, which has the ATI Mobility Radeon HD5450 as an option.

## Features

In addition to the host of features found on regular laptops, tablet PCs may also possess:

- Capacitive contact technology, which can sense finger(s) on the screen without needing significant pressure for system to recognize an input.[9]
- Palm recognition, which prevent inadvertent palms or other contacts from disrupting the pen's input.[9]
- Multi-touch abilities, which can recognize multiple simultaneous finger touches, allowing for enhanced manipulation of on-screen objects.[10]

## Popular models

Most of the major PC manufacturers also make tablet PCs which run Microsoft Windows. These include Acer, Hewlett-Packard, Lenovo Group and Toshiba.

## Application software

- Comfort On-Screen Keyboard [22] - advanced on-screen keyboard for Tablet PC
- Microsoft Windows Journal
- Microsoft Office OneNote
- Einstein Technologies Tablet Enhancements for Outlook
- FutureWave Smartsketch drawing program published by FutureWave Software
- GO Corporation
- Agilix GoBinder
- Mobilis - Protectis Range
- EverNote
- InkSeine [23]: Prototype Tablet GUI/Interface - Microsoft Research
- IHMC CmapTools [24] - a free concept mapping application
- Xournal - a Linux notetaking application
- OnSite Companion Construction Software for Tablet PC
- MusicPad Pro [25]: MusicReader - Electronic Music Stand - sheet music display on Tablet PC
- Documentor [26]: A Documentation Engine for Health Care Professionals
- StarDraw Contol - room automation, home cinema control system

## Screen size trends

Many Tablet PC makers have standardized on a 12" widescreen format, with a resolution of 1280x800 pixels. The Fujitsu T5010 has a larger 13.3" display, but still uses 1280x800 pixel resolution.[11] The Acer TravelMate C300 has a 14.1" screen at 1024x768.

The 12" form factor is optimal for the power, size and weight considerations needed for portability. Although there is some demand for larger Tablet PC screen sizes from consumers, larger screens add significant weight and bulk to Tablet PCs. They also need more power, therefore larger, heavier batteries or shorter battery life.

## References

[1] Microsoft Tablet PC (http://msdn.microsoft.com/en-us/library/ms840465.aspx)

[2] List of Tablet PC since 2002 (Italian) (http://tabletpcitalico.blogspot.com/2009/01/lista-dei-tablet-pc-prodotti.html)

[3] Microsoft (2005), *Windows XP Tablet PC Edition 2005 Hardware Requirements* (http://users.erols.com/rwservices/pens/biblio10.html#Microsoft06i), www.microsoft.com, , retrieved 2009-03-14

[4] *MSDN: Windows XP Tablet PC Edition: Tablet PC: An Overview* (http://users.erols.com/rwservices/pens/biblio05.html#Microsoft04a), Microsoft, 2004-08-24, , retrieved 2008-09-04

[5] *Windows XP Tablet PC Edition: Tablet PC: An Overview* (http://www.itxcgc.com/images/Brochures/Microsoft/TabletPCOverview.pdf), Microsoft, 2002-06-01, , retrieved 2008-09-04

[6] MSDN (http://msdn.microsoft.com/en-us/library/ms701180(VS.85).aspx) Ink collection

[7] http://www.microsoft.com/windows/windows-7/features/tablet-pc.aspx

[8] Convertibles: The new laptop bling? - CNET News.com (http://news.com.com/Convertibles+The+new+laptop+bling/2100-1044_3-5900655.html)

[9] Tablet PC offers capacitive touch sensing capability., Dell, Inc (http://news.thomasnet.com/fullstory/811421)

[10] jkOnTheRun:So what is multi-touch? (http://jkontherun.blogs.com/jkontherun/2007/12/so-what-is-mult.html)

[11] http://www.fujitsu.com/au/services/technology/pc/notebooks/tseries/t5010/specs.html

- See Stargate Atlantis they used Tablet PC. JLSXS2010

## External links

- Tablet PCs (http://www.dmoz.org/Computers/Systems/Tablet_PCs/) at the Open Directory Project
- Jeff Han Talks About Touch-Driven Computer Screens (http://www.howstuffworks.com/1787-jeff-han-talks-about-touch-driven-computer-screens-video.htm) at HowStuffWorks
- Annotated bibliography of references to handwriting recognition and pen computing (http://rwservices.no-ip.info:81/biblio.html)
- Comparison table of convertible tablets (http://thetabletpc.net/comparison-convertibles.htm)
- Microsoft Center for Research on Pen-Centric Computing (http://pen.cs.brown.edu/)

# Encipher Inye

**Encipher Inye** The Encipher Inye is a tablet PC developed by The Encipher Group. It was announced on 8 May 2010 and released in Nigeria that same year. It is powered by an Telechips Tcc8902 ARM 11 800Mhz processor and runs on Android version 2.1 aka Eclair.

## Specifications

**Power:** 2600 mAh battery

**Storage capacity:** 16Gb

**Memory:** 512MB .

**Input:** Resistive touchscreen.

**I/O PORTS:** Mic- in, DC-in, 35mm stereo headphone jack, HDMI 1.3, Output 1080P 1xUSB Host 1.1, Highspeed USB OTG 2.0.

**Camera:** 1.3MP

**AUDIO:** MP3,WMA,MP2,OGG,AAC,M4A,MA4,FLAC,APE,3GP,WAV

**Video playback:** Capable of HD playback (1080P)

**Connectivity:** Wifi 802.11 (a/b/g). 3G.

**Online services:** Android Market.

## Name

The name "Inye" means 'The One' in Igala, a language in Nigeria.

## References

## External links

- Enipher group.com (http://www.enciphergroup.com/)

Android

# EO Personal Communicator

### EO Communicator 440/880

| EO Communicator 440/880 | |
|---|---|
| **Release date** | April 1993 |
| **CPU** | AT&T Hobbit |

The **EO** was an early commercial tablet computer created by GO/Eo (both later acquired by AT&T) and released in April 1993.[1] Eo (Latin for "GO") was the hardware spin-out of GO. Officially named the **AT&T EO Personal Communicator**, it was similar to a large personal digital assistant with wireless communications,[2] and competed against the Apple Newton. The unit was produced in conjunction with the Frog design, Matsushita, Olivetti and Marubeni corporations.

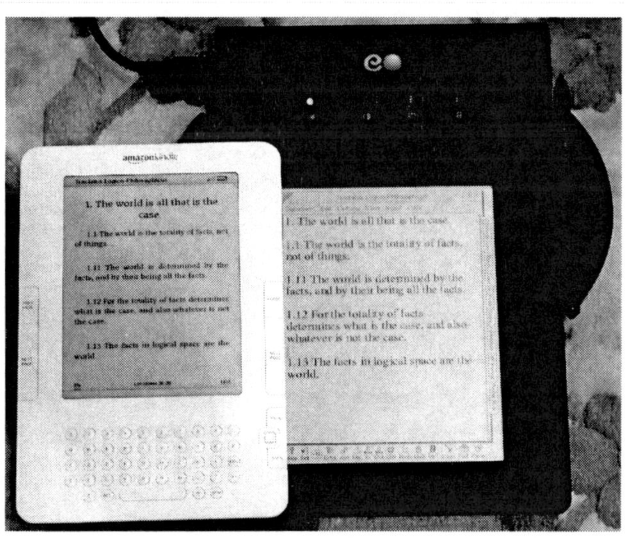

Comparison of the EO 440 Personal Communicator (1993) and the Amazon Kindle 2 e-book reader (2009). Both have transreflective (no backlight) displays. The EO has liquid crystal display, the Kindle an Electrophoretic one

Among the EO customers AT&T claimed were: The New York Stock Exchange, Andersen Consulting, Lawrence Livermore Laboratories, FD Titus & Sons and Woolworths.

EO, Inc., 52 percent owned by AT&T, shut down operations on July 29, 1994 after failing to meet its revenue targets and to secure the funding to continue.

## Product specifics

Two models, the Communicator 440 and 880, were produced and measured about the size of a small clipboard. Both were powered by the AT&T Hobbit chip, created by AT&T specifically for running code from the C programming language. They also contained a host of I/O ports - modem, parallel, serial, VGA out and SCSI. The device came with a wireless cellular network modem, a built-in microphone with speaker and a free subscription to AT&T EasyLink Mail for both fax and e-mail messages.

Perhaps the most interesting part was the operating system, PenPoint OS, created by GO Corporation. Widely praised for its simplicity and ease of use, the OS never gained widespread use. Also equally compelling was the tightly integrated applications suite, Perspective, licensed to EO by Pensoft.

## External links

- Cerda, Michael (September 11, 1995). "EO Interest Document" [3]. Retrieved May 15, 2009.
- EO 440 and 880 specs [4]
- The EO 440 And EO 880 [5] (subscription required)
- EO 440 receives one of 1993 Byte Awards [6]
- Personal retrospective about working for EO [7]

## Notes

[1] Jerry Kaplan. (1994). *Startup : a Silicon Valley adventure*. New York: Penguin Books. ISBN 0140257314.
[2] Ken Maki. (1993). *The AT&T EO travel guide*. New York: Wiley. ISBN 0471007838.

# Fujitsu Lifebook T900

**Fujitsu Lifebook T900** is a new Tablet PC from Fujitsu. It runs the new Windows 7 operating system. It comes with a Core i5, and DDR3 RAM (running at 1067 MHz) on the standard configurations.

The T900 comes with a new Dual Digitizer (Not available on models with indoor/outdoor display option enabled), a LED backlit display, and a WXGA display with wide viewing angles. The new Lifebook T900 offers the 2010 Core i5 provides performance greater over any of the current Intel Core 2 Duo. The new Core i5 models include a new technology by Intel called Turbo Boost which can increase clock speeds when needed. Although the Core i5 offers superior performance to the Previous generation, the Core 2 Duo, there is an option to upgrade to a Core i7 620m (a Non Quad Core version) which has a slightly better performance. The clocks range from 2.4 to 2.66 GHz with Turbo Boosts from 2.93 to 3.33 GHz (Note that all processors come with a level 3 cache of 3 MB, except for the Core i7 620m which has 4MB).

**Graphics:** The HD graphics in the Lifebook T900 is integrated with the new Core i's (3, 5, and 7) on the same chip. A DataSheet provided by Intel is provided Here [1] on page 11. The graphics are still not comparable to the Nvidia's GeForce series, or AMD's Mobility HD Radeon series, and can be used as a cheap alternative for costumers wanting to get a computer for some of the most basic of tasks; like Web Surfing, or Checking E-Mail.

**Design** The Design of the T900 remains pretty much the same as its predecessor the T5010. It has a black exterior, while retaining a white keyboard and plastic casing. The Keyboard has remained the same since the T4220 which is a 12in discontinued tablet PC; widely popular before the release of the 5010. Speakers have been placed in a inconvenient place, the back behind the screen. Also the scroll bar under the screen for 'Tablet Mode', can cause annoyances while writing. Overall the design of the T900, while stylish, fits the need of an everyday on the go business man.

**Batteries and other accessories**

The Fujitsu Lifebook T900 comes standard with a 6-cell, 10.8 Volt, 5800 mAh, primary battery. An optional second battery (which replaces the CD drive temporarily) is available for an extra $134 that provides 6-cells 3800 mAh, and 10.8 Volts.

## References

[1] [2]

[1] Intel.com
[2] Fujitsu.com

## External links

- Fujitsu T900 (http://store.shopfujitsu.com/fpc/Ecommerce/buildseriesbean.do?series=T900)
- Core i5 Mobile Processor Technical Documents (http://www.intel.com/products/processor/corei5/mobile/techdocs.htm)

# Gateway C-Series

## C-Series

| Developer | Gateway, Inc. |
| --- | --- |
| Type | Convertible Tablet PC |
| Release date | June 28, 2007 |
| Introductory price | USD$899 |
| CPU | (Early 2008) 1.46 / 1.6 GHz Intel Core 2 Duo |
| Website | Gateway C-Series storefront [1] |

The **C-Series** is a line of notebook computers with convertible tablet PC form factors manufactured by Gateway, Inc. It replaced the CX series convertible tablet in Gateway's lineup.

The flagship product in the C-Series, the **C-140**, was released on June 28, 2007. The 14-inch notebook utilizes Intel Core Duo processors, with optional discrete ATI graphics solutions. C-Series notebooks are convertible tablet PCs, meaning that they have the shape of a traditional notebook computer while possessing the ability to have their screens rotated through 180 degrees, and laid flat against the keyboard, essentially converting the notebook into a slate-form factor tablet PC.

As of the beginning of February 2007 the C-Series line includes only the low-priced C-140S and the higher-end C-141. Discontinued models include the C-140X and C-140XL. Models for sale to small business customers carry the **S-7235** designation, while the product is sold to the educational market as the **E-295C**. Another member of the C-Series which is currently unavailable from Gateway is the C-120, a similar design to the C-140, but featuring a 12-inch, rather than 14-inch screen.

C-Series models purchased through Gateway's online store offer few possibilities or customization, a move which allows for more aggressive pricing by sacrficing the ability to custom-build a system that customers are used to. Faster processors and a variety of different configurations are available through MPC, which purchased Gateway, Inc.'s Professional Services Unit business line on September 5, 2007. C-140s sold through MPC carry the E-295C designation.

## Overview (C-140)

The C-140/E-295C/S-7235 (henceforth referred to as the "C-140") features a widescreen 14.1" LCD display ith a 1280x768 resolution. This display features a Wacom Penabled touchscreen with an active digitizer, allowing the user to use an included electromagnetic stylus pen to interact with the computer, through handwriting recognition or using the pen as a replacement for a standard computer mouse or touchpad. Input and output ports include VGA, built-in Ethernet, 802.11 a/b/g Wi-Fi, Bluetooth capability, three USB ports, one Firewire 400 port, and a proprietary Gateway port for connecting to a docking station. The notebook also possesses a "5-in-1" memory card reader (which can access Secure Digital, Memory Stick, and xD Picture Card, among others), as well as a single PCMCIA Type II Cardbus PC Card slot. The chassis incorporates a Synaptics touchpad, an integrated microphone, and provides biometric security in the form of a fingerprint reader. The C-140's optical drive is removable and is replaceable with a modular battery (although this product is now largely discontinued); the drive is capable of reading and writing to most popular forms of DVD and CD-ROM media. The laptop has a single hard disk bay, and two available slots for connecting RAM memory boards (no memory is hard-wired to the motherboard. A PCI-Express slot is available for future expansion. The C-140's battery extends out beyond the rear edge of the computer, acting as a handgrip when the computer is in slate-tablet mode; a 6-cell battery is included, while heavier

8-cell and physically larger 12-cell batteries are also available.

The C-140 comes pre-loaded with Microsoft Windows Vista, which includes the rudimentary Microsoft Works productivity suite, Windows Media Player 11, and Internet Explorer 7.

# HP Compaq TC1100

The **HP Compaq TC1100** is a tablet PC sold by Hewlett-Packard that was the follow up to the Compaq TC1000. The TC1100 had either an Intel Celeron or an Intel Pentium M chip set and could be upgraded to a maximum amount of 2 gigabytes of memory. These upgrades from the TC1000 were much welcomed after numerous complaints about the poor performance of the TC1000. The TC1100 was the last version from HP in this style of tablet. It was replaced by the HP Compaq TC4200, which featured a more traditional non-detachable design.

TC1100 in slate mode with the keyboard removed

## Design

The TC1100 has a 10.4 inch LCD display and pressure-sensitive pen that shares the same basic design as its predecessor, the TC1000. It has a unique design that has been coined by many as a hybrid tablet. This refers to the fact that it has the properties of both a convertible and slate tablet. All the necessary hardware components are stored within the casing of the display and digitizer. This allows it to work with or without a keyboard attached. With the keyboard attached it can either be used in the same fashion as a laptop, with the keyboard supporting the rest of the tablet, or with the back of the tablet folded into the keyboard allowing the user to write on the screen easily. This sort of design gives much versatility and has gathered a cult-like following due to the lack of similar designs on the market.

TC1100 unfolded with keyboard attached

The range of processors includes Pentium-M 1.0Ghz, 1.1Ghz, and 1.2Ghz. The high end TC1100 features the 1.2 GHz Intel Pentium M 753 Ultra Low Voltage processor(1.20 GHz, 2MB L2 cache, 400 MHz FSB), 60 GB hard drive, 512 MB (333 MHz) of installed RAM (2 GB max), 54g wi-fi connectivity (802.11b/g), Bluetooth wireless connectivity, Secure Digital memory card slot, and Windows XP Tablet PC Edition operating system.

The TC1100 allows for easy access to its memory, hard drive, and wireless card. The memory comes standard as either 256MB or 512MB and can be upgraded to 2GB. The hard drive is also easily upgradeable, most 2.5-inch IDE hard drives are compatible with it but the tablet will only address up to 137GB due to a lack of LBA48 support. The wireless card can be accessed from the same area as the memory, but some tablets that did not originally have a wireless card installed may not have the antenna installed either making a new installation either hard or impossible.[1]

HP implemented 6 customizable controls: 3 physical buttons along the side of the unit, and 3 stylus-sensitive spots in the bezel of the display. In addition, there is a "jog dial" in line with the physical buttons, which can be used for scrolling or zooming, as controlled by software.

Two small retractable "feet" were also included on the back on the tablet, allowing for an angled writing surface when extended, and ventilation when placed on a flat surface.

## Discontinued

By the end of 2005, HP had discontinued the TC1100. It retained a loyal following, however, due to its uncommon design. HP's official response to questions asked about the TC1100's discontinuation is that "HP remains committed to the Tablet PC platform".[2]

## TX1000 Series

Since discontinuing the TC1100, HP has released a new line of tablets, the TX1100US and the TX1200US being the first of the line. These updated versions are substantially more powerful than the TC series, but are of the more conventional convertible design.

## References

[1] Christopher J. James (2005). "TC Upgrades" (http://81.5.185.34/tc-one-thousand/upgrades.html). . Retrieved 2006-11-29.

[2] Mark Payton (2005). "What is HP Thinking" (http://vermontslate.blogspot.com/2005/11/what-is-hp-thinking.html). *Vermont Slate*. . Retrieved 2006-11-26.

## Further reading

- HP Compaq Tablet PC TC1100 Reviews (http://reviews.cnet.com/HP_Compaq_Tablet_PC_TC1100/4505-3126_7-30573412.html)
- Windows Vista Installation Notes (http://mobilepcwiki.com/mpc/index.php?title=HP/TC1100/Windows_Vista_Installation_Notes)
- Manual and User Guide (http://h20000.www2.hp.com/bizsupport/TechSupport/Home.jsp?lang=en&cc=us&prodTypeId=321957&prodSeriesId=376810&lang=en&cc=us)
- Upgrade info (http://www.tabletpcbuzz.com/showthread.php?s=8f92b29e421048c0cdea55668073e539&t=34009&page=3)
- Linux on TC1100 - LinuxQuestions wiki (http://wiki.linuxquestions.org/wiki/TC1100)
- OpenSuse Linux on a tc1100 (http://dorienherremans.blogspot.com/2010/08/how-to-install-opensuse-113-on-hp.html)

# HP Compaq TC4200

The **HP Compaq TC4200** is a Tablet PC that was released on March 1, 2005 and has since been discontinued. It is believed to be the successor to the TC1100, which was discontinued in Q4 of 2005. The TC4200 boasted many powerful features that could be found on mid to high-range laptops and competing tablets during its production. The higher-end equivalent of the TC4200 is the HP Compaq TC4400, which is still available.

## Specifications

| | |
|---|---|
| **Operating System** | Windows XP Tablet PC Edition 2005 |
| **Processor Type** | Intel Pentium M |
| **Display** | 12.1-inch Color TFT XGA wide viewing angle display with digitizer (1024 x 768 resolution and 16 M colors) |
| **Maximum Memory** | 2GB |
| **Wireless** | Intel PRO/Wireless 2915ABG 802.11 a/b/g WLAN Bluetooth V1.2 Compliant |
| **Maximum Hard Drive** | 80GB SMART |
| **Ports** | 1 External Monitor 1 Microphone In<br>1 Headphone/Line-out<br>1 DC Power<br>1 RJ-11 (Modem)<br>1 RJ-45 (NIC)<br>1 Infrared Port<br>1 S-Video<br>3 USB 2.0<br>1 Docking Connector |

More extensive specs list [1]

## Further reading

- CNet.com Review [2]

# HP Compaq TC4400

The **HP Compaq TC4400** is of the convertible Tablet PC design (as opposed to hybrid or slate). This design allows it to be used in the position of a normal laptop or have the screen turned and folded down for writing on.

## Specifications

As with many manufactured tablets, there are multiple pre-configured models with various options, as well as the ability to cusomize your own model. The following is a list of common specs on current models:

| | |
|---|---|
| **Operating System** | Windows XP Tablet PC Edition 2005 |
| **Processor** | Intel Core Duo or Intel Core 2 Duo 1.83 GHz - 2.16 GHz |
| **Display** | 12.1-inch Color TFT XGA WVA, optional enhanced Outdoor-viewable Display |
| **Graphics** | Intel Graphics Media Accelerator 950 |
| **Memory** | 512MB - 2GB available upradable Max of 4GB |
| **Wireless** | 802.11a/b/g Standard, optional Bluetooth V1.2 Compliant |
| **Maximum Hard Drive** | 60GB - 100GB SATA (5400RPM) |
| **Ports** | 1 External Monitor 1 Microphone In<br>1 Headphone/Line-out<br>1 Accessory Battery Connector<br>1 RJ-11 (Modem)<br>1 RJ-45 (NIC)<br>1 Infrared Port<br>1 S-Video<br>3 USB 2.0<br>1 Docking Connector |

[1] [2]

## Pricing

As of November 2006, prices on pre-configured models range from US$1,449 to US$1,849.[2] Creating a custom model can bring the price over US$3,000.[3]

## Further reading

- Laptop Magazine's Review [4]
- Use of the Compaq at a suburban intermediate school [5]

## References

[1] "HP Compaq tc4400 Tablet PC - specifications and warranty" (http://h10010.www1.hp.com/wwpc/us/en/sm/WF06a/321957-304452-306995-304455-306995-1847962.html). 2006. . Retrieved 2006-11-28.
[2] "HP Compaq tc4400 Tablet PC- models" (http://h10010.www1.hp.com/wwpc/us/en/sm/WF25a/321957-304452-306995-304455-306995-1847962.html). 2006. . Retrieved 2006-11-28.
[3] "-Configurable- HP Compaq tc4400 Tablet PC" (http://h71016.www7.hp.com/dstore/MiddleFrame.asp?page=config&ProductLineId=540&FamilyId=2404&BaseId=19384&jumpid=re_R2515_store/smProdCat/PSG/tablets/HP_tc4400_tablets). 2006. . Retrieved 2006-11-28.

# HP Pavilion TX1000 Series Tablet PC

**HP Pavilion TX1000 Series Tablet PC** is a series of notebook computers from Hewlett Packard introduced in February 2007. These notebooks are designed for Windows Vista. The TX series uses the AMD Turion 64 X2 processors. This series has a 12.1-inch touch screen, a DVD+RW and competed well with the top-of-the-line tablets at the time of release. All models came with a NVIDIA GeForce Go 6150 graphics system, which features 128 MB integrated graphics and extra shared graphics memory of up to 916 MB. This model has been superseded by the HP Touchsmart tx2 Series, and subsequently by the HP Touchsmart tm2.

## Design

The series is delivered with the HP Imprint Finish.[1] The form factor is referred to as a "convertible tablet", that is, the screen can be rotated to use the notebook as a slate with the included stylus. The current model has a glossy, black plastic casing and a perforated touchpad. The speakers are located near the hinge, on the screen and the webcam on the top of the screen. The stereo microphones are also mounted on the screen and the tablet comes with an optional fingerprint reader. The standard 6-cell battery juts out to form a hand-grip and the DVD drive can be replaced with a plastic "weight-saver".

## Specifications

- AMD Turion(TM) 64 X2 Dual-Core Processor
- 12.1″ WXGA BrightView LED back-lit [semi-glossy/matte] Widescreen (1280×800) with passive touchscreen (without Wacom Penabled digitizer)
- NVIDIA GeForce Go 6150 graphics
- Webcam + Dual Mic
- Fingerprint Reader (Optional)
- PC-5300 RAM 1GB [base config], 2GB, 3GB, 4GB
- SATA Hard Drive, 160GB [base config], 250GB, 320GB
- Removable LightScribe DVD+/-RW w/Double Layer
- Networking - 802.11 a/b/g/draft n WLAN [base config]
- Bluetooth 2.1 (optional)
- Verizon Wireless V740 ExpressCard (requires data plan)

Lithium Ion Battery 6 Cell [base config], 4 Cell 8 Cell

## Criticism

Within a few months of release of the tx1000 series, numerous technical failures were reported on internet blogs, review sites and HP's own support websites. These included webcam, audio, speaker, BIOS, power management, overheating, booting, and wireless adapter problems. Some were addressed in a timely manner with driver updates, but other users were still had to turn the notebook on and off repeatedly, until it booted up and some were left with a non-working "bricked" unit. HP released an updated model, the HP Pavilion tx2, which in turn was followed by the HP TouchSmart tm2, HP never issued a recall for its tx1 model.

## References

[1] HP Imprint Finish (http://h71036.www7.hp.com/hho/cache/581662-0-0-225-121.html)

## External links

- Notebook Review of the tx1000 (http://www.notebookreview.com/default.asp?newsID=4741)
- HP TX2000 (http://h30429.www3.hp.com/?fr_story=59d39c8be359575dffa201bfdc2670c0280d60f7&rf=sitemap) later version

# HP Slate 500

## HP Slate 500

| Manufacturer | Hewlett-Packard |
|---|---|
| Type | Tablet PC |
| Release date | 22 October 2010 |
| Introductory price | $799 |
| Operating system | Windows 7 |
| CPU | Intel Atom Z540 processor @1.86 GHz |
| Storage capacity | 64 GB, |
| Memory | 2 GB |
| Display | 8.9″ screen (1024×600 px) |
| Input | Multi-touch touchscreen display; active digitizer with pen support |
| Camera | Front Webcam (0.3 MPx), rear camera (3 MPx) |
| Connectivity | Wi-Fi, USB 2.0, Bluetooth |
| Dimensions | 9.21 in (23.4 cm) (h)<br>5.7 in (14.5 cm) (w)<br>0.57 in (1.4 cm) (d) |
| Website | /slate [1] |

The **HP Slate 500** is a multi-touch capable Windows 7 slate PC that was announced at CES 2010 and launched on 22 October 2010.[1] [2]

## History

The Slate 500 began as an e-reader concept,[3] but after further study of the uses for such devices, HP realigned their goal to deliver a product that provided a "rich user experience; to browse, listen to music, watch videos and enjoy media".[4]

HP Chief Technology Officer, Phil McKinney, stated that "2010 is the optimal year...there is now this convergence of low cost, low power processors, with an Operating System - Windows 7 that is touch aware."[4]

## Hardware

The Slate 500 has a three-megapixel camera on its back panel and a VGA resolution webcam on the front panel, a 8.9" capacitive multi-touch screen supporting 1024×600 pixel resolution with digitizer and pen support.[1] The Slate is powered by a 1.86 GHz Intel Atom Z540 processor with 2GB DDR2 of RAM, 64GB of onboard solid state flash storage and one standard USB 2.0 port.[1] [5] The device supports 1080p playback powered by the Intel GMA 500 integrated graphics chipset in addition to a Broadcom Crystal HD media accelerator card for hardware assisted video playback.[1] [5] Wireless capabilities include the built-in WiFi and Bluetooth support. Power is supplied by a 2-cell 30WHr Lithium-Ion battery with an average runtime of 5 hours.[5]

The Slate 500 also has support for a stylus pen/digitizer, to enable on-screen freehand drawing and writing.[1]

## Software

The Slate 500 runs Windows 7, which includes native touch technology.[1] Adobe Systems and HP confirmed that the "full web" experience will be available on the Slate 500, including full hardware accelerated Adobe Flash content and Adobe AIR applications.[6] HP Taiwan also confirmed that Palm's WebOS will be used on "smartphones and tablets", a category that would include an HP Slate.[7]

## Release

HP announced that the device was available for purchase on 22 October 2010, initially with a cost of US$799.[2] A month after launch, HP announced that the device was back ordered for six weeks due to "extraordinary demand," though Engadget claimed that a source said that HP had planned to build only 5,000 Slates, but received orders for 9,000, forcing the delay.[8] Another Slate-like tablet computer using the WebOS operating system is expected to be released several weeks after HP's "WebOS Event" scheduled for February 9th.[9] [10]

### Reception

The Slate 500 (at the time known simply as the Slate) received a positive reception when it was shown at CES 2010. CNBC said "HP's Slate has been the big buzz".[11]

Initial reviews have not met a general consensus yet. CNET said the device was a "lightweight, sturdy device, with...a slick industrial design and several hardware advantages over the iPad."[12] Its only criticism was the lack of a specialized interface for touchscreen use; rather, the Slate has no additional software beyond what is included with Windows 7 Professional, and the CNET review considered this a limitation for productivity uses.[12]

## References

[1] "HP Slate 500 finally (finally!) official, rings up at $799" (http://www.engadget.com/2010/10/21/hp-slate-finally-finally-official-rings-up-at-799/). Engadget. 21 October 2010. . Retrieved 22 October 2010.
[2] "HP's Slate 500 Tablet Goes on Sale for $800" (http://www.pcworld.com/businesscenter/article/208511/hps_slate_500_tablet_goes_on_sale_for_800.html). PCWorld. 21 October 2010. . Retrieved 22 October 2010.
[3] "HP's eBook reader" (http://www.youtube.com/watch?v=uXGB2m3EqOU). .
[4] "SPECIAL REPORT! The HP Slate" (http://www.youtube.com/watch?v=apwliqIKf84). .
[5] http://www.hpslate.org/featured-2/hp-slate-500-specs-revealed-what-was-confirmed-plus-one-big-suprise/
[6] "Adobe Demos Flash & Air on HP's Slate Device" (http://www.youtube.com/watch?v=-p-RZAwQq0E). .
[7] "HP-slate.com: HP promises Windows slate and Palm slate too" (http://www.hp-slate.com/hp-slate-both-windows-and-palm.htm). .
[8] "HP Slate 500 sees 'extraordinary demand,' experiences six-week shipping delay (update)" (http://www.engadget.com/2010/11/13/hp-slate-500-sees-extraordinary-demand-experiences-six-week-s/). Engadget. 13 November 2010. . Retrieved 3 December 2010.
[9] "HP delays slate to February while RIM PlayBook remains elusive too" (http://www.guardian.co.uk/technology/2011/jan/05/hp-slate-delayed-rim-playbook-not-seen). guardian. 5 January 2011. . Retrieved 13 January 2011.
[10] "HP: New WebOS products shipping soon, another unveil set for March 14" (http://www.cnet.com/8301-17918_1-20029947-85.html). cnet. 28 January 2011. . Retrieved 7 February 2011.
[11] "HP's Slate: PC of Profits?" (http://www.cnbc.com/id/34805830). .
[12] "Hands-on with the HP Slate 500" (http://news.cnet.com/8301-17938_105-20020363-1.html). CNET. 21 October 2010. . Retrieved 23 October 2010.

## External links

- Official Site (http://www.hp.com/slate)
- HP Slate YouTube Page (http://www.youtube.com/view_play_list?p=912FC4549847323A)

# HP TouchSmart

The Touchsmart 2 (shown) can be used like a traditional computer (left) or by using the touchscreen (right).

**HP TouchSmart** is a series of tablet PC laptops and touchscreen all-in-one desktop computers designed by HP. It features various Intel or AMD processors and runs Windows Vista or Windows 7 as standard.

## HP TouchSmart All-in-One

### Consumer version

#### HP TouchSmart Crossfire

**HP TouchSmart Crossfire**

HP TouchSmart IQ770

| | |
|---|---|
| **Manufacturer** | Hewlett-Packard |
| **Type** | All-in-one |
| **Release date** | January 7, 2007 |
| **Operating system** | Windows Vista Home Premium |
| **CPU** | AMD Turion 64 X2 TL-52 processor |
| **Storage capacity** | 320 GB HDD |
| **Memory** | 2 GB SDRAM |
| **Display** | 19" Touchscreen |
| **Camera** | Yes |
| **Connectivity** | FM and ATSC HDTV tuners; Bluetooth, 802.11a/b/g wireless, and gigabit Ethernet connectivity |
| **Successor** | HP TouchSmart IQ500 |

The HP TouchSmart was first introduced by Bill Gates on January 7, 2007,[1] becoming the first mass market touchscreen desktop PC.[2]

Also known as the "Crossfire", the HP TouchSmart IQ770 featured a 19 inch touchscreen, an AMD Turion 64 X2 TL-52 processor, NVIDIA GeForce Go 7600. It had a wide array of ports, including Ethernet, two FireWire, six USB 2.0 ports, one with HP printer power Y-cable connector, 5.1 + digital audio out, IR out, mini-VGA, FM coax, TV coax, ATSC, and two S-Video; however, the IQ770 did not have HDMI ports. PC World gave the machine a "very good" rating of 81/100, but noted that the use of mobile components slowed the computer[3]

### HP TouchSmart 2

On June 10, 2008, HP unveiled their new HP TouchSmart IQ500 series. The series featured a 22-inch widescreen touchscreen display, an Intel Core 2 Duo processor, a 500GB disk, 256MB NVIDIA GeForce 9300 M HS HD graphics, and 802.11n WiFi, along with an Energy Star qualification.[4] The new TouchSmart featured a sleeker 2 inch profile in a piano-black finish.[5]

The IQ500 series was followed by the IQ800 series, featuring a larger 25.5 inch touchscreen. Other features included a TV tuner with remote, integrated webcam, Bluetooth, HP Pocket Media drive bay and an ambient light to illuminate the keyboard. The more expensive IQ816 featured a 2.10GHz T8100 Core 2 Duo on a 800MHz bus with a 3MB cache, Blu-ray drive / dual-layer burner, and a GeForce 9600M GS chip.[6] There is a choice of 640GB or 1TB hard drives.

### TouchSmart 300

The TouchSmart 300 was released on October 13, 2009.[7]

### TouchSmart 600

**HP TouchSmart 600**

| | |
|---|---|
| **Manufacturer** | Hewlett Packard |
| **Type** | All-in-one |
| **Release date** | October 22, 2009 |
| **Introductory price** | Starting at $1049 |
| **Operating system** | Windows 7 or Windows Vista |
| **Power** | Energy star |
| **CPU** | Intel Core 2 Duo T7450 (2.13 GHz) |
| **Storage capacity** | 750 GB |
| **Memory** | 4GB DDR3 |
| **Display** | 23" |
| **Camera** | Yes |
| **Predecessor** | HP TouchSmart IQ500/800 |

The TouchSmart 600 was released on October 13, 2009.[8]

## Business version

### HP TouchSmart 9100

The HP TouchSmart 9100 is a business oriented all-in-one PC that bears a strong resemblance to its consumer counterpart, the HP TouchSmart 600.

# Tablet

## TouchSmart tx2z

Released in December 2008, the TouchSmart tx2 was touted as the first consumer notebook and tablet PC with on-screen multi-touch control. The TouchSmart tx2 replaced the older HP Pavilion tx series.[9]

## TouchSmart tm2

The HP TouchSmart tm2 is a convertible laptop, with a multi-touch touch-screen. Converted into slate mode, the tm2 allows artists to draw using the included digital pen and also allows students to take notes in classes.[10]

HP tm2 laptop in slate mode

## TouchSmart Mini 5102

HP's first touch-enabled netbook, enabling multitouch gestures and menus. It features an anodized aluminum case in black, red or blue and weights 2.6 lbs. It offers face recognition for easy log-on to Windows 7. The series features Intel Atom N450 CPU, mobile broadband, HP video playback and 10 hour battery run time.[11]

## Slate

At CES 2010, in conjunction with Steve Ballmer, CEO of Microsoft, HP announced the Windows 7 HP Slate PC.[12]

# References

[1] Dybwad, Barb (January 7, 2007). "Microsoft announces the HP TouchSmart PC" (http://www.engadget.com/2007/01/07/microsoft-announces-the-hp-touchsmart-pc/). engadget. . Retrieved 2009-01-28.

[2] Block, Ryan (November 30, 2006). "HP IQ770 "Crossfire" 19-inch touchscreen Vista PC revealed!" (http://www.engadget.com/2006/11/30/hp-iq770-crossfire-19-inch-touchscreen-media-pc-revealed//). engadget. . Retrieved 2009-01-28.

[3] Perensen, Melissa J. PC World. Jan 7 2007. Accessdate = 10 August 2009http://www.pcworld.com/reviews/product/29673/review/touchsmart_iq770_pc.html

[4] Hewlett Packard Development Company, LP (June 10, 2008). "HP Redefines Home Computing, Putting the Digital Lifestyle at People's Fingertips with New TouchSmart PCs" (http://www.hp.com/hpinfo/newsroom/press/2008/080610xb.html?mtxs=rss-corp-news). . Retrieved 2009-01-28.

[5] Ricker, Thomas (June 10, 2008). "HP slips into thin with TouchSmart 2 all-in-ones" (http://www.engadget.com/2008/06/10/hp-slips-into-thin-with-touchsmart-2-all-in-ones/). engadget. . Retrieved 2009-01-28.

[6] Patel, Nilay (16 September 2008). "HP announces the TouchSmart IQ800 series" (http://www.engadget.com/2008/09/16/hp-announces-the-touchsmart-iq800-series/). engadget. . Retrieved January 28, 2009.

[7] HP http://www.hp.com/hpinfo/newsroom/press/2009/091013xc.html

[8] HP http://www.hp.com/hpinfo/newsroom/press/2009/091013xc.html

[9] Jackson, Jerry (22 December 2008). "HP TouchSmart tx2 Review" (http://www.notebookreview.com/default.asp?newsID=4741). www.notebookreview.com. . Retrieved January 28, 2009.

[10] "HP Unveils Touch-enabled Notebook and Minis in Stylish Designs" (http://www.hp.com/united-states/personal_again/press/touch_mini_pr.pdf). .

[11] "HP Unveils Touch-enabled Notebook and Minis in Stylish Designs" (http://www.hp.com/united-states/personal_again/press/touch_mini_pr.pdf). .
[12] "The HP Slate" (http://www.engadget.com/2010/01/06/the-hp-slate/). .

## External links

- HP TouchSmart US microsite (http://www.hp.com/united-states/campaigns/touchsmart/)
- HP TouchSmart Australian microsite (http://h20426.www2.hp.com/campaign/touchsmart/au/en/mouseisdead/touchsmart.asp)
- HP TouchSmart PC Community and Forum (http://www.touchsmartcommunity.com/)
- HP TouchSmart IQ770 Review (http://reviews.cnet.com/desktops/hp-touchsmart-iq770/4505-3118_7-32305738.html) (cnet.com)
- HP TouchSmart IQ506 Review (http://www.entirestore.net/hp-touchsmart-iq506-review-entertainment-with-a-touch-screen/) EntireStore.net

# HTC Flyer

## HTC Flyer/ HTC EVO View

| | |
|---|---|
| **Manufacturer** | HTC Corporation |
| **Type** | Tablet media player |
| **Release date** | May 2011 |
| **Operating system** | Android 2.3.3 with HTC Sense UI [1] [2] |
| **CPU** | 1.5 Ghz |
| **Storage capacity** | Flash memory: 32 GB |
| **Memory** | 1 GB DDR2 RAM |
| **Display** | 7-inch 1024×600 px |
| **Input** | Multi-touch capacitive touchscreen display<br>HTC Scribe Capacitive Stylus |
| **Camera** | 5.0 megapixel rear-facing |
| **Connectivity** | HSDPA<br>Wi-Fi 802.11n<br>Bluetooth 3 (with A2DP)[1] |
| **Dimensions** | 195.4 mm (7.69 in) *(h)*<br>122 mm (4.8 in) *(w)*<br>13.2 mm (0.52 in) *(d)* |
| **Weight** | 415 g (14.6 oz) |
| **Website** | HTC Flyer [3] at HTC.com |

The **HTC Flyer** (also known as the **HTC EVO View 4G**) is an upcoming tablet computer by HTC Corporation. It was announced at the Mobile World Congress (MWC) 2011 and is scheduled to be released in the second quarter of 2011.[3] Unlike other tablets announced at MWC, the Flyer will have a single-core 1.5 Ghz CPU[4] and will run Android 2.3.3 (Gingerbread) instead of 3.0 (Honeycomb).[1] [2] An HTC representative has been quoted as saying "I can confirm that we are working to bring a Honeycomb update to Flyer in short order – however, I don't have any specific information on what the timing may be."[5] It will have a 7 inch TFT display and include some special features, such as pen input as well as touch input.[6] [7] [8] A Wi-Fi variant is expected to be launched at a lower price soon after the 3G variant is released.[9]

## Key features of the HTC Flyer include

- An optional HTC Scribe™ digital pen that unlocks HTC Scribe technology, which enables the ability to capture and annotate any on-screen content with notes and drawings
- Integration/compatibility with Wi-Fi and Bluetooth® 3.0
- 7" 1024×600 display with multi-touch capability and an optional digital pen that enables users to take synchronized notes and annotate content
- Built-in dual microphones for noise reduction
- Android™operating system
- Adobe® Flash® 10.1 support

## Hardware Specs

- 5 MP Color CMOS camera with auto focus
- 1.3MP front camera for video chatting
- 16GB eMMC memory plus microSD card slot
- 4,000 mAh battery

"The HTC Flyer features an immersive 3D user experience that brings to life, all your favorite content - weather, email and even ebooks [10] ." Best Buy will be the exclusive retailer for the Spring 2011 launch of the HTC Flyer [11] Currently, Sprint will be the only carrier to sell a 4G model with black and red instead of white and silver.

## References

[1] Bray, Jonathan (15 February 2011). "HTC Flyer review: first look" (http://www.pcpro.co.uk/blogs/2011/02/15/htc-flyer-review-first-look/). PC Pro UK. . Retrieved 17 February 2011.
[2] "Version confusion on Google's Android resolved" (http://www.h-online.com/open/news/item/Version-confusion-on-Google-s-Android-resolved-1195322.html). 23 February 2011. . Retrieved 6 March 2011.
[3] "HTC Flyer Tablet launched at Mobile World Congress 2011" (http://www.newsden.net/htc-flyer-tablet-specs-review-hands-on-video-6660/). .
[4] Palmer, Jacob (17 February 2011). "LG Optimus Pad vs HTC Flyer vs Samsung Galaxy Tab 2" (http://www.gizmocrunch.com/computing/5391-htc-flyer-lg-optimus-pad-samsung-galaxy-tab-2). Gizmocrunch. . Retrieved 17 February 2011.
[5] "HTC confirms that Honeycomb will be coming to the Flyer - no time frame though" (http://www.phonearena.com/news/HTC-confirms-that-Honeycomb-will-be-coming-to-the-Flyer---no-time-frame-though_id16805). Phone Arena. 15 February 2011. .
[6] Kremp, Matthias (17 February 2011). "Schlaumeier-Handys und Facebook überall" (http://www.spiegel.de/netzwelt/gadgets/0,1518,745673,00.html) (in German). Der Spiegel. . Retrieved 17 February 2011.
[7] Briggeman, Mark (15 February 2011). "Hands-on with the new HTC Flyer" (http://www.mobilityminded.com/12194/hands-on-with-the-new-htc-flyer). Mobility Minded. . Retrieved 17 February 2011.
[8] "MWC2011: HTC Flyer Android 2.4 Tablet with 1 GB RAM and 1.5 GHz processor" (http://mobilesmug.com/news/49-tablets/785-mwc2011-htc-flyer-android-24-tablet-with-1-gb-ram-and-15-ghz-processor-release-date-available). .
[9] "HTC Flyer set for cheaper Wi-Fi option News TechRadar UK" (http://www.techradar.com/news/mobile-computing/htc-flyer-set-for-cheaper-wi-fi-option-928670). .
[10] HTC Flyer coming to Singapore in May (http://www.vr-zone.com/articles/htc-flyer-coming-to-singapore-in-may/11968.html)
[11] "Best Buy Gets Exclusive Agreement to Sell HTC Flyer" (http://www.htctablet.net/2011/best-buy-gets-exclusive-agreement-to-sell-htc-flyer/). *HTCFlyer.net*. March 23, 2011.

## External links

- Official website (http://www.htc.com/www/product/flyer/overview.html)
- Official website: product specs (http://www.htc.com/www/product/flyer/specification.html)

# Ink Serialized Format

**Ink Serialized Format** or ISF is a Microsoft format to store written ink information. The format is mainly used for mobile devices like Personal digital assistants, tablet PCs and Ultra-Mobile PCs to store data entered with a stylus.

An ink object is simply a sequence of strokes, where each stroke is a sequence of points, and the points are X, and Y coordinates. Many of the new mobile devices can also provide information such as pressure, and angle. In addition can be used to store custom information along with the ink data.

## Availability

Its specification is freely available for download [1]. Microsoft has added the ISF format to its technologies available under the Open Specification Promise making ISF related technology patent claims available for everybody to use or implement ISF.

This allows for ISF format to be used even together with open source software licensing like GPL2.

## External links

- Integrating Ink on mobile devices [2] Ink article on MSDN

# MobileDemand

**MobileDemand** is a provider of rugged Tablet PC mobile computer systems headquartered in Hiawatha, Iowa with manufacturing facilities in Taiwan.[1] [2] The products are built for use by mobile workers in harsh environments to survive falls, extreme temperatures and exposure to liquids.[2] [3] The company specializes in complete mobile automation systems by integrating data collection technologies including barcode scanning, numeric keypad, credit card reader, color photography, GPS and touch screen in its PC tablets.[3]

## History

MobileDemand was founded in 2003 by Matt Miller.[1] At that time, the company specialized in manufacturing portable, rugged Tablet PCs with laser-based bar code scanning for the wholesale beer sector.[4] [5] With the introduction of smaller Rugged Tablet PC systems and accessories, MobileDemand expanded to a wide variety of vertical markets that employ a mobile workforce including hospitality, manufacturing, military, public safety, retail, transportation and logistics, and warehousing.[2] [5]

Under Mr. Miller's leadership, the company has grown to 10 full-time employees in the company's headquarters.[3] US-based software partners are responsible for 76 percent of MobileDemand's sales.[3]

## Products

xTablet T7000 [6]
Released in October 2009, the xTablet T7000 ultra-mobile rugged mini tablet computer is small, lightweight (2.6 lbs), and rugged for use in harsh environments.[2] [5] It functions like a notebook with a full Windows 7 [7] operating system and has significant memory capacity and Intel Atom processing power unlike traditional Windows® Mobile handhelds.[5] Data input into the Tablet PC is flexible with a built-in numeric keypad, optional QWERTY keyboard, bar code and credit card readers, color camera and 7-inch high-resolution all-light-readable touch screen display.[2] [6]

xTablet T8700 [9]

Announced in January 2008, the xTablet T8700 is used by food and beverage distributors for direct store delivery (DSD) tracking and inventory management.[5] The new Tablet PC retains the form factor and overall concept of the xTablet series, runs on a full Microsoft Windows 7 operating system, is powered by the Intel Core Duo processor, has faster wireless communications and an 8.7" sunlight readable display.[7]

xTablet C1200 [11]

The xTablet C1200 is a rugged convertible tablet PC. It transforms from a rugged laptop to a Tablet PC [12] and can be used outdoors by mobile workers in field service, military, public sector, health care, agriculture and delivery applications. Like a laptop [13], it runs on a full Windows Operating System [14] and like a tablet PC, it has touch data entry, signature capture, and a color camera. A unique spill-guard design allows liquids to dissipate, reducing the risk of damage. [8]

# Competitors

Panasonic, Dell, Fujitsu [1] [5]

# References

[1] Corridor Business Journal Entrepreneur:101 "Benefit from success, own up to failures" p. 12-13, 2010 Edition

[2] " MobileDemand Expands Public Sector Offerings With Addition Of MobileFrame Software Solutions For Law Enforcement, EMS, Investigative Services (http://www.fieldtechnologiesonline.com/article.mvc/MobileDemand-Expands-Public-Sector-Offerings-0001?VNETCOOKIE=NO)" Integrated Solutions, October 16, 2010

[3] Google Adwords Success Story: Mobile Demand (http://www.google.com/adwords/select/success/mobiledemand.html). Accessed November 2, 2010

[4] MobileDemand Poised for Growth with New Computer, Markets (http://www.easterniowabusiness.com/2010/08/03/mobiledemand-poised-for-growth-with-new-computer-markets/) Eastern Iowa Business, August 3, 2010

[5] " Entrepreneur of the Year (http://www.corridorbiznews.com/aspx/NewsDetail.aspx?ItemID=1396)" Corridor Business Journal

[6] MobileDemand announces availability of ultra-compact xTablet 7000 (http://www.ruggedpcreview.com/3_slates_tabletpc_mobiledemand_t7000.html), Rugged PC Review, January 15, 2010

[7] " MobileDemand xTablet T8700 Tablet PC (http://ruggedpcreview.com/3_slates_tabletpc_mobiledemand_t8700.html)" Rugged PC Review, Accessed November 2, 2010

[8] (http://www.ruggedtabletpc.com/Default.aspx?app=LeadgenDownload&shortpath=docs/xtablet+c1200+press+release.pdf), MobileDemand Introduces the xTablet C1200 Convertible Tablet PC, February 2, 2011

# OLPC XO-3

**XO-3** is the upcoming planned tablet/laptop/e-book reader that is intended to be developed under One Laptop per Child initiative. The shaping is that of a tablet PC, replacing the canceled two sheet design concept of the XO-2. The inner workings are those of the XO 1.75[1] that will use an ARM processor. It is planned to be released in 2012 with a price goal below $100.[2]

## References

[1] http://blog.laptop.org/2009/12/24/xo-3-concept/
[2] OLPC News: " First Version XO-3 Laptop to be Released by Marvell (http://www.olpcnews.com/laptops/xo-3/first_version_xo-3_laptop_to_b.html)"

# Pepper Pad

The **Pepper Pad** is a Linux-based mobile computer with Internet capability and doubles as a handheld game console. It also serves as a portable multimedia device. The device uses Bluetooth and Wi-Fi technologies for Internet connection.

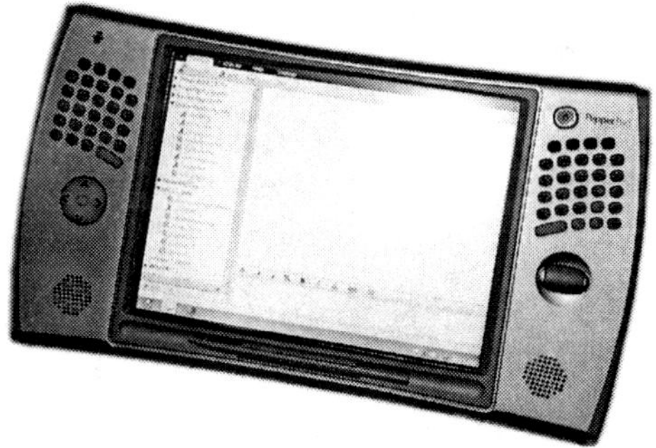

Photo of a Pepper Pad 2.

The Pepper Pad 3 has a split QWERTY button keyboard, built-in microphone, video camera, composite video output, and stereo speakers, Infra-Red receiver and transmitter, 800x480 7 inch LCD touchscreen (with stylus), SD/MMC Flash memory slot, 20 or 30 GB hard disk, 256MB RAM, 256KB ROM, AMD CPU, and both Wi-Fi (b/g) and Bluetooth 2.0. The built-in software is a variant of Linux (2.6 kernel) with an extensive variety of Open Source software.

## Support

Pepper Computer, Inc. has ceased operations and is no longer providing support or sales for Pepper Pad web computers or Pepper Linux.

## Software ported to the Pepper Pad

- FCE Ultra (NES emulator)
- Adobe Systems/Macromedia Flash 7
- Java
- X11
- GTK+
- Mozilla Firefox
- Real Player
- Helix
- Squeak

*This list is incomplete.*

## Hardware

- Mass: 2.1 pounds (985g)
- Size: 29 cm x 14.9 cm x 2.3 cm (11.4" x 5.9" x 0.9")

### Mainboard

- AMD Geode CPU, 533MHz clock speed, x86 instruction set with MMX and 3DNow extensions, integrated north bridge, graphics controller and PCI bridge
- AMD CS5536 Companion device (south bridge), USB 2.0 / IDE / IR / SMBus / APM interface
- Wolfson WM9713 [1] AC97 Audio / Touchscreen interface
- 256MB DDR SDRAM (DDR-333 SO-DIMM)
- 256KB BIOS ROM
- Chrontel CH7013B NTSC/PAL TV signal encoder
- IrDA and TvIR emitters/receivers

### Subsystems

- Hitachi TravelStar 20GB 1.8" IDE disk drive
- Atheros AR2413A-based mini-PCI 802.11b/g WiFi interface, with externally-attached antenna (external to the card, internal to the Pepper)
- Bluetooth 2.0
- AU Optronics A070VW01 [2] 7.0" 800x480 TFT LCD
- Integrated 62-key clicky keyboard, including 4-way cursor array and scroll wheel
- 3800mAh Lithium-Ion Battery
- Stereo Speakers
- Microphone
- 640x480 digital camera, fixed focus

### External Ports

- USB 2.0 host port
- USB 2.0 device port
- 1/8" Stereo headphone out
- 1/8" Composite video out
- 1/8" Microphone In

### Internal Ports

- miniPCI (occupied by WiFi interface)
- JTAG test-access port.
- Serial port with console

## External links

- Pepper Computer, Inc. [3]
- DOWN 2011-02-24 Hanbit America [4], hardware manufacturer website
  - Archive of Hanbit America [5] Web archive of hardware manufacturer website
- Pepper Pad Community Forums [6], official discussion forums
- DOWN 2011-02-24 Pepper Wiki [7], Pepper Pad information repository
  - Web archive of wiki [8] Archive
- Pepper Linux 4.0 Application Launching Preview [9] (Video)

# Soft Input Panel

The **Soft Input Panel** (also called **S.I.P.**) is a special on-screen input method for devices which do not have standard keyboards. SIP is commonly used in Microsoft Pocket PC and Tablet PC devices, where there is no room for a keyboard. In Microsoft Windows there is a similar on-screen keyboard used as a Microsoft Active Accessibility (MSAA) which also has an ability to change its layout according to current keyboard language and key layout. It was patented by Microsoft in November 2004 under the patent number **6819315**.[1]

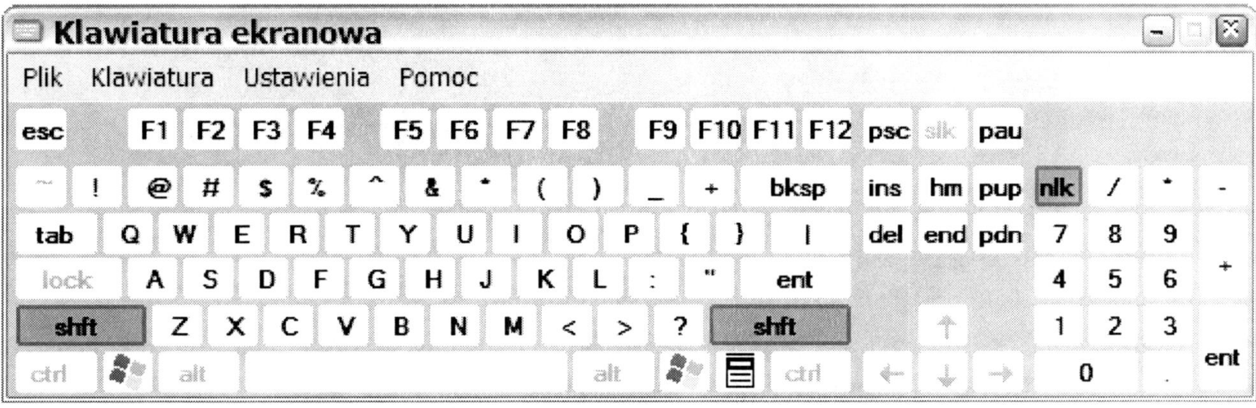


*Picture 1: Windows XP on-screen keyboard*

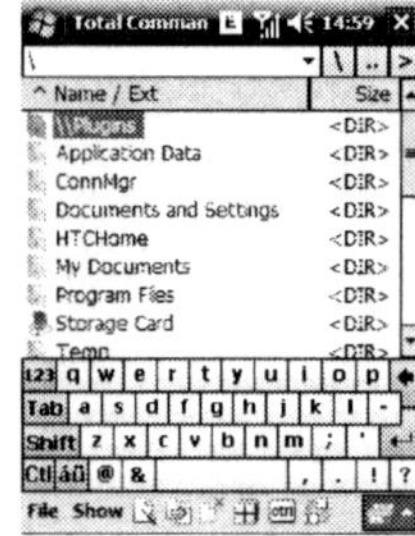


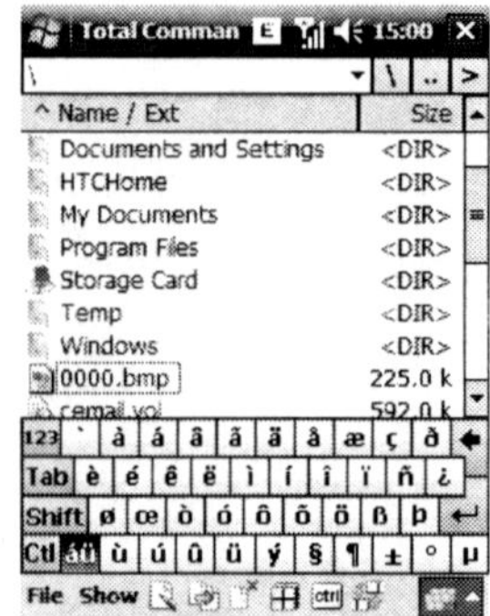


*Picture 2: Windows Mobile SIP Picture 3: Windows Mobile SIP with additional characters*

## References

[1] US Patent 6819315 - Soft input panel system and method (http://www.patentstorm.us/patents/6819315.html)

# Tablet personal computer

A **tablet personal computer** (**Tablet PC**) is tablet computer having the main characteristics of a personal computer in the tradition of the Microsoft Tablet PC, as a machine operated by an end-user with no intervening computer operator. A portable tablet PC is equipped with a touchscreen as a primary input device[1] and designed to be operated and owned by an individual.[2] The term was made popular as a concept presented by Microsoft in 2001,[3] but tablet PCs now refer to any tablet-sized personal computer, even if it's not using Windows but another PC operating system.[4] Tablets may use virtual keyboards and handwriting recognition for text input through the touchscreen.

HP Compaq tablet PC with rotating/removable keyboard

All tablet personal computers have a wireless adapter for Internet and local network connection. Software applications for tablet PCs include office suites,[5] web browsers,[6] games and a variety of applications. However, since portable computer hardware components usually have lower performance, demanding PC applications may not provide an ideal experience to the user.[7]

According to a study released by the law firm Olswang in early 2011, the tablet market is in an early stage with 3% of Americans owning an iPad and 2% owning some other kind of tablet, with Apple users being more likely to show brand loyalty.[8]

# System software

| Quantity of OS market shares by Gartner (new sales)[9] | |
|---|---|
| **Operating system** | **Percent** |
| Apple iOS Q3 2010 | 95.5% |
| Apple iOS Q4 2010 | 75.3% |
| Android Q3 2010 | 2.3% |
| Android Q4 2010 | 21.6% |
| Others Q3 2010 | 2.3% |
| Others Q4 2010 | 3.1% |

## Microsoft Windows

Following Windows for Pen Computing, Microsoft has been developing support for tablets running Windows under the Microsoft Tablet PC name.[10] According to a 2001 Microsoft definition[11] of the term, "Microsoft Tablet PCs" are pen-based, fully functional x86 PCs with handwriting and voice recognition functionality. Tablet PCs use the same hardware as normal laptops but add support for pen input. For specialized support for pen input, Microsoft released Windows XP Tablet PC Edition. Today there is no tablet specific version of Windows but instead support is built in to both Home and Business versions of Windows Vista and Windows 7. Tablets running Windows get the added functionality of using the touchscreen for mouse input, hand writing recognition, and gesture support. Following Tablet PC, Microsoft announced the UMPC initiative in 2006 which brought Windows tablets to a smaller, touch-centric form factor. This was relaunched in 2010 as Slate PC, to promote tablets running Windows 7, ahead of Apple's iPad launch.[12] Slate PCs are expected to benefit from mobile hardware advances derived from the success of the netbooks.

While many tablet manufacturers are moving to the ARM architecture with lighter operating systems, Microsoft has stood firmly by Windows.[13] [14] [15] Though Microsoft has Windows CE for ARM support it has kept its target market for the smartphone industry with Windows Mobile and the new Windows CE 6 based Windows Phone 7. Some manufacturers, however, still have shown prototypes of Windows CE-based tablets running a custom shell.[16]

The succession of Windows Vista has meant that Tablet PC functionality no longer requires a separate edition; with the exception of Home Basic and Starter, Tablet PC support is built into all editions of Windows Vista. This extends the handwriting recognition, ink collection,[17] and additional input methods to any computer running Vista even if the input device is an external digitizer, a touch screen, or even a regular mouse. Vista also supports multi-touch functions and gestures (originally developed for the Microsoft Surface version of Vista) and is now usable by the public with the release of multi-touch tablets. Windows Vista also significantly improved handwriting recognition functionality with the introduction of a handwriting recognition personalization tool as well as an automatic handwriting learning tool.

Tablet functionality is available in all editions of Windows 7 except the Starter edition. It introduces a new Math Input Panel that recognizes handwritten math expressions and formulas, and integrates with other programs. Windows 7 also significantly improved pen input and handwriting recognition by becoming faster, more accurate, and supportive of more languages, including East Asian writing systems. Personalized custom dictionaries help with the recognition of specialized vocabulary (like medical and technical terms), and text prediction speeds up the input process to make note-taking faster. Multi-touch technology is also available on some tablet PCs, enabling more advanced interaction using touch gestures with your fingers the same way a mouse is used.[18] Despite such advances, problems may arise with tablet functions of the OS, when, for instance, touch screen drivers are recognized as PS/2 mouse input rather than a touch input device. In such instances tablet functions may be unavailable or severely restricted in functionality.

Windows 7 touch capability is built with Microsoft Surface technologies. This is a gesture and touch-centric UI enhancement that works with most current touch computers. Among the first tablet PCs launched in 2010 based on the Windows 7 operating system are bModo12 from bModo[19] and Samsung Galaxy. Windows has a history of tablet technology including Windows XP Tablet PC Edition.[20] [21] Tablet PC Edition is a superset of Windows XP Professional, the difference being tablet functionality, including alternate text input (Tablet PC Input Panel) and basic drivers for support of tablet PC specific hardware. Requirements to install Tablet PC Edition include a tablet digitizer or touchscreen device, and hardware control buttons including a Ctrl-Alt-Delete shortcut button, scrolling buttons, and at least one user-configurable application button.

### Windows applications

Applications developed for the tablet PC cater to the form factor and functionality available on the platform. Many forms of applications incorporate a pen-friendly user interface and/or the ability to hand write directly in the document or interface.

A brief description of the applications included follows:

Experience Pack

- Ink Desktop: an Active Desktop control designed to run in the background and allow the user to write directly on the desktop.
- Snipping Tool: a screen capture application which allows the tablet pen to be used to select a portion of the screen and then annotate it and save as a file or send in an email.
- Ink Art: a painting application developed by Ambient Design originally as ArtRage, licensed to Microsoft for release to Tablet PC users.
- Ink Crossword: a crossword application developed to mirror the experience of a paper crossword puzzle on a tablet PC.
- Media Transfer: a synchronization utility designed to download music, pictures, and videos from computers in the same network.

Education Pack

- Ink Flash Cards [8]: an application designed to assist memorization by using a flash card approach, enabling the user to hand write their own flash cards and display them back in a slide show.
- Equation Writer [9]: a recognition tool specializing in converting handwritten mathematical equations to a computer-generated image for pasting into other documents.
- GoBinder Lite [10]: an organization and note-taking application developed by Agilix Labs.
- Hexic Deluxe [11]: a game with a tablet PC specific gesture enabled for easier use with the tablet.

## Linux

One early implementation of a Linux tablet was the ProGear by FrontPath. The ProGear used a Transmeta chip and a resistive digitizer. The ProGear initially came with a version of Slackware Linux, but could later be bought with Windows 98. Because these computers are general purpose IBM PC compatible machines, they can run many different operating systems. However, the device is no longer for sale and FrontPath has ceased operations. It is important to note that many touch screen sub-notebook computers can run any of several Linux distributions with little customization.

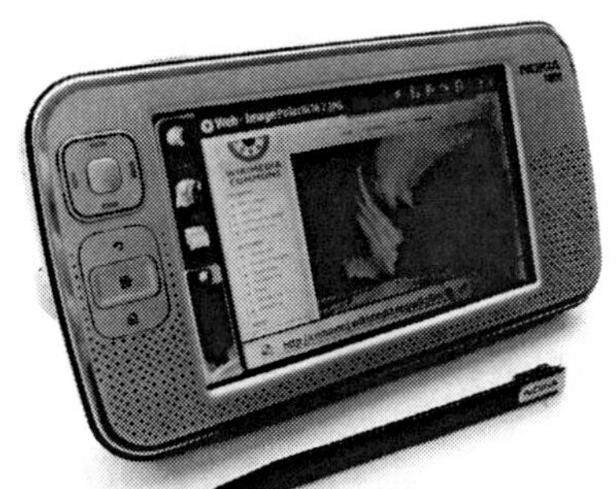

The Nokia N800

X.org now supports screen rotation and tablet input through Wacom drivers, and handwriting recognition software from both the Qt-based Qtopia and GTK+-based Internet Tablet OS provide promising free and open source systems for future development.

Open source note taking software in Linux includes applications such as Xournal (which supports PDF file annotation), Gournal (a Gnome based note taking application), and the Java-based Jarnal (which supports handwriting recognition as a built-in function). Before the advent of the aforementioned software, many users had to rely on on-screen keyboards and alternative text input methods like Dasher. There is a stand alone handwriting recognition program available, CellWriter, in which users must write letters separately in a grid.

A number of Linux based OS projects are dedicated to tablet PCs. Since all these are open source, they are freely available and can be run or ported to devices that conform to the tablet PC design. Maemo (rebranded MeeGo in 2010), a Debian Linux based graphical user environment, was developed for the Nokia Internet Tablet devices (770, N800, N810 & N900). It is currently in generation 5, and has a vast array of applications available in both official and user supported repositories. The Ubuntu Netbook Remix edition, as well as the Intel sponsored Moblin project, both have touchscreen support integrated into their user interfaces. Canonical has hinted at better supporting tablets with the Unity UI for Ubuntu 10.10.[22]

TabletKiosk currently offers a hybrid digitizer / touch device running openSUSE Linux. It is the first device with this feature to support Linux.

### Android

Google's Linux-based Android operating system has been targeted by manufacturers for the tablet market following its success on smartphones due to its open nature and support for low-cost ARM systems much like Apple's iOS. In 2010, there have been many announcements of such tablets.[23] However, much of Android's tablet initiative comes from hardware makers, as Google focuses its development mainly on smartphones and restricts the Android Market from non-phone devices.[24] However, there is talk of tablet support from Google coming to its web-centric Chrome OS.[25] [26] Some vendors such as Motorola are delaying deployment of their tablet computers until 2011, after Android is reworked to include more tablet features.[27] [28] Android 3.0 (Honeycomb) is the latest version of the Android platform. It is optimized specifically for devices with larger screen sizes, mainly tablets. Android is the software stack for mobile devices that includes operating system, middleware and key applications.

### MeeGo

Nokia entered the tablet space with the Nokia 770 running Maemo, a Debian-based Linux distribution custom-made for their Internet Tablet line. The product line continued with the N900 which is the first to add phone capabilities. Intel, following the launch of the UMPC, started the Mobile Internet Device initiative, which took the same hardware and combined it with a Linux operating system custom-built for portable tablets. Intel co-developed the lightweight Moblin operating system following the successful launch of the Atom CPU series on netbooks.

MeeGo is a new operating system developed by Intel and Nokia supports Netbooks, Smartphones and tablet PCs. In 2010, Nokia and Intel combined the Maemo and Moblin projects to form MeeGo. The first MeeGo powered tablet PC is the Neofonie WeTab. The WeTab uses an extended version of the MeeGo operating system called WeTab OS. WeTab OS adds runtimes for Android and Adobe AIR and provides a proprietary user interface optimized for the WeTab device.

## Apple

### Mac OS X

Apple has never sold a tablet PC-style computer running Mac OS X, although OS X does have support for handwriting recognition via Inkwell. However, Apple sells the iOS-based iPad, introduced in 2010 and iPad 2, released in 2011.

Before the introduction of the iPad, Axiotron introduced the Modbook, a heavily modified Apple MacBook, Mac OS X-based tablet computer at Macworld in 2007.[29] The Modbook used Apple's Inkwell handwriting and gesture recognition, and used digitization hardware from Wacom. To support the digitizer on the integrated tablet, the Modbook was supplied with a third-party driver called TabletMagic [59]. Wacom does not provide drivers for this device.

### Jailbroken iPad

The jailbreaking operation on an Apple iPad allows the end user to gain full software control of the hardware, avoiding the walled garden approach designed by Apple for the product. A jailbroken iPad may be used and administered as a personal computer by its owner. This allows the ability to install arbitrary or self-developed software not approved and signed by Apple, which is the only possibility with regular iPads

# Display size trends

As with other portable computers, larger size brings easier usability but less portability and higher power needs.

As of 2011, the usual tablet computer display size is 10" (for iPad) or 7" (for many Android tablets). Many tablet PC makers have standardized on a 12" widescreen format, with a resolution of 1280x800 pixels. The Fujitsu T5010 has a larger 13.3" display, but still runs at the 1280x800 pixel resolution.[30] The Acer TravelMate C300 has a 14.1" screen at 1024x768.

April 2011: Sony has announced Honeycomb Android Tablet S2 with dual 5.5-inch screens.[31]

# Timeline of tablet PC history

The following timeline list gives some of the highlights of this history:

- Before 1950
  - 1888: U.S. Patent granted to Elisha Gray on electrical stylus device for capturing handwriting.[32]
  - 1915: U.S. Patent on handwriting recognition user interface with a stylus.[33]
  - 1942: U.S. Patent on touchscreen for handwriting input.[34] [35]
  - 1945: Vannevar Bush proposes the Memex, a data archiving device including handwriting input, in an essay As We May Think.[36]
- 1950s
  - Tom Dimond demonstrates the Styalator electronic tablet with pen for computer input and software for recognition of handwritten text in real-time.[37]
- Early 1960s
  - RAND Tablet invented.[38] [39] The RAND Tablet is better known than the Styalator, but was invented later.

- Late 1960s
  - Alan Kay of Xerox PARC proposed a notebook computer, optionally using pen input, called the Dynabook: however the device is never constructed or implemented with pen input.
- 1966
  - In the science fiction television series Star Trek, crew members carry large, wedge-shaped electronic clipboards, operated through the use of a stylus.
- 1982
  - Pencept of Waltham, Massachusetts markets a general-purpose computer terminal using a tablet and handwriting recognition instead of a keyboard and mouse.[40]
  - Cadre System markets the Inforite point-of-sale terminal using handwriting recognition and a small electronic tablet and pen.[41]
- 1985
  - Pencept[42] and CIC[43] both offer PC computers for the consumer market using a tablet and handwriting recognition instead of a keyboard and mouse. Operating system is MS-DOS.
- 1989
  - The first commercially available tablet-type portable computer was the GRiDPad[44] from GRiD Systems released in September. The GridPad was manufactured by Samsung,[45] modified from the Samsung PenMaster which never made it to commercial distribution. Its operating system was based on MS-DOS.
  - Wang Laboratories introduces Freestyle. Freestyle was an application that would do a screen capture from a DOS application, and let users add voice and handwriting annotations. It was a sophisticated predecessor to later note-taking applications for systems like tablet PCs.[46] The operating system was MS-DOS
  - In partnership with Fujitsu [18], the Poqet Computer Corporation announced the arrival of the Poqet PC.
- 1991
  - The Momenta Pentop was released.[47]
  - GO Corporation announced a dedicated operating system, called PenPoint OS, featuring control of the operating system desktop via handwritten gesture shapes.[48] [49] Gestures included "flick" gestures in different directions, check-marks, cross-outs, pig-tails, and circular shapes, among others.
  - NCR released model 3125 pen computer running MS-DOS, Penpoint OS or Pen Windows.[50]
  - The Apple Newton entered development; although it ultimately became a PDA, its original concept (which called for a larger screen and greater sketching abilities) resembled the hardware of a tablet PC.
- 1992
  - GO Corporation shipped the PenPoint OS for general availability and IBM announced IBM 2125 pen computer (the first IBM model named "ThinkPad") in April.[51]
  - Microsoft releases Windows for Pen Computing as a response to the PenPoint OS by GO Corporation.
- 1993
  - Fujitsu releases the Poqet PC the first pen tablet to use an integrated wireless LAN[52]
  - Apple Computer announces the Newton PDA, also known as the Apple MessagePad, which includes handwriting recognition with a stylus.
  - The IBM releases the ThinkPad, IBM's first commercialized portable tablet computer product available to the consumer market, as the IBM ThinkPad 750P and 360P[53]
  - AT&T introduced the EO Personal Communicator combining PenPoint with wireless communications.
  - BellSouth released the IBM Simon Personal Communicator, an analog cellphone using a touch-screen and display. It did not include handwriting recognition, but did permit users to write messages and send them as faxes on the analog cellphone network, and included PDA and Email features.
- 1996

  - ViA, Inc. releases the *ViA Tablet PC*.
- 1999
  - The "QBE" pen computer created by Aqcess Technologies wins Comdex Best of Show.[54]
- 2000
  - PaceBlade [27] develops the first device that meets the Microsoft's Tablet PC standard[55] and received the "Best Hardware" award at VAR Vision 2000
  - The "QBE Vivo" pen computer created by Aqcess Technologies ties for Comdex Best of Show.
- 2001
  - Bill Gates of Microsoft demonstrates the first public prototype of a Tablet PC (defined by Microsoft as a pen-enabled computer conforming to hardware specifications devised by Microsoft and running a licensed copy of the "Windows XP Tablet PC Edition" operating system)[56] at Comdex.
- 2003
  - PaceBlade [30] receives the "Innovation des Jahres 2002/2003" award for the PaceBook [31] tablet PC from PC Professionell Magazine at the Cebit
  - Fingerworks[57] develops the touch technology and touch gestures later used in the Apple iPhone.
- 2006
  - Samsung introduces the Samsung Q1 UMPC.
  - Windows Vista released for general availability. Vista included the functionality of the special Tablet PC edition of Windows XP.
  - On Disney Channel Original Movie, *Read It and Weep*, Jamie uses a tablet PC for her journal.
- 2007
  - Axiotron introduces Modbook, the first (and only) tablet computer based on Mac hardware and Mac OS X at Macworld.[29]
- 2008
  - In April 2008, as part of a larger federal court case, the gesture features of the Windows Tablet PC operating system and hardware were found to infringe on a patent by GO Corp. concerning user interfaces for pen computer operating systems.[58] Microsoft's acquisition of the technology is the subject of a separate lawsuit.[59] [60]
  - HP releases the second Multi-Touch capable tablet: the HP TouchSmart tx2 series.[61]
- 2009
  - Asus netbook, the EEE PC T91 and T91MT, the latter which features a multi-touch screen.
  - Always Innovating announced a new tablet netbook with an ARM CPU.
  - Motion Computing launched the J3400.
- 2010
  - MobileDemand launches the xTablet T7000 Rugged Tablet PC [38] which runs a full Windows OS and features include an integrated numeric keypad, bar code scanner, credit card reader, etc.
  - Apple unveils the iPad, running Apple iOS.
  - Quaduro Systems [62] unveils the 10" QuadPad 3G Plus [63], a 900 gram Microsoft Windows based 3G tablet PC with 8 hours of battery life.
  - Samsung unveils the Galaxy Tab, running Google Android.
  - bModo [64] launches the bModo12 [65] which runs the Windows 7 OS and features include 11.6" TFT-LCD display, 3G, Wi-Fi, GPS, Bluetooth® 2.1, USB2.0, SDHC slot, unlocked SIM card Slot, miniHDMI connector, OMTP Jack, a webcam, a mic, etc.
  - Neofonie releases the WeTab, a MeeGo-based slate tablet PC, featuring an 11.6 inch multi-touch screen at 1366×768 pixels resolution.[62]

- Dixons Retail plc unveils the Advent Vega, a 10" tablet PC running Android 2.2, having a 1 GHz NVIDIA Tegra chipset, 512 Mb of RAM and ROM, 1.3 MP camera, WiFi b/g connectivity, Bluetooth 2.1, a micro SD card slot, a USB port and a 16h battery life for audio playback and 6.5h for 1080p video.[63]
- Dell Announces the Inspiron Duo A flip screen Netbook and Tablet PC hybrid
- HP releases the Slate 500, running a full-version of Windows 7
- 2011
  - Motorola announces Xoom Tablet, a 10 inch tablet powered by the upcoming Android 3.0 Honeycomb
  - Asus announces the EEE Pad MeMO (7 inch tablet), EEE Slate EP121 (Windows 7 tablet), EEE Pad Transformer (10 inch tablet with Android and docking keyboard that transforms it into a laptop form factor) and EEE Pad Slider (10 inch tablet with sliding screen over the QWERTY keyboard) [all tablets use IPS display]
  - Dell showcases the Streak 7 tablet and says it's working on the 10 inch Streak 10
  - ZTE announces the *ZTE V11* that runs Android 3.0, and the *Z-pad*.[64]
  - Apple announces the iPad 2
  - Toshiba announces the Toshiba Tablet [2], a 10 inch tablet powered by a Tegra 2 process and Android 3.0 Honeycomb [65]

# References


[1] Beck H *et al*, *Business Communication and Technologies in a Changing World*, Macmillan Education Australia, 2009, p 402
[2] Haven, Kendall F. *100 greatest science inventions of all time*, Libraries Unlimited, 2006, p 191
[3] Page, M Microsoft Tablet PC Overview (http://www.transmetazone.com/articleview.cfm?articleID=499), TransmetaZone, 2000-12-21
[4] Kuhn, Bradley M. Free software and cellphones (http://www.fsf.org/working-together/next-steps/free-software-phones), Free Software Foundation, 2010
[5] WeTab running OpenOffice (http://www.youtube.com/watch?v=KPDfHWAEV8A), NewGadgetsDE, 2010
[6] Beavis, Gareth Firefox for Android coming 'late this year' (http://www.techradar.com/news/phone-and-communications/mobile-phones/firefox-for-android-coming-late-this-year--670810), Techradar, 2010
[7] Van West, Jeff Tablet PC vs. Laptop: How Do You Choose? (http://replay.web.archive.org/20090315054203/http://www.microsoft.com/windowsxp/using/tabletpc/expert/vanwest_05feb11tabvlap.mspx), Microsoft, 2005
[8] http://www.tvgenius.net/blog/2011/03/17/mobile-tv-convergence/
[9] https://secure.globeadvisor.com/servlet/ArticleNews/story/gam/20110326/RBRIMSTOCKPRINTATL Retrieved at March 28, 2011
[10] http://msdn.microsoft.com/en-us/library/ms840465.aspx
[11] "Tablet PC Brings the Simplicity of Pen and Paper to Computing" (http://www.microsoft.com/presspass/features/2000/nov00/11-13tabletpc.mspx). .
[12] "Live from Steve Ballmer's CES 2010 keynote" (http://www.engadget.com/2010/01/06/live-from-steve-ballmers-ces-2010-keynote/). Engadget. . Retrieved 4 August 2010.
[13] "Ballmer Admits Apple is Beating Microsoft in the Tablet Sector" (http://www.dailytech.com/Ballmer+Admits+Apple+is+Beating+Microsoft+in+the+Tablet+Sector/article19215.htm). DailyTech. . Retrieved 6 August 2010.
[14] Windows 7 is not yet optimized for fingertip events - 2010-09-24 (http://arstechnica.com/gadgets/news/2010/09/hp-slate-video-shows-all-thats-wrong-with-windows-7-on-tablets.ars)
[15] Windows 7 will not be optimized for slates; that will have to wait for Windows 8 (http://www.foxnews.com/scitech/2010/10/05/microsofts-ipad-answer-coming-christmas-holiday/)
[16] "Asus launches Eee Pad tablets and Eee Tablet note-taking thingie" (http://www.liliputing.com/2010/05/asus-launches-two-tablets-the-eee-pad-and-eee-tablet.html). liliputing. . Retrieved 6 August 2010.
[17] MSDN (http://msdn.microsoft.com/en-us/library/ms701180(VS.85).aspx) Ink collection
[18] http://www.microsoft.com/windows/windows-7/features/tablet-pc.aspx
[19] http://www.bmodo.com
[20] *MSDN: Windows XP Tablet PC Edition: Tablet PC: An Overview* (http://users.erols.com/rwservices/pens/biblio05.html#Microsoft04a), Microsoft, 2004-08-24, , retrieved 2008-09-04
[21] *Windows XP Tablet PC Edition: Tablet PC: An Overview* (http://web.archive.org/web/20080719105920/http://www.itxcgc.com/images/Brochures/Microsoft/TabletPCOverview.pdf), Microsoft, 2002-06-01, archived from the original (http://www.itxcgc.com/images/Brochures/Microsoft/TabletPCOverview.pdf) on 19 July 2008, , retrieved 2008-09-04
[22] "Ubuntu gets multitouch support, Unity netbook UI" (http://www.linuxfordevices.com/c/a/News/Canonical-uTouch-and-Ubuntu-Maverick-Meerkat/). eWeek. .

[23] "9 Upcoming Tablet Alternatives to the Apple iPad" (http://mashable.com/2010/01/27/9-upcoming-tablet-alternatives-to-the-apple-ipad/ ). Mashable. . Retrieved 7 August 2010.
[24] "Don't bank on KMart's $150 Augen tablet getting Android Market access" (http://www.liliputing.com/2010/08/dont-bank-on-kmarts-150-augen-tablet-getting-android-market-access.html). liliputing. . Retrieved 7 August 2010.
[25] "Forget all these Android tablets, let me at that Chrome OS" (http://www.crunchgear.com/2010/07/20/forget-all-these-android-tablets-let-me-at-that-chrome-os/). CrunchGear. . Retrieved 7 August 2010.
[26] "Google Chrome OS Tablet Brings Ties With Verizon" (http://www.informationweek.com/news/services/data/showArticle.jhtml?articleID=226700487)
[27] http://www.marketwatch.com/video/asset/digits-motorola-plans-tablet-device-2010-09-16/7CC13B36-0A8B-42E0-AD1A-72FF9BF04348 Motorola Android tablet in 2011
[28] The successor to *Gingerbread*, Android project *Honeycomb* is targeted for tablet computers. — Daniel Lyons ( Oct. 11, 2010), *Newsweek* p. 49
[29] (http://www.tabletpcreview.com/default.asp?newsID=695)
[30] http://www.fujitsu.com/au/services/technology/pc/notebooks/tseries/t5010/specs.html
[31] http://techcrunch.com/2011/04/25/sony-announces-s1-and-dual-screen-s2-android-tablets/?utm_source=feedburner&utm_medium=feed&utm_campaign=Feed%3A+Techcrunch+%28TechCrunch%29
[32] Gray (1888-07-31), *Telautograph* (http://rwservices.no-ip.info:81/pens/biblio70.html#Gray1888b), United States Patent 386,815,
[33] Goldberg, H.E. (1915-12-28), *Controller* (http://users.erols.com/rwservices/pens/biblio70.html#GoldbergHE15), United States Patent 1,117,184,
[34] Moodey, H.C. (1942-12-27), *Telautograph System* (http://users.erols.com/rwservices/pens/biblio70.html#Moodey40), United States Patent 2,269,599,
[35] Moodey, H.C. (1942-12-27), *Telautograph System* (http://www.freepatentsonline.com/2269599.pdf), United States Patent 2,269,599 (full image),
[36] Bush, Vannevar (1945-07-15), *As We May Think* (http://rwservices.no-ip.info:81/pens/biblio70.html#BushV45), The Atlantic Monthly,
[37] Dimond, Tom (1957-12-01), *Devices for reading handwritten characters* (http://rwservices.no-ip.info:81/pens/biblio70.html#Dimond57), Proceedings of Eastern Joint Computer Conference, pp. 232–237, , retrieved 2008-08-23
[38] *RAND Tablet* (http://users.erols.com/rwservices/pens/biblio70.html#RAND61), 1961-09-01,
[39] *50 Years of Looking Forward* (http://www.rand.org/publications/randreview/issues/rr.fall.98/50.html), RAND Corporation, 1998-09-01,
[40] *Pencept Penpad (TM) 200 Product Literature* (http://rwservices.no-ip.info:81/pens/biblio83.html#Pencept83), Pencept, Inc., 1982-08-15,
[41] *Inforite Hand Character Recognition Terminal* (http://rwservices.no-ip.info:81/pens/biblio83.html#Inforite82), Cadre Systems Limited, England, 1982-08-15,
[42] *Users Manual for Penpad 320* (http://users.erols.com/rwservices/pens/biblio85.html#Pencept84d), Pencept, Inc., 1984-06-15,
[43] *Handwriter (R) GrafText (TM) System Model GT-5000* (http://rwservices.no-ip.info:81/pens/biblio85.html#CIC85), Communication Intelligence Corporation, 1985-01-15,
[44] *The BYTE Awards: GRiD System's GRiDPad* (http://rwservices.no-ip.info:81/pens/biblio90.html#GridPad90a), BYTE Magazine, Vol 15. No 1, 1990-01-12, pp. 285,
[45] "GRidPad 1910" (http://www.computinghistory.org.uk/det/6565/GRidPad-1910/). ComputingHistory. . Retrieved 19 February 2011.
[46] *WANG Freestyle demo* (http://rwservices.no-ip.info:81/pens/images.html#WangFreestyle), Wang Laboratories, 1989, , retrieved 2008-09-22
[47] Lempesis, Bill (1990-05), *What's New in Laptops and Pen Computing* (http://rwservices.no-ip.info:81/pens/biblio90.html#Momenta90), Flat Panel Display News,
[48] Agulnick, Todd (1994-09-13), *Control of a computer through a position-sensed stylus* (http://users.erols.com/rwservices/pens/biblio95.html#Agulnick94), United States Patent 5,347,295,
[49] Agulnick, Todd (1994-09-13), *Control of a computer through a position-sensed stylus* (http://www.freepatentsonline.com/5347295.pdf), United States Patent 5,347,295 (full image),
[50] (– Scholar search (http://scholar.google.co.uk/scholar?hl=en&lr=&q=intitle:NCR+announces+pen-based+computer+press+release&as_publication=&as_ylo=&as_yhi=&btnG=Search)) *NCR announces pen-based computer press release* (http://findarticles.com/p/articles/mi_m0NEW/is_1991_June_24/ai_10957018), FindArticles, , retrieved 2007-04-20
[51] (– Scholar search (http://scholar.google.co.uk/scholar?hl=en&lr=&q=intitle:Penpoint+OS+shipping+press+release&as_publication=&as_ylo=&as_yhi=&btnG=Search)) *Penpoint OS shipping press release* (http://web.archive.org/web/20070830050237/http://findarticles.com/p/articles/mi_m0NEW/is_1992_April_17/ai_12165379), FindArticles, archived from the original (http://findarticles.com/p/articles/mi_m0NEW/is_1992_April_17/ai_12165379) on 30 August 2007, , retrieved 2007-04-20
[52] (http://solutions.us.fujitsu.com/www/content/products/Tablet-PCS/index.php)
[53] Lenovo - The history of ThinkPad (http://www.pc.ibm.com/us/thinkpad/anniversary/history.html)
[54] *Trends at COMDEX Event 1999* (http://www.guiart.fi/gobr01en.htm), , retrieved 2008-08-11
[55] PaceBlade launches Tablet PC (http://www.allbusiness.com/electronics/computer-equipment-personal-computers/6004956-1.html)

[56] Microsoft (2005), *Windows XP Tablet PC Edition 2005 Hardware Requirements* (http://users.erols.com/rwservices/pens/biblio10.html#Microsoft06i), www.microsoft.com, , retrieved 2009-03-14
[57] Fingerworks, Inc. (2003), *iGesture Game Mode Guide* (http://rwservices.no-ip.info:81/pens/biblio05.html#Fingerworks03), www.fingerworks.com, , retrieved 2009-04-30
[58] Mintz, Jessica (2008-04-04), *Microsoft to Appeal $367M Patent Ruling* (http://www.usatoday.com/tech/products/2008-04-04-2507619152_x.htm), The Associated Press, , retrieved 2008-09-04
[59] http://news.com.com/Go+files+antitrust+suit+against+Microsoft/2100-7343_3-5772534.html
[60] http://www.groklaw.net/article.php?story=20050704045343631
[61] *HP TouchSmart tx2z* (http://www.shopping.hp.com/webapp/shopping/computer_can_series.do?storeName=computer_store&category=notebooks&a1=Category&v1=Mobility&series_name=tx2z_series), HP, , retrieved 2008-11-28
[62] "WeTab ships in Germany" (http://www.h-online.com/open/news/item/WeTab-ships-in-Germany-1083804.html). *The H*. 22 September 2010. .
[63] "Full tech specification of the Dixons Advent Vega Android 2.2 tablet" (http://www.eurodroid.com/2010/10/update-full-tech-specification-of-the-dixons-advent-vega-android-2-2-tablet). *Gary C*. 8 October 2010. .
[64] ZTE Launches Two Android Tablets: Dual-core Z-pad and Android 3.0 V11 at MWC (http://www.gadgetsbing.com/2011/02/zte-launches-two-android-tablets-dual-core-z-pad-and-android-3-0-v11-at-mwc/)
[65] Toshiba Announces 10.1-inch Tegra 2 Tablet (http://www.tomshardware.com/news/Toshiba-Tablet-Tegra-2-Tegra-Tablets,11909.html)

# External links

- Tablet PCs (http://www.dmoz.org/Computers/Systems/Tablet_PCs/) at the Open Directory Project
- Jeff Han Talks About Touch-Driven Computer Screens (http://www.howstuffworks.com/1787-jeff-han-talks-about-touch-driven-computer-screens-video.htm) at HowStuffWorks
- Microsoft Center for Research on Pen-Centric Computing (http://pen.cs.brown.edu/)

# Tablet PC Input Panel

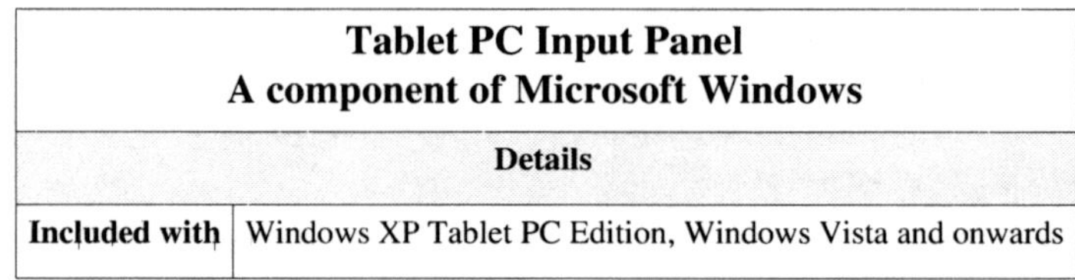

| Tablet PC Input Panel<br>A component of Microsoft Windows | |
|---|---|
| **Details** | |
| **Included with** | Windows XP Tablet PC Edition, Windows Vista and onwards |

The **Tablet PC Input Panel** is an accessory included in Microsoft Windows that allows input of text using a pen and digitizing tablet, touch screen, an on-screen soft keyboard or mouse. It performs handwriting recognition and converts handwriting into text for use in most non-full-screen Windows applications. It was included first in Windows XP Tablet PC Edition and is included in subsequent client versions of Microsoft Windows.

## Features

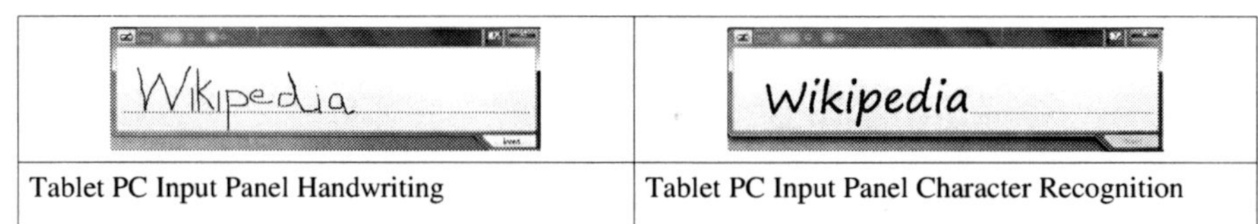


| Tablet PC Input Panel Handwriting | Tablet PC Input Panel Character Recognition |
|---|---|

- Users can use a writing pad or soft keyboard to convert handwriting to text. The writing pad recognises single characters, entire words and shortcut strokes or gestures. The Tablet PC Input Panel also supports AutoComplete in Windows Vista and later.
- The Tablet PC Input Panel can be docked to the top or bottom of the screen or floating.
- The integrated handwriting recognition features can recognize print, cursive, or mixed writing. Accuracy can be increased by configuring the recognizer to expect left-handed writing or right-handed writing. For Windows XP Tablet PC Edition which does not support all languages out of the box, recognition in a variety of languages is available with the install of a recognizer pack [1]. Windows Vista and Windows 7 users can get additional language support for handwriting recognition by installing the respective MUI pack (also called language pack).
- The soft keyboard supports viewing the keyboard layout of the selected input language chosen from the language bar. Windows XP users need to install the Tablet PC Recognizer Pack to support switching of the soft keyboard to the default input language. [1]
- Handwriting recognition accuracy can be improved by training using the handwriting recognition personalization tool.
- Windows 7 improves the Tablet PC Input Panel to make faster corrections, supports text prediction in the soft keyboard and introduces a new Math Input Panel for inputting math into programs that support MathML. It recognizes handwritten math expressions and formulas.

## History

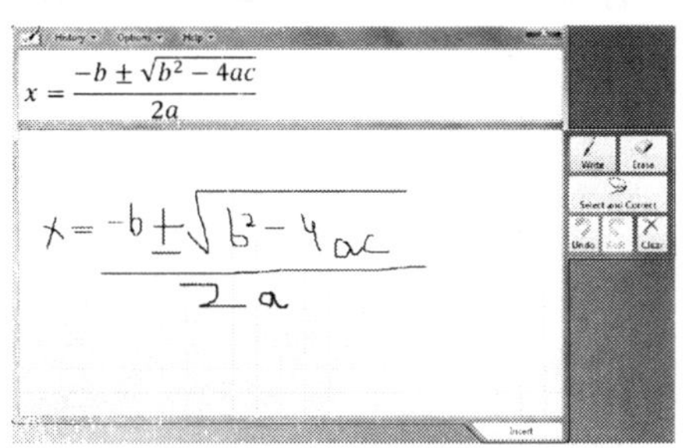

Math Input Panel in Windows 7 editing the Quadratic Formula.

When first introduced, Tablet PC Input Panel was only included with the Windows XP Tablet PC Edition of Windows XP and had limited application text entry support. Windows XP Service Pack 2 for Windows XP Tablet PC Edition which was incorporated into Windows XP Tablet PC Edition 2005 brought improved the handwriting recognition and allowed the Tablet PC Input Panel to be used in almost every application. The Tablet PC Input Panel was also revised to extend speech recognition services (input and correction) to other applications.

With the release of Windows Vista, the Tablet PC Input Panel is built into all editions of Windows Vista with the exception of Home Basic and Starter editions. The speech recognition features were moved into Windows Speech Recognition.

## References

[1] Tablet PC Recognizer Pack frequently asked questions (http://support.microsoft.com/kb/828729)

# TabletKiosk

**TabletKiosk**

| Type | Private |
|---|---|
| Industry | Electronics |
| Founded | 2003 |
| Headquarters | Torrance, California |
| Products | Tablet PC and UMPC |

**TabletKiosk** is a manufacturer of Tablet PCs and UMPCs located in Torrance, California, United States. All mobile computers produced by TabletKiosk fall into the slate category, featuring touchscreen or pen (active digitizer) input, in lieu of integrated or convertible keyboards. Current products include the Sahara Slate PC i400 series, designed in-house at TabletKiosk's Taiwan R&D facility, the original eo line of UMPC's was a collaboration with outside designers and the TabletKiosk team, while the second generation of this brand is being designed exclusively inhouse.

TabletKiosk is a wholly owned subsidiary of Sand Dune Ventures, based in Torrance, California.

In 2006, TabletKiosk delayed shipment of its "eo" brand tablet after discovering problems with the device's fan.[1]

SoftBrands announced in 2007 that it would use TabletKiosk's Sahara Slate PC line to distribute SoftBrands software to hotel companies.[2]

Parkland Memorial Hospital in Dallas, Texas, United States has patients visiting its emergency department fill in their details using a TabletKiosk machine.[3] [4]

## References

[1] Fried, Ina (May 1, 2006). "Origami PC maker has to scribble 'wait'" (http://news.zdnet.com/2100-9584_22-147852.html). *ZDNet News*. . Retrieved 2008-10-31.

[2] "SoftBrands Links With TabletKiosk to Offer Mobile Software to Hoteliers" (http://www.accessmylibrary.com/coms2/summary_0286-31813385_ITM). *Wireless News*. July 4, 2007. . Retrieved 2008-10-31.

[3] "TabletKiosk Greets Patients in ER" (http://www.medgadget.com/archives/2007/06/tabletkiosk_greets_patients_in_er.html). *MedGadget.com*. June 11, 2007. . Retrieved 2008-10-31.

[4] Breen, Kim (Thursday, June 7, 2007). "Parkland's kiosks speed check-in. Parkland computer kiosks eliminate lines, frustrate some" (http://www.dallasnews.com/sharedcontent/dws/dn/latestnews/stories/060707dnmeterkiosk.37be576.html). *The Dallas Morning News*. . Retrieved 2008-10-31.

- O'Reilly, Dennis (May 12, 2006). "First Look: Ultra Mobile PC Head-to-Head" (http://www.washingtonpost.com/wp-dyn/content/article/2006/05/11/AR2006051101865_pf.html). *PC World via The Washington Post*. Retrieved 2008-10-31.
- Kwan, Michael (March 26, 2007). "Video: TabletKiosk Sahara i215 Not Designed for Vista" (http://www.mobilemag.com/content/100/341/C12155/). *Mobile Magazine*. Retrieved 2008-10-31.

## External links

- Company website (http://www.tabletkiosk.com/)

# Ultra-mobile PC

An **ultra-mobile PC**[1] (**ultra-mobile personal computer** or **UMPC**) is a small form factor version of a pen computer, a new class of laptop whose specifications were launched by Microsoft and Intel in spring 2006. Sony had already made a first attempt in this direction in 2004 with its Vaio U series, which was however only sold in Asia. UMPCs are smaller than subnotebooks, have a TFT display measuring (diagonally) about 12.7 to 17.8 cm, and are operated like tablet PCs using a touchscreen or a stylus. There is no clear boundary between subnotebooks and ultra-mobile PCs.

The Wibrain B1 UMPC is a UMPC based on the VIA Ultra Mobility Platform featuring a 1.2 GHz VIA C7-M processor, 4.8" touchscreen, split thumb keyboard, touchpad, and webcam.

The first-generation UMPCs were simple PCs running Linux or an adapted version of Microsoft's tablet PC operating system. With the announcement of the UMPC, Microsoft dropped the licensing requirement that tablet PCs must support proximity sensing of the stylus, which Microsoft termed "hovering".

Second-generation UMPCs use less electricity and can therefore be used longer (up to five hours) and also support Windows Vista.

Originally codenamed **Project Origami**, the project was launched in 2006 as a collaboration between Microsoft, Intel, Samsung, and a few others. Despite prediction of the demise of UMPC device category according to CNET[2] and the comparatively dominant sale of netbooks, the UMPC category appears to continue to be in existence and may possibly see a rise in demand[3] as a media consumption device as evidenced by the introduction of Apple iPad, Google Android (and the upcoming Chrome OS), BlackBerry Tablet OS, Nokia's upcoming MeeGo and HP's upcoming webOS 2.0.

## History

In February 2006, a viral marketing campaign was quietly launched for the UMPC, then still referred to by its codename, "Project Origami". Speculation over "what is Origami?" and pictures of the rumored prototypes were passed around and covered extensively on Engadget, Scobleizer,[4] Thatedeguy[5] and other technology sites. Finalization of the Origami project was announced in time to keep the excitement level high for CeBIT.

Much speculation positioned Origami as a portable gaming device that would directly compete with Nintendo's DS and Sony's PSP. This rumor gained credibility after videos were leaked showing *Halo: Combat Evolved* being played on a UMPC. While the movie was quickly taken down from its original source, mirrors exist on many other sites. Later in the week, the Associated Press confirmed that "Origami" was actually to be a regular PC with "limited gaming capabilities".[6]

## First two devices

The first UMPCs on the market were AMtek's T700 and Samsung's Q1.

Samsung Q1 Ultra UMPC

The AMtek T700 is sold in the USA as the *TabletKiosk eo v7110*, *agoPC ago7*, and *Azentek GB-810*, in Europe as the *PaceBlade* [30] *EasyBook P7* [7] and *its Label Origami*, and in Australia the *TabletKiosk eo v7110* and the *Pioneer DreamBook UMPC 700* and in Japan the *PBJ SmartCaddie*.

## 2006

In late August 2006, TabletKiosk launched a line of Intel based UMPCs, the eo i7210 and i7209. They followed this up in March 2007 with a ruggedized VIA based UMPC, the eo TufTab v7112XT.[7]

OQO is also selling UMPCs. The OQO model 01 was actually launched well before the ultra-mobile PC craze began, but its specifications were very similar to the UMPC specifications.

In September 2006, Raon Digital launched the Vega running a AMD Geode LX800, 256 MB of RAM, and a 30 GB hard drive. It has a 4.3" screen, a 500 MHz processor, and a battery life of 5.5 hours. It runs Microsoft Windows XP Home Edition and retails for 680,000 Korean won (U$700–750). However it does not have WiFi capability.

In early October 2006 Samsung quietly launched the Q1B, bringing the Ultra Mobile platform closer to the vision that Microsoft created. The Q1b features a VIA C7-M ULV processor running at 1 GHz, up to five hours of battery life, and a lower price point than the Samsung Q1. It also has optional modules for HSDPA or WiBro for ubiquitous internet connectivity in major cities around the world. Also a new UMPC on the market is the T770 from AMtek. It is a Windows Vista powered device with a 1200 MHz processor and 1024 MB of RAM. It has a 40 GB hard disk (or 60 GB on another cheaper brand, and also the same device) and a 7" screen. It is available for 899 € (the cheaper brand is 849 €).

## 2007

Wibrain[8] launched the first UMPC model B1E and B1H in December 2007.

In 2007, Bill Gates introduced [10] the OQO model 02 in his keynote at CES 2007 [11]. The OQO model 02 [12] is now shipping with a 5-inch/12.7-cm screen, EV-DO WWAN, Bluetooth, 802.11 a/b/g WiFi, running Microsoft Windows XP and Vista. OQO has won quite a few computer and design awards, including Guinness World Records [13] recognition of OQO model 02 as the world's smallest fully functional computer [14].

In August 2007, Raon Digital launched their second UMPC 'Everun' which has built in WiFi and HSDPA. It uses the AMD Geode (processor) LX900. Everun is introduced as the UMPC with the longest battery life—as much as 6–7 hours with its standard battery and 12 hours with a large battery. Unlike its previous model 'VEGA', Everun has a full qwerty key pad, aesthetically similar to a Smartphone, which appeals to the mobile commuter.

On September 17, 2007, OQO launched the model e2[9] for the European audience with a localized keyboard, 1.6 GHz VIA C7-M processor, 120 GB hard drive or a 32 GB SSD option.

Also, in October 2007 the Asus EEE PC (model 701) was launched. With a 7 inch screen, full keyboard and wifi, running Linux, it started the netbook revolution.[10]

### 2008

Wibrain launched the second models of B1L series with Ubuntu Linux on February 27, 2008. Their starting price is around $500.00. Wibrain UMPC features a 4.8 inch touch enabled LCD screen at 1024x600 resolution, a 1.0 GHz or 1.2 GHz VIA C7M CPU, 512 MB or 1 GB of memory, a 30 GB or 60 GB harddisk, a full qwerty keyboard and built-in WiFi (802.11b/g).

Around the same date, CHIP.DE[11] featured an article about the R2H from ASUS, which runs a Windows Tablet PC edition OS on its Intel Celeron system. It has a VGA-TV output, GPS, 3 USB ports, 60 GB hard drive and 512 MB RAM. It also offers wired/wireless network capabilities. In Germany, its current price is €939 at Amazon.de.

In September 2008 Nova Mobility[12] announced its second generation Side Arm 2 Industrial UMPC. This unit is designed around the Intel Atom processor and is the first industrial grade UMPC released on that platform. It has GPS, WiFi and Bluetooth standard and 3G as an option. You can also have EVDO via the PCI Express card slot in the top of the unit. Two USB ports, a 7" touch screen and one hand-typeable QWERTY keyboard are available. The device weighs less than 2 lbs and offers up to ten hours of battery life.

### 2009–2010

Viliv introduced the S5 in mid 2009 followed by X70 models. In July 2010 the Vliv N5 was introduced. The N5 is a small notebook-style UMPC whereas the S5 and the X70 are tablets. They all feature GPS, Wifi, Bluetooth, 3G availability, SSD options with Intel Z520 and integrated GMA500 graphics with hardware acceleration for H264 HD video playback. The starting prices are around US$ 599 with battery life of five hours or longer.[13]

MobileDemand [37] introduced the 2.5 lb, 7" xTablet T7000 Rugged Tablet PC [38] UMPC, which meets MIL-STD810G and IP65 standards for ruggedability. Options include bar code scanner, credit card reader, GPS, Bluetooth, RFID, SSD, full QWERTY keyboard, docking systems, high-capacity batteries, etc.

### 2011

Ocosmos is planning to launch the OCS1, a gaming UMPC with the latest CPU from Intel and will feature Windows 7 Home Edition and front- and rear-facing cameras.

## Features

Project Origami defines a specification for computers with a 20 cm (8-inch) or smaller touch sensitive screen at a minimum resolution of 800 × 480. To make it more suited for the small form factor, Windows XP Tablet PC Edition was originally used with slight tweaks to the interface and a software add-on known as the *Touch Pack Interface* to make the interface more suitable for use of a stylus as well as hands. When the UMPC was disclosed at CeBIT 2006, Samsung, ASUS, and Founder had near-complete devices on display. Recently, the UMPC initiative has included later Windows versions.

UMPCs with Windows XP installed are able to run any software that has been written for the Windows XP platform, though the small form factor often mandates some changes to the interface. The standard Windows XP interface is the default, though a choice of having an interface more suited for the small form factor is available with the *Touch Pack Interface*. As the units are so small, many UMPCs do not feature a physical keyboard, but an on-screen virtual keyboard provided in the Touch Pack Interface (such as the DialKeys, below). Also, since the device has standard USB 2.0 connectivity, external keyboards and mice can be attached.

UMPC devices include either Intel or VIA processors, 256 MB to 2 GB of RAM, and a 30 to 160 GB hard disk, depending on the manufacturer.[14] Other ultra mobile devices feature AMD or Transmeta Crusoe CPUs. Ultra-mobile PCs can also feature Global Positioning System (GPS) devices, webcams, fingerprint readers, stereo speakers, TV tuners, and memory card readers. Bluetooth, Wi-Fi, Ethernet and WWAN connections are sometimes included as well.

UMPCs have enough processing power to support audio, video, and gaming, in addition to having rich support for browsing the internet as well as for other communication and networking applications. Windows Media Player is included, with a special skin designed to provide a better experience on the small screen. The devices also feature DirectX 9–class graphics, and all applications available for standard Tablet PCs are expected to be compatible.

Prices of UMPCs are gradually coming down to the US$500 range. Battery life is expected to increase from the initial 2½ hours to 8 hours.[15] Most UMPCs are now available with Windows 7 although many new UMPCs come with the option to have XP or Linux installed, as some devices are too sluggish to run the Vista kernel on which 7 is based. One example of this is the Samsung Q1 Ultra which originally launched with only Vista versions, but has subsequently launched Windows XP versions.[16] This is largely due to the fact that current UMPC hardware may be too close to the minimum Vista requirements to be comfortably used.

### DialKeys

A new text input method was implemented for ultra-mobile PCs. Consisting of two rings of keys around the lower corners of the screen, DialKeys is intended for use with the thumbs.

### Accessories

There are currently several companies developing accessories exclusively for the 7" UMPC platform. These include carry cases, screen protectors, styli, protective bump cases and docking stations. In addition, several prototypes of "mounting solutions" have been previewed which permit the UMPC device to be mounted in the car, on the wall or attached to an adjustable arm. User interface software that enables UMPC's to become portable "infotainment" devices is evolving. There are touch-friendly, voice-controlled, user interface software platforms designed to run on Windows XP and Vista-based UMPCs that allows users to control Windows without the need of a mouse and keyboard.

## Programs

- Microsoft Office OneNote
- GO Corporation
- Agilix GoBinder
- Mobilis – Protectis Range
- EverNote
- InkSeine
- StarDraw Control[17]

## References

[1] Spelled lower case because it's a type of computer, not a specific product, see Microsoft's description (http://www.microsoft.com/windows/products/winfamily/umpc/default.mspx).

[2] http://reviews.cnet.com/2300-33_7-10001201-33.html?s=0&o=10001201&tag=mncolpage

[3] iPad vs. netbook: direct cannibalization and collateral damage, see (http://arstechnica.com/apple/news/2010/09/ipad-vs-netbook-direct-cannibalization-and-collateral-damage.ars).

[4] What is the Origami Project? « Scobleizer — Tech geek blogger (http://scobleizer.wordpress.com/2006/02/23/what-is-the-origami-project/)

[5] What is Origami? Microsoft's Origami Project | Thatedeguy (http://www.thatedeguy.com/archives/2006/02/what-is-origami)

[6] "Microsoft Unveils Project Origami" (http://news.yahoo.com/s/ap/20060309/ap_on_hi_te/origami_unfolded_5;_ylt=AuWUS4JrWARgcFBhri0vdySi1SoA;_ylu=X3oDMTBiMW04NW9mBHNlYwMlJVRPUCUl). Yahoo! News. 9 March 2006. .

[7] TabletKiosk (March 20, 2007). "TabletKiosk Now Shipping Sahara Slate PC i440D with Windows Vista" (http://www.tabletkiosk.com/company/press_releases.asp#tuftab). Press release. .

[8] Welcome to Wibrain! (http://www.wibrain.com)

[9] http://www.engadget.com/2007/09/17/oqo-brings-the-oqo-model-e2-to-europe/OQO brings the OQO model e2 to Europe
[10] http://money.cnn.com/2008/10/13/technology/copeland_asus.fortune/index.htm Asus launches the netbook revolution with the EEE PC
[11] CHIP.DE (http://www.chip.de/news/c1_news_18962740.html)
[12] Nova Mobility Systems Announces NEW Side Arm 2 UMPC (http://www.novamobility.com)
[13] Viliv X70 EX UMPC Full Review with Videos (http://www.umpcportal.com/2009/06/viliv-x70-ex-umpc-full-review-with-videos/)
[14] Engadget - Hands-on with the WiBrain B1 UMPC (http://www.engadget.com/2008/01/07/hands-on-with-the-wibrain-b1-umpc/)
[15] "Microsoft Preps Ultramobile PC for Second Chance" (http://www.thechannelinsider.com/article/Microsoft+Preps+Ultramobile+PC+for+Second+Chance/181124_1.aspx). eWeek Channel Insider. June 19, 2006. .
[16] "New Samsung Q1 Ultra models ditch Vista for XP" (http://www.pocketables.net/2007/08/new-samsung-q1-.html). Pocketables. August 28, 2007. .
[17] Artical about using a UMPC to control a whole house home audio system (http://www.cepro.com/article/dealer_taps_stardraw_software_for_multiroom_audio/)

# External links

- Microsoft's official ultra-mobile PC website (http://www.microsoft.com/windows/products/winfamily/umpc/default.mspx)
- UMPC comparison website (http://www.umpcportal.com/products/)
- Annotated bibliography of references to handwriting recognition and pen computing (http://rwservices.no-ip.info:81/biblio.html)

# Windows Journal

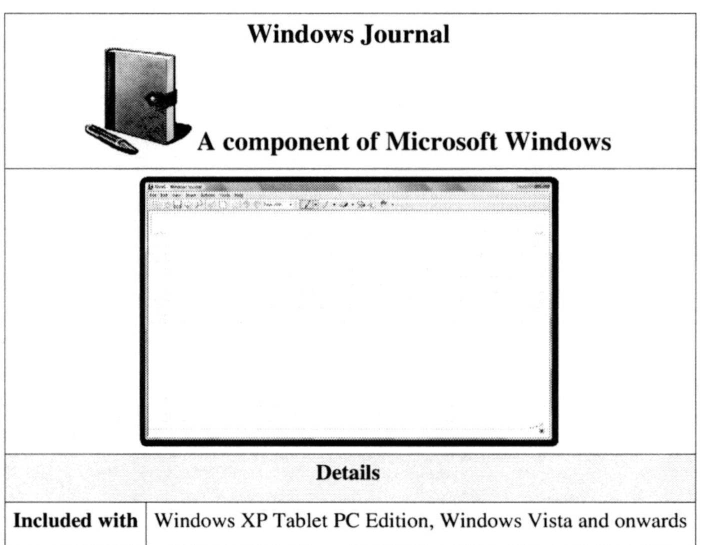

| Windows Journal | |
|---|---|
| A component of Microsoft Windows | |
| Details | |
| **Included with** | Windows XP Tablet PC Edition, Windows Vista and onwards |

**Windows Journal** is a notetaking application, created by Microsoft and included in tablet editions of Windows XP, Windows Vista, and Windows 7. It allows the user to create and organize handwritten notes and drawings. It is also able to simply use an ordinary computer mouse to compose a handwritten note, as well as a graphics tablet or a Tablet PC.

## Availability

When first introduced, Windows Journal was only included with Windows XP Tablet PC Edition. Currently, it is also included in the Home Premium and higher editions of Windows Vista and Windows 7.

## Viewer

**Windows Journal Viewer** is an application, created by Microsoft, that allows viewing the *.JNT files on other systems without the Tablet PC software. The current version (v1.5 2005) is available for Windows 2000, XP and Server 2003.

## External links

- Getting to Know Windows Journal for Tablet PC [1]
- Download details: Windows Journal Viewer 1.5 [2]

# Mobile operating system

A **mobile operating system**, also known as a **mobile OS**, a **mobile platform**, or a **handheld operating system**, is the operating system that controls a mobile device or information appliance—similar in principle to an operating system such as Windows, Mac OS, or Linux that controls a desktop computer or laptop. However, they are currently somewhat simpler, and deal more with the wireless versions of broadband and local connectivity, mobile multimedia formats, and different input methods.

Typical examples of devices running a mobile operating system are smartphones, personal digital assistants (PDAs), tablet computers and information appliances, or what are sometimes referred to as smart devices, which may also include embedded systems, or other mobile devices and wireless devices.

## History

The increasing importance of mobile devices has triggered intense competition amongst software giants such as Google, Microsoft, and Apple, as well as mobile industry leaders Nokia, Research In Motion (RIM), and Palm, in a bid to capture the largest market share pre-emptively.[1]

With the release of the iPhone in 2007, Apple significantly disrupted the mobile industry and effectively ushered in a new era of smartphone operating systems that focus on user experience and rely on touch-based interaction. In November 2007, Google formed the Open Handset Alliance with 79 other hardware, software, and telecom companies to make inroads into the smartphone market through its new Android operating system.[2] Though its reception was mainly positive from the media and public, the release of Android created a rift between Apple and Google, eventually leading to the resignation of Google's CEO, Eric Schmidt, from Apple's board of directors.[3]

Since the launch of both Apple's iOS and Google's Android, the smartphone market has exploded in popularity and in May 2010, accounted for more than 17.3% of all mobile phones sold.[4] This has led to greater consumer awareness of the various mobile operating systems, with telecoms and manufacturers regularly advertising the advantages of their OS. As of January 2011, Google holds 33.3% of the smartphone market worldwide, demonstrating amazing growth for Android which held only 4.7% a year earlier. Nokia, Apple, RIM, and Microsoft hold 31%, 16.2%, 14.6%, and 3.1% respectively.[5]

## Market projection

Mobile platforms are in the nascent stage and any projection regarding market growth is hard to make at the present time. However, a clear trend is the surging growth of mobile operating systems which are developed for smart devices, rather than for feature phones. As of February 2011, Nokia has announced a partnership with Microsoft which effectively ends the development of Symbian OS, the most popular feature phone OS, by the end of 2011 in favor of Windows Phone.

It is noteworthy that Intel is taking the initiative to focus on portable devices other than mobile phones. They are Mobile Internet Devices (MID) and Ultra-Mobile PC (UMPC). Meantime, Palm abandoned its plan to develop Foleo, which was to be a companion device for a smartphone.

## Mobile navigation

Canalys has estimated that in 2009 the installed base of smartphones with integrated GPS was 163 million units worldwide, of which Nokia accounted for more than half (51%), having shipped cumulatively 83 million GPS devices. On January 22, 2010, Nokia released a free version of Ovi Maps in an effort to increase its number of users.

## Smartphone operating systems

Operating systems that can be found on smartphones include Nokia's Symbian, Google's Android, Apple's iOS, RIM's BlackBerry OS, Microsoft's Windows Phone, Linux, Palm/HP's WebOS, Samsung's Bada, Nokia's Maemo and MeeGo among many others. Android, Bada, WebOS and Maemo are built on top of Linux, and iOS is derived from the BSD and NeXTSTEP operating systems, which are all related to Unix.

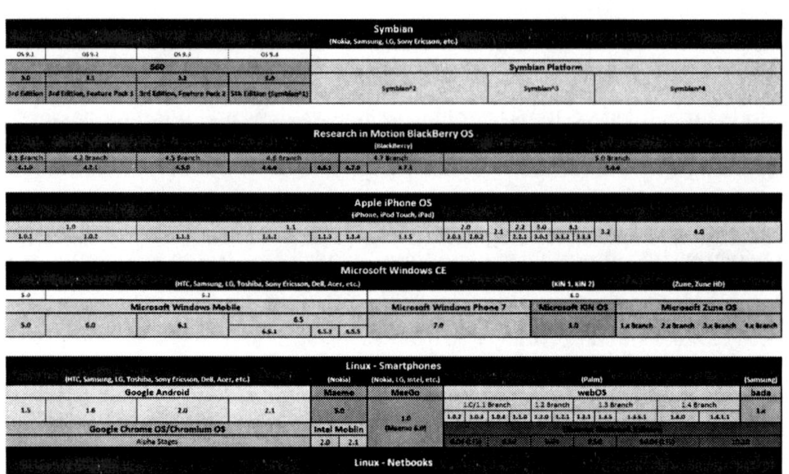


Table showing most of the current mobile operating systems for smartphones, PDAs and netbooks in 2010

The most common operating systems (OS) used in smartphones by Q3 2010 sales are:

The Symbian OS and its successor Symbian platform from the Symbian Foundation (36.6% Market Share Sales Q3 2010)[7] (open public license)

Symbian has the largest share in most markets worldwide, but lags behind other companies in the relatively small but highly visible North American market.[8] This matches the success of its largest shareholder[9] and customer, Nokia, in all markets except Japan. In Japan Symbian is strong due to a relationship with NTT DoCoMo, with only one of the 44 Symbian handsets released in Japan coming from Nokia.[10] It has been used by many major handset manufacturers, including BenQ, Fujitsu, LG, Mitsubishi, Motorola, Nokia, Samsung, Sharp, and Sony Ericsson. Current Symbian-based devices are being made by Fujitsu, Nokia, Samsung, Sharp, and Sony Ericsson. Prior to 2009 Symbian supported multiple user interfaces, i.e. UIQ from UIQ Technologies, S60 from Nokia, and MOAP from NTT DOCOMO. As part of the formation of the Symbian platform in 2009 these three UIs were merged into a single platform which is now fully open source. Recently, though

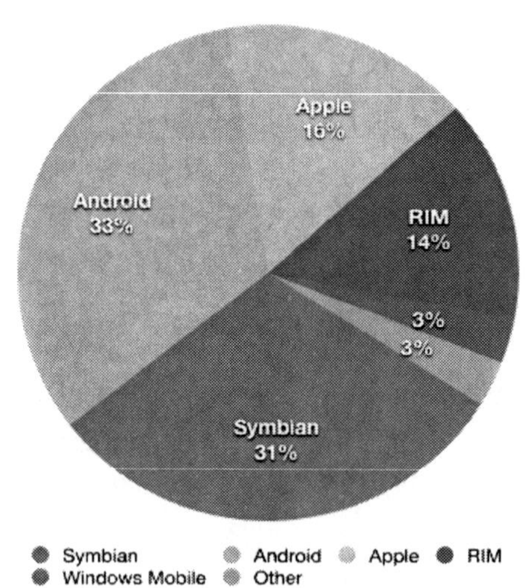


Share of worldwide 2010 Q4 smartphone sales to end users by operating system, according to Canalys.[6]

shipments of Symbian devices have increased, the operating system's worldwide market share has declined from over 50% to just over 40% from 2009 to 2010.

Android from Google Inc. (25.5% Market Share Sales Q3 2010)[7] (open source, Apache)

Android was developed by a small startup company that was purchased by Google Inc., and Google continues to update the software. Android is an open source, Linux-derived platform backed by Google, along with major hardware and software developers (such as Intel, HTC, ARM, Samsung, Motorola and eBay, to name a few), that form the Open Handset Alliance.[11] Released on November 5th 2007, the OS has a following among programmers.[12] There have been seven releases of Android- Android 1.0, 1.5, 1.6, 2.0, 2.1, 2.2 and 2.3. All are nicknamed after a dessert item like Cupcake (1.5) or Frozen Yogurt (2.2). Most major mobile service providers carry an Android device.

Since the HTC Dream (T-Mobile G1) was introduced, there has been an explosion in the number of devices that carry Android OS. From Q2 of 2009 to the second quarter of 2010, Android's worldwide market share rose 850% from 1.8% to 17.2%.

The Apple iPad tablet computer uses a version of iOS.

iOS from Apple Inc. (16.7% Market Share Sales Q3 2010)[7] (closed source, proprietary)

The Apple iPhone, iPod Touch and iPad all use an operating system called iOS, which is derived from Mac OS X. Third party applications were not officially supported until the release of iOS 2.0 on July 11th 2008. Before this, "jailbreaking" allowed third party applications to be installed, and this method is still available. Currently all iOS devices are developed by Apple and manufactured by Foxconn or another of Apple's partners.

RIM BlackBerry OS (14.8% Market Share Sales Q3 2010)[7] (closed source, proprietary)

This OS is focused on easy operation and was originally designed for business. Recently it has seen a surge in third-party applications and has been improved to offer full multimedia support. Currently Blackberry's App World has over 15,000 downloadable applications.

Windows Mobile from Microsoft (2.8% Market Share Sales Q3 2010)[7] [13] (closed source, proprietary)

The Windows CE operating system and Windows Mobile middleware are widely spread in Asia. The two improved variants of this operating system, Windows Mobile 6 Professional (for touch screen devices) and Windows Mobile 6 Standard, were unveiled in February 2007. It has been criticized for having a user interface which is not optimized for touch input by fingers; instead, it is more usable with a stylus. However, unlike iPhone OS, it does support both touch screen and physical keyboard configurations.

Windows Mobile's market share has sharply declined in recent years to just 5% in Q2 of 2010.[14] Microsoft is phasing out the Windows Mobile OS to specialized markets and is instead focusing on it's new platform, Windows Phone.

Windows Phone from Microsoft (negligible Market Share Sales in October 2010) (closed source, proprietary)

On February 15th, 2010 Microsoft unveiled its next-generation mobile OS, Windows Phone 7. The new mobile OS includes a completely new over-hauled UI inspired by Microsoft's "Metro Design Language". It includes full integration of Microsoft services such as Windows Live, Zune, Xbox Live and Bing, but also integrates with many other non-Microsoft services such as Facebook and Google accounts. The new OS platform has received some positive reception from the technology press.[15] [16] [17] As Windows Phone 7 is a new platform, there is no backwards compatibility with Windows Mobile applications and some power-user features that were in Windows Mobile will not be present until near-future updates.

Linux operating system (open source, GPL) (2.1% Market Share Sales Q3 2010, non-Android Linux-based OS's only)[7]

Linux is strongest in China where it is used by Motorola, and in Japan, used by DoCoMo.[18] [19] Rather than being a platform in its own right, Linux is used as a basis for a number of different platforms developed by several vendors, including Android, LiMo, Maemo, Openmoko and Qt Extended, which are mostly incompatible.[20] [21] PalmSource (now Access) is moving towards an interface running on Linux.[22] Another platform based on Linux is being developed by Motorola, NEC, NTT DoCoMo, Panasonic, Samsung, and Vodafone.[23]

The Palm Pre running HP (formerly Palm) webOS. HP purchased Palm in 2010.

Palm webOS from HP (certain parts open sourced) and Palm OS/Garnet OS from Access Co. (closed source, proprietary)

Palm webOS is Palm's next generation operating system. PalmSource traditionally used its own platform developed by Palm Inc. Access Linux Platform (ALP) is an improvement that was planned to be launched in the first half of 2007. It will use technical specifications from the Linux Phone Standards Forum. The Access Linux Platform will include an emulation layer to support applications developed for Palm-based devices.

bada from Samsung Electronics (closed source, proprietary)

This is a mobile operating system being developed by Samsung Electronics. Samsung claims that bada will rapidly replace its proprietary feature phone platform, converting feature phones to smartphones.The name 'bada' is derived from 바다, the Korean word for ocean or sea. The first device to run bada is called 'Wave' and was unveiled to the public at Mobile World Congress 2010. The Wave is a fully touchscreen phone running the new mobile operating system. With the phone, Samsung also released an app store, called Samsung Apps, to the public. It has close to 3000[24] mobile applications.

Samsung has said that they don't see Bada as a smartphone platform, but as a platform with a kernel configurable architecture, which allows the use of either proprietary Real-time operating system (RTOS) kernel, or the Linux kernel. Though Samsung plans to install bada on many phones, the company still has a large lineup of Android phones.

MeeGo from Nokia and Intel (open source, GPL)

At the 2010 Mobile World Congress in Barcelona, Nokia and Intel both unveiled 'MeeGo' a brand new mobile operating system which would combine the best of Moblin and the best of Maemo to create a truly open-sourced experience for users across all devices. As of 2011, Nokia has announced that it will no longer be pursuing MeeGo and will instead adopt Windows Phone 7 as its primary mobile OS.

Maemo from Nokia (open source, GPL)

Maemo is a software platform developed by Nokia for smartphones and Internet Tablets. It is based on the Debian operating system.

Maemo is mostly based on open source code, and has been developed by Maemo Devices within Nokia in collaboration with many open source projects such as the Linux kernel, Debian and GNOME.

Maemo is based on Debian GNU/Linux and draws much of its GUI, frameworks and libraries from the GNOME project. It uses the Matchbox window manager and the GTK-based Hildon as its GUI and application framework.

Limo

Brew OS from Qualcomm

Brew OS is used by a some mobile phone manufacturers and mobile networks, however most often the end-user does not know this since mobile phones running Brew most often lack any Brew OS branding and Brew runs in the background with the custom "skins" of the mobile phone manufacturer or operator on-top. Brew OS is used by Sprint Nextel, metroPCS, U.S. Cellular and Verizon in the US and by the Three network in much of Europe, the UK and Australia on many mobile phones produced especially for their network. Manufacturers such as Huawei, INQ Mobile, Amoi Samsung Mobile amongst others use Brew OS in some of their mobile phones and it is featured in Three UK phones such as the 3 Skypephone, INQ1 and Huawei u7510 (3 Touch). A few HTC mobile phone use this platform, for example is HTC Freestyle.

## Market share by OS

| Source | Year | Symbian | Android | RIM | iOS | Microsoft | Other OSs |
|---|---|---|---|---|---|---|---|
| Gartner [25] | 2010 | 37.6% | 22.7% | 16.0% | 15.7% | 4.2% | 3.8% |
| Gartner [25] [26] | 2009 | 46.9% | 3.9% | 19.9% | 14.4% | 8.7% | 6.1% |
| Gartner [26] [27] | 2008 | 52.4% | 0.5% | 16.6% | 8.2% | 11.8% | 10.5% |
| Gartner [27] | 2007 | 63.5% | N/A | 9.6% | 2.7% | 12.0% | 12.1% |

# Smartphone OS comparison

Only the latest versions are shown in this table, even though old versions may still be marketed.

| re | iOS | Android | webOS | Windows Mobile | Windows Phone | BlackBerry OS | Symbian | Maemo | MeeGo | Bada |
|---|---|---|---|---|---|---|---|---|---|---|
| | Apple | Open Handset Alliance(Google) | HP/Palm, Inc | Microsoft | Microsoft | RIM | Symbian Foundation | Nokia | Linux Foundation | Samsung |
| rsion | 4.3.3 | 3.0.1 | 2.* | 6.5.3 | 7.0.7390.0 | 6.0.0 | 9.5 | 5.0 | 1.1.2 | 1.2 |
| | Mac OS X/Unix-like | Linux | Linux | Windows CE 5.2 | Windows CE 7 | Mobile OS | Mobile OS | Linux | Linux | Linux |
| CPU e | ARM | ARM, MIPS, Power Architecture, x86 | ARM | ARM | ARM | ARM | ARM | ARM | ARM, x86 | ARM |
| d in | C, C++, Objective-C | C, C++, Java | C | C++ | Many[28], .NET (Silverlight/XNA) | Java | C++ | C/C++ | C++ | C++ |
| | Proprietary EULA except for open source components | Free and open source (Android 2.3.4) and closed source (Android 3.0.1) | Free and open source except closed source modules | Proprietary | Proprietary | Proprietary | Eclipse Public License | Free and open source except closed source components | Free and open source | Proprietary |
| es list | No, but there is a unofficial tracker[29] | Yes[30] | No | No | No, but there is a unofficial collection[31] | No | Not anymore[32] | Yes[33] | Yes[34] | No |

| Package manager | iTunes | APK | Preware (3rd party homebrew) | Windows Mobile Device Center/ActiveSync | Zune Software | Blackberry Desktop Manager | Nokia Ovi Suite | dpkg+apt-get | rpm+yum+zypper |
|---|---|---|---|---|---|---|---|---|---|
| Multi-user | No[35] | No[36] | No | ? | ? | ? | ? | ? | ? |
| Per application runtime modifiable permissions | Only location access[37] | No[38] | ? | ? | No[39] | ? | ? | ? | ? |
| Non english languages support | Yes | Limited[40] | ? | Yes | Yes | Yes | Yes | Yes | Yes |
| Underlining spell checker | Yes[41] | No[42] | No | ? | Yes[43] | Yes | Yes | Yes | ? |
| Keeps browser state on shutdown or crash | Yes | Limited[44] | No | No | Yes | ? | ? | Yes | ? |
| Search multiple internal applications at once | Yes | Calendar has no search[45] | Yes | Yes | No[46] | Yes | Yes | Yes | ? |
| Search all fields of internal objects | iOS will not search Contacts notes field[47] | Only search Contacts name field but not any other field[48] | Yes | Yes | Contacts are only search by name[49] | Limited on most models[50] | Yes | Yes | ? |
| Proxy server | Yes | No[51] | No[52] | Yes | Yes | Yes | Yes | Yes | ? |
| On-device encryption | Yes[53] | No[54] | No | Yes[55] | No[56] | Yes[57] | ? | Yes | ? |
| Sync to Cloud communication encryption | Yes[58] | No[59] | ? | ? | ? | Yes[60] | ? | Yes, with 3rd party apps | ? |
| Desktop Sync | Yes | No[61] | No[62] | Yes | No[63] | Yes | Yes | Yes[64] | Yes |
| cut, copy, and paste | Yes[65] | Yes[66] | Yes | Yes | Yes[67] [68] | Yes | Yes | Yes | ? |
| undo | Yes[70] | No[71] | Limited | Yes (via Ctrl+Z using default keyboard | No | No | ? | Yes | ? |
| Phone number linking to dialer | Yes | No[72] | Yes | Yes (but not in browser) | Yes | Yes | No | Yes | ? |
| Default Web Browser/Engine | Webkit | Webkit | Webkit | Trident | Trident | Webkit | Webkit | Gecko | Webkit |
| Browser Save Page | No | No[73] | No | ? | No | ? | ? | ? | ? |

| | | | | | | | | | | |
|---|---|---|---|---|---|---|---|---|---|---|
| t | No[74] | Yes | No[75] | ? | No | ? | No | ? | ? | No |
| | No[76] | Yes[77] | ? | ? | Yes | Yes | Yes | ? | ? | Yes |
| Store | App Store | Android Market | App Catalog | Windows Marketplace for Mobile | Windows Phone Marketplace | App World | Symbian Horizon,Ovi store | maemo.org,Ovi store | ? | Samsung Apps |
| inatory | Apple discriminates based on country[78] and own Apple policies[79] | ? | Discriminates by country[80] | ? | ? | ? | ? | ? | ? | ? |
| x | Yes | No[81] | Yes | Yes | No[46] | Yes | Yes | ? | ? | Yes |
| | POP3, IMAP, MAPI | POP3, IMAP, MAPI | POP3, IMAP, MAPI | POP3, IMAP, MAPI | POP3, IMAP, MAPI | BES, BIS, Push e-mail | POP3, IMAP | POP3, IMAP, Exchange | POP3, IMAP | POP3, IMAP |
| e s | No[82] | Yes | Yes | ? | Yes[83] | ? | ? | ? | ? | ? |
| ations | Yes Apple Push Notification Service | Yes[84] | Yes | ? | Yes[85] | Yes | Yes | | | Yes |
| gtones | Yes | Yes | Yes | Yes | With Mango update[86] | Yes | Yes | Yes, with 3rd party apps[87] | ? | Yes |
| gnition | Only simple voice commands | Yes[88] | Yes (in version 2.1 or higher) | Yes | Yes | Yes | Yes | | Yes | |
| rder | Limited(Not voice controlled) | Very Limited(Does not work in background[89] and not voice controlled) | 3rd party apps available | ? | 3rd party and Very Limited(Does not work in background and not voice controlled) | Very Limited(Does not work in background and not voice controlled) | ? | Yes, with 3rd party apps[90] | ? | ? |
| er | Prevented by OS restrictions | Prevented by OS restrictions[91] | ? | Yes[92] | No | ? | Yes | Yes, with 3rd party apps[93] | ? | ? |
| tter | In silence mode[94] | In silence mode[95] | In silent mode | ? | No[96] | ? | ? | ? | ? | ? |
| | No | Yes | via 3rd party apps | ? | No | ? | ? | Yes | ? | Yes |
| | Yes | No[97] | Yes | ? | No | ? | ? | ? | ? | Yes |
| | Yes | No[98] | ? | ? | No sound recorder | ? | ? | ? | ? | ? |

| Tethering | Bluetooth, USB (carrier dependent), Personal Hotspot (Wi-Fi Tethering) (carrier dependent, since iOS 4.2.5/4.3 (iPhone only) or with 3rd party software and "jail break") | Mobile Wi-Fi Hotspot, USB, Bluetooth | Mobile Wi-Fi Hotspot (officially Verizon Wireless only) | USB, Bluetooth, Mobile Wi-Fi Hotspot (with 3rd party software) | Not officially, supported through homebrew[99] [100] | USB, Bluetooth, Mobile Wi-Fi Hotspot | USB, Bluetooth, Mobile Wi-Fi Hotspot (with 3rd party software | microUSB, Bluetooth, Mobile Wi-Fi Hotspot | |
|---|---|---|---|---|---|---|---|---|---|
| USB On-The-Go | No[101] | No[102] | ? | ? | No | ? | Yes[103] | ? | ? |
| Text/Document Support | Read only: Microsoft Office, iWork, PDF, Images, TXT/RTF, VCF | | Microsoft Office, PDF | Microsoft Office Mobile, PDF | Microsoft Office Mobile, PDF | Microsoft Office, PDF | Microsoft Office Mobile, PDF,djvu | text files, PDF, HTML, Multiple office formats with free 3rd party software | |
| Audio Playback | AAC (8 to 320 Kbps), Protected AAC (from iTunes Store), HE-AAC, MP3 (8 to 320 Kbps), MP3 VBR, Apple Lossless, AIFF, WAV | AAC LC/LTP 3GPP, HE-AACv1 (AAC+), HE-AACv2 (enhanced AAC+), AMR-NB, AMR-WB, MP3 (Mono/Stereo 8-320 kbit/s constant or variable bit-rate, MIDI (MIDI Type 0 and 1. DLS Version 1 and 2., Ogg Vorbis, PCM/WAVE (8- and 16-bit linear PCM (rates up to limit of hardware), WAVE [104] | MP3, AAC, AAC+, AMR, QCELP, WAV | | MP3, AAC, AAC+, eAAC+, WAV, WMA pro, AMR-NB, MIDI | MP3, WAVE, WMA, AAC+, MIDI, AMR, eAAC+, FIAC, OGG | All | All (some require optional debian packages) | |
| Video Playback | H.264 AVC, MPEG-4, M-JPEG | H.263, H.264 AVC, MPEG-4 SP, DivX, XviD, VP8 [104] | MPEG-4, H.263, H.264 | | H.263, H.264, WMV, MPEG4, MPEG4@ HD 720p 30fps, DivX, XviD | MP4, WMV, H.263, H.264, DivX, WMV, XviD, 3gp | H.263, H.264, WMV, MPEG4, MPEG4@ HD 720p 30fps, MKV, DivX, XviD | All (some require optional debian packages) | |
| Media Player Fine Scrubbing | Yes[105] | No[106], but there are 3rd party apps[107] | No | ? | No | ? | ? | ? | ? |
| Media Player Double Speed Playing | Yes[108] | No[109] | ? | ? | No | ? | ? | ? | ? |

| n GPS | 3rd Party software | Google Maps Navigation (will not work with limited phone coverage)[110] or 3rd Party software | Carrier software, 3rd Party Software | 3rd Party Software | 3rd Party software[111] | 3rd Party Software | 3rd Party Software, free global Nokia Ovi Maps | 3rd Party Software, Nokia Ovi Maps | | Samsung LBS (Route 66)) |
|---|---|---|---|---|---|---|---|---|---|---|
| | VGA, up to 576p,480p | 1080p on select devices | No | | Play To[112] | None | Nokia AV Out (PAL/NTSC), HDMI | Nokia AV Out (PAL/NTSC) | | DLNA |
| g | Limited[113] | Yes | Yes | Yes | Tombstoning[114] | Yes | Yes | Yes | Yes | Limited |
| eractive | No | Yes | No | Yes | Yes (through "live tiles") | No | Yes | Yes | Yes | Yes |
| | Yes[115] | Yes, third party software[116] | Yes (in version 2.0 or higher) | Yes | No[117] | Yes | Yes | Yes, with plugins | ? | ? |
| rence camera | Yes (Currently iPhone 4 and iPod Touch 4 Only) | Yes (Hardware Currently Available on Some Models) | Yes (Pre3 and TouchPad only) | No | ? | Yes | Yes | Yes | Yes | Yes |
| le | No[118] | Yes[119] | No | Yes | No[99] | Yes | Yes | Yes | Yes | ? |
| IP | 3rd Party (like Skype) | 3rd Party (like Skype) | No[120] | 3rd party (like fring) | With Mango update[121] | 3rd party[122] | Yes (SIP) or 3rd Party (like Skype) | Yes (SIP)[123] | ? | No[124] |
| | Jailbreaking Required and OpenSSH Installed (free from Cydia Application) | Yes | Homebrew required | No | No | Yes | ? | Yes | Yes | ? |
| | ? | ? | ? | Remote Desktop | ? | Yes | Yes(3rd Party Software) | Yes | Yes | ? |
| P | Yes[125] | No[126] | ? | ? | ? | ? | ? | ? | ? | ? |
| me | ? | ? | ? | ? | ? | ? | ? | Yes | Yes | ? |
| | Yes[127] | Jailbreak required and 3rd-party apps[128] [129] | Yes | Yes[130] | With Mango update[131] Possible through homebrew or SDK.[132] [133] | Yes (3rd Party Software) | Yes[134] | Yes | ? | Yes |
| erated | Yes | Yes (Released in Honeycomb)[135] | ? | No | Yes[136] | ? | Yes | Yes | ? | ? |
| K | Mac OS X | Multiplatform[137] | Multiplatform | Windows | Windows | Windows | Windows/Multiplatform (Qt) | GNU/Linux[138] | GNU/Linux | Windows |
| **re** | **iOS** | **Android** | **webOS** | **Windows Mobile** | **Windows Phone 7** | **BlackBerry OS** | **Symbian** | **Maemo** | **MeeGo** | **Bada** |

## Featurephone operating systems

Common operating systems for feature phones include Nokia OS with user interfaces S30 or S40.[139] S40 offers APIs for Java ME.[139]

## References


[1] Can Mac OS X succeed as a mobile platform? (http://blogs.computerworld.com/node/4407) 2007-01-22

[2] Google Enters the Wireless World (http://www.nytimes.com/2007/11/05/technology/05cnd-gphone.html?ex=1352005200&en=d7a169e184415788&ei=5088&partner=rssnyt&emc=rss)

[3] Breakin' up is hard to do: Schmidt leaves Apple board (http://arstechnica.com/apple/news/2009/08/breakin-up-is-hard-to-do-schmidt-leaves-apple-board.ars)

[4] Mobile market up, smartphones up, Android and iPhone way up (http://arstechnica.com/gadgets/news/2010/05/mobile-market-up-smartphones-up-iphone-and-android-way-up-1.ars)

[5] Android tops everyone in 2010 market share; 2011 may be different (http://arstechnica.com/gadgets/news/2011/01/android-beats-nokia-apple-rim-in-2010-but-firm-warns-about-2011.ars)

[6] http://www.canalys.com/pr/2011/r2011013.html

[7] "Gartner Says Worldwide Mobile Phone Sales Grew 35 Percent in Third Quarter 2010; Smartphone Sales Increased 96 Percent" (http://www.gartner.com/it/page.jsp?id=1466313). Gartner, Inc. 2010-11-10. Table 2. . Retrieved 2011-02-21.

[8] North American Market (http://uk.theinquirer.net/?article=35179)

[9] Symbian Shareholders (http://www.symbian.com/about/overview/ownership/ownership.html)

[10] Symbian Facts (http://www.symbian.com/about/fastfacts/fastfacts.html)

[11] http://www.openhandsetalliance.com/oha_members.html

[12] http://www.pcworld.com/businesscenter/article/146450/developers_praise_android_at_google_io.html?tk=rl_noinform

[13] "CEO Ballmer Reportedly Says Microsoft 'Screwed Up' with Windows Mobile" (http://www.eweek.com/c/a/Windows/Microsoft-CEO-Steve-Ballmer-Says-Company-Screwed-Up-Windows-Mobile-241614/). *eWeek*. 28 September 2009. .

[14] (http://www.appleinsider.com/articles/10/09/16/iphone_drops_to_23_8_smartphone_market_share_android_jumps_to_17.html)

[15] http://www.engadget.com/2010/02/15/windows-phone-7-series-is-official-and-microsoft-is-playing-to/

[16] http://gizmodo.com/5471805/windows-phone-7-series-everything-is-different-now

[17] http://www.crunchgear.com/2010/02/15/windows-phone-7-series-our-take/

[18] Shipping Linux-based Phones at *Technology News Daily* (http://www.technologynewsdaily.com/node/3904)

[19] Microsoft Excluded from DoCoMo at *The Register* (http://www.theregister.co.uk/2004/11/26/microsoft_excluded_from_docomo/)

[20] Incompatibility in Mobile Linux at *OS News* (http://www.osnews.com/story.php/15040/Editorial-The-Chaos-of-Incompatibility-in-Mobile-Linux)

[21] Search Mobile Computing (http://searchmobilecomputing.techtarget.com/originalContent/0,289142,sid40_gci1218922,00.html)

[22] Running on Linux (http://news.com.com/Can+Linux+save+the+Palm+OS/2008-1045_3-6110042.html)

[23] Motorola Press Release on Partnership on Linux Platform (http://www.motorola.com/mediacenter/news/detail.jsp?globalObjectId=6872_6826_23)

[24] Samsung s8530 Wave II review (http://www.gsmarena.com/samsung_s8530_wave_ii-review-538p7.php)

[25] "Gartner Says Worldwide Mobile Device Sales to End Users Reached 1.6 Billion Units in 2010; Smartphone Sales Grew 72 Percent in 2010" (http://www.gartner.com/it/page.jsp?id=1543014). Gartner, Inc. 2011-02-09. Table 2. . Retrieved 2011-02-16.

[26] "Gartner Says Worldwide Mobile Phone Sales to End Users Grew 8 Per Cent in Fourth Quarter 2009; Market Remained Flat in 2009" (http://www.gartner.com/it/page.jsp?id=1306513). Gartner, Inc. 2010-02-23. Table 2. . Retrieved 2011-02-16.

[27] "Gartner Says Worldwide Smartphone Sales Reached Its Lowest Growth Rate With 3.7 Per Cent Increase in Fourth Quarter of 2008" (http://www.gartner.com/it/page.jsp?id=910112). Gartner, Inc. 2009-03-11. Table 4. . Retrieved 2011-02-16.

[28] List_of_CLI_languages .Net CLI Languages

[29] PleaseFixTheiPhone (http://pleasefixtheiphone.com/)

[30] Android Issues Tracker (http://code.google.com/p/android/issues/list)

[31] The WP7 list of BUGS' Thread (or design inconsistencies) NoDo fixed almost None! (http://forum.xda-developers.com/showthread.php?t=836373)

[32] Symbian Foundation is completing its transition to a licensing body (http://blog.symbian.org/2010/12/17/symbian-foundation-is-completing-its-transition-to-a-licensing-body/)

[33] Maemo Issues Tracker (https://bugs.maemo.org/)

[34] MeeGo Issues Tracker (http://meego.com/community/bug-tracking)

[35] Does the iPad support multiple users? (http://www.theipadguide.com/faq/does-ipad-support-multiple-users)

[36] Android Issue 15030: Multi user support (http://code.google.com/p/android/issues/detail?id=15030)

[37] iOS 4 New Features: New Location Services settings (http://www.youtube.com/watch?v=XH0kvnFEi_0)

[38] Android Issue 3778: Feature request: Application permissions should be individually grantable by the user (http://code.google.com/p/android/issues/detail?id=3778)

[39] Zune Marketplace requires user-confirmed permissions, similar to Android (http://windowsphone7central.com/news/zune_marketplace_requires_userconfirmed_permissions_similar_to_android-10-11-10.php)
[40] Android Issue 3732: Search Improve contact search (http://code.google.com/p/android/issues/detail?id=3732) Android Issue 3393: No Unicode support on SMS sending (http://code.google.com/p/android/issues/detail?id=3393) Android Issue 9199: SQLite3 Unicode Case not working (only ASCII case works) (include ICU support) (http://code.google.com/p/android/issues/detail?id=9199)
[41] iOS 4 features: Spell-check and text replace (http://www.tipb.com/2010/07/13/ios-4-features-spellcheck-text-replace/)
[42] Android Issue 10332: Retrospective spell checking on all input fields as an OS feature (input device agnostic) (http://code.google.com/p/android/issues/detail?id=10332)
[43] http://www.engadget.com/2010/10/20/windows-phone-7-review/
[44] Android Issue 8880: Keep open URLs/windows on shutdown or crash (http://code.google.com/p/android/issues/detail?id=8880)
[45] Android Issue 2518: Calendar app has no search. (http://code.google.com/p/android/issues/detail?id=2518)
[46] Bonnie Cha (27 October 2010). "Top 5 things I dislike about Windows Phone 7" (http://www.cnet.com/8301-17918_1-20020922-85.html). CNET. .
[47] iOS will not search Contacts notes field (http://discussions.apple.com/message.jspa?messageID=12439417)
[48] Android Issue 3732: Only search Contacts name field but not any other field (http://code.google.com/p/android/issues/detail?id=3732)
[49] WP7 on HTC Mozart - Unable to search for additional Contact fields - by design or bug? (http://social.answers.microsoft.com/Forums/en-US/windowsphone7/thread/b29e7b1a-c870-4061-bad7-9669187a465f)
[50] Notes search not available in BB Torch (http://supportforums.blackberry.com/t5/BlackBerry-Torch-9800-smartphone/Notes-search-not-available-in-BB-Torch/m-p/675645)
[51] Android Issue 1273: IP Proxy Settings for Wifi Network (http://code.google.com/p/android/issues/detail?id=1273)
[52] webOS Software : No proxy support when using WiFi on Pre (http://forums.palm.com/t5/webOS-Software/No-proxy-support-when-using-WiFi-on-Pre/td-p/208059)
[53] iOS 4: Understanding data protection (http://support.apple.com/kb/HT4175)
[54] Android Issue 3748: Add support for partition/block device encryption (http://code.google.com/p/android/issues/detail?id=3748) Android Issue 11211: Android too insecure - Encryption of the SDcard is crucial (http://code.google.com/p/android/issues/detail?id=11211)
[55] Microsoft Windows Mobile encryption (http://msdn.microsoft.com/en-us/library/bb416357.aspx)
[56] Galen Gruman (8 November 2010). "Windows Phone 7 lacks on-device encryption" (http://www.infoworld.com/d/mobilize/windows-phone-7-lacks-device-encryption-585). *InfoWorld*. .
[57] BlackBerry Stored Data Security (http://us.blackberry.com/ataglance/security/features.jsp#tab_tab_stored_data)
[58] Apple - iPhone in Business - Integration (http://www.apple.com/iphone/business/integration/)
[59] Android Sync Communication is not encrypted (http://android.stackexchange.com/questions/3129/what-android-syncd-data-is-encrypted)
[60] Standard BlackBerry encryption (http://docs.blackberry.com/en/admin/deliverables/12873/Standard_BlackBerry_message_encryption_193608_11.jsp)
[61] Android Issue 66: OpenSync desktop synchronisation support (http://code.google.com/p/secrets-for-android/issues/detail?id=66)
[62] Palm needs to develop a Palm Pre desktop sync application. (http://forums.palm.com/t5/Synergy-webOS/Palm-needs-to-develop-a-Palm-Pre-desktop-sync-application/td-p/209510)
[63] How to Sync Windows Phone 7 with Outlook (http://pocketnow.com/windows-phone/how-to-sync-windows-phone-7-with-outlook)
[64] Maemo Sync (http://wiki.maemo.org/Sync)
[65] Nilay Patel (2009-03-17). "iPhone finally gets copy and paste!" (http://www.engadget.com/2009/03/17/iphone-finally-gets-copy-and-paste/). *Engadget*. .
[66] Android Issue 3190: Improve copy-paste in Browser/WebView (http://code.google.com/p/android/issues/detail?id=3190)
[67] Microsoft's Windows Phone 7 'NoDo' update starts rolling out, brings copy / paste and other fun additions (http://www.engadget.com/2011/03/22/microsofts-windows-phone-7-nodo-update-starts-rolling-out-br/)
[68] http://www.engadget.com/2010/10/11/copy-and-paste-coming-to-windows-phone-7-in-early-2011/
[69] Does Bada OS have Cut, Copy & Paste? (http://forum2.mobile-review.com/showthread.php?t=92645)
[70] Phat^Trance (2009-05-23). "iPhone: Undo Typing – Cool feature in iPhone 3.0" (http://dailymobile.se/2009/05/23/iphone-undo-typing-nice-feature-in-iphone-30/). dailymobile. .
[71] Android Issue 6458: Enhancement: Undo (http://code.google.com/p/android/issues/detail?id=6458)
[72] Android Issue 4575: Phone number linking to dialer (http://code.google.com/p/android/issues/detail?id=4575)
[73] Android Issue 6399: Save current web page (http://code.google.com/p/android/issues/detail?id=6399)
[74] Safari for iOS needs a text size preference and text reflow (http://www.456bereastreet.com/archive/201101/safari_for_ios_needs_a_text_size_preference_and_text_reflow/)
[75] Palm, please add Text Reflow to the Web Browser (http://forums.precentral.net/palm-pre/253307-palm-please-add-text-reflow-web-browser.html)
[76] Uploading files using HTML file input on iphone (http://stackoverflow.com/questions/1577003/uploading-files-using-html-file-input-on-iphone)
[77] Android Issue 2519: Browser should support file uploads (input type="file") (http://code.google.com/p/android/issues/detail?id=2519)

[78] iphone - How to change the language of the App store (and iTunes)? - Apple - Stack Exchange (http://apple.stackexchange.com/questions/3897/how-to-change-the-language-of-the-app-store-and-itunes)
[79] Apple Releases Its Rules for App Store Censoring (http://www.campusprogress.org/articles/apple_releases_its_rules_for_app_store_censoring/)
[80] webOS Billing countries (http://forum.xda-developers.com/archive/index.php/t-990047.html)
[81] Android Issue 8261: Unified Inbox (Gmail & other mailboxes in 1 place) (http://code.google.com/p/android/issues/detail?id=8261)
[82] iOS vs Android vs WebOS: Who's Doing Mobile Notifications Right? (http://www.tested.com/news/ios-vs-android-vs-webos-whos-doing-mobile-notifications-right/1918/)
[83] http://www.anandtech.com/print/3982
[84] Android Cloud To Device Messaging (http://android-developers.blogspot.com/2010/05/android-cloud-to-device-messaging.html)
[85] Push Notifications for Windows Phone (http://msdn.microsoft.com/en-us/library/ff402537(v=vs.92).aspx)
[86] http://pocketnow.com/windows-phone/seven-great-new-features-of-mango-for-windows-phone-7
[87] Maemo Custom ringtones for your contacts (http://maemo.org/packages/view/per-contact-ringtones/)
[88] Android does not natively support voice commands, but Google provides a cloud based closed source implementation ( Voice Actions for Android (http://www.google.com/mobile/voice-actions/index.html)) that will only work when online Android Issue 11062: Offline voice commands for opening apps, controlling music player, and making calls (http://code.google.com/p/android/issues/detail?id=11062)
[89] Android Issue 14462: Sound Recorder does not work on background (http://code.google.com/p/android/issues/detail?id=14462)
[90] Maemo Recorder (http://maemo.org/downloads/product/Maemo5/recorder/)
[91] Android Issue 2117: Enhancement: Call Recorder (http://code.google.com/p/android/issues/detail?id=2117)
[92] Two-Way In Call Recording on Windows Mobile (http://www.brighthub.com/mobile/windows-mobile-platform/articles/30136.aspx)
[93] Maemo Recorder (http://maemo.org/downloads/product/Maemo5/recorder/)
[94] Apple Support Communities > iPhone > iPhone Hardware > Discussions > Shutter noise (https://discussions.apple.com/thread/2496491)
[95] Android Issue 9854: Cannot disable shutter sound (http://code.google.com/p/android/issues/detail?id=9854)
[96] Disabling the shutter sound in Windows Phone 7 (http://windowsphone7central.com/news/disabling_the_shutter_sound_in_windows_phone_7-02-11-11.php)
[97] Android Issue 9507: Basic video editor (at least time trim and split) (http://code.google.com/p/android/issues/detail?id=9507)
[98] Android Issue 14553: Basic sound editor (at least time trim and split) (http://code.google.com/p/android/issues/detail?id=14553)
[99] "Windows Phone 7 OS review: From scratch" (http://www.gsmarena.com/windows_phone_7-review-521.php). *GSM Arena*. 8 October 2010. .
[100] http://wmpoweruser.com/hackstethering-come-to-htc-wp7-handsets-htc-hub-comes-to-all-other-wp7-devices/
[101] Nokia N8 vs iPhone 4 – Ten Things Why Nokia N8 Is Better (http://symbianworld.org/5003-nokia-n8-vs-iphone-4â��ten-things-why-nokia-n8-is-better/)
[102] Android Issue 738: I hope Android will implement and support the USB host feature (http://code.google.com/p/android/issues/detail?id=738)
[103] Nokia N8's USB On-The-Go support demoed, lesser phones turned into slaves (http://www.engadget.com/2010/05/30/nokia-n8s-usb-on-the-go-support-demoed-lesser-phones-turned-in/)
[104] Android Core Media Formats (http://developer.android.com/guide/appendix/media-formats.html#core)
[105] iOS has fine scrubbing (http://www.youtube.com/watch?v=klRDYXutEWA#t=03m11s)
[106] Android Issue 15505: Media player fine scrubbing (swipe to seek) (http://code.google.com/p/android/issues/detail?id=15505)
[107] Meridian Player (http://www.androidtapp.com/meridian-player/)
[108] Listen to podcasts in half the time (http://www.nevsblog.com/2006/06/23/listen-to-podcasts-in-half-the-time/)
[109] Android Issue 1961: MediaPlayer Adjustable SampleRate/Playback Speed support (http://code.google.com/p/android/issues/detail?id=1961)
[110] Android Issue 4471: Downloadable maps for offline navigation/location (http://code.google.com/p/android/issues/detail?id=4471)
[111] http://mobilitydigest.com/turn-by-turn-directions-comes-to-windows-phone-via-a-to-b-free/
[112] http://www.engadget.com/2010/10/22/lg-optimus-7-review/
[113] http://www.maximumpc.com/article/features/smartphone_face-_ios_vs_android_vs_blackberry_vs_maemo
[114] http://blogs.microsoft.co.il/blogs/alex_golesh/archive/2010/07/14/silverlight-for-windows-phone-7-tombstoning.aspx
[115] Finally, Bluetooth keyboard support for the iPhone (http://www.mobilecrunch.com/2010/04/08/finally-bluetooth-keyboard-support-for-the-iphone/)
[116] KeyPro - Bluetooth keyboard manager (http://www.mymobilegear.com/AndroidKBDriver.php), 12/09/09
[117] Bluetooth Keyboards On Windows Phone 7 (http://gadgetix.com/2010/12/31/bluetooth-keyboards-on-windows-phone-7/)
[118] Apple Support Communities > Peripherals > Bluetooth > Discussions > Bluetooth file transfer (https://discussions.apple.com/message/13009289?messageID=13009289)
[119] Android Issue 1725: Bluetooth File Transfer (http://code.google.com/p/android/issues/detail?id=1725)
[120] Regarding VoIP client (SIP) implementation on Palm webOS (https://developer.palm.com/distribution/viewtopic.php?f=21&t=7879)
[121] http://www.engadget.com/2011/04/13/microsofts-joe-belfiore-confirms-skype-coming-to-windows-phone/
[122] The Best BlackBerry VoIP Apps & Services (http://www.voip-sol.com/the-best-blackberry-voip-apps-services/)
[123] Internet Communications Software Update for N800: Development version (http://rtcomm.garage.maemo.org/)

[124] bada VoIP applications finally allowed (http://www.joernesdohr.com/bada/bada-voip-applications-finally-allowed/)
[125] (http://manuals.info.apple.com/en_US/Enterprise_Deployment_Guide.pdf)
[126] Android Issue 1386: Feature req: support WPA2-Enterprise with EAP extensions (http://code.google.com/p/android/issues/detail?id=1386)
[127] Screenshot#iOS
[128] Android Issue 6547: Screen shots (http://code.google.com/p/android/issues/detail?id=6547)
[129] Screenshot-it (http://www.appbrain.com/app/screenshot-it/com.edwardkim.android.screenshotitfull)
[130] How to make Windows Mobile screenshots? (http://forum.xda-developers.com/showthread.php?t=363028)
[131] http://itsalltech.com/2011/04/13/microsoft-demoes-next-windows-phone-7-update-updates-on-app-numbers/
[132] Take a screenshot on Windows Phone 7 (http://superuser.com/questions/216092/take-a-screenshot-on-windows-phone-7)
[133] http://wmpoweruser.com/home-brew-delivers-againscreen-shot-functionality-arrive-on-the-htc-hd7/
[134] Screenshot for Symbian OS (http://www.antonypranata.com/screenshot)
[135] Stewart Mitchell, "Android lets developers work closer to the metal" (http://www.pcpro.co.uk/news/365215/android-lets-developers-work-closer-to-the-metal), *PC Pro*, 11/02/11
[136] http://www.anandtech.com/show/2969/windows-phone-7-series-the-anandtech-guide/13
[137] http://developer.android.com/sdk/index.html
[138] http://wiki.maemo.org/Documentation/Maemo_5_Final_SDK_Installation#Installing_Maemo_5_SDK_using_GUI_Installer
[139] http://www.forum.nokia.com/Technology_Topics/Device_Platforms/Series_40/

# External links

- Mobile Platform (http://www.mobileplatform.com/)
- Java ME (http://java.sun.com/javame/index.jsp)
- Intel Mobile Platform (http://softwarecommunity.intel.com/articles/eng/1331.htm)
- Android-based smartphone shipments leapfrog Apple's iPhone (http://www.appleinsider.com/articles/10/08/12/android_based_smartphone_shipments_leapfrog_apples_iphone.html)
- Qualcomm Uplinq Mobile OS Developer Conference (Annual) (http://www.uplinq.com/)

# Linaro

**Linaro**

| | |
|---|---|
| **Type** | Not-for-Profit |
| **Founded** | June 2010 |
| **Company** | ARM, Freescale, IBM, Samsung, ST-Ericsson, Texas Instruments |
| **Programmed In** | C, C++ |
| **OS Family** | Linux |
| **Working State** | Beta |
| **Initial Release** | 10 November 2010 (10.11) |
| **Target Markets** | Mobile, Mobile computing, Digital Home, Infotainment |
| **Supported Platforms** | ARMv7A |
| **Kernel Type** | Linux |
| **Website** | www.Linaro.org [1] |

**Linaro** is a not-for-profit (NFP) engineering organization that works on Linux-based open source software and tools which was announced at Computex in June 2010 by ARM, Freescale Semiconductor, IBM, Samsung, ST-Ericsson, and Texas Instruments in a joint press conference [1] . It also provides aligned engineering and investment in upstream open source projects, a six monthly release of tools and software[2] and support to silicon companies in upstreaming their system-on-a-chip (SoC) support.

Linaro focuses mostly on optimized open source support of the ARM v7A architecture, for example SoCs which contain a Cortex-A8 or dual-core Cortex-A9 processor(s). Engineering is planned in six month periods working in upstream projects on a set of requirements that are determined by the Technical Steering Committee [3] . At the end of each cycle there is a release of tools and software that acts as a staging tree for code that will be pushed upstream. Linaro works on software that is close to the silicon such as kernel, multimedia, power management, graphics and security. Linaro aims to provide stable, optimised and tested tools and code for multiple software distributions to use and hence reduce low level fragmentation and improve the optimisation of embedded Linux software[4] .

## History

In 2010 ARM joined with Freescale Semiconductor, IBM, Samsung, ST-Ericsson and Texas Instruments (TI) in forming a not for profit open source engineering company, Linaro [6], to enhance open source innovation for the next wave of always-connected, always-on computing[5] . In the first engineering cycle 10.11 (November 2010) Linaro has worked with the open source community on improving tools (GCC, Valgrind, OProfile) and kernel consolidation[6] . Multimedia and graphics working groups are planned for the second cycle. Canonical is using the Linaro GCC 4.5.2 branch for their latest Ubuntu builds (natty narwhal 11.04)[7] .

## Milestones

March 2010 – Company founded

- Membership agreements initiated
- Engineering begins

June 2010 – Company launch

- Website and wiki opened
- Engineering organization ramps
- Open engineering

November 2010 – First release

- Linaro's 10.11 release is announced at TechCon

## Release schedule

It was announced in June 2010 at Computex that Linaro would follow a six month engineering cycle that would culminate in a release of tools and software that represents an integrated build of software worked on during the cycle[8] . Linaro version 10.11 was released on November 10, 2010. Linaro's cycle almost coincides with Ubuntu.

## System requirements

Linaro is optimized to run on the ARMv7A Architecture which is implemented in SoCs such as TI's OMAP 3 and OMAP 4, Samsung's Orion processor, ST-Ericsson's U8500 and Freescale's i.MX51.

## Downloads

There are three types of software download available from Linaro:

1. At the end of each six month cycle Linaro release an integrated build including all the software worked on during the cycle. These images are available from releases.linaro.org [11].
2. There are monthly versions of upstream software, such as GCC or QEMU. These are downloads from places such as launchpad.net/gcc-linaro [12].
3. Linaro maintains public staging trees of upstream code they are working on. For example the kernel and u-boot trees are kept on git.linaro.org [13]; while others are kept under code.launchpad.net [14].

## License

All code developed within Linaro working groups is open source and therefore available under standard Open Source Initiative (OSI) license terms. For more details see Linaro Membership Rules [15] and Linaro Articles of Association [16].

## Core OS

Linaro is Linux-based and works with the open source community by providing aligned upstream engineering investment[9] .

## References

[1] http://www.dailytech.com/IBM+Freescale+Samsung+Form+Linaro+to+Aid+in+Developing+ARMcompatible+Software/article18611.htm Daily Tech 5 June 2010
[2] http://arstechnica.com/open-source/news/2010/06/linaro-nonprofit-aims-to-fight-arm-linux-fragmentation.ars ARS Technica 3 June 2010
[3] http://www.linaro.org/how-linaro-works/
[4] http://lwn.net/Articles/391189/lwn.net 9 June 2010
[5] http://www.geek.com/articles/chips/arm-ibm-and-other-industry-leaders-form-linaro-to-speed-roll-out-of-linux-based-devices-2010063/ Geek.com 3 June 2010
[6] http://chipdesignmag.com/sld/blog/2010/09/23/moving-to-open-source-software/Chip design magazine 5 October 2010
[7] http://packages.ubuntu.com/natty/devel/gcc Ubuntu -- Details of package GCC in natty
[8] http://www.dailytech.com/IBM+Freescale+Samsung+Form+Linaro+to+Aid+in+Developing+ARMcompatible+Software/article18611.htm Daily Tech 5 June 2010
[9] http://www.linaro.org/faqs/Linaro FAQs

## External links

- Linaro.org (http://www.linaro.org/)
- Linaro FAQ (http://www.linaro.org/faqs)
- Linaro Wiki (https://wiki.linaro.org/)
- Launch video (http://www.linaro.org/watch-the-announcement-of-linaro-at-computex/)

# Maemo

**Maemo**

maemo™

Screenshot of Maemo 5

| **Company / developer** | open source community Maemo organisation while Nokia is a primer company to help in it and use its OS. top user are NOKIA,OPTIMA,ZTE |
|---|---|
| **Programmed in** | C, C++ |
| **OS family** | Linux |
| **Working state** | working, and it is too a part of MeeGo for Internet tablets |
| **Source model** | Largely open source with mandatory proprietary components |
| **Latest stable release** | 5.0 PR1.3 / 25 October 2010 |
| **Available language(s)** | Multilingual |
| **Update method** | APT and Flashing |
| **Package manager** | dpkg |
| **Supported platforms** | ARM architecture |
| **Kernel type** | Monolithic (Linux) |
| **Default user interface** | Hildon UI |
| **Official website** | maemo.org [1] |

**Maemo** is a software platform developed by the Maemo community for smartphones and Internet tablets.[1] It is based on the Debian Linux distribution.

The platform comprises the Maemo operating system and the Maemo SDK.

Maemo is mostly based on open source code, and has been developed by Maemo Devices within Nokia in collaboration with many open source projects such as the Linux kernel, Debian, and GNOME. Maemo is based on Debian GNU/Linux and draws much of its GUI, frameworks, and libraries from the GNOME project. It uses the Matchbox window manager, and the GTK-based Hildon as its GUI and application framework.

The UI in Maemo 4 is similar to many handheld interfaces, and features a "home" screen, which acts as a central point from which all applications and settings are accessed. The home screen is divided into areas for launching applications, a menu bar, and a large customisable area that can display information such as an RSS reader, Internet radio player, and Google search box.

The Maemo 5 UI is slightly different: The menu bar and info area are consolidated to the top of the display, and the four desktops can be customized with shortcuts and widgets.

At the Mobile World Congress in February 2010, it was announced that the Maemo project would be merging with Moblin to create the MeeGo mobile software platform.

# User Interface

## OS2005–OS2008

Up to Maemo 4 (AKA OS2008), the default screen is the "Home" screen—the central point from which all applications and settings are accessed. The Home Screen is divided into the following areas:

- Vertically down the left hand side of the screen is the Taskbar, with applets for the web browser, communications, and application menu by default, but these can be modified using third party plugins (to provide a favorites menu, or a command menu, for example).
- Horizontally across the top left half is the menu bar, which shows the application name and window title and gives access to the application's menu (which contains the typical, File, Edit, View, Tools, etc., menus and submenus)
- Horizontally across the top right half is the status bar, containing icons such as battery life, wireless connection, volume, Bluetooth, and brightness by default, but these can be expanded using third party plugins in the same manner as the Taskbar.
- The remaining large part of the display contains Home applets (roughly analogous to Apple Inc.'s Dashboard widgets), which can display data as well as being a shortcut to applications. These include an RSS reader, Internet radio player, Google search box and contact list by default, but can also be expanded with third party plugins.

The interface uses either the touch screen, or a directional pad and select button, with separate back, menu, and home buttons. It is capable of two modes of text input: handwriting recognition, and two different sizes of onscreen keyboard, as well as hardware keyboard input with the N810.[2]

## Maemo 5 (Fremantle)

The UI in Maemo 5 has changed with respect to its predecessors. It provides four fully customizable (add/remove widgets, move widgets around, change the background, shortcut to applications/contacts) "Home" screens,[3] called Panorama Desktop.[4] Switching from one desktop to the others is done by sliding one's finger horizontally on the background. The dashboard is accessed via the upper left icon and shows all the running applications, in a manner similar to the Exposé feature in Apple's Mac OS X operating system. From the dashboard, running applications can be brought back to fullscreen by tapping the preview window or applications can be closed by tapping an X-symbol located in the top right corner of the preview window, similar to the concept of closing applications in other operating systems. The application launcher, where all the installed applications can be launched, can be accessed as well from the dashboard by tapping the same area again in the upper left corner of the screen which invokes the dashboard.[5] [6] If no task or application is running in the background, tapping the top left icon skips the dashboard and directly displays the application launcher.

Maemo provides the Mozilla-based MicroB web-browser with complete Adobe Flash support, which can operate over a wireless connection. It supports an 800x480 display resolution, so some web pages can be viewed without horizontal scrolling. It can automatically connect to known wireless networks and download RSS feeds and email and disconnect automatically without user intervention.[7]

Software is installed or uninstalled using the Application manager. The X Terminal can also be used to install applications using the "apt-get" command (Although this is discouraged for inexperienced users). Users can subscribe to different software repositories which can then be used to automatically keep software up to date. The Application manager also provides an overview of everything currently installed on the system. Data can be synchronized with a PC via a USB connection, and the users files can be accessed using the standard Removable Storage Device protocol.[7]

# Features

## Updating

Maemo devices can be updated using a simple flashing method with a computer over USB.

Since Diablo (Maemo 4.1), Maemo supports "Seamless Software Update" (SSU), which allows incremental operating system upgrades "over the air" using apt without the need for a full flash with every update.[8]

Flashing remains available as a way to start over from scratch with a clean install (much like formatting your hard drive and reinstalling your OS on a PC).[9]

## Security

The quick start guide for developers warns that Maemo security concentrates on preventing remote attacks (e.g. by wireless networking and Bluetooth). It also warns that Maemo's root account has a trivial default password (user: gainroot, password:rootme) which needs to be changed before enabling remote access.[10]

Maemo provides a numeric access code as a way to lock the device's controls and display independently of the root password; this has been done in order to help prevent unauthorised access.[11]

# Components

Maemo is a modified version of the Debian Linux distribution, slimmed down for mobile devices.[12] It uses an X Window System-based graphical user interface using Xomap and the Matchbox window manager; the GUI uses the GTK+ toolkit and Hildon user interface widgets and API.[13]

BusyBox, a software package for embedded and mobile devices, replaces the GNU Core Utilities used in Debian-proper to reduce memory usage and storage requirements (at the expense of some functionality).[14]

ESD is used as the primary sound server, and GStreamer is used by the shipped media player to play back sounds and movies. The formats supported by GStreamer can be extended by compiling GStreamer plugins in scratchbox (Maemo SDK), which was done, for example, to bring Ogg support to the platform,[15] as well as experimental features such as WebM and VP8 after they were announced by Google.[16] third-party party media players can access GStreamer directly or via "osso-media-server".

Window management is handled by the Matchbox window manager, which limits the screen to showing a single window at a time (Ubuntu Netbook Edition implements a similar system). This is to improve handheld usability on a mobile device with a small screen.

Although Maemo is based on Linux and open source software, some parts of Maemo remain closed source. These include some user-space software, like certain statusbar and taskbar applets (including the display brightness applet) and applications, and some system daemons related to connectivity and power management. [17]

## Software

Maemo comes with a number of built-in applications, but additional applications can be installed from a number of sources, including various official and community software repositories and deb files through either the built-in package manager "Application manager" or apt and dpkg.

Bundled applications include the Mozilla-based MicroB browser, Macromedia Flash, Gizmo5, and Skype.[18]

### Third-party applications

Due in part to the free and open source nature of Linux and Maemo, porting applications to Maemo is a straightforward procedure. Because of this, there are many third-party applications available for the platform. Some applications are original software written specifically for Maemo, while other applications are straight ports of existing Linux programs. Some notable software includes:

Media players

Canola (with network streaming), MPlayer

Internet

Claws Mail, Modest, Midori, Firefox for mobile

Office applications

Gnumeric (spreadsheet), Abiword (word processing)

Instant Messaging

Pidgin

VOIP

Gizmo5, Skype

Games

The Battle for Wesnoth, Wormux, Doom, Angry Birds

Others

FBReader (e-book reader), GPE (OpenSync compatible PIM), rdesktop (RDP remote access), Rhapsody (subscription music, US only), ScummVM (game emulator), Free42S (HP 42S calculator emulator), gPodder (podcast client), Maemo Mapper (includes GPS functionality), MaemoMyth (MythTV frontend that uses GMythStream), Monsoon HAVA (TV viewer and controller), Navit (GPS navigation software), Obscura Photo Manager, Palm Emulator from Access (ARM based Palm emulator), Phonelink (SMS and voice caller via BT), Quiver Image Viewer, SDict Viewer (sdict-based dictionary/encyclopedia viewer), Vagalume (Last.FM player), VNC, YouAmp (music player), LogMeIn Browser Plugin

Fremantle Stars

Applications developed by the community and supported by Nokia as Fremantle Stars will be part of Maemo 5.[19] Some notable applications: Mauku (micro-blogging client),[20] Maemo Mapper (map application),[21] Numpty Physics (game),[22] ScummVM (game, includes Beneath a Steel Sky),[23] Xournal (notes/sketch utility),[24] Fennec (web browser)[26], FBReader (e-book reader),[25] OSM2Go (OpenStreetMap editor)[26]

Debian

The complete ARM Debian distribution can be installed as a Maemo application.[27] , making thousands of software packages available (including OpenOffice.org, Mozilla Firefox, Java, the GNOME and LXDE desktops, etc.). Debian ARM packages can also be used if they are modified with the maemo-optify tool for example.[28] The ability to run largely-unmodified linux packages is the main difference compared to other *Linux based* mobile operating systems such as Android and webOS.

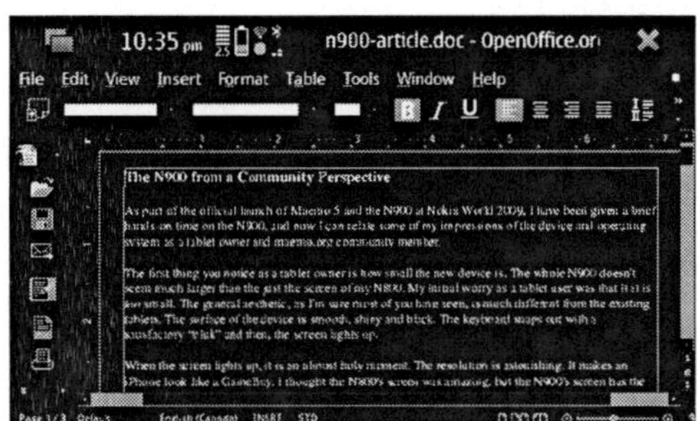

OpenOffice.org running on Maemo 5 using Easy Debian.

## Media support

Other media types, such as the audio format .OGG, can be added with the use of community plug-ins.

Video

MPEG-1, MPEG-4 ASP (H.263), RealVideo, AVI, 3GP

Audio/playlists

MP3, RealAudio, MPEG-4, AAC, WAV, AMP, MP2, AMR, AWB, M4A, WMA. OGG/Vorbis (requires addon package), M3U, PLS

Image/Animation

JPEG, BMP, TIFF, PNG, SVG Tiny, ICO

Text/layout

text files, PDF, HTML.

# Software development

Software can be developed in C using the Maemo SDK, in Java which is supported by the Jalimo JVM,[29] in Python, in Ruby, and Mono.

The Maemo SDK is based around the Debian-oriented Scratchbox Cross Compilation Toolkit, which provides a sandbox environment in which development may take place. Scratchbox uses Qemu to emulate an ARM processor or sbrsh to remotely execute instructions. Scratchbox-compatible rootstraps are available for both x86 and ARM, so the majority of development and debugging takes place on x86, with final packaging being for ARM.[30]

As a new feature to the Maemo operating system, Maemo 5 brings the Qt library as a community-supported component alongside the officially supported GTK+ backend. This is going to change with the Harmattan release which will bring in the Qt library as the default, GTK+ becoming community-supported.[31] The programming languages Python, C and C++ will also be supported.

The Forum Nokia Wiki has quality-controlled articles which support Qt development. The Maemo operating system has a development group at Forum Nokia Wiki Maemo.

## Hardware

The Maemo operating system is designed for Nokia Internet Tablets, which feature very similar specifications to Nokia's high-end N-series and E-series cellphones, with TI OMAP ARM SoCs, large screens, and expandable internal storage.[32] Although the highly optimized, hardware-specific nature of Maemo means running all of it on non-Internet Tablet hardware would be very difficult, most of the important non-proprietary parts of the OS and some of the available third-party party applications are actively being packaged for Debian and are available for use on other distributions, which will open up a large range of other hardware options.[33]

Nokia runs the Maemo operating system on the Nokia N900.

## Version history

### OS2005

Shipped with the 770 in November 2005, this is the original Internet Tablet OS. It came bundled with the Opera web browser, Flash 6, basic Email and RSS clients, audio and video players, PDF and image viewers, a graphical APT front-end (dubbed simply "Application manager"), and a variety of simple games and utilities.[34]

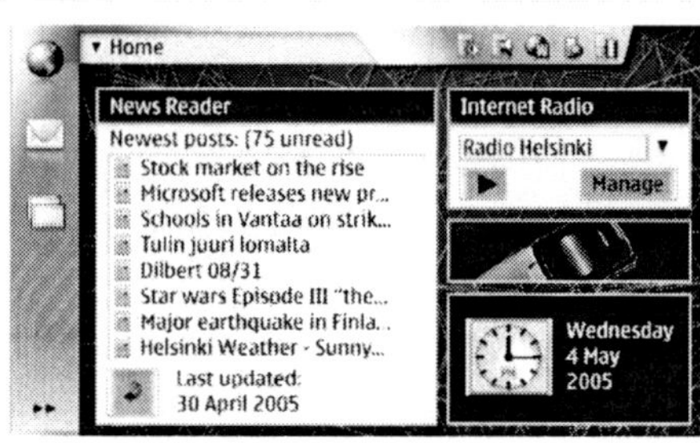

OS2005 Desktop

### OS2006

On May 16, 2006 Nokia announced a new version of Internet Tablet OS,[35] which was subsequentially released as a beta version for the 770 on June 9, 2006 and as a final on June 20, 2006.[36] The update featured improved performance and stability, a built-in Google Talk client, a refreshed look, and a new full-screen finger keyboard. Because of significant API and architecture changes, existing applications required recompiling. It is the last officially supported Internet Tablet OS release for the 770.

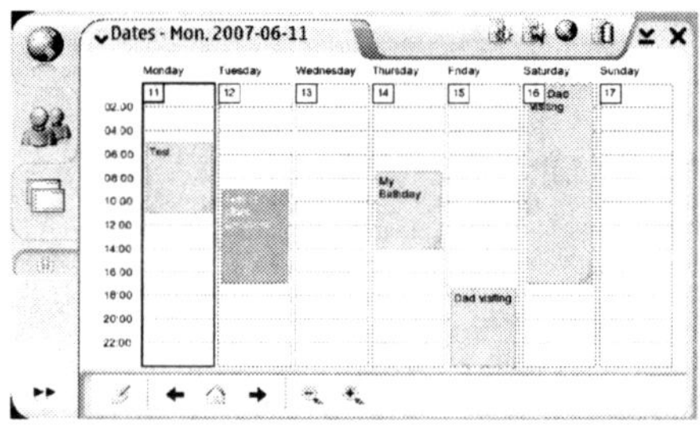

OS2006 showing Pimlico Dates

Also included was the ability to support 2 GB RS-MMC cards (formatted FAT). The Linux kernel was upgraded to 2.6.16 with the associated patches for the OMAP platform. This new version uses kernel preemption for improved interactivity.

## OS2007

OS2007 was released and bundled with the N800 on January 8, 2007 after its announcement at the Las Vegas CES 2007 summit. It featured significant bug fixes and performance improvements in almost all areas of the OS, bringing updated versions of Opera 8 and Flash 7, an updated interface and various API and library updates.

OS2007 Desktop showing OMWeather

## OS2008

OS2008 was released with the N810 in November 2007, based on Linux 2.6.21, and featuring MicroB, a new Mozilla-based web browser that replaces Opera, integrated Samba file sharing and additional support for Windows Media Player Formats and H.264, improved support for USB devices,[37] [38] among other incremental UI improvements (particularly in the direction of finger-friendliness).[39] Dynamic frequency scaling (between 165 MHz and 400 MHz) was also implemented, which gave the N800 a 70 MHz speed increase.[40]

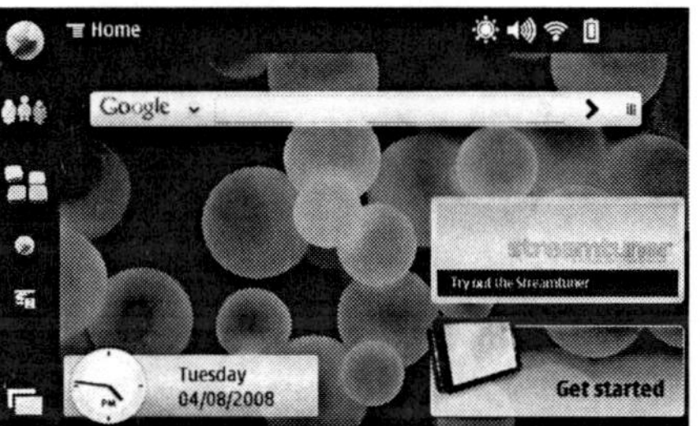

OS2008 Desktop

### Diablo

Diablo is the codename for the OS2008 Feature Upgrade (corresponding to Maemo 4.1).,[41] released in June 2008.[42] Major features include significant improvements to the built-in Application manager, incremental operating system upgrades without reflashing ("Seamless Software Update", SSU), Modest as the default mail client, and a new version of the MicroB browser with more optimizations and some interface improvements (though still based on the same Gecko release as Chinook's MicroB).[43] [44] Diablo also included an implementation of the WiMAX stack for the short-lived N810 variation called N810 WiMAX edition.[45]

### SSU

SSU, in particular, is one of the most significant parts of the Diablo release, as it eliminates the flash-based upgrade system of previous Maemo releases which required the user to completely wipe their device with each upgrade. With SSU, the user can receive "over-the-air" updates to the live system. This also decouples bundled software updates from the major system updates as was required with the flash-based method, so Nokia can release more frequent updates to individual packages than before.[46]

The first SSU update was pushed on August 11, 2008, and brought Diablo up to version 4.2008.30-2. The update primarily features MicroB, Modest, and connectivity framework updates as well as a number of other minor bugfixes.

## Maemo 5

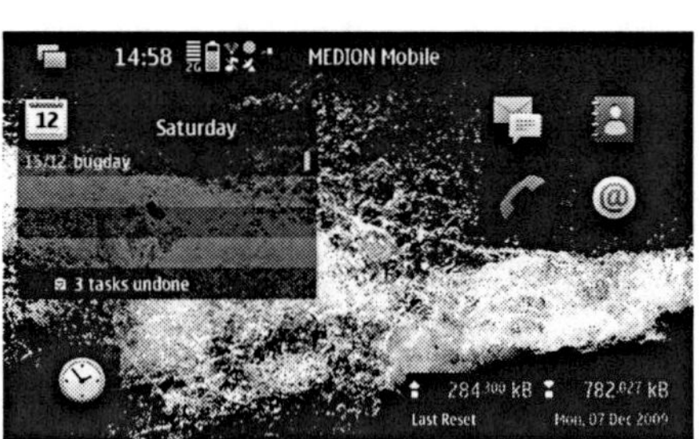

Maemo 5 Screenshot

Maemo 5, also known as Fremantle,[41] is the default operating system on the Nokia N900. The release features a much more finger-friendly and consistent UI, and an X-server based on Xorg rather than KDrive.[47] [48] It features several new technologies, including the Tracker search system, PulseAudio (replacing ESD), the OHM hardware management daemon, the gUPnP UPnP framework, enhanced location framework, and Upstart. Several existing technologies have also been updated, including Gecko, BlueZ, gstreamer (will include OpenMAX), GTK+, and Telepathy.[49] [50]

Maemo 5 comes with new hardware, the Nokia N900 featuring a Texas Instruments OMAP3 SoC, with an HSPA modem and HD camera, which provides significant improvements in the areas of speed, 3D acceleration, and media playback. It has been decided by Nokia that the commercial Maemo 5 platform releases will not be available on N800/N810 hardware, for compatibility reasons.[51] An open source Linux project called Mer, a variant of Maemo, has been formed to provide an alternative, fully open operating system for mobile devices including the Nokia N800 and N810.[52]

Unlike most smartphones, the end-user is able to gain root access by issuing the command "sudo gainroot" in the terminal in Maemo 5.[53] The device does not need to be unlocked or "jailbroken" in order to install an unsupported application. The UK cellular operator Vodafone has its own branded, somewhat more restricted version of the Maemo 5 operating system. Users can flash (change) to the Global variant of the operating system.

The Maemo 5 operating system comes preloaded with a variety of applications such as:

Web

Maemo Browser (Mozilla based web browser with Adobe Flash 9.4[54] ), RSS reader

Phone application

VoIP

Session initiation protocol, Skype[55]

Conversations **(IM chat and SMS, no MMS[56] )**

Media

Camera, Photos, Media player

Production

Email, Calendar, PDF reader, Contacts

Ovi Maps **(Find position on a map using the GPS, Search an address or location, Plan routes)**

Utilities

Clock, Notes, Calculator, Sketch

System Tools

File manager, Application manager for downloads, Widgets

Games

Bounce, Chess, Blocks, Marbles and Mahjong

Nokia expects the open source community to play a large part in the development of applications for Maemo 5.[57] As an example, Nokia has launched a contest at the onedotzero festival in London called PUSH N900 aimed at designers, artists, hackers and modders. The contest invites participants "*to connect the N900 to something you love.*"[58]

More than 1500 additional applications (an overwhelming majority of them free to download and use) have been created by third-party party developers.[59]

## Hacker Editions

Nokia's release of the N800 in January 2007 brought Internet Tablet OS 2007. OS2007 ran only on the N800 and Nokia initially had no plans to release it for the 770; however feedback from disgruntled 770 owners[60] led Nokia to release an unsupported hybrid of OS2006 and OS2007, dubbed Internet Tablet OS 2007 Hacker Edition, in February 2007.[61] OS2007HE combined the binary parts of OS2006 with most of the updated libraries and user-space applications of OS2007.

Nokia followed the release of the N810 and OS2008 in November 2007 with the OS2008 Hacker Edition for the 770 on February 14, 2008, following a similar method to the OS2007HE release to create a hybrid between OS2006 and OS2007. The Hacker Editions allow 770 users to access the latest Internet Tablet OS releases and third-party software, although due to the 770's hardware limitations and the increased CPU requirements of OS2008, performance is inferior to that of OS2007 HE in most areas.[62]

## Alternative desktops

In addition to the officially supported Hildon environment that comes standard on the tablets, several alternate desktop systems are available. Penguinbait, a member of the Internet Tablet Talk community, has successfully ported KDE 3,[63] Openbox,[64] and XFCE[65] to the N800 and N810 (the 770 is able to run an early version of the KDE port). KDE 4 is being ported at the present time.[66] LXDE is the default desktop for the "Easy Debian" distribution, which is installed as a single application under Maemo but provides access to the full range of software in the ARM Debian distribution (including GIMP, Iceweasel/Firefox and OpenOffice) [27] via a chroot environment.

### Mer

Mer is a completely open-sourced alternative operating system for the N800 and N810 (collectively known as the N8x0 devices). It is based on Ubuntu 9.04, and with the release of Maemo 5/Fremantle, a new goal has emerged: "[To bring] as much of Fremantle as we can get on the N8x0."

Mer has halted further development, at release 0.17, and the former developers have begun focusing on building MeeGo for the N800 and N810 devices.

### Harmattan

Little is known about Harmattan except for the plans to bundle officially supported Qt libraries with it in place of GTK+/Hildon, as well as improved power profiles.[67] [68]

Harmattan, with the MeeGo announcement, is set to be the "first" MeeGo incarnation on a Nokia device, rather than Maemo 6.

### MeeGo

After the release of the MeeGo code base, there are two main community efforts to bring MeeGo to the current Maemo devices (N800, N810, and N900).

There is the MeeGo adaptation for the N800 and N810 devices,[69] [70] and the MeeGo to N900 project [71]

### Qt

In January 2008, Nokia began the process of acquiring Trolltech, the developer of the Qt application framework. Nokia has since announced plans for the Qt libraries to be bundled with Maemo by Q4 2008, though without a platform-specific "hildonized" UI as is offered with GTK (meaning Qt applications will look different from hildonized GTK ones).[72] [73] This will make porting of Qt applications to the platform easier for developers and make new applications available to users. Qt support on S60 devices will likely lead to cross-platform application sharing between the two platforms.[74] [75] The announcement has met with mixed reaction in the developer community.[76] [77]

## Release history

### Naming

Maemo Codenames are named for winds. For example, the latest release, codenamed "Fremantle," is a reference to the Fremantle Doctor, the Western Australian vernacular term for the cooling afternoon sea breeze which occurs during summer months in south west coastal areas of Western Australia.

| | Version | Codename | Build identifier | Release date | First device shipped with | Notes | Devices Supported |
|---|---|---|---|---|---|---|---|
| **OS2005** | 1.1 | - | 2.2005.45-1 | November 2005 | 770 | | 770 |
| | | | 3.2005.51-13 | December 2005 | | | 770 |
| | | | 5.2006.13-7 | April 2006 | | | 770 |
| **OS2006** | 2.0 | Mistral | 0.2006.22-21 | May 2006 | | Beta release | 770 |
| | | | 1.2006.26-8 | May 2006 | | | 770 |
| | 2.1 | Scirocco | 2.2006.39-14 | November 2006 | | | 770 |
| | 2.2 | Gregale | 3.2006.49-2 | January 2007 | 770 | | 770 |
| **OS2007** | 3.0 | Bora | 2.2006.51-6 | January 2007 | N800 | | 770*, N800 |
| | 3.1 | | 3.2007.10-7 | March 2007 | | | 770*, N800 |
| | 3.2 | | 4.2007.26-8 | July 2007 | | | 770*, N800 |
| | | | 4.2007.38-2 | October 2007 | | SDHC corruption fix | 770*, N800 |

| | | | | | | | |
|---|---|---|---|---|---|---|---|
| **OS2008** | 4.0 | Chinook | 1.2007.42-18 | November 2007 | N810 | (N810 only) | N810 |
| | | | 1.2007.42-19 | November 2007 | | Kernel upgrade only (N810 only) | N810 |
| | | | 1.2007.44-4 | November 2007 | | Beta release (N800 only) | N800 |
| | | | 2.2007.50-2 | November 2007 | | | 770*, N800, N810 |
| | | | 2.2007.51-3 | January 2008 | | NOLO (Nokia bootloader) upgrade only | 770*, N800, N810 |
| | 4.1 | Diablo | 4.2008.23-14 | June 2008 | | Adds SSU (Seamless Software Update) support | N800, N810 |
| | | | 4.2008.30-2 | August 2008 | | First SSU update | N800, N810 |
| | | | 4.2008.36-5 | September 2008 | | | N800, N810 |
| | | | 5.2008.43-7 | December 2008 | | | N800, N810 |
| **Maemo 5** | 5.0 | Fremantle | 1.2009.42-11 | November 2009 | N900 | Bundled officially supported Qt libraries (PR1.2), Emphasis on finger use rather than stylus use | N900 |
| | | | 1.2009.44-1 | January 2010 | | Preparatory release for the 2.2009.51-1 firmware, released only OTA (Over-the-air) to 1.2009.42-11 users | N900 |
| | | | 2.2009.51-1 | January 2010 | | Also known as PR1.1. Changes[78] | N900 |
| | | | 3.2010.02-8 | February 2010 | | Preparatory release for the PR1.2 firmware. Also known as PR1.1.1. Changes[79] | N900 |
| | | | 10.2010.12-9 | May 2010 | | PR1.2, Hong Kong only, with Chinese input methods,[80] with Chinese input support. Changes[81] | N900 |
| | | | 10.2010.19-1 | May 2010 | | PR1.2, Skype and Google video calls, Facebook IM chat, Improved Maps, Portrait browsing, Improved email, Qt 4.6 enabling new applications[81] | N900 |
| | | | 20.2010.36-2 | October 25 2010 | | PR1.3, Qt 4.7.0, Full OVI-Suite support, updated kernel with kexec patches for MeeGo, bug fixes. | N900 |

*: Hacker Editions, Nokia-released, but Community-maintained. Primarily used by developers to continue developing programs while using older hardware.

## Maemo Summit

In 2008 and 2009 the Maemo developers and users gathered at Maemo Summit. The registration for the summit was free. Each participant got a badge and a Maemo T-shirt.

The 2009 Maemo Summit was held in Amsterdam on October 9–11.[82] The first day was the Nokia day while the other two days were the community days. Nearly 400 developers attended the summit. Nokia gave out 300 N900 devices to independent developers during the summit.

The 2009 Maemo Summit was also the last Maemo Summit since MeeGo was launched. The event was replaced by the MeeGo Conference.

# References


[1] "Maemo Trademark" (http://maemo.org/legal/terms_of_use/trademarks/). Maemo.org. 2008-09-23. . Retrieved 2009-08-29.

[2] http://www.reghardware.co.uk/2007/01/26/review_nokia_n800/

[3] "Flickr Photo Download: My Nokia #N900 Panoramic Desktop" (http://www.flickr.com/photos/chanse/3911804566/sizes/l/). Flickr.com. 2009-09-11. . Retrieved 2010-01-01.

[4] "Panorama desktops" (http://maemo.nokia.com/features/panorama-desktop/). maemo.nokia.com. . Retrieved 16 September 2009.

[5] *YouTube – Nokia N900 hands-on* (http://www.youtube.com/watch?v=ZrYqemylplo). YouTube, LLC. 2 September 2009. . Retrieved 16 September 2009.

[6] *YouTube – Hands-on with Nokia N900* (http://www.youtube.com/watch?v=RG4qPv2k4Ak). YouTube, LLC. 2 September 2009. . Retrieved 16 September 2009.

[7] Bangeman, Eric (2007-02-12). "Ars Technica review of the N800" (http://arstechnica.com/reviews/hardware/n800.ars). Arstechnica.com. . Retrieved 2010-12-08.

[8] "It's Official N810 WiMAX Announced" (http://www.internettablettalk.com/2008/04/01/its-official-n810-wimax-announced/). Internettablettalk.com. 2008-04-01. . Retrieved 2010-12-08.

[9] Gil, Quim (2007-06-01). "Nokia and Maemo in the new GNOME mobile context" (http://www.slideshare.net/qgil/nokia-and-maemo-in-the-new-gnome-mobile-context/3) (FLV). p. 22. . Retrieved 28 April 2008.

[10] "maemo 4 Quick Start Guide" (http://maemo.org/development/documentation/maemo-quick-start-guide.pdf) (PDF). Nokia. 2007. p. 11. . Retrieved 2011-04-16.

[11] "Internet Tablet OS 2008 edition User Guide" (http://nds1.nokia.com/files/support/nam/phones/guides/N810_US_en.PDF) (PDF). Nokia. 2007. p. 14. . Retrieved 2009-06-24.

[12] "maemo Getting Started – maemo Platform Overview" (http://web.archive.org/web/20080616191310/http://maemo.org/maemo_training_material/maemo4.x/html/maemo_Technology_Overview/Chapter_03_maemo_Platform_Overview.html). Nokia Corporation. Archived from the original (http://maemo.org/maemo_training_material/maemo4.x/html/maemo_Technology_Overview/Chapter_03_maemo_Platform_Overview.html) on June 16, 2008. . Retrieved 2008-08-15.

[13] "maemo Getting Started – What is maemo?" (http://maemo.org/maemo_training_material/maemo4.x/html/maemo_Getting_Started/Chapter_01_What_is_maemo.html). Nokia Corporation. . Retrieved 2008-08-14.

[14] Abinader, Bruno (2008-04-01). "Re: Systemtap testsuite report for arm architecture" (http://sources.redhat.com/ml/systemtap/2008-q2/msg00002.html). *systemtap mailing list*. . Retrieved 2008-04-28.

[15] Maemo 4.x: Getting started with multimedia (http://maemo.org/development/documentation/how-tos/4-x/getting_started_with_multimedia.html)

[16] "N900 and Maemo5 playing vp8/webm live stream" (http://zaheer.merali.org/articles/2010/05/24/n900-and-maemo5-playing-vp8webm-live-stream/). Zaheer.merali.org. 2010-05-24. . Retrieved 2010-12-08.

[17] Freeing Maemo (http://wiki.maemo.org/Free_Maemo) On wiki.maemo

[18] Nokia N810 Specifications (http://nokia.us/A4626059) List of bundled applications

[19] "Fremantle Stars – maemo.org wiki" (http://wiki.maemo.org/Fremantle_Stars). Nokia Corporation. . Retrieved 16 September 2009.

[20] "Downloads: Mauku" (http://maemo.org/downloads/product/OS2008/mauku/). maemo.org. . Retrieved 2010-07-14.

[21] "Downloads: Maemo Mapper" (http://maemo.org/downloads/product/OS2008/maemo-mapper/). maemo.org. . Retrieved 2010-01-01.

[22] "Downloads: NumptyPhysics" (http://maemo.org/downloads/product/OS2008/numptyphysics/). maemo.org. . Retrieved 2010-07-14.

[23] "Downloads: ScummVM" (http://maemo.org/downloads/product/OS2008/scummvm/). maemo.org. . Retrieved 2010-07-14.

[24] "Downloads: Xournal" (http://maemo.org/downloads/product/OS2008/xournal/). maemo.org. . Retrieved 2010-07-14.

[25] "Downloads: FBReader - e-book reader" (http://maemo.org/downloads/product/OS2008/fbreader/). maemo.org. . Retrieved 2010-07-14.

[26] "Downloads: OSM2Go" (http://maemo.org/downloads/product/OS2008/osm2go/). maemo.org. . Retrieved 2010-07-14.

[27] Qole Pejorian (2008-10-12). "Easy Debian moves to Extras" (http://qole.blogspot.com/2008/10/easy-debian-moves-to-extras-devel.html). .

[28] "README – maemo-optify in Maemo Application Framework – Gitorious" (http://gitorious.org/maemo-af/maemo-optify/blobs/master/README). Shortcut AS. . Retrieved 17 September 2009.

[29] "Maemo – Jalimo" (http://wiki.evolvis.org/jalimo/index.php/Maemo) (in **German**). Wiki.evolvis.org. . Retrieved 2010-12-08.

[30] Overview of the software development process using the maemo SDK environment (http://maemo.org/maemo_training_material/maemo4.x/html/maemo_Technology_Overview/Chapter_05_Software_Development_Process_for_maemo_SDK.html#OverviewofthesoftwaredevelopmentprocessusingthemaemoSDKenvironment)

[31] "Maemo Harmattan Qt And More" (http://www.slideshare.net/qgil/maemo-harmattan-qt-and-more). SlideShare Inc.. 4 July 2009. . Retrieved 17 September 2009.

[32] "Device Specifications" (http://www.forum.nokia.com/devices/matrix_maemo_1.html). Forum.nokia.com. 2010-12-01. . Retrieved 2010-12-08.

[33] "Debian Maemo packaging team" (http://wiki.debian.org/pkg-maemo). Wiki.debian.org. 2009-03-16. . Retrieved 2010-12-08.
[34] 770 Device Profile (http://linuxdevices.com/articles/AT5858395674.html) List of bundled applications for OS2005
[35] "Nokia – The Nokia 770 Internet Tablet adds Internet calls and Instant Messaging support" (http://press.nokia.com/PR/200605/1051308_5.html). Press.nokia.com. 2006-05-16. . Retrieved 2010-12-08.
[36] Nokia 770 Tablet "OS 2006" arrives (http://www.linuxdevices.com/news/NS9255811301.html) News article on OS2006 release
[37] USB in OS2008 (http://www.ibrado.org/2008/02/usb-in-os2008.html) Article on OS2008 USB support
[38] USB On-The-Go (http://blogs.forum.nokia.com/blog/kate-alholas-forum-nokia-blog/maemo/2008/01/21/usb-on-the-go) Kate Alhola's Forum Nokia Blog USB On-The-Go
[39] "Nokia Europe – Nokia N810 – OS2008 features" (http://europe.nokia.com/A4579471). .
[40] "Maemo-Developers Mailing List: Frequencies scaling with OS2008" (http://lists.maemo.org/pipermail/maemo-developers/2007-December/049275.html). .
[41] "Codenames" (http://wiki.maemo.org/Codenames). *maemo.org Wiki*. . Retrieved 25 June 2008.
[42] "OS2008 Feature Upgrade: reflash your tablet (for the last time?)" (http://maemo.org/news/announcements/os2008_feature_upgrade-reflash_your_tablet-for_the_last_time/). Maemo.org. . Retrieved 2010-12-08.
[43] "What do we know about Diablo (Maemo 4.1)" (http://www.internettablettalk.com/forums/showthread.php?t=17727). *Internet Tablet Talk forums*. 2008-03-09. . Retrieved 28 April 2008.
[44] Greene, Jonathan (2007-10-24). "A not so modest update to email is coming" (http://www.maemoapps.com/2007/10/24/a-not-so-modest-update-to-email-is-coming/). *Featured Maemo Apps*. . Retrieved 28 April 2008.
[45] "Nokia 810 WiMAX edition" (http://www.nokiausa.com/find-products/phones/nokia-n810-wimax-edition). .
[46] "Interview with Urho Konttori" (http://www.nseries.com/index.html#l=workshop,articles,414). Nseries.com. . Retrieved 2010-12-08.
[47] Bug 2564 – No consistency on scrolling/scrollbars in bundled OS2008 applications (https://bugs.maemo.org/show_bug.cgi?id=2564#c6)
[48] Bug 1897 – Mouse support (Bluetooth and on 770 USB support) (https://bugs.maemo.org/show_bug.cgi?id=1897#c6)
[49] "OSiM Maemo Developer Session" (http://www.internettablettalk.com/2008/09/18/osim-maemo-developer-session/). Internettablettalk.com. 2008-09-18. . Retrieved 2010-12-08.
[50] Maemo Roadmap – Fremantle (https://wiki.maemo.org/Task:Maemo_roadmap/Fremantle)
[51] "Comment on talk.maemo.org by Gil Quim, Nokia employee" (http://talk.maemo.org/showpost.php?s=3b2f5dfc74e359ee7cbbcb895f23287c&p=279460&postcount=4). Talk.maemo.org. 2009-04-14. . Retrieved 2010-12-08.
[52] "Mer – a Mobile Linux Distribution" (http://mer-project.blogspot.com/). Blogspot. . Retrieved 10 November 2009.
[53] "Software freedom lovers: here comes Maemo 5 « flors" (http://flors.wordpress.com/2009/08/27/software-freedom-lovers-here-comes-maemo-5/). WordPress. 27 August 2009. . Retrieved 16 September 2009.
[54] "Maemo software | Nokia › Maemo Browser" (http://maemo.nokia.com/features/maemo-browser/). Maemo.nokia.com. . Retrieved 2010-01-01.
[55] "Maemo software – Nokia > Phone" (http://maemo.nokia.com/features/phone/). Nokia Corporation. . Retrieved 16 September 2009.
[56] "maemo.org – Talk – View Single Post – Now it's official: Maemo 5 and the N900 launch!" (http://talk.maemo.org/showpost.php?p=318414&postcount=419). Nokia Corporation. 30 August 2009. . Retrieved 18 September 2009.
[57] *YouTube – Who will create applications for Nokia N900?* (http://www.youtube.com/watch?v=GzNbPAgcHMw). YouTube, LLC. 6 September 2009. . Retrieved 16 September 2009.
[58] "What is PUSH N900" (http://blogs.nokia.com/pushn900/index.php/what-is-push/). Nokia Corporation. . Retrieved 16 September 2009.
[59] Complete Maemo 5 Software Directory at My-Maemo.com (http://my-maemo.com/software/)
[60] We're getting some feedback .. and we've got a plan now (http://jaaksi.blogspot.com/2007/01/were-getting-some-feedback-and-weve-got.html) Ari Jaaksi's blog post on OS2007 for 770
[61] First release of OS 2007 / 770 hacker edition out (http://www.notacloud.com/blog/?p=27) Announcement of first OS2007 HE release on Carlos Guerreiro's blog
[62] Internet Tablet Hacker Edition pushed at Chinook level (http://maemo.org/news/announcements/internet_tablet_hacker_edition_pushed_at_chinook_level/) Announcement of the first OS2008 HE release
[63] "KDE/Koffice Install made easy for everyone" (http://www.internettablettalk.com/forums/showthread.php?t=14680). Internettablettalk.com. . Retrieved 2010-12-08.
[64] "OPENBOX-ROX Now Available" (http://www.internettablettalk.com/forums/showthread.php?t=5126). Internettablettalk.com. . Retrieved 2010-12-08.
[65] " XFCE Available" (http://www.internettablettalk.com/forums/showthread.php?t=9678). Internettablettalk.com. 2007-09-13. . Retrieved 2010-12-08.
[66] "Why Not Skip Ahead? (KDE4 for ITs)" (http://geekpenguin.blogspot.com/2008/04/why-not-skip-ahead.html). Geekpenguin.blogspot.com. 2008-04-22. . Retrieved 2010-12-08.
[67] "Maemo Harmattan Qt and More" (http://www.slideshare.net/qgil/maemo-harmattan-qt-and-more). Slideshare.net. 2009-07-04. . Retrieved 2010-12-08.
[68] Bug 1046 – RFE: Power Management Profiles (AC/Battery, Timed, Environment and screen saver) (https://bugs.maemo.org/show_bug.cgi?id=1046)

[69] "MeeGo hardware adaptation for N8x0 - maemo.org - Talk" (http://talk.maemo.org/showthread.php?t=48929). Talk.maemo.org. . Retrieved 2010-07-14.
[70] "Unofficial MeeGo hardware adaptation for Nokia N8x0" (http://forum.meego.com/showthread.php?t=317). meego.com. .
[71] "Brief status of "MeeGo to N900" project - maemo.org - Talk" (http://talk.maemo.org/showthread.php?t=50763). Talk.maemo.org. 2010-04-22. . Retrieved 2010-07-14.
[72] "Qt to be supported in addition to GTK+" (http://web.archive.org/web/20080420031623/http://maemo.org/news/announcements/view/qt_to_be_supported_in_addition_to_gtk.html). *maemo.org Announcements*. 2008-04-15. Archived from the original (http://maemo.org/news/announcements/view/qt_to_be_supported_in_addition_to_gtk.html) on April 20, 2008. . Retrieved 28 April 2008.
[73] Jaaksi, Ari (2008-04-14). "CTIA and Qt" (http://jaaksi.blogspot.com/2008/04/ctia-and-qt.html). *Ari Jaaksi's Blog*. . Retrieved 28 April 2008.
[74] Gil, Quim (2008-01-29). "Gnomes, trolls and the Maemo lands" (http://flors.wordpress.com/2008/01/29/gnomes-trolls-and-the-maemo-lands/). *flors*. . Retrieved 27 April 2008.
[75] Paul, Ryan (2008-04-23). "Nokia Internet Tablets get Ubuntu and Qt" (http://arstechnica.com/journals/linux.ars/2008/04/23/nokia-internet-tablets-get-ubuntu-and-qt). *Ars Technica*. . Retrieved 27 April 2008.
[76] van den Oever, Jos (2008-01-28). "digesting the Trolltech acquisition" (http://www.kdedevelopers.org/node/3233). *oever's blog*. . Retrieved 27 April 2008.
[77] Wilcox, Mark (2008-02-03). "Trolltech, Linux, Open Source, the future?" (http://blogs.forum.nokia.com/blog/mark-wilcoxs-forum-nokia-blog/general/2008/02/03/trolltech-linux-open-source-the-future). *Mark Wilcox's Forum Nokia Blog*. . Retrieved 27 April 2008.
[78] "Maemo 5/PR1.1 - maemo.org wiki" (http://wiki.maemo.org/Maemo_5/PR1.1). Wiki.maemo.org. . Retrieved 2010-07-14.
[79] "Maemo 5/PR1.1.1 - maemo.org wiki" (http://wiki.maemo.org/Maemo_5/PR1.1.1). Wiki.maemo.org. . Retrieved 2010-07-14.
[80] "The N900 (With PR 1.2) Launches In Hong Kong With An Awesome Promo Video | The MeeGo Blog - Formerly Maemo Central" (http://maemocentral.com/2010/04/30/the-n900-with-pr-1-2-launches-in-hong-kong-with-an-awesome-promo-video/). Maemocentral.com. 2010-04-30. . Retrieved 2010-07-14.
[81] "Maemo 5/PR1.2 - maemo.org wiki" (http://wiki.maemo.org/Maemo_5/PR1.2). Wiki.maemo.org. . Retrieved 2010-07-14.
[82] "Maemo Summit 2009" (http://wiki.maemo.org/Maemo_Summit_2009). Wiki.maemo.org. 2010-08-30. . Retrieved 2010-12-08.

## External links

- Official homepage (http://www.maemo.org/)
- Maemo home page (http://maemo.nokia.com/)

# MeeGo

**WARNING: Article could not be rendered - ouputting plain text.**
Potential causes of the problem are: (a) a bug in the pdf-writer software (b) problematic Mediawiki markup (c) table is too wide

MeeGoNotebook EditionSoftware industryCompany / Software developerdeveloperLinux Foundation, Intel CorporationIntel, Nokia, Novell, AMD "AMD to contribute to MeeGo development". The H open. 2010-11-15. . Retrieved 2011-01-27. MeeGo CommunityProgrammed inC++OS familyLinuxWorking state CurrentInitial release 26 May 2010Software release life cycleLatest stable release 1.1.4 / 7 April 2011Marketing target MobilePackage managerRPM Package ManagerSupported platformsARM architectureARM and x86Kernel (computing)Kernel typeMonolithic kernelMonolithic (Linux kernelLinux)Software licenseLicense Various, see MeeGo#LicensesbelowOfficial website meego.com MeeGo is a Linux-based open source mobile operating system project.Grabham, Dan (2010-02-15). "Intel and Nokia merge Moblin and Maemo to form MeeGo". techradar.com. . Retrieved 15 February 2010. Primarily targeted at mobile devices and information appliances in the consumer electronics market, MeeGo is designed to act as an operating system for hardware platforms such as netbooks, entry-level desktops, nettops, tablet computers, mobile computing and communications devices, in-vehicle infotainment devices, SmartTVSmartTV / ConnectedTV, IPTV-boxes, smart phones, and other embedded systems. "openSUSE News - Announcing Smeegol 1.0". . Retrieved 2010-10-06. MeeGo is today hosted by the Linux Foundation. "FAQ on MeeGo website, retrieved 29 May 2010". Meego.com. . Retrieved 2010-12-08.It was first announced at Mobile World Congress in February 2010 by Intel and Nokia in a joint press conference. The stated aim is to merge the efforts of Intel's Moblin and Nokia's Maemo former projects into one new common project. According to Intel, MeeGo was developed because Microsoft did not offer comprehensive Windows 7 support for the Intel AtomAtom processor. "Intel: MeeGo exists because Microsoft let us down". TechRadar. 20 April 2010. . Novell also plays a large part in the MeeGo effort, working with the Linux Foundation on their build infrastructure and official MeeGo products, and MeeGo is increasingly using more of Novell's technology that was originally developed for openSUSE, (including openSUSE Build Service, ZYpp for package management, and other system management tools). "openSUSE Releases MeeGo-based Smeegol Linux". . Retrieved 2010-10-06. In November 2010, Advanced Micro DevicesAMD also joined the alliance of companies that are actively developing MeeGo. "AMD will contribute 'engineering expertise' to MeeGo development project". Engadget. 2010-11-15. . Retrieved 2010-12-08.Maemo Harmattan#FutureHarmattan, originally slated to become Maemo 6, is now considered to be a MeeGo instance (though not a MeeGo product), and Nokia is giving up the Maemo branding for Harmattan and beyond (Maemo 5, aka Fremantle, and previous versions will still be referred to as Maemo). ""maemo.org - Talk - Renaming Maemo 6 to MeeGo/Harmattan"". . Retrieved 2010-02-27.In February 2011 Nokia announced a partnership with Microsoft for mobile handsets "Nokia and Microsoft form partnership". BBC News. 2011-02-11. . and the departure of Nokia's MeeGo team manager Alberto Torres, "Nokia execs reshuffled in Microsoft-centered Elopcalypse". Engadget.com. 2011-02-11. . leading to speculation as to Nokia's future participation in MeeGo development. Overview MeeGo is intended to run on a variety of hardware platforms including handhelds, in-car devices, netbooks and televisions. "Devices". MeeGo. . Retrieved 2010-12-08. All platforms share the MeeGo core, with different graphical user interface"User Experience" ("UX") layers for each type of device. System requirements MeeGo provides support for both ARM architectureARM and Intel x86 processors with SSSE3 enabled "MeeGo FAQ". . Retrieved 2010-02-15. and uses btrfs as the default file system. "MeeGo project chooses Btrfs as standard file system". The H. 12 May 2010. .User interfaces Screenshot of MeeGo's Netbook UX Within the MeeGo project there are several graphical user interfaces – internally called User Experiences ("UX").Netbook The Netbook UX is a continuation of the Moblin interface. It is written using the Clutter (toolkit)Clutter based Mx (toolkit)Mx toolkit, and uses the Mutter (window manager)Mutter window manager. MeeGo's netbook version uses several Linux applications in the background, such as Evolution (software)Evolution (Email, calendar), Empathy (software)Empathy (instant messaging), Gwibber (microblogging), Chromium (web browser)Chromium (web browser), and Banshee (media player)Banshee (multimedia player), all integrated into the graphical user interface. Handset Handset UX from MeeGo 1.1 "Day 1" The Handset UX is based on Qt (framework)Qt, but GTK+ and Clutter (toolkit)Clutter will be included to provide compatibility for Moblin applications. To support the hundreds of Hildon based Maemo applications, users have to install the Hildon library ported by the maemo.org community. Depending on the device, applications will be provided from either the Intel AppUp or the Nokia Ovi (Nokia)Ovi digital software distribution systems. "MeeGo Press Release". . Retrieved 2010-02-15.The MeeGo Handset UX's "Day 1" prerelease was on June 30, 2010. The preview was initially available for the Aava Mobile Intel Moorestown platform, and a 'kickstart' file provided for developers to build an image for the Nokia N900. "MeeGo Handset UX Day 1 Blog Post". . Retrieved 2010-06-30. "MeeGo Handset UX Developer Preview". . Retrieved 2010-06-30.Tablet MeeGo's Tablet UX as a pre-alpha version Intel demonstrated the Tablet UX on a Moorestown (computing platform)Moorestown-based tablet PC at COMPUTEX Taipei in early June 2010. Since then some information appeared on MeeGo website indicating there will be a Tablet UX part of the MeeGo project, but it is not known if this UX will be the one demonstrated by Intel. This Tablet UX will be fully open source like the rest of the MeeGo project and will be coded with Qt and the MeeGo Touch Framework. "MeeGo tablet UX". . Retrieved 2010-08-31. Intel has revealed interest in combining Qt with Wayland (display server)Wayland display server instead of the often seen Qt/X11 combination in MeeGo Touch in order to utilize the latest graphics technologies supported by Linux kernel, which should improve user experiences and reduce system complexity.Michael Larabel (September 16, 2010). "Where Wayland May First Appear In Use By A Distro". Phoronix. . Retrieved 11 October 2010.Michael Larabel (September 21, 2010). "Qt Is Now Drawing On Wayland". Phoronix. . Retrieved 11 October 2010.Minimum hardware requirements are currently unknown. The WeTab runs MeeGo with a custom user interface and has been available since September 2010 "WeTab is based on MeeGo". The H. October 13, 2010. .In-Vehicle Infotainment MeeGo's IVI UX as shipped with MeeGo 1.1 The GENIVI Alliance, a consortium of several car makers and their industry partners, uses Moblin with Qt as base for its 'GENIVI 1.0 Reference Platform' for In car entertainmentIn-Vehicle Infotainment (IVI) and automotive navigation system as a uniformed mobile computing platform. Graham Smethurst of GENIVI Alliance and BMW Group announced in April 2010 the switch from Moblin to MeeGo. "Linux Foundation Press Releases » Blog Archive » Public Support for the MeeGo Project". Linux-foundation.org. . Retrieved 2010-12-08.http://www.linuxfordevices.com/c/a/News/Genivi-selects-MeeGo/Licenses MeeGo is a complex project that involves many vendors and organizations. Its license policy is mainly documented at the "MeeGo License Policy" "MeeGo License Policy". . Retrieved 2010-07-07. page. Consider the nature of MeeGo's targeting markets – the mobile and handset sectors – which, unlike the desktop software market that tends to adopt one or two major software vendor's operating systems, is highly diversified and hence differentiation is taken as of vital importance by both device makers and software vendors. Therefore MeeGo's license policy is, at one hand, trying to encourage the fostering of derivative work while at the same time, keep the project as open as possible. From the distribution point of view, MeeGo is a collection of open source software, which are distributed conforming to their respective licenses. From the development point of view, which mainly addresses the way of adopting software from the free software community on account of license, MeeGo software can be classified into two categories: the Operating System (OS) software and User Experience (UX) software. The OS software should mainly be using a copyleftcopyleft license to ensure the openness of the underlying system, while the UX software could be of BSD licensesBSD-style licenses, which do not mandate code modifications to be open sourced.The licenses of MeeGo developed technologies, such as fast-boot, power and speed optimizations are of interest to derivative products and projects. Those technologies spread among the system and can't be easily isolated out. For example, the fast-boot technology consists mainly of the fast and small Syslinux bootloader, "Syslinux Wiki". Syslinux.zytor.com. . Retrieved 2010-12-08. a new system service and software launcher called "uxlaunch", the optimized read-ahead component, little tweaking and tuning among many software services. The license policy is that these changes should follow the base work's license upon which they are made, that is to say, the corresponding upstream project's license policy. For example, MeeGo's work on the Linux kernel is available under the license of the Linux kernel. Technical foundations Core OS The MeeGo Core operating system is a Linux distribution, drawing on Nokia's Debian-based Maemo and Intel's Fedora (operating system)Fedora-based Moblin. "Intel switches from Ubuntu to Fedora for Mobile Linux". . Retrieved 2010-06-21. MeeGo is one of the first Linux distributions to use the Btrfs file system as default, and uses RPM Package ManagerRPM repositories. Architecture Software development The officially endorsed way to develop MeeGo applications is to use the Qt (framework)Qt framework and Qt Creator as Integrated development environmentdevelopment environment, but writing GTK+GTK applications is also supported. "MeeGo Netbook and GTK - MeeGo wiki". Wiki.meego.com. 2010-08-19. . Retrieved 2010-12-08.openSUSEopenSUSE's openSUSE Build ServiceBuild Service is used to compile the applications. "Build Infrastructure - MeeGo wiki". Wiki.meego.com. 2010-11-20. . Retrieved 2010-12-08.Derivatives As with Moblin before, MeeGo also serves as a technology pool that software vendors can access to build their products from. So far only ports of the graphical user interfaces to other Linux distributions have been announced. MeeGo/Harmattan Even though MeeGo was initiated as collaboration between Nokia and Intel, the collaboration was formed when Nokia was already developing the next incarnation of its Maemo Linux distribution. As a result, the Maemo 6 base operating system will be kept intact while the Handset UX will be shared, with the name changed to "MeeGo/Harmattan".SUSE and Smeegol Linux On June 1st, 2010 Novell announced that they would ship a SUSE Linux distributionsSUSE Linux incarnation with MeeGo's Netbook UX (MeeGo User Experience) graphical user interface. "Novell Announces Support for MeeGo". . Retrieved 2010-06-21.A MeeGo-based Linux distribution with this user interface is already available from openSUSE's Goblin Team under the name Smeegol Linux, this project combines MeeGo with openSUSE to get a new netbook-designed Linux distribution. What makes Smeegol Linux unique when compared to the upstream MeeGo or openSUSE is that this distribution is at its core based on openSUSE but has the MeeGo User Experience as well as a few other changes such as adding the Mono (software)Mono-based Banshee (media player) Banshee media player, NetworkManager-powered network configuration, a newer version of Evolution (software)#Evolution ExpressEvolution Express, and more. Any end-users can also build their own customized Smeegol Linux OS using SUSE Studio. "openSUSE MeeGo repo". . Retrieved 2010-06-21.Fedora Fedora (operating system)Fedora 14 contains a selection of software from the MeeGo project. Changes in Fedora for Desktop UsersLinpus Linpus Technologies is working on bringing their services on top of MeeGo Netbook and MeeGo Tablet. "Linpus Lite for MeeGo". . Retrieved 2010-08-31. "Slides about Linpus Lite MeeGo". . Retrieved 2010-08-31.Splashtop The latest version of the instant-on OS Splashtop-platform (by Splashtop Inc. which was previously named DeviceVM Inc.) is compliant with MeeGo, and future version of Splashtop will be based on MeeGo and will be available for commercial use in the first half of 2011. "DeviceVM Goes MeeGo-Compliant with Splashtop Product". . Retrieved 2010-09-14. "Remember SplashTop? Here's An Update On Them". Phoronix.com. 2010-10-30. . Retrieved 2010-12-08.Release Schedule It was announced at the Intel Developer Forum 2010 that MeeGo would follow a six month release schedule. Version 1.0 for Atom netbooks and a code drop for the Nokia N900 became available for download as of Wednesday, 26 May 2010. Version Linux kernelKernel version Release date Notes Devices Supported (Netbooks) Devices Supported (Handsets) Codename MeeGo 1.0 2.6.33 "Intel and Nokia release MeeGo v1.0", The H, 27 May 2010, 26 May 2010 "MeeGo at IDF. Netbook and Handheld Eye Candy, Chrome, Fennec and Lots of Developer Details", Carrypad, 13 April 2010, Primarily a Netbook release; only a code drop was released for mobile devices (the Nokia N900). Asus EeePC 901, 1000H, 1001P, 1005HA, 1005PE, 1008HA, Eeetop ET1602, Dell mini10v, Inspiron Mini 1012, Acer Aspire One D250, AO532-21S, Revo GN40, Aspire 5740-6025, Lenovo S10, MSI U100, U130, AE1900, HP mini 210-1044, Toshiba NB302. Nokia N900 (No handset UX). Arch 1.0.1 2.6.33.5 "MeeGo 1.01 for Netbooks update", All About MeeGo, July 12, 2010, July 2010 Update to MeeGo 1.0; Kernel updated to 2.6.33.5, USB device loading time improved, improved 3D performance, browser enhancements, resolved multiple e-mail client issue, enhanced netbook window manager, improved visuals, full support for GNOME proxy configuration in the media player, more control over DNS settings. All Netbooks supported by MeeGo 1.0; see above. None Bubble 1.0.2 2.6.33.5 MeeGo v1.0.2 Core Update, September 21, 2010, 9 August 2010 Update to MeeGo 1.0; X-Server Update, Connection Manager Update, Package Manager UI Update, Perl Update and several more. All Netbooks supported by MeeGo 1.0; see above. None Carte 1.0.3 2.6.33.5 MeeGo v1.0.3 Core Update, September 21, 2010, 10 September 2010 Update to MeeGo 1.0; several Updates, e.g. Chromium (web browser)Chromium browser, Connection Manager All Netbooks supported by MeeGo 1.0; see above. None Dutchwell 1.0.4 2.6.33.5 MeeGo v1.0.4 Core Update, October 19, 2010, 12 October 2010 Update to MeeGo 1.0; several security updates, better support for Lenovo IdeaPad S10-3sLenovo S10-3, ... All Netbooks supported by MeeGo 1.0; see above. None Ebota 1.0.5 Unknown 28 November 2010 MeeGo core update. MeeGo v1.0.5 Core Update I MeeGo All Netbooks supported by MeeGo 1.0; see above. None Faketi 1.0.6 Unknown 4 January 2011 MeeGo core update. MeeGo v1.0.6 Core Update I MeeGo All Netbooks supported by MeeGo 1.0; see above. None Garnet 1.0.7 Unknown 24 February 2011 MeeGo Netbook software update. MeeGo v1.0.7 Netbook Update I MeeGo All Netbooks supported by MeeGo 1.0; see above. None Herder 1.1 2.6.35 "MeeGo project releases preview source code", The Tech Journal, July 2, 2010, 28 October 2010 "MeeGo 1.1 Release". MeeGo.com. October 28, 2010. . Touch-based devices support proposed with the Handset UX "MeeGo v1.0 Core Software Platform & Netbook User Experience project release". Meego.com. . Retrieved 2010-12-08. Unknown Aava and Nokia N900 Indonesia 1.1.1 2.6.35 "MeeGo v1.1.1 Core Update". Dezember 7, 2010. . 28 November 2010 Several Fixes and Updates Unknown Aava and Nokia N900 Jupiter 1.1.2 2.6.35 "MeeGo v1.1.2 Core Update". January 12, 2011. . 07 January 2011 Several security issues fixed, update syncevolution and connman Unknown Kelly 1.1.3 2.6.35 "MeeGo v1.1.3 Core Update". March 16, 2011. . 24 February 2011 Fixed many important security issues, enabled all programs to access remote files over network and updated translation Unknown Line 1.2 2.6.37 19 May 2011 Unknown Marble 1.3 2.6.37 October 2011 Unknown Nadine Project planningLaunch Nokia announced it's first MeeGo phone Nokia N950 which is to be launched in 2011. First MeeGo based tablet WeTab was launched in 2010 by Neofonie. Companies supporting project Acer Inc.Acer, Amino, Asianux, Asus, basysKom, BMW Group, CollaboraCollabora, Ltd., CS2C, DeviceVM, EA Mobile, Gameloft, GM, Hancom, Igalia, Jaguar Land Rover, Linpus, Maemo Community Council, Mandriva, Metasys, Miracle, MontaVista Software, Novell, PixartPixArt, PSA Peugeot Citroen, Red Flag, ST-Ericsson, Tencent, TurboLinux, VietSoftware, Wind River SystemsWind River, WTEC and Xandros. More companies can be found in http://meego.com/about/public-support-meego and http://www.linuxfoundation.org/node/6144.References External links MeeGo website MeeGo FAQ MeeGo Community

# MotoMagx

## MOTOMAGX

| Company / developer | Motorola |
|---|---|
| Working state | Discontinued |
| Kernel type | Monolithic (Linux) |
| Official website | MOTODEV > Technologies > MOTOMAGX [1] |

**MOTOMAGX** is an operating system developed, and launched in 2007 by Motorola to run on their mobile phones. The system is based on MontaVista Linux. Originally intended for the 60% of their upcoming devices[1], it was soon dropped in favor of Android and Windows Mobile operative systems[2].

## Devices

Phones based on this OS are:

- Motorola EM30
- Motorola ROKR E2
- Motorola ROKR E8
- Motorola ROKR/RIZR Z6
- Motorola U9
- Motorola RAZR2 V8
- Motorola VE66
- Motorola ZINE ZN5
- Motorola Tundra V76r
- Motorola ROKR EM35

## References

[1] Motorola Unveils MOTOMAGX Mobile Linux Platform. (http://www.prnewswire.com/news-releases/motorola-unveils-motomagx-mobile-linux-platform-57935622.html) *PR Newswire*

[2] Albanesius, Chloe. Motorola Delays Cell-Phone Spinoff, Drops Platforms. (http://www.pcmag.com/article2/0,2817,2333601,00.asp) *pcmag.com*. October 30, 2008.

- Introducing MOTOMAGX (http://www.motorola.com/content.jsp?globalObjectId=8411)
- MOTODEV > Technologies > MOTOMAGX (http://developer.motorola.com/technologies/motomagx/)

# Palm OS

## Palm OS (Garnet OS)

Palm m505, running Palm OS 4.0

| Company / developer | Palm, Inc., ACCESS (Garnet OS) |
|---|---|
| OS family | Palm OS |
| Working state | Current |
| Source model | Closed source |
| Initial release | 1996 |
| Latest stable release | Garnet OS 5.5 / 2007 |
| Available programming languages(s) | C/C++ |
| Supported platforms | ARM architecture |
| License | Proprietary EULA |
| Official website | Garnet OS [1] |

**Palm OS** (also known as **Garnet OS**) is a mobile operating system initially developed by Palm, Inc., for personal digital assistants (PDAs) in 1996. Palm OS is designed for ease of use with a touchscreen-based graphical user interface. It is provided with a suite of basic applications for personal information management. Later versions of the OS have been extended to support smartphones. Several other licensees have manufactured devices powered by Palm OS.

Following Palm's purchase of the Palm trademark, the currently licensed version from ACCESS was renamed *Garnet OS*. In 2007, ACCESS introduced the successor to Garnet OS, called Access Linux Platform and in 2009, the main licensee of Palm OS, Palm, Inc., switched from Palm OS to webOS for their forthcoming devices.

## Creator and ownership

Palm OS was originally developed under the direction of Jeff Hawkins at Palm Computing, Inc.[1] Palm was later acquired by U.S. Robotics Corp.,[2] which in turn was later bought by 3Com,[3] which made the Palm subsidiary an independent publicly traded company on March 2, 2000.[4]

In January 2002, Palm set up a wholly owned subsidiary to develop and license Palm OS,[5] which was named PalmSource. PalmSource was then spun off from Palm as an independent company on October 28, 2003.[6] Palm (then called palmOne) became a regular licensee of Palm OS, no longer in control of the operating system.

In September 2005, PalmSource announced that it was being acquired by ACCESS.[7]

In December 2006, Palm gained perpetual rights to the Palm OS source code from ACCESS.[8] With this Palm can modify the licensed operating system as needed without paying further royalties to ACCESS. Together with the May 2005 acquisition of full rights to the *Palm* brand name,[9] only Palm can publish releases of the operating system under the name 'Palm OS'.

As a consequence, on January 25, 2007 ACCESS announced a name change to their current Palm OS operating system, now titled *Garnet OS*.[10]

## OS overview

Palm OS is a proprietary mobile operating system. Designed in 1996 for Palm Computing, Inc.'s new Pilot PDA, it has been implemented on a wide array of mobile devices, including smartphones, wrist watches, handheld gaming consoles, barcode readers and GPS devices.

Palm OS versions earlier than 5.0 run on Motorola/Freescale DragonBall processors. From version 5.0 onwards, Palm OS runs on ARM architecture-based processors.

The key features of the current Palm OS Garnet are:

- Simple, single-tasking environment to allow launching of full screen applications with a basic, common GUI set
- Monochrome or color screens with resolutions up to 480x320 pixel
- Handwriting recognition input system called Graffiti 2
- HotSync technology for data synchronization with desktop computers
- Sound playback and record capabilities
- Simple security model: Device can be locked by password, arbitrary application records can be made private
- TCP/IP network access
- Serial port/USB, infrared, Bluetooth and Wi-Fi connections
- Expansion memory card support
- Defined standard data format for personal information management applications to store calendar, address, task and note entries, accessible by third-party applications.

Included with the OS is also a set of standard applications, with the most relevant ones for the four mentioned PIM operations.

## Version history and technical background

Manufacturers are free to implement different features of the OS in their devices or even add new features. This version history describes the officially licensed version from Palm/PalmSource/ACCESS.

### Palm OS 1.0

Palm OS 1.0 is the original version present on the Pilot 1000 and 5000. This version and all versions prior to Palm OS 5 are based on top of the AMX 68000[11] kernel licensed from KADAK Products Ltd [13]. While this kernel is technically capable of multitasking, the "terms and conditions of that license specifically state that Palm may not expose the API for creating/manipulating tasks within the OS."[12]

Palm OS does not differentiate between RAM and file system storage. Applications are installed directly into RAM and executed in place. As no dedicated file system is supported, the operation system depends on constant RAM refresh cycles to keep its memory. The OS supports 160x160 monochrome output displays. User input is generated through the Graffiti handwriting recognition system or optionally through a virtual keyboard. The system supports data synchronization to another PC via its HotSync technology over a serial interface. The latest bugfix release is version 1.0.7.

Version 1.0 features the classic PIM applications *Address*, *Date Book*, *Memo Pad*, and *To Do List*. Also included is a calculator and the Security tool to hide records for private use.

## Palm OS 2.0

Palm OS 2.0 was introduced on March 10, 1997 with the PalmPilot Personal and Professional.[13] This version adds TCP/IP network, network HotSync, and display backlight support. The last bugfix release is version 2.0.5.

Two new applications, *Mail* and *Expense* are added, and the standard PIM applications have been enhanced.

## Palm OS 3.0

Palm OS 3.0 was introduced on March 9, 1998 with the launch of the Palm III series.[14] This version adds IrDA infrared and enhanced font support. This version also features updated PIM applications and an update to the application launcher.

**Palm OS 3.1** adds only minor new features, like network HotSync support. It was introduced with the Palm IIIx and Palm V.[15]

**Palm OS 3.2** adds Web Clipping support, which is an early Palm-specific solution to bring web-content to a small PDA screen. It was introduced with the Palm VII organizer.

**Palm OS 3.3** adds faster HotSync speeds and the ability to do infrared hotsyncing. It was introduced with the Palm Vx organizer.

**Palm OS 3.5** is the first version to include native 8-bit color support. It also adds major convenience features that simplify operation, like a context-sensitive icon-bar or simpler menu activation. The datebook application is extended with an additional agenda view. This version was first introduced with the Palm IIIc device.[16] The latest bugfix release is version 3.5.3.

As a companion, Palm later offered a *Mobile Internet Kit* software upgrade for Palm OS 3.5.[17] This included Palm's Web Clipping software, MultiMail (which was later renamed to VersaMail) Version 2.26 e-mail software, handPHONE Version 1.3 SMS software, and Neomar Version 1.5 WAP browser.

## Palm OS 4.0

Palm OS 4.0 was released with the new Palm m500 series on March 19, 2001.[18] This version adds a standard interface for external file system access (such as SD cards). External file systems are a radical change to the operating system's previous in-place execution. Now, application code and data need to be loaded into the device's RAM, similar to desktop operating system behavior. A new Universal Connector with USB support is introduced. The previous optional Mobile Internet Kit is now part of the operating system. Version 4.0 adds an attention manager to coordinate information from different applications, with several possibilities to get the user's attention, including sound, LED blinking or vibration. 16-bit color screens and different time zones are supported. This version also has security and UI enhancements.

**Palm OS 4.1** is a bugfix release. It was introduced with the launch of the Palm i705. The later minor OS update to version 4.1.2 includes a backport of Graffiti 2 from Palm OS 5.2.

**Palm OS 4.2 Simplified Chinese Edition** is targeted especially for the Chinese market with fully Simplified Chinese support, co-released with Palm OS 5.3. No device has been manufactured with this version up to now.

## Palm OS 5

Palm OS 5 (not called 5.0) was unveiled by the Palm subsidiary PalmSource in June 2002[19] and first implemented on the Palm Tungsten T. It is the first version released to support ARM devices, with support for DragonBall applications through the *Palm Application Compatibility Environment* (PACE) emulator. Even with the additional overhead of PACE, Palm applications usually run faster on ARM devices than on previous generation hardware. New software can take advantage of the ARM processors with small units of ARM code, referred to as *ARMlets*.

With a more powerful hardware basis, Palm OS is substantially enhanced for multimedia capabilities. High density 320x320 screens are supported together with a full digital sound playback and record API. Palm's separate Bluetooth stack is added together with an IEEE 802.11b Wi-Fi stack. Secure network connections over SSL are supported. The OS can be customized with different color schemes.

For Palm OS 5 PalmSource developed and licensed a web browser called *PalmSource Web Browser*,[20] which is based on ACCESS' NetFront 3.0 browser.

**Palm OS 5.2** is mainly a bugfix release, first implemented in the Samsung SGH-i500.[21] It provides support for 480x320 resolutions and introduces a new handwriting input system called Graffiti 2, due to the lost lawsuit against Xerox. Graffiti 2 is based on *Jot* from CIC [24]. The latest bugfix release is version 5.2.8.

**Palm OS 5.3 Simplified Chinese Edition** provides full Simplified Chinese support,[22] further adds support for QVGA resolutions, and a standard API for virtual Graffiti called *Dynamic Input Area*. This version was first introduced with Lenovo's P100 and P300 handhelds.[23]

**Palm OS Garnet** (5.4) officially provides support for multiple screen resolutions, ranging from 160x160 up to 480x320. It also features updated Bluetooth libraries. This version introduces the *Garnet* moniker to distinguish it from Palm OS Cobalt 6.0. The latest bugfix release is version 5.4.9.

**Garnet OS 5.5** is the current version developed by ACCESS. This version is dedicated to be run inside the *Garnet VM* virtual machine. Garnet VM is a core part of Access Linux Platform and also available for Nokia Internet Tablets.

## Palm OS Cobalt

Palm OS Cobalt (6.0) was the designated successor for Palm OS 5. It was introduced on February 10, 2004,[24] but is not offered anymore from ACCESS (see next section). Palm OS 6.0 was renamed to Palm OS Cobalt to make clear that this version was initially not designated to replace Palm OS 5, which adopted the name Palm OS Garnet at the same time.

Palm OS Cobalt introduced modern operating system features to an embedded operating system based on a new kernel with multitasking and memory protection, a modern multimedia and graphic framework (derived from Palm's acquired BeOS), new security features, and adjustments of the PIM file formats to better cooperate with Microsoft Outlook.

**Palm OS Cobalt 6.1**[25] presented standard communication libraries for telecommunication, Wi-Fi, and Bluetooth connectivity. Despite other additions, it failed to interest potential licensees to Palm OS Cobalt.

## Third party OS enhancements

Several licensees have made custom modifications to the operating system. These are not part of the official licensed version.

- Palm developed a Bluetooth API for external Bluetooth SDIO Cards for Palm OS 4.0 devices. The Bluetooth stack was later included in Palm OS 5[26]
- Palm added a virtual graffiti input area API especially for their Tungsten T3 device. This API was later superseded by the official Dynamic Input Area API in Palm OS 5.3.
- Palm added to Palm OS 5.4 the Non-Volatile File System, and used Flash for storage instead of DRAM, preventing data-loss in the event of battery drain. However, this fundamentally changed the way programs were executed from the Execute-in-Place system that Palm OS traditionally used, and has been the source of many compatibility problems, requiring many applications to have explicit NVFS support added for them to become stable.
- For their camera-equipped devices Palm added the CameraLib API.
- Sony added a library to support JogDial input available on their CLIÉ organizers.

## Modernization

For several years PalmSource had been attempting to create a modern successor for Palm OS 5 and have licensees implement it. Although PalmSource shipped Palm OS Cobalt 6.0 to licensees in January 2004, none adopted it for release devices. PalmSource made major improvements to Palm OS Cobalt with the release of Palm OS Cobalt 6.1 in September 2004 to please licensees, but even the new version did not lead to production devices.

In December 2004, PalmSource announced a new OS strategy. With the acquisition of the mobile phone software company China Mobilesoft, PalmSource planned to port Palm OS on top of a Linux kernel, while still offering both Palm OS Garnet and Palm OS Cobalt.[27] This strategy was revised in June 2005, when still no device with Palm OS Cobalt was announced. PalmSource announced it was halting all development efforts on any product not directly related to its future Linux based platform.[28]

With the acquisition of PalmSource by ACCESS, Palm OS for Linux was changed to become the ACCESS Linux Platform which was first announced in February 2006.[29] The initial versions of the platform and software development kits for the ACCESS Linux Platform were officially released in February 2007.[30] As of January 2011, the ACCESS Linux Platform has yet to ship on devices, however development kits exists and public demonstrations have been showcased.

Palm, Inc. the main licensee of Palm OS Garnet did not license ACCESS Linux Platform for their own devices. Instead, Palm developed another Linux-based operating system called Palm webOS.[31] On February 11, 2009 Palm CEO Ed Colligan said there would be no additional Palm OS devices (excepting the Centro being released to other carriers). Palm is focusing on Palm webOS and Windows Mobile devices.[32] On April 1, 2009 Palm announced the availability of a Palm OS emulator for its webOS.[33]

## Built-in applications

Palm OS licensees decide which applications are included on their Palm OS devices. Licensees can also customize the applications.

### Standard Palm OS applications

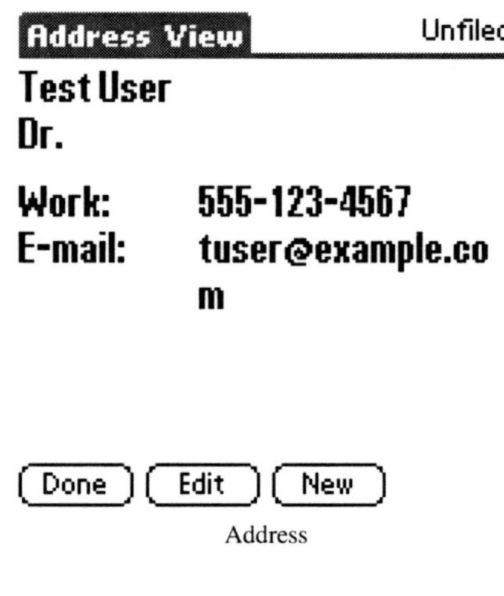

Address

Note : On the newer models, the standard PIM apps "Address", "Date Book", "Memo Pad" and "ToDos" have been replaced by their improved counterparts "Contacts", "Calendar" "Memos" and "Tasks".

The Palm's **Address** program stores contact information, keyed by any of several user-definable categories. Entries are displayed and sorted in last name, first name order (this can be changed only to Company, Last Name order). There are five slots for phone or e-mail, each of which may be designated Work, Home, Fax, Other, E-mail, Main, Pager or Mobile (the slot designations cannot be changed). The newer **Contacts** app adds the following features : several addresses, 9 new fields : Website, Birthday, More phone numbers, Instant Messaging with quick connect.

**Calc** turns the Palm into a standard 4-function pocket calculator with three shades of purple and blue buttons contrasting with the two red clear buttons. It supports square root and percent keys and has one memory.

It also has an option to display a running history of the calculations, much like the paper-tape calculators that were once common.

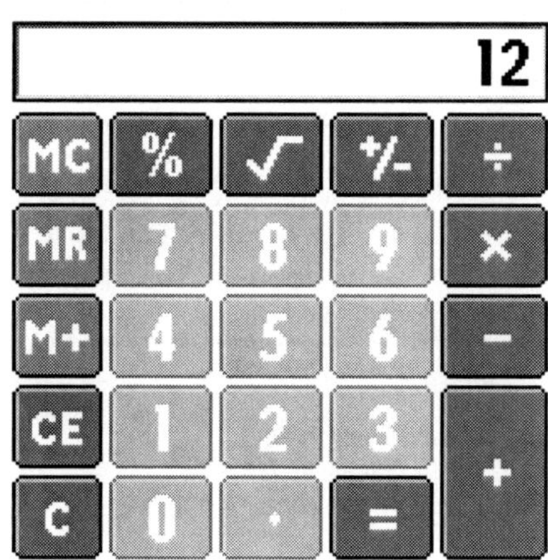


Calculator as seen on Palm OS 4.1

Date Book

**Date Book** shows a daily or weekly schedule, or a simple monthly view. The daily schedule has one line per hour, between user-selected begin and end times. Clicking on an empty line creates a new event. Empty lines are crowded out by actual events, whose start and stop times are shown by default bracketed in the left margin. The newer **Calendar** app adds the following features : New Day view, use of categories for events, event location, event can span midnight, event details, birthdays as timeless events. It supports timezone designation for events, a feature lacking in some more recent competitors.

An event, or appointment, can be heralded by an alarm, any number of minutes, hours or days before it begins. These alarms sound even when the unit is switched off.

Appointments can recur in a specified number of days, weeks, months or years and can contain notes.

**Expense** tracks common business expenses. No totals are calculated on the Palm. The user must sync with a host computer and view the expense data in a worksheet (templates for Microsoft Excel are supplied).

**HotSync** integrates with the user's PC. Usually activated by a press of the physical HotSync button on the Palm's cradle (a dock station), this application communicates with various conduits on the desktop PC to install software, backup databases, or merge changes made on the PC or the handheld to both devices. It can communicate with the PC through a physical connection (USB on newer models; although drivers for Windows x64 based platforms are still unavailable, 32 bit editions work well), Bluetooth or IrDA wireless connections, and direct network connections on devices with networking capability.

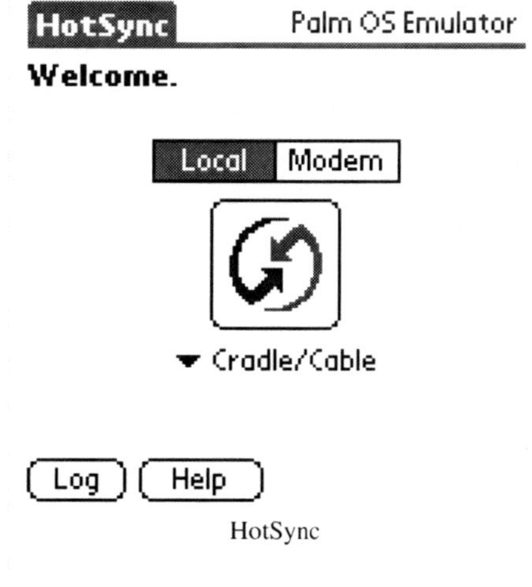


HotSync

In addition to the conduits provided by the licensee, developers can create their own conduits for integration with other Palm OS applications and desktop products. For example, a time tracking package could provide a conduit to communicate information between Palm OS and Windows executables.

A Backup conduit included with the HotSync software backs up (and restores, if necessary) most of the data on a Palm OS device. This allows users to hard reset their Palm—thus clearing all of the data—with few noticeable consequences. This also allows users to migrate to new Palm devices of the same Palm OS version, a feature that is helpful to those who lose or damage their device.

Some models of Palm keep their data storage in volatile memory and require constant power to maintain their memory. Although these handhelds attempt to save the contents of memory in low battery situations by not "turning on," leaving a "dead" handheld for an extended period of time can cause this reserve power to be used up and the contents of storage memory to be lost. Some later Palms use NVRAM or microdrive for storage.

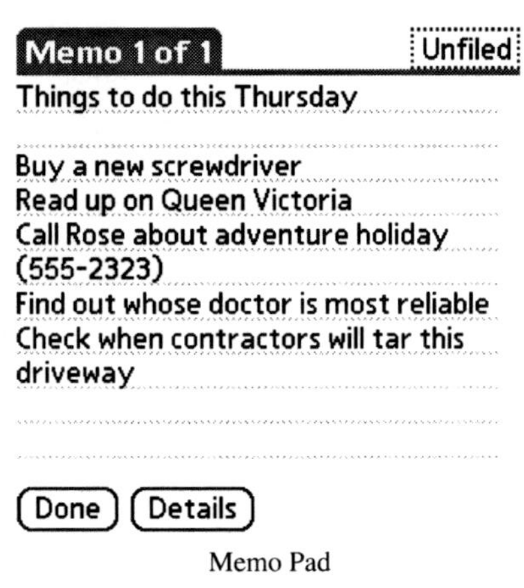

Memo Pad

**Memo Pad** can hold notes of up to 4,000 characters each; the newer **Memos** app increases field size from 3 to 30 kB. Memos are ordered in two ways: alphabetically, and manually (which allows the user to choose the order of the memos), and memos can be grouped in user-configurable categories. Memo Pad is for text only, not for drawings, and text can be entered using the Graffiti alphabet, using hardware or software keyboards, or using the 'paste' function. When Palm devices first became available, some Palm users started to create and exchange Memo Pad documents containing generally useful information, which came to be known as Memoware.

**To do list** creates personal reminders and prioritizes the things the user has to do. Each To Do List item may also have: a priority, categories (to organize and view items in logical groups), attached Note (to add more description and clarification of the task).
To Do List item can be sorted by: due date, priority or category. The newer **Tasks** app features the following improvements : new interface, repeating tasks, alarms, etc.

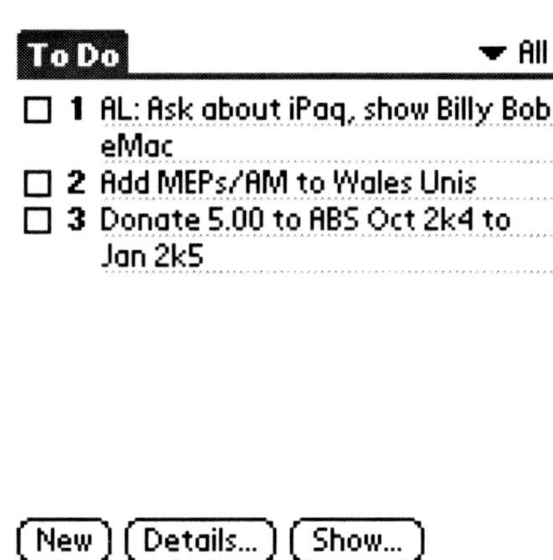

To Do list

**Preferences** (also referred to as Prefs) shows program files with a special preference panel type which are not shown by the normal launcher. Programs can be changed by switching the 'appl' type to 'panl' and vice versa. Palm OS contains approximately 15 preference panels by default and new preference panels can be added just like any other application.

Preference panels allow users to manage a number of setting including Graffiti settings, sound settings, text shortcuts, network settings and the system time.

**Security** (which is a panel on newer Palm OS devices) is used to configure Palm OS's security settings. These include the password needed to display hidden records and unlock the device when locked, as well as setup an automatic lock down time or inactivity threshold. On the PC, only Palm Desktop honors this password but other PC programs can view everything—in other words, all the data protected by this password can be seen by anyone opening the .dat files using a text editor or word processor.

## Common 3rd party core OS applications

Starting with Palm OS version 5.2, Palm created customized versions of the common PIM application. Some new features have been added, e.g. support for Address categories, Ringtone associations to users, longer memo texts, etc.. They were also renamed to reflect designations from Microsoft Outlook, thus Address became *Contacts*, Datebook became *Calendar*, Memo Pad became *Memos* and To do list became *Tasks*.

Blazer is a web browser for Palm handhelds. The versions 1.0 and 2.0 run on Palm OS 3.1 or higher handhelds, but they needed a proxy server which has been shut down, so they can no longer be used. Version 3.0 is used on the Treo 600 smartphone. The current version of Blazer is Blazer 4.5, which is compliant with most major standards. It is generally bundled with newer smartphones and newer Palm devices capable of accessing the Internet.

Palm's **Note Pad** can be used for quick drawings. With neat handwriting, 20-30 words will fit on one page; for more text, Memo Pad is the better choice. There are three sizes of pen width, plus an eraser and a background color change feature in some models. It is possible to draw a very simple map. The more "advanced" desktop version saves the Memo pad drawings to the desktop.

Note Pad

As of 2006, most new Palm handhelds include **Photos**, which creates a digital photo album used to view pictures on a Palm OS device. As with all the other photo programs, photos can be beamed to other mobile devices. Each photo can be labeled and organized into separate photo albums. A slideshow can also be shown for a specific album, and each photo in the album will be shown full screen.

Photos can be edited with the Palm Photos PC software (Windows only), and when the photos are transferred to the handheld they will contain all changes made to the photo.

The Palm Photos software is available in the Zire 71, Tungsten C, Tungsten E, Tungsten T2, Tungsten T3 and several others.

With the support for Video, Palm Photos was later renamed to *Media* and even later to *Pics& Videos*.

Some models feature the ability to make voice recordings which are synced using the Voice conduit and can be viewed on a desktop with the **Voice Memo** application which is part of the Palm Desktop Suite.

# Third-party applications

There are many successful applications that can be installed on a Palm OS device. As of 2008, there are more than 50,000 third-party applications available for the Palm OS platform,[34] which have various licensing types, including open-source, and various closed licensing schemes such as freeware,[35] shareware, and traditional pay-up-front purchase.

# Application development

Palm OS Garnet applications are primarily coded in C/C++. Two officially supported compilers exist: a commercial product, CodeWarrior Development Studio for Palm OS, and an open source tool chain called prc-tools, based on an old version of gcc. CodeWarrior is criticized for being expensive and is no longer being developed, whereas PRC-Tools lacks several of CodeWarrior's features. A version of PRC-Tools is included in a free Palm OS Developer Suite (PODS).

OnBoardC is a C compiler, assembler, linker and programming editor that runs on the Palm itself.

Palm OS Cobalt applications are also coded in a variation of gcc, but the Cobalt compilers have fewer limitations.

There are development tools available for Palm programming that do not require low-level programming in C/C++, such as PocketC/PocketC Architect, CASL, AppForge Crossfire (which uses Visual Basic, Visual Basic.NET, or C#), Handheld Basic, Pendragon Forms, Satellite Forms [39] and NSBasic/Palm (Visual Basic like languages). A Java Virtual Machine was previously available for the Palm OS platform, however on 2008-01-12 Palm, Inc. announced that it would no longer be available. Palm, Inc. further said "There is no alternate Java Virtual Machine that we are aware of for Palm OS."[36] Waba and a derivative of it, SuperWaba, provide a Java-like virtual machine and programming language. A version of the Lua language, called Plua, is also available for Palm; however, due to the fact that it requires an additional runtime to be installed along with the application, it is only used for mainstream applications by a minority of software companies. Quartus Forth [41] is an ISO/ANSI Standard Forth compiler that runs on the Palm itself. It also has an interactive console for dynamic development and debugging.

Two environments allow programming in Pascal for Palm OS. The free PP Compiler[37] runs directly on the handheld computer, while PocketStudio is a Delphi-like IDE for Windows Computers that has a visual form designer and generates PRC files for being transferred to handhelds via HotSync.

As Palm has no connection drivers that enable the transfer of data with a server DBMS (Oracle, mySQL, MS SQL Server), the programmer can use Middleware software that enables this connectivity.

A roughly R4RS-compatible implementation of Scheme, LispMe, provides the Palm platform with a GPL-licensed onboard Lisp REPL with some Palm OS-specific adaptations, but although it is functionally a compiler it does not produce code that operates outside the development environment, so its use is restricted to prototyping.

A free development tool, LaFac, works directly on the Palm device, using the Memo Pad for source code editing, and provides support for a limited subset of C, Pascal, and Basic.

## Legal issues

Palm OS has been involved in various lawsuits over the years.

**Xerox vs. Palm Computing (1997)** In 1997, Xerox was granted a patent (5,596,656) on "unistroke." It filed suit against Palm (then U.S. Robotics), alleging that Graffiti infringed on this patent. The Palm OS switch from Graffiti 1 to Graffiti 2 was triggered by Palm losing this suit to Xerox. The patent was overturned in May 2004 due to prior art.[38]

**Pilot Pen Corporation vs. Palm Computing (1998)** The original name for Palm OS handhelds was Pilot. However, a lawsuit from Pilot Pen Corporation forced a name change to PalmPilot, then eventually to Palm.

**Palm vs. Microsoft (1998)** In 1998, Microsoft planned to name the next version of their handheld computing platform "Palm PC". Palm filed suit against Microsoft, forcing the name change to, first, Palm-sized PC, and later, Pocket PC.

**E-Pass Technologies vs. Palm, Microsoft and HP (2000)** In 2000, E-Pass Technologies filed suit against Palm, alleging that its handhelds infringed on an E-Pass's patent (#5,276,311) for a multi-function, credit card-sized computer that allows users to securely store account numbers, PIN codes, etc.. This lawsuit continues.

**NCR vs. Handspring and Palm (2001)** In 1987, NCR was granted a patent for a portable e-commerce terminal. In 2001, NCR sued Handspring and Palm. This case was ruled without merit in 2002, a decision that was upheld on appeal.

**RIM vs. Handspring (2002)** In 2002, Research In Motion (makers of the BlackBerry), sued Handspring. By year end, both Handspring and Palm licensed the patents and the suit was dropped.

**Peer-to-Peer Systems vs. Palm (2002)** Also in 2002, Peer-to-Peer systems filed lawsuit against Palm that alleges Palm infringed on its patent for wireless gaming. This lawsuit has been settled as of Feb 9th 2005.

**Forgent Networks vs. HP, Toshiba, palmOne, etc., etc. (2004)** Starting in 2002, Forgent Networks began offering licenses for a patent that encumbers JPEG. In 2004, it filed suit against various companies, including palmOne. The

JPEG or 672 patent has been reviewed by the U.S. Patent and Trademark Office which has rejected 19 of the 47 claims based on prior art.[39]

# References


[1] *Piloting Palm,* Andrea Butter & David Pogue, Wiley 2002, p. 82.

[2] *Piloting Palm,* chapter 8, *passim.*

[3] *Piloting Palm,* pp. 179–189.

[4] Palm, Inc. Sets IPO Price at $38 per Share (http://investor.palm.com/releasedetail.cfm?releaseid=339213), 3Com / Palm press release, March 1, 2000

[5] Palm Completes Formation of Palm OS Subsidiary as Palm Powered Devices Hit 20 Million Sold (http://www.access-company.com/news/press/PalmSource/2002/012102.html), Palm / PalmSource press release, January 21, 2002

[6] PalmSource Spins Out From Palm, Inc. (http://www.access-company.com/news/press/PalmSource/2003/102803_palmsourcespin.html), PalmSource press release, October 28, 2003

[7] ACCESS to Extend Leadership in Mobile Device Software with Acquisition of PalmSource (http://www.access-company.com/news/press/PalmSource/2005/090905_access.html), PalmSource / ACCESS press release, September 9, 2005

[8] Palm Signs Perpetual License for Palm OS Garnet Source Code and Expanded Patent Rights From ACCESS Systems Americas (http://investor.palm.com/releasedetail.cfm?releaseid=344677), Palm press release, December 7, 2006

[9] palmOne Acquires Rights to Palm Brand (http://investor.palm.com/releasedetail.cfm?ReleaseID=341907), palmOne press release, May 24, 2005

[10] ACCESS Debuts New ACCESS Powered Mark (http://www.access-company.com/news/press/ACCESS/2007/20070125_powered_logo.html), ACCESS press release, January 25, 2007

[11] KADAK Partner Web Site (http://www.kadak.com/html/kdkp1620.htm#Palm,)

[12] Palm OS is a multitasking operating system. How can I create a task? (http://kb.palmsource.com/cgi-bin/palmsource.cfg/php/enduser/std_adp.php?p_faqid=72), ACCESS Palm OS Developer Knowledge Base entry

[13] U.S. Robotics Announces Two New Models of the Best Selling Pilot Connected Organizer (http://investor.palm.com/releasedetail.cfm?ReleaseID=335827), U.S. Robotics / Palm press release, March 10, 1997

[14] 3Com Delivers the Palm III Connected Organizer, the Third Generation of the Industry-Leading PalmPilot Handheld Computer (http://investor.palm.com/releasedetail.cfm?releaseid=336734), 3Com / Palm press release, March 9, 1998

[15] 3Com Unveils the Palm V and Palm IIIx Connected Organizers (http://investor.palm.com/releasedetail.cfm?releaseid=338042), 3Com / Palm press release, February 22, 1999

[16] Palm, Inc. Introduces The Palm IIIc Product Industry's Smallest, Lightest Color Handheld Computer (http://investor.palm.com/releasedetail.cfm?ReleaseID=339196), Palm press release, February 22, 2000

[17] Palm Mobile Internet Kit Ships, Links Palm Handhelds With Mobile Phones To Connect Wirelessly to the Web (http://investor.palm.com/releasedetail.cfm?ReleaseID=339878), Palm press release, November 13, 2000

[18] New Sleek Palm m500 and m505 Handhelds Add Expansion, Mobile Connectivity and Vibrant Color (http://investor.palm.com/releasedetail.cfm?ReleaseID=344698), Palm press release, March 19, 2001

[19] PalmSource Ships Faster, More Powerful Palm OS 5 (http://www.access-company.com/news/press/PalmSource/2002/061002_1.html), PalmSource press release, June 10, 2002

[20] First PalmSource ARM-Native Proxy-less Web Browser Ships to Licensees (http://www.access-company.com/news/press/PalmSource/2002/091702.html), PalmSource press release, Sept. 17, 2002

[21] Samsung reveals feature-packed SGH-i500 (http://www.infosyncworld.com/news/n/3238.html), infoSync News Article, March 13, 2003

[22] PalmSource Ships Palm OS 5 Simplified Chinese Edition (http://www.access-company.com/news/press/PalmSource/2003/091003_chineseEd.html), PalmSource press release, Sept. 9, 2003

[23] PalmSource Welcomes First Palm OS 5 Simplified Chinese Edition Handhelds from Lenovo (http://www.access-company.com/news/press/PalmSource/2003/120803_lenovo.html), PalmSource press release, Dec. 8, 2003

[24] PalmSource Introduces Palm OS Cobalt (http://www.access-company.com/news/press/PalmSource/2004/021004_cobalt.html), PalmSource press release, Feb 10, 2004

[25] PalmSource Introduces Palm OS Cobalt 6.1 (http://www.access-company.com/news/press/PalmSource/2004/092804_cobalt.html), PalmSource press release, Sep 28, 2004

[26] Palm Delivers SIG-Compliant Bluetooth Software to Massive Palm OS Developer Base (http://investor.palm.com/releasedetail.cfm?ReleaseID=341039), Palm press release, January 14, 2001

[27] PalmSource to Extend Leadership in Phone Software with Acquisition of China MobileSoft (http://www.access-company.com/news/press/PalmSource/2004/120804_cms.html), PalmSource press release, December 8, 2004

[28] PalmSource halts development on Garnet and Cobalt (http://www.vnunet.com/vnunet/news/2139110/palmsource-linux-phone-promised), VUnet News entry

[29] ACCESS and PalmSource Announce the ACCESS Linux Platform (http://www.access-company.com/news/press/ACCESS/2006/021406.html), ACCESS/PalmSource press release, February 14, 2006

[30] ACCESS Releases ACCESS Linux Platform PDK and SDK to Licensees and Developers (http://www.access-company.com/news/press/ACCESS/2007/20070212d_alp_pdk.html), ACCESS press release, February 12, 2007
[31] Colligan Talks About Next Generation Palm OS Progress (http://www.palminfocenter.com/news/8301/colligan-talks-about-next-generation-palm-os-progress/), PalmInfoCenter news entry
[32] Palm CEO Ed Colligan Talks Pre with Investors (http://www.precentral.net/palm-ceo-ed-colligan-talks-pre-investors)
[33] "PalmOS Emulation on webOS CONFIRMED: will be done by Motion Apps" (http://www.precentral.net/palmos-emulation-webos-confirmed-will-be-done-motion-apps) precentral (http://www.precentral.net/)
[34] Treo and Centro Software - Top 100 Gold List (http://blog.treonauts.com/2008/01/treo-and-cent-1.html)
[35] Palm Freeware Directory (http://www.palm-freeware.org/), Wiki-like Palm Freeware Directory, August 15, 2008
[36] JVM download for Palm OS devices no longer available from Palm (http://www.palm.com/us/support/jvm/), Palm Support Site, 2008-01-12
[37] PP Compiler Pascal & Palm
[38] Xerox loses patent claim against PalmOne (http://www.computerweekly.com/Articles/2004/05/26/202705/xerox-loses-patent-claim-against-palmone.htm)
[39] Forgent JPEG Related Patent (http://www.pubpat.org/forgentjpeg.htm)

## External links

- Palm.com (http://www.palm.com/)
- Palm OS 4.1 Screenshots (http://members.shaw.ca/guis/palmos41.html)
- Palm OS (http://www.dmoz.org/Computers/Systems/Handhelds/Palm_OS//) at the Open Directory Project

# Pilot-link

## Pilot-link

| Developer(s) | David A. Desrosiers[1] |
|---|---|
| Stable release | 0.12.5, "No Codename" / March 1, 2010 |
| Operating system | Unix-like, Linux |
| Platform | Palm OS |
| Type | library |
| License | open source |
| Website | http://www.pilot-link.org/ |

**pilot-link** is a library of utilities for connecting to and synchronising with Palm OS-based PDAs on Unix and Unix-based operating systems. It uses a set of 'conduits' for the exchange of information from different Palm applications.

pilot-link provides command line tools to perform synchronisation tasks, such as the pilot-xfer command, which can install the standard Palm database (PDB) files to the connected device. Graphical User Interfaces for the pilot-link software include KPilot, part of the KDE's Personal Information Management applications, and JPilot, a GTK+-based interface.

## References

[1] CV for David A. Desrosiers; Open Source Developer, Engineer and Entrepreneur (http://resume.gnu-designs.com/)

## External links

- Pilot-link community home page (http://www.pilot-link.org/)
- Pilot-link (http://sourceforge.net/projects/pilot-link/) at SourceForge.net
- KPilot home page (http://cvs.codeyard.net/kpilot/)
- JPilot (http://www.jpilot.org/requirements.html)

[Category:Computer libraries| ]]

# PlayStation Portable system software

**PlayStation Portable System Software** is the official, updatable firmware for the PlayStation Portable. Updates add new functionality as well as security patches to prevent homebrew applications being run on the system. Updates can be obtained in four ways:

- Direct download to the PSP over Wi-Fi. This can be performed by choosing [Settings], [System Update] from the XMB.
- Download to a PC, then transfer to the PSP via a USB cable or Memory Stick.
- Included on the UMD of some games. These games may not run with earlier firmware than the version on their UMD.
- Download from a PS3 to a PSP system via USB cable. (Japanese and American version only)

While system software updates can be used with consoles from any region, Sony recommends only downloading system software updates released for the region corresponding to the system's place of purchase. System software updates have added various features including a web browser, Adobe flash player 6 support, additional codecs for images, audio, and video, PlayStation 3 connectivity, as well as patches against several security exploits, vulnerabilities, and execution of homebrew programs.[1] The battery must be at least 75% charged or else the system will prevent the update code from installing. If the power supply is lost while writing to the system software, the console will no longer be able to operate unless the system is booted in service mode or sent to Sony for repair if still under warranty.

The latest reported firmware version shipping pre-installed on new PSP systems is 6.20[2] (as of November 24, 2010). The latest version of the system software is 6.38 (as of April 12, 2011).[3]

## Versions

| Version | Date Released[4] | Description |
|---|---|---|
| **6.38**[5] | April 12, 2011 | • Enhances system stability under certain conditions.<br>• Allows access to the Qriocity service. |
| **6.37**[6] | January 20, 2011 | • The *Everybody's Sukkiri* #1 Save Game Exploit was patched.<br>• The scepower kernel exploit was patched.<br>• Required version to run:<br>  • *Dissidia 012 Final Fantasy* |
| **6.36**[7] | *UMD Only* First found on December 1, 2010 | • Required version to run:<br>  • *Monster Hunter Portable 3rd* |
| **6.35**[3] | November 24, 2010 | • Prepares the PSP system for Qriocity,[8] a cloud-based music service.<br>• The *Hot Shots Golf* Save Game Exploit was silently patched. |
| **6.31**[9] | July 29, 2010 | • The system stability of certain titles has been improved<br>• Fixed a bug in *Persona 3 Portable* when you couldn't play the game after the PSP was put in standby. |
| **6.30**[10] | June 29, 2010 | • Games can now be sorted by their format (PSP, minis, PlayStation, PC Engine, and Neo Geo.)<br>• PlayStation Plus compatibility.<br>• The *Patapon 2* Save Game Exploit was silently patched.<br>• The Datel cheat device was silently patched.[11] |

| | | |
|---|---|---|
| **6.20**[12] | November 18, 2009 | *Initial release for a revision of PSP-3000 with TA-093 motherboard.*<br>• The 'Archer MaClean's Mercury Exploit' was patched.<br>• The importing of playlists from the Media Go application is now supported under [Video].<br>• The importing of playlists from the PlayStation 3 system or the Media Go application is now supported under [Photo].<br>• The [TV] category has been integrated into the new [Extras] category in the XMB (XrossMediaBar) menu. 2000 3000 N1000 (Japanese Version)<br>• [Digital Comics] reader added under [Extras].<br>• Wireless LAN LED no longer flashes when online<br>• Some enhancements were added for Media Go<br>• Required version to run:<br>◦ *Kingdom Hearts Birth by Sleep*<br>◦ *Metal Gear Solid: Peace Walker*<br>◦ *God Eater* (Japanese Version)<br>◦ *Naruto Shippūden: Ultimate Ninja Heroes 3*<br>◦ *Modnation Racers*<br>◦ *BlazBlue Portable* |
| **6.10**[13] [14] | September 30, 2009 | • SensMe Channels added<br>• Playlist support has been added for playlists imported from Media Go<br>• Some enhancements were added for Media Go<br>• [Update] has been added to the list of options for games and applications.<br>• [Version] has been added as new metadata information for content stored under [Game]<br>• Bluetooth Tethering for Internet Access. N1000<br>• The [Standard] option for [Display Panel Close Options] has been changed. N1000<br>• [Memory Stick] has been added as a save destination for content downloaded from PlayStation Store. N1000<br>• The Dial-Up Networking profile has been added as one of the supported Bluetooth profiles. N1000<br>• Required version to run:<br>◦ *Tekken 6* |
| **6.00**[15] | September 10, 2009 | *This firmware does not contain the 05g model (PSP-N1000 (PSPgo)) according to psardumper.*<br>• New colors have been added to the XMB. 2000 3000<br>• A security patch has been added.<br>• Under [System Update], you can now choose how to update the system software.<br>• Games can now be grouped and displayed in folders based on their expire date under [Game].<br>• Group Content under the following new folders: With Expire Date, Expired, and Without Expire Date.<br>• The battery icon now animates differently while charging.<br>• The PS1 emulator has been updated.<br>• When highlighting a background under [Theme Settings] in [Background], the PSP automatically changes the background for a preview<br>• Required version to run:<br>◦ *Metal Gear Solid: Peace Walker* Demo [16]<br>◦ *Gran Turismo* [17]<br>◦ *Invizimals* |
| **5.70** | *Pre-installed Only*<br>First found on October 1, 2009 | This firmware is only available pre-installed on new PSP-N1000 models and some later PSP 3000 models and cannot be downloaded.[18]<br>• [Network Update] has been renamed to [System Update].<br>• [Your Birth Date] option has been added to [System Settings]. N1000<br>• [Bluetooth Device Settings] has been added to the [Settings] menu. N1000<br>• [Display Panel Close Option] has been added to [System Settings]. N1000<br>• Calendar has been added to the [Display Panel Close Option] screensaver setting. N1000<br>• [System Settings] icon has been redesigned. |

| | | |
|---|---|---|
| **5.55**[19] | *UMD Only*<br>First found on July 5, 2009 | • Provided only with some UMD games, including:<br>  • *Soul Calibur: Broken Destiny*<br>  • *G.I. Joe: The Rise of Cobra*<br>  • *Tales of VS.*<br>  • *Armored Core 3 Portable*<br>  • *Disgaea 2 Dark Hero Days*<br>  • *Dissidia: Final Fantasy* (Europe version)<br>  • *MotorStorm: Arctic Edge*<br>  • *Colin McRae: Dirt 2*<br>  • *AFL Challenge*<br>  • *Cloudy With a Chance of Meatballs*<br>  • *IL-2 Sturmovik: Birds of Prey*<br>  • *Shin Megami Tensei: Persona*<br>  • *Rugby League Challenge*<br>  • *Gran Turismo*<br>  • *Macross Ultimate Frontier*<br>  • *WWE SmackDown vs. Raw 2010*<br>• Required to play the above games<br>• Security on 5.55+ titles has been increased |
| **5.51**[20] | June 11, 2009 | • System software stability during use of some features has been improved.<br>• 5.03-5.05 ChickHEN kernel-level exploit silently patched.<br>• Patched 5.50 gamesave exploit for Need for Speed Underground (US) and Monster Hunter Freedom (JPN) |
| **5.50**[21] | April 20, 2009 | • [Information Board] has been added<br>• Memory Stick improvements<br>  • Sub-folder support has been added for music, videos, and photos<br>  • Space required to download a file from PlayStation Store to your Memory Stick has been reduced significantly.<br>• [Internet Search] for games directly from the XMB has been added<br>• An [Internet Search] icon has been added within the web browser<br>• Trend Micro trial has been added for the Web Browser.<br>  • Trend Micro Web Security<br>  • Trend Micro Kids' Safety<br>• The new TIFF exploit (3rd of 3) by MaTiAz was patched.<br>• You can now access the PlayStation Store even if you do not have an account.<br>• An option to sign-in automatically is now available on the PlayStation store sign-in screen.<br>• [Download All] has been added as an option when purchasing multiple items from the store.<br>• Removal of Go!Messenger under Network (European versions only)<br>• Consumption capacity calculation problem with download contents for The Idolm@ster has been fixed.[22] |
| **5.05**[23] | *UMD Only*<br>First found on February 19, 2009 | *Provided only with the Japanese release of* The Idolm@ster<br>• Rumored changes relating to *The Idolm@ster*:<br>  • In-game PlayStation Store interface—it is said that *The Idolm@ster* is the first title that has this interface.[24]<br>  • Support for PlayStation Home rewards added—rumor spread from the false report by some websites that prizes in PlayStation Home resulted from player in-game accomplishments from *The Idolm@ster*.[25] |
| **5.03**[26] | January 19, 2009 | • System software stability during use of some features has been improved.<br>• Patches the Gripshift buffer overflow exploit via modified game save data.[27]<br>• Support for Premium Themes has been added. |
| **5.02**[28] | November 20, 2008 | • System software stability including the use of the PlayStation(R) Store has been improved.<br>Japanese only feature:<br>• One-segment TV channel list for Takada, Nigata and Koga, Shiga has been updated. 2000 3000 |
| **5.01**[29] | October 21, 2008 | • Fixes a bug in the PlayStation Store with 8GB and 16GB Memory Sticks, causing the system to display "Not Enough Space" while downloading content. |

| Version | Date | Changes |
|---|---|---|
| **5.00**[30] [31] | October 15, 2008 | *First "universal" firmware version for the original PSP-1000, PSP-2000 PSP Slim & Lite and PSP-3000 series*<br>• [PlayStation Network] has been added as a category on the XMB<br>• [PlayStation Store] has been added under [PlayStation Network] menu<br>• [Account Management] has been added under [PlayStation Network] menu<br>• Sleep Timer Function for [Music]<br>• [USB Auto-Connect] Feature added for PSP-1000 and PSP-2000 under [System Settings]<br>• A new full-screen keyboard; press [Select] when the On-Screen Keyboard is displayed.<br>• A new redesigned XMB Background [Original] added as an option under [Theme Settings]<br>• A new video format is supported (MPEG-4 AVC (H.264) Video Main Profile (AVC CABAC) in 640 × 480 pixels)<br>• [Title Display] feature added under [Video Settings]<br>• Screen capture has been added as a feature within games and the internet browser (this is up to the game developer or the web site developer to support though).<br>• PlayStation format software can now be output in full-screen size on a connected device, even if it doesn't have progressive input capability. Still PSP format software can only be output on devices that have progressive input capability. 2000 3000 |
| **4.21** | *Pre-installed Only*<br>First found on December 5, 2008 | *Only available pre-installed on the initial release of the black* Rachet & Clank *Entertainment Pack PSP-3000 series in North America and possibly some later production units of the Silver* Rachet & Clank *and* Gran Turismo *bundles in North America and other colors and regions worldwide.*<br>• Fixed a bug in Libtiff feature. |
| **4.20**[32] | *Pre-installed Only*<br>First found on October 14, 2008 | No update to this firmware was ever made available. This firmware was only available pre-installed on the initial release of the PSP-3000 series<br>• [USB auto-connect] feature in [System Settings] under [Settings]. (This feature was made available in a subsequent update to other PSP systems)<br>• [Flicker Reduction] under the [Connected Display] menu in [Settings]. 3000<br>• [Noise Reduction] under the [Connected Display] menu in [Settings]. 3000<br>• [Color Space] under the [System Settings] menu in [Settings]. 3000 |
| **4.05**[33] | July 13, 2008 | • Added new visualization effect under [Music].<br>• Added support for viewing rentals and purchased videos downloaded from the [PlayStation Store] (temporarily US version only)<br>Japanese only features:<br>• Up to 8 programs may now be scheduled for record using the One-segment TV Tuner 2000<br>• You may now set up a whole series of programs to record using the One-segment TV Tuner 2000<br>• You may now record TV using the One-segment TV Tuner without having to also watch it 2000 |
| **4.01**[34] | June 25, 2008 | *Initial release for the TA-088 v3 motherboard, non-compatible with the Pandora Battery.*<br>• Display of search results under [Internet Search] has been improved for certain languages.<br>• Playback of video content under [Video] has been improved for certain file types. |
| **4.00**[35] | June 18, 2008 | • [Internet Search] has been added as a feature under [Network]<br>• Functionality allowing for altered playing speeds under [Video]<br>• Added Subtitle support for UMD Movies under [Video] |
| **3.96** | *UMD Only*<br>First found on June 3, 2008 | *Provided only with the North American version of* Hot Shots Golf: Open Tee 2<br>• Support for PlayStation Network titles has been expanded. |
| **3.95** | April 8, 2008 | • Support for PlayStation Network titles has been expanded.<br>• Downloaded PlayStation game controls can now be further customized.<br>• The method for turning the PS3 off using [Remote Play] has been altered. |
| **3.93** | March 18, 2008 | • The Internet Radio feature has been expanded.<br>• Skype feature has been added under Network. (Japanese version only) 2000 |

| | | |
|---|---|---|
| **3.90** | January 29, 2008 | • Support for PlayStation Network titles has been expanded.<br>• Support for the Go!Messenger service (under [Network]). (European version only)[36]<br>• *Skype feature has been added under Network.* (Excluding Japanese version) 2000 |
| **3.80** | December 17, 2007 | • Streaming internet radio player<br>• Added new music visualization effect<br>• Video scene search<br>• RSS now supports OPML and pictures<br>• PlayStation Spot now available at BB Mobile Point (Japanese version only)<br>• Added ability to play PlayStation games from disc or hard drive via Remote Play with the PlayStation 3 system<br>Japanese only features:<br>• One-segment broadcasting recordings 2000 |
| **3.73** | November 29, 2007 | *Initial release for a revision of the Slim & Lite with TA-085 v2 motherboard.*<br>• Improved system stability by fixing problems where the UMD drive would occasionally suspend and then fail to reload data. |
| **3.72** | October 30, 2007 | • Support for PlayStation Network titles expanded.<br>• Remote Start now available under Remote Play. Remote Start requires a PlayStation 3 system with system software version 2.00. |
| **3.71** | September 13, 2007 | • Revisions to strengthen security have been added.<br>• Support for PlayStation Network titles expanded.<br>• A correction has been made to the settings for some regions (i.e., the PlayStation Spot icon was removed for regions other than Japan) |
| **3.70** | September 11, 2007 | *First "universal" firmware version for both the original PSP-1000 and PSP-2000 PSP Slim & Lite series*<br>• Custom themes<br>• Support has been added for assigning buttons in [Remote Play]<br>• A scene search feature has been added under [Video]<br>• Sequential playback is now supported under [Video]<br>• Simultaneous playback of content under [Music] and [Photo] is now supported<br>• PlayStation Spot icon added under [Network] for regions other than Japan<br>• Video bitrate limit raised to 2Mbit/s from 768kbit/s |
| **3.60** | *Pre-installed Only*<br>First found on September 10, 2007 | *No update to this firmware was ever made available. This firmware was only available pre-installed on the initial release of the PSP Slim & Lite with TA-085 motherboard.*<br>• TV output added 2000<br>• Support for the 1-Seg Tuner *(Japanese version only)* 2000<br>• UMD cache support 2000<br>• USB Charge option 2000<br>• Additional color themes for XMB 2000 |
| **3.52** | July 24, 2007 | • Support for PlayStation Network titles expanded. |
| **3.51** | June 29, 2007 | • Illuminati exploit has been patched. |
| **3.50** | May 31, 2007 | • Allows Remote Play to be used via an internet connection.<br>• "RSS Channel Guide" has been added as a feature under "RSS Channel".[37]<br>• CPU speed limit removed, allowing CPU to run at 333 MHz rather than 266 MHz.[38] |
| **3.40** | April 20, 2007 | • Support for PlayStation Network titles expanded..<br>• "Certificate Utility" option erased. (Can still be accessed by pressing triangle on the selected game)<br>• Saved data from PlayStation format software can be used on both PSP and PS3 systems.[39] |
| **3.30** | March 28, 2007 | Security added to detect TA-082 / TA-086 motherboards which have been downgraded to 1.50 and prevent upgrading to 3.30 or newer. Easily fixed by using IDstorage Key Cleaner.<br>• Support for thumbnail images within RSS channel and in video folder.<br>• MPEG-4/H.264 support for 720×480, 352×480, and 480×272 (native resolution).<br>• "Wireless Hotspot" added (6 months of free T-Mobile Hotspot wireless internet access was added for US users)[40] |

| | | |
|---|---|---|
| **3.11** | February 8, 2007 | • Added:<br>• Reset option for PlayStation Network games.<br>• "Portable TV" menu under "Network". (Japanese version only)[41] |
| **3.10** | January 30, 2007 | • Added:<br>• Dynamic normalizer.<br>• Conserve memory option.<br>• [PlayStationSpot] menu under [Network]. (Japanese version only)<br>• Secret patching of sceRegOpenRegistry and GTA exploits. |
| **3.03** | December 20, 2006 | • Support for PlayStation Network titles expanded.<br>• Added:<br>• Support for taking photos and videos using the camera. |
| **3.02** | December 6, 2006 | • Support for PlayStation Network titles expanded. |
| **3.01** | November 22, 2006 | • Support for PlayStation Network titles expanded. |
| **3.00** | November 21, 2006 | • Support for:<br>• PlayStation 3 Remote Play.<br>• Classic PSone games.<br>• Added a music visualizer. |
| **2.82** | October 26, 2006 | • Revisions to strengthen security have been added. |
| **2.81** | September 7, 2006 | • Support for memory sticks with a capacity greater than 4GB.<br>• Patched a libtiff exploit (2nd of 3). |
| **2.80** | July 27, 2006 | • Support for Video RSS feeds.<br>• Update for LocationFree Player to support AVC video codec.<br>• Secret patching of sceKernelLoadExec bug, but opening sceRegOpenRegistry exploit. |
| **2.71** | May 30, 2006 | • Support to download Game Demos from the Internet Browser. |
| **2.70** | April 25, 2006 | • Support for Adobe Flash Player (Version 6). |
| **2.60** | November 29, 2005 | • First attempt at patching the 2.00-2.50 GTA exploit. Security update was later found not to work correctly in every version through 3.03 (Grand Theft Auto: Liberty City Stories exploit).<br>• Support for Audio RSS feeds.<br>• An overclock bug (or limit?) was introduced with this update preventing the CPU from going above 222mHz while WiFi is activated. This is a predictable and reproductive behavior where if the CPU is overclocked (such as 266-333) before activating wifi, the behavior is nullified until the next complete shutdown. This is still present in the latest firmware. This could have been an attempted limit by Sony to anticipate the lower voltage of the battery in the PSP-2000 to prevent drawing too much power at once. |
| **2.50** | October 13, 2005 | • Network<br>• LocationFree Player added.<br>• [Auto-Select] and [Unicode (UTF-8)] added to the browser.<br>• Settings for [Text Size] and [Display Mode] and the input history of online forms accessed can now saved in the browser.<br>• Video<br>• Copyright-protected video can now be played.<br>• Settings<br>• [Set via Internet] has been added to [Date and Time] in [Date & Time Settings].<br>• [WPA-PSK (AES)] has been added as a security method under [Network Settings].<br>• Other<br>• Korean input mode has been added to the on-screen keyboard. |
| **2.01** | October 3, 2005 | • Security update to patch the original (first of 3) TIFF exploit. |

| | | |
|---|---|---|
| **2.00** | September 1, 2005 | *Initial UK release (with included update disc)*<br>• [Network] (added in this release)<br>  • [Internet Browser] added.<br>• Video<br>  • 4:3 Screen Mode has been added (for video saved on Memory Stick Duo media).<br>  • Go To feature has been added (for UMDVIDEO and UMDMUSIC).<br>  • A-B Repeat feature has been added (for UMDVIDEO, UMDMUSIC and video saved on Memory Stick Duo media).<br>  • Audio options have been added (for video saved on Memory Stick Duo media).<br>  • MP4 (AVC) has been added as a playable file format (for video saved on Memory Stick Duo media).<br>• Music<br>  • The combination of SonicStage version 3.2 (or later) and PSP system software 2.00 (or later) has made it possible for music files in ATRAC3 plus format to be transferred to a Memory Stick PRO Duo<br>  • MP4 (the audio codec for MP4 format audio files is MPEG-4 AAC) and WAV (Linear PCM) have been added as playable file formats (for music saved on Memory Stick Duo media).<br>• Photo<br>  • Wallpaper feature has been added.<br>  • Image transfer feature has been added.<br>  • TIFF, GIF, PNG and BMP have been added as viewable file formats.<br>• Settings<br>  • Korean has been added as a system language in [System Settings].<br>  • [Character Set] has been added in [System Settings].<br>  • [Theme Settings] has been added.<br>  • [Internet Browser Start Control] has been added as a security mode in [Security Settings].<br>  • WPA-PSK (TKIP) has been added as a security mode in [Network Settings].<br>  • Web address shortcut feature has been added as an input mode for the on-screen keyboard. |
| **1.52** | June 15, 2005 | *Initial UK release*<br>• Revisions to strengthen security have been added.<br>• Support for UMD music. |
| **1.51** | May 18, 2005 | • Security update to patch "KXploit" exploit |
| **1.50** | March 24, 2005 | *Initial North American release*<br>• Support for:<br>  • content authorization.<br>  • new video codecs.<br>  • multiple languages. |
| **1.00** | *Pre-installed Only*<br>First found on December 12, 2004 | *Initial Japanese release*<br>• Original release<br>• No content authorization system. |

## References


[1] "Sony releases anti-piracy PSP update" (http://www.theinquirer.net/default.aspx?article=26662). The Inquirer. 2005-10-03. .

[2] "PSP-3000 rocking new motherboard" (http://www.qj.net/qjnet/psp/psp-3000-rocking-new-motherboard.html). QJ.net. 2010-03-13. .

[3] Lempel, Eric (2010-11-23). "Updates to PSP System Software, Media Go" (http://blog.us.playstation.com/2010/11/23/updates-to-psp-system-software-media-go/). Sony Computer Entertainment America. . Retrieved 2011-04-11.

[4] "Update History" (http://www.us.playstation.com/Support/SystemUpdates/PSP/history.html). Sony Computer Entertainment America. . Retrieved 2011-04-11.

[5] Bendel, Mike (April 12, 2011). "PSP Firmware 6.38 Released" (http://exophase.com/22429/psp-firmware-6-38-released/). eXophase. . Retrieved 2011-04-11.

[6] Bendel, Mike (January 19, 2011). "PSP Firmware 6.37 Detailed" (http://exophase.com/20928/psp-firmware-6-37-detailed//). eXophase. . Retrieved 2011-04-11.

[7] Bendel, Mike (November 29, 2010). "PSP Firmware 6.36 Spotted On UMD" (http://exophase.com/19918/psp-firmware-6-36-spotted-on-umd/). eXophase. . Retrieved 2011-04-11.

[8] "Qriocity Official Website (US)" (http://www.qriocity.com/us/en/music.html). Sony. . Retrieved 2011-04-11.

[9] Karl B. (Jul 27, 2010). "PS3 FW 3.41 is live, PSP FW 6.31 also coming" (http://www.qj.net/qjnet/news/ps3-fw-341-is-live-psp-fw-631-also-coming.html). QJ.net. . Retrieved 2011-04-11.

[10] Lempel, Eric (2010-07-28). "PlayStation 3 System Software Update v3.40 Available Now" (http://blog.us.playstation.com/2010/06/28/playstation-3-system-software-update-v3-40-available-soon-2/). Sony Computer Entertainment America. . Retrieved 2011-04-11.

[11] "Le Firmware 6.30 n'aime pas les tricheurs..." (http://www.pspgen.com/firmware-6-30-aime-pas-tricheurs-article-194257-1.html) (in French). PSPGEN.com. June 29, 2010. . Retrieved 2011-04-11.

[12] Lempel, Eric (2009-11-18). "PSP Firmware (v6.20) Update" (http://blog.us.playstation.com/2009/11/psp-firmware-v6-20-update/). Sony Computer Entertainment America. . Retrieved 2011-04-11.

[13] Lempel, Eric (2009-09-30). "PSP Firmware Update (v6.10)" (http://blog.us.playstation.com/2009/09/psp-firmware-update-v6-10/). Sony Computer Entertainment America. . Retrieved 2011-04-11.

[14] "Support: System Software Update (v6.10)" (http://www.us.playstation.com/Support/SystemUpdates/PSP/PSP_610_update.html). Sony Computer Entertainment America. . Retrieved 2011-04-11.

[15] Lempel, Eric (2009-09-09). "PSP Firmware Update (v6.00)" (http://blog.us.playstation.com/2009/09/09/psp-firmware-v6-00-update/). Sony Computer Entertainment America. . Retrieved 2011-04-11.

[16] "Peace Walker - More TGS details... and Ashley Wood?" (http://thesnakesoup.org/?section=announcements&content=index&t=3464). The Snake Soup. September 16, 2009. . Retrieved 2011-04-11.

[17] "Gran Turismo PSP requires OFW 6.00" (http://pspupdates.qj.net/Gran-Turismo-PSP-requires-OFW-6-00/pg/49/aid/134492). QuickJump. September 10, 2009. . Retrieved 2011-04-11.

[18] "Hands On With The PSP Go" (http://www.sonyinsider.com/2009/09/22/hands-on-with-the-psp-go-check-it-out-wednesday-at-sonystyle/). Sony Insider. September 22, 2009. . Retrieved 2011-04-11.

[19] Glenn M. (Jul 5, 2009). "PSP FW 5.55 spotted in Japan Expo" (http://www.qj.net/psp/firmware/psp-fw-555-spotted-in-japan-expo.html). QuickJump. . Retrieved 2011-04-11.

[20] Lempel, Eric (2009-06-10). "PSP Firmware (v5.51) Update" (http://blog.us.playstation.com/2009/06/10/psp-firmware-v551-update/). Sony Computer Entertainment America. . Retrieved 2011-04-11.

[21] Lempel, Eric (2009-04-20). "PSP Firmware (v5.50) Update" (http://blog.us.playstation.com/2009/04/20/psp-firmware-v550-update/). Sony Computer Entertainment America. . Retrieved 2011-04-11.

[22] "Media Go - プレイステーション オフィシャルサイト" (http://www.jp.playstation.com/psn/store/mediamanager/infoimas.html) (in Japanese). Sony Computer Entertainment. . Retrieved 2011-04-11.

[23] Yoon, Andrew (Feb 19th 2009). "PSP Firmware 5.05 released, available on UMD only" (http://playstation.joystiq.com/2009/02/19/psp-firmware-5-05-released-available-on-umd-only/). Joystiq. . Retrieved 2011-04-11.

[24] "THE IDOLM@STER DLC released story mode and more information" (http://game.watch.impress.co.jp/docs/20090107/imas.htm) (in Japanese). Game Watch. . Retrieved 2011-04-11.

[25] "PS3『Home』で『アイドルマスター SP』の特製アイテムを配布" (http://www.gpara.com/article/cms_show.php?c_id=11699&c_num=14) (in Japanese). Gpara. 2009.02.10. . Retrieved 2011-04-11.

[26] "PSP (PlayStation Portable) v5.03 Update" (http://uk.playstation.com/psp/support/system-software/detail/item139250/Update-features-(ver-5-03)/). Sony Computer Entertainment Europe. . Retrieved 2011-04-11.

[27] "PSP Firmware 5.03 Released" (http://www.psp-hacks.com/2009/01/20/psp-firmware-503-released/). PSP Hacks. January 20, 2009. . Retrieved 2011-04-11.

[28] "PSP (PlayStation Portable) v5.02 Update" (http://uk.playstation.com/psp/support/system-software/detail/item131634/Update-features-(ver-5-02)/). Sony Computer Entertainment Europe. . Retrieved 2011-04-11.

[29] "PSP (PlayStation Portable) v5.01 Update" (http://uk.playstation.com/psp/support/system-software/detail/item125743/Update-features-(ver-5-01)/). Sony Computer Entertainment Europe. . Retrieved 2011-04-11.

[30] Lempel, Eric (2008-10-13). "Firmware Updates: PS3 (v2.50) / PSP (v5.00)" (http://blog.us.playstation.com/2008/10/13/firmware-updates-ps3-v250-psp-v500/). Sony Computer Entertainment America. . Retrieved 2011-04-11.

[31] "PSP®向けPlayStation®Storeを利用するには? " (http://www.jp.playstation.com/store/psp/index.html) (in Japanese). Sony Computer Entertainment. . Retrieved 2011-04-11.
[32] Tanaka, John (September 2, 2008). "PSP-3000 Firmware Changes Discovered" (http://psp.ign.com/articles/907/907086p1.html). IGN. . Retrieved 2011-04-11.
[33] Lempel, Eric (2008-07-13). "PSP (PlayStation Portable) v4.05 Update" (http://blog.us.playstation.com/2008/07/13/psp-playstation-portable-v405-update/). Sony Computer Entertainment America. . Retrieved 2011-04-11.
[34] Lempel, Eric (2008-06-24). "PSP (PlayStation Portable) v4.01 Update" (http://blog.us.playstation.com/2008/06/24/psp-playstation-portable-v401-update/). Sony Computer Entertainment America. . Retrieved 2011-04-11.
[35] Lempel, Eric (2008-06-16). "PSP (PlayStation Portable) v4.00 Update" (http://blog.us.playstation.com/2008/06/16/psp-playstation-portable-v400-update/). Sony Computer Entertainment America. . Retrieved 2011-04-11.
[36] "BT Go!Messenger website" (http://gomessenger.bt.com/). BT Group. . Retrieved 2011-04-11.
[37] "Firmware 3.50 now available on Network Update" (http://www.pspfanboy.com/2007/05/31/firmware-3-50-now-available-on-network-update/). PSP fanboy. . Retrieved 2007-05-31.
[38] "PSP CPU power unlocked" (http://www.gamesindustry.biz/content_page.php?aid=26057). GamesIndustry.biz. . Retrieved 2007-06-26.
[39] "PSP Firmware 3.40 for the US" (http://www.qj.net/PSP-FW-3-40-for-the-US/pg/49/aid/89907). QuickJump. . Retrieved 2007-04-20.
[40] "Sony PSP Firmware Update 3.30: Free T-Mobile Wireless Access Included" (http://www.gamingbits.com/content/view/1889/2/). Gaming Bits. . Retrieved 2006-04-05.
[41] "PSP Updated : New firmware lets you reset" (http://psp.ign.com/articles/762/762675p1.html). IGN. . Retrieved 2007-04-03.

# External links

**Official PlayStation Portable System Software Update page**

- "Asia" (http://asia.playstation.com/eng_hk/index.php?q=psp-sysupdate). • Australia (http://au.playstation.com/help-support/psp/system-software/download/) • "Japan" (http://www.jp.playstation.com/psp/update/ud_01.html). • "Korea" (http://do01a.psp.update.playstation.org/update/psp/image/oa/2007_0913_6babee6e1415ae27999928566adbd569/EBOOT.PBP). • New Zealand (http://www.nz.playstation.com/support/psp/faqs/psp_system_software_updates.jhtml) • United Kingdom (http://uk.playstation.com/help-support/psp/guides/detail/item54261/PSP-system-software-updates/) • United States (http://www.us.playstation.com/PSP/Downloads/SystemUpdate)

# Series 30 (software platform)

The **Series 30** software platform is an application user interface used on Nokia's broad range of entry-level mobile devices. Most, if not all of Nokia's no-frills phones such as the Nokia 1600, Nokia 2310 and Nokia 5030 XpressRadio run on the Series 30 platform[1] , although some now use the more advanced Series 40 interface[2] , albeit lacking some certain features common on mid-range Series 40 phones.

The Nokia 1600, which runs on the Series 30 platform.

The Nokia 3510i, an early Series 30 phone released in 2002 was equipped with Series 40 capabilities to gain Java ME and polyphonic MIDI sound experience[3] . Later Series 30 devices dropped some of the said features in favor of embedded content and less emphasis on extra features such as Internet connectivity.

## References

[1] Nokia 5030 spec sheet (http://www.maps.nokia.com/find-products/devices/nokia-5030/specifications)

[2] Nokia 2330 spec sheet (http://www.maps.nokia.com/find-products/devices/nokia-2330-classic/specifications)

[3] Nokia software platforms (http://www.filesaveas.com/nokia.html)

## External links

- Nokia Series 40 Developer Platform (http://www.forum.nokia.com/main/platforms/s40/index.html)

# Series 40

**Series 40** is a software platform and application user interface (UI) software on Nokia's broad range of mid-tier mobile phones, as well as on the Vertu line of luxury phones. It is the world's most widely used mobile phone platform and found in hundreds of millions of devices.[1]

Series 40-based Nokia 6300

## Features

### Applications

It provides communication applications such as telephone, internet telephony (VoIP), messaging, email client with POP3 and IMAP4 capabilities and Web browser; media applications such as camera, video recorder, music/video player and FM radio; and phonebook and other personal information management (PIM) applications such as calendar and tasks. Basic file management, like in Series 60, is provided in the Applications and Gallery folders and subfolders. Gallery is also the default location for files transferred over Bluetooth to be placed. User-installed applications on Series 40 are generally mobile Java applications. Flash Lite applications are also supported, but mostly used for screensavers.[2]

### Web browser

The integrated web browser can access most web content through the service provider's XHTML/HTML gateway. The latest version of Series 40, called Series 40 6th Edition, introduced a new browser based on the WebKit open source components WebCore and JavaScriptCore. The new browser delivers support for HTML 4.01, CSS2, JavaScript 1.5, and Ajax. Also, like the higher-end Series 60, Series 40 can run the Opera Mini web browser to enhance the user's web browsing experience.

### Synchronization

Support for SyncML synchronization with external services of the address book, calendar and notes is present. However with many S40 phones, these synchronization settings must be sent via an OTA text message.

## Technical

### Software platform

Series 40 is an embedded software platform that is open for software development via standard or de-facto content and application development technologies. It supports Java MIDlets, i.e. Java MIDP and CLDC technology, which provide location, communication, messaging, media, and graphics capabilities.[3] S40 also supports Flash Lite applications.[2]

## Operating system

Series 40 is a simpler operating system variant than the higher end S60 (which is based on the multi-tasking Symbian OS). Because S40 devices do not support true multi-tasking and do not have a native code API for third parties, its user interface may appear to be more responsive and faster than other Nokia platforms.[4]

## History

The first Series 40 devices (introduced in 2002) had only 128x128 pixel large displays with lower color capabilities. Over the years, the S40 UI has evolved from a low resolution UI to a high resolution color UI with an enhanced graphical look. The third generation of Series 40 that became available in 2005 introduced support for devices with resolutions as high as QVGA (240x320).[5] It is possible to customize the look-and-feel of the UI via comprehensive themes.[6] A list of all Series 40 devices can be found on the Nokia web site.[7]

## References

[1] "Forum Nokia - Nokia Series 40 Platform" (http://www.forum.nokia.com/Devices/Series_40/). Nokia. . Retrieved 2010-10-27.

[2] "Working with Nokia Series 40 Flash Lite content – Adobe Developer Center" (http://web.archive.org/web/20080518220200/http://www.adobe.com/devnet/devices/articles/nokia_series40_pt1_print.html). Adobe Systems. Archived from the original (http://www.adobe.com/devnet/devices/articles/nokia_series40_pt1_print.html) on 2008-05-18. . Retrieved 2008-09-26.

[3] "Developing Scalable Series 40 Applications, A Guide for Java Developers" (http://www.pearsoned.co.uk/BOOKSHOP/detail.asp?item=100000000075919). Addison-Wesley. . Retrieved 2008-09-26.

[4] "Comparing Series 40 against S60 (as of 2007) – All about Symbian" (http://www.allaboutsymbian.com/features/item/Series_40_vs_S60.php). . Retrieved 2008-09-26.

[5] "Series 40 UI Style Guide – Forum Nokia" (http://www.forum.nokia.com/info/sw.nokia.com/id/73e935fe-8b59-43b2-ab3e-1c5f763672db/Series_40_UI_Style_Guide.html). Nokia. . Retrieved 2008-09-26.

[6] "Carbide.ui Theme Edition (can be used to create S40 themes) – Forum Nokia" (http://www.forum.nokia.com/main/resources/tools_and_sdks/carbide_ui/features.html). Nokia. . Retrieved 2008-09-26.

[7] "Series 40 Platform SDKs" (http://www.forum.nokia.com/Library/Tools_and_downloads/Other/Series_40_platform_SDKs/). Nokia. . Retrieved 2010-09-19.

# Smarterphone

### Smarterphone

| Type | Private[1] |
|---|---|
| Industry | Software |
| Founded | 1993[2] |
| Headquarters | Oslo, Norway |
| Key people | Egil Kvaleberg CEO |
| Products | Mobile operating system and application suite |
| Employees | 30 |
| Website | www.smarterphone.com [3] |

**Smarterphone** is a company making software for mobile phones. The company was founded in 1993 as **Kvaleberg AS**, but was renamed to Smarterphone in December 2010. [3] In June 2007, venture capital investor Ferd invested €2 million in the company. [4] By January 2010, further €3.6 million was invested. [5] The head office is in Oslo, Norway, but the company also has offices in Taiwan, South Korea, Japan and the United States.

Smarterphone develops mobile software for handsets, with mobile phone OEMs, ODMs and chipset vendors as customers. The company also provides professional services in the above areas.

In 2008, then as Kvaleberg, the company joined the LiMo Foundation, [6] and at the 2009 Mobile World Congress they presented the *Madrid* handset, in cooperation with Compal Communications. [7]

## Smarterphone OS

### Smarterphone OS

Mimiria 2.2

| Company / developer | **Smarterphone** |
|---|---|
| Programmed in | Scheme (UI) and C++ (core) |
| Working state | Current |
| Source model | Closed source software |
| Initial release | 21 October 2008 |
| Latest stable release | 2.4 |
| Supported platforms | ARM/Qualcomm, ARM/Broadcom, ARM/TI |

| Kernel type | Realtime kernel |
|---|---|
| Default user interface | Graphical touch and/or keypad (ITU or QWERTY) |
| Official website | smarterphone.com [9] |

The company's main product is **Smarterphone OS** which is a platform independent full mobile phone operating system and applications suite for the feature phone segment. Smarterphone OS, then called **Mimiria**, was first unveiled at the Mobile World Congress show in February 2008, and has been used for such handsets as the Vibo T588, and the *Madrid* LiMo device. The Smarterphone architecture is *clean-room*, with a very strict model-view-controller design that enables variations to be implemented with little effort. [8] The user interface of Smarterphone OS is programmed in a scripting language, which is a variant of Scheme with object oriented extensions.

Smarterphone OS includes a user interface (MMI) software stack, implementing a full user interface and middleware for 2G and 3G feature phones. It also integrates a range of 3rd-party modules such as Java ME JVM from Sun Microsystems, mobile browser from Obigo, MMS and SMS stack from Mobile Messaging Factory, predictive text input from Nuance and Cootek, and handwriting recognition from Sinovoice.

# References


[1] Company registration data (http://w2.brreg.no/enhet/sok/detalj.jsp?orgnr=968304283) From the Norwegian register authority, in Norwegian

[2] Siving Egil Kvaleberg AS (http://investing.businessweek.com/research/stocks/private/snapshot.asp?privcapId=34766657), Bloomberg

[3] Name change record (http://w2.brreg.no/kunngjoring/hent_en.jsp?kid=20100000572344&sokeverdi=968304283) from the Norwegian register authority

[4] "Kvaleberg receives EUR 2 million in funding from Ferd Venture" (http://www.ferd.no/lang/en/show.do?page=12;22&articleid=1556), *Ferd - Press release 6 June 6, 2007*, , retrieved 2010-12-10

[5] "Ferd calls on Smarterphone" (http://realdeals.eu.com/venture_capital/ferd-calls-on-smarterphone), *RealDeals Europe*, , retrieved 2011-01-27

[6] "LiMo fights back on Linux for phones as Mozilla signs up" (http://www.guardian.co.uk/technology/blog/2008/may/14/limofightsbackonlinuxfor). The Guardian. 2008-05-14. . Retrieved 2010-12-15.

[7] "LiMo Foundation Members Showcase Next-Generation Handsets, Toolkits, and Applications at MWC 2009" (http://www.limofoundation.org/zh/Press-Releases/limo-foundation-members-showcase-next-generation-handsets-toolkits-and-applications-at-mwc-2009.html), *Limo Foundation press release - February 16, 2009*, , retrieved 2010-12-10

[8] "Under-the-radar trends at Mobile World Congress: Quantum leap in mobile devices" (http://www.visionmobile.com/blog/2010/02/2010-in-review-under-the-radar-trends-at-mobile-world-congress/), *Vision Mobile blog - Andreas Constantinou*, , retrieved 2010-12-10

# Smeegol Linux

**Smeegol Linux**

| Company / developer | Novell, openSUSE Goblin Team, the openSUSE community |
|---|---|
| OS family | Linux |
| Working state | Current |
| Initial release | 6 October 2010 |
| Latest stable release | 1.0 / 6 October 2010 |
| Marketing target | Mobile |
| Package manager | RPM Package Manager |
| Supported platforms | x86 / IA-32 and x86-64 |
| Kernel type | Monolithic (Linux) |
| Official website | {{URL\|*example.com*\|*optional display text*}} |

**Smeegol Linux** is a new MeeGo and openSUSE Linux-based open source mobile operating system made available from Novell and their openSUSE Goblin Team under the name Smeegol Linux.[1] [2] [3] [4] [5] [6]

This Linux distribution combines openSUSE with MeeGo's netbook oriented user interface to get a new Linux distribution designed for netbooks. What makes Smeegol Linux unique when compared to the upstream MeeGo or openSUSE is that this distribution is at its core based on openSUSE but has the MeeGo User Experience as well as a few other changes such as adding the Mono-based Banshee media player, NetworkManager-powered network configuration, a newer version of Evolution Express, and a range of social networking features for Facebook, Twitter, MySpace, Flickr and Digg, plus FireFox and Chromium web browsers already pre-installed. Any end-users can also build their own customized Smeegol Linux OS using SUSE Studio.[1] [2] [3]

## References

[1] "openSUSE MeeGo repo" (http://download.opensuse.org/repositories/Meego:/). . Retrieved 2010-06-21.

[2] "openSUSE Releases MeeGo-based Smeegol Linux" (http://www.phoronix.com/scan.php?page=news_item&px=ODY1Ng). . Retrieved 2010-10-06.

[3] "openSUSE News - Announcing Smeegol 1.0" (http://news.opensuse.org/2010/10/06/announcing-smeegol-1-0/). . Retrieved 2010-10-06.

[4] http://www.tuxmachines.org/node/48230 Announcing Smeegol 1.0

[5] http://www.linuxcompatible.org/news/story/smeegol_10_released.html Smeegol 1.0 released

[6] http://distrowatch.com/?newsid=06301 Distribution Release: Smeegol 1.0

## External links

- Smeegol Linux ISO images download (http://download.opensuse.org/repositories/Meego:/Netbook/images/iso/)
- Smeegol Linux Repo (http://download.opensuse.org/repositories/Meego:/)

# Symbian Foundation

## Symbian Foundation Ltd.

| SYMBIAN | |
|---|---|
| **Founded** | 24 June 2008 |
| **Location** | London, United Kingdom |
| **Origins** | Symbian Ltd |
| **Products** | The Symbian platform |
| **Focus** | Open mobile software platform |
| **Website** | symbian.org [1] |

The **Symbian Foundation** is a non-profit organisation that stewards the Symbian platform; an operating system for mobile phones, based on Symbian OS, which was previously owned and licensed by Symbian Ltd.. Symbian Foundation has never directly developed the platform, but evangelised, co-ordinated and ensured compatibility. It also provided key services to its members and the community such as collecting, building and distributing Symbian source code. During its operational phase (from 2009 to 2010), it also provided:

- platform development kits and tools
- documentation and example code
- discussion forums and mailing lists
- application signing (Symbian Signed)[1]
- application distribution (Symbian Horizon)[2]
- idea gathering and feedback (Symbian Ideas)[3]
- an annual conference (Symbian Exchange and Exposition, abbreviated "SEE")

The Foundation was founded by Nokia, Sony Ericsson, NTT DoCoMo, Motorola, Texas Instruments, Vodafone, LG Electronics, Samsung Electronics, STMicroelectronics and AT&T.[4] Due to a change in their device strategy, LG and Motorola left the Foundation board soon after its creation. They were later replaced by Fujitsu[5] and Qualcomm Innovation Center[6] .

Following "a change in focus for some of [the] funding board members", the Symbian Foundation announced in November 2010 that it would transition to "a legal entity responsible for licensing software and other intellectual property", with no operational responsibilities or staff.[7] . Along with this announcement, Nokia announced it would take over governance of the Symbian platform. Nokia has been the major contributor to the code, and has been maintaining their own code repository for the platform development ever since the purchase of Symbian Ltd., regularly releasing their development to the public repository. [8] After the transition completes in April 2011, the Symbian Foundation will remain as the trademark holder and licensing entity, and will only have non-executive directors involved. All Symbian Foundation public web sites, wiki and code repositories were shut down on December 17, 2010[9] , and on that date Nokia launched a new Symbian site[10] .

## Members

The Symbian Foundation invited companies to join as members, and attracted over 200, from a large number of categories[11]:

- Device manufacturers (e.g. Nokia, Fujitsu)
- Financial services companies (e.g. Visa)
- Semiconductor vendors (e.g. ARM, Broadcom)
- Mobile network operators (e.g. China Mobile, Vodafone, AT&T)
- Software companies
- Professional services firms

## References

[1] "Symbian Signed" (http://developer.symbian.org/main/services/symbian_signed/index.php). . Retrieved 2009-08-04.
[2] "Symbian Horizon" (http://horizon.symbian.org). .
[3] "Symbian Ideas" (http://ideas.symbian.org). .
[4] Nokia (24 June 2008). "Mobile leaders to unify the Symbian software platform and set the future of mobile free" (http://www.nokia.com/press/press-releases/showpressrelease?newsid=1230416). Press release. . Retrieved 2010-01-22.
[5] http://www.fujitsu.com/global/news/pr/archives/month/2009/20091029-01.html
[6] http://www.prnewswire.com/news-releases/qualcomm-innovation-center-joins-the-symbian-foundation-67131667.html
[7] http://blog.symbian.org/2010/11/08/symbian-foundation-to-transition-to-a-licensing-operation/
[8] http://eu.techcrunch.com/2010/11/08/guest-post-symbian-os-one-of-the-most-successful-failures-in-tech-history/
[9] http://blog.symbian.org/2010/12/17/symbian-foundation-is-completing-its-transition-to-a-licensing-body/
[10] http://symbian.nokia.com/2010/12/16/welcome-to-symbian-blog-from-nokia/
[11] http://www.symbian.org/members/member-directory

## External links

- Official Symbian blog (http://blog.symbian.org/)

# Symbian

## Symbian

| SYMBIAN | |
|---|---|
| **Company / developer** | Nokia |
| **Programmed in** | C++[1] |
| **OS family** | Embedded operating system |
| **Working state** | Partially Discontinued |
| **Source model** | Proprietary[2] |
| **Latest stable release** | Symbian^3 / October 2010 |
| **Marketing target** | Smartphones |
| **Supported platforms** | ARM, x86[3] |
| **Kernel type** | Microkernel |
| **Default user interface** | Currently based on S60 platform, later to use Qt |
| **License** | Proprietary |
| **Official website** | [symbian.nokia.com symbian.nokia.com] |

**Symbian** is an operating system (OS) and software platform designed for smartphones and currently maintained by Nokia. The Symbian platform is the successor to Symbian OS and Nokia Series 60; unlike Symbian OS, which needed an additional user interface system, Symbian includes a user interface component based on S60 5th Edition. The latest version, Symbian^3, was officially released in Q4 2010, first used in the Nokia N8.

*Symbian OS* was originally developed by Symbian Ltd.[4] It is a descendant of Psion's EPOC and runs exclusively on ARM processors, although an unreleased x86 port existed.

Devices based on Symbian accounted for 29.2% of worldwide smartphone market share in 2011 Q1.[5] Some estimates indicate that the cumulative number of mobile devices shipped with the Symbian OS up to the end of Q2 2010 is 385 million.[6]

By April 5, 2011, Nokia released Symbian under a new license and converted to a proprietary shared-source model as opposed to an open source project.[2]

# History

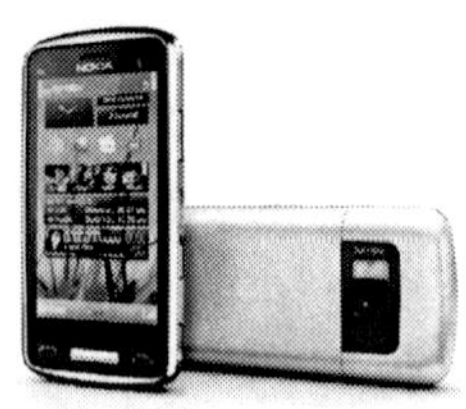
Nokia C6-01, running Symbian^3

The **Symbian** platform was created by merging and integrating software assets contributed by Nokia, NTT DoCoMo, Sony Ericsson and Symbian Ltd., including Symbian OS assets at its core, the S60 platform, and parts of the UIQ and MOAP(S) user interfaces.

In December 2008, Nokia bought Symbian Ltd., the company behind Symbian OS; consequently, Nokia became the major contributor to Symbian's code, since it then possessed the development resources for both the Symbian OS core and the user interface. Since then Nokia has been maintaining its own code repository for the platform development, regularly releasing its development to the public repository.[7] File Symbian was intended to be developed by a community led by the Symbian Foundation,[8] which was first announced in June 2008 and which officially launched in April 2009. Its objective was to publish the source code for the entire Symbian platform under the OSI- and FSF-approved Eclipse Public License (EPL). The code was published under EPL on 4 February 2010; Symbian Foundation reported this event to be the largest codebase transitioned to Open Source in history.[9] [10]

However, some important components within Symbian OS were licensed from third parties, which prevented the foundation from publishing the full source under EPL immediately; instead much of the source was published under a more restrictive Symbian Foundation License (SFL) and access to the full source code was limited to member companies only, although membership was open to any organisation.[11]

In November 2010, the Symbian Foundation announced that due to a lack of support from funding members, it would transition to a licensing-only organisation; Nokia announced it would take over the stewardship of the Symbian platform. Symbian Foundation will remain the trademark holder and licensing entity and will only have non-executive directors involved.

On February 11, 2011, Nokia announced a partnership with Microsoft which would see it adopt Windows Phone 7 for smartphones, reducing the number of devices running Symbian over the coming two years.[12]

By April 5, 2011, Nokia ceased to open source any portion of the Symbian software and reduced its collaboration to a small group of pre-selected partners in Japan.[2] Source code released under the EPL remains available in third party repositories.[13] [14]

## Version history

Symbian releases are styled **Symbian^1**, **Symbian^2** etc. (vocalised as "Symbian one", "Symbian two").

**Symbian^1**, being the first release, forms the basis for the platform. It incorporates Symbian OS and S60 5th Edition (which is built on Symbian OS 9.4) and thus it was not made available in open source.[15]

**Symbian^2** was the first royalty-free version of Symbian.[16] While portions of Symbian^2 are EPL licensed, most of the source code is under the proprietary SFL license and available only to members of the Symbian Foundation. On June 1, 2010, a number of Japanese companies including DoCoMo and Sharp announced smartphones using Symbian^2.[17]

**Symbian^3** was announced on 15 February 2010.[18] It was designed to be a more 'next generation' smartphone platform. The Symbian^3 release introduced new features like a new 2D and 3D graphics architecture, UI improvements, and support for external displays via HDMI.[19] [20] It has single tap menus and up to three customizable homescreens. The Symbian^3 SDK (Software Development Kit) was released September 2010.[21]

Six smartphones with the Symbian^3 operating system have been released so far; the Nokia N8, Nokia C6-01, Nokia E7-00, Nokia C7-00, Nokia E6, and Nokia X7.[22] [23]

In April 2011, an update to Symbian^3, known as 'Symbian Anna', was released by Nokia as part of the launch of the X7 and E6 smartphones.[24] Symbian Anna includes such improvements as a new browser, a virtual keyboard in portrait orientation, and real-time homescreen scrolling.[25] Nokia has indicated that the Anna update will be also be available for previous Symbian^3 devices such as the N8 and C7.[26]

**Symbian^4** was expected to be released in the first half of 2011. However, Nokia announced in October 2010 that Symbian^4 will not ship in a separate release. Instead, improvements to Symbian will be delivered in software updates to all current Symbian^3 devices.[27]

## Features

### User interface

Symbian has had a native graphics toolkit since its inception, known as AVKON (formerly known as Series 60). S60 was designed to be manipulated by a keyboard-like interface metaphor, such as the ~15-key augmented telephone keypad, or the mini-QWERTY keyboards. AVKON-based software is binary-compatible with Symbian versions up to and including Symbian^3.

Symbian^3 includes the Qt framework, which is now the recommended user interface toolkit for new applications. Qt can also be installed on older Symbian devices.

Symbian^4 was planned to introduce a new GUI library framework specifically designed for a touch-based interface, known as "UI Extensions for Mobile" or UIEMO (internal project name "Orbit"), which was built on top of Qt; a preview was released in January 2010, however in October 2010 Nokia announced that Orbit/UIEMO has been cancelled.

Nokia currently recommends that developers use Qt Quick with QML, the new high-level GUI and scripting framework for creating visually rich touchscreen interfaces that allows development for both Symbian and MeeGo; it will be delivered to existing Symbian^3 devices as a Qt update. When more applications gradually feature a user interface reworked in Qt, the legacy S60 framework (AVKON) will be deprecated and no longer included with new devices at some point, thus breaking binary compatibility with older S60 applications.[27] [28]

### Browser

Symbian^3 and earlier have a native WebKit based browser; indeed, Symbian was the first mobile platform to make use of WebKit (in June 2005).[29]

Nokia plans to introduce a new Qt-based browser as a free update for Symbian^3 devices.

### Application development

From 2010, Symbian switched to using standard C++ with Qt as the SDK, which can be used with either Qt Creator or Carbide. Qt supports the older Symbian S60 3rd and 5th editions, as well as the new Symbian platform. It also supports Maemo and MeeGo, Windows, Linux and Mac OS X.[30] [31]

Alternative application development can be done using Python (see Python for S60), Adobe Flash or Java ME.

Symbian OS previously used a Symbian specific C++ version along with Carbide.c++ integrated development environment (IDE) as the native application development environment.

Web Runtime (WRT) is a portable application framework that allows creating widgets on the S60 Platform; it is an extension to the S60 WebKit based browser that allows launching multiple browser instances as separate JavaScript applications.[32] [33]

# Architecture

## Technology domains and packages

Symbian's design is subdivided into **technology domains,**[34] each of which comprises a number of software **packages.**[35] Each technology domain has its own roadmap, and the Symbian Foundation has a team of technology managers who manage these technology domain roadmaps.

Every package is allocated to exactly one technology domain, based on the general functional area to which the package contributes and by which it may be influenced. By grouping related packages by themes, the Symbian Foundation hopes to encourage a strong community to form around them and to generate discussion and review.

The Symbian System Model[36] illustrates the scope of each of the technology domains across the platform packages.

Packages are owned and maintained by a package owner, a named individual from an organization member of the Symbian Foundation, who accepts code contributions from the wider Symbian community and is responsible for package.

## Symbian kernel

The Symbian kernel (EKA2) supports sufficiently-fast real-time response to build a single-core phone around it—that is, a phone in which a single processor core executes both the user applications and the signalling stack.[37] The real-time kernel has a microkernel architecture containing only the minimum, most basic primitives and functionality, for maximum robustness, availability and responsiveness. It has been termed a nanokernel, because it needs an extended kernel to implement any other abstractions. It contains a scheduler, memory management and device drivers, with networking, telephony and file system support services in the OS Services Layer or the Base Services Layer. The inclusion of device drivers means the kernel is not a *true* microkernel.

## Design

Symbian features pre-emptive multitasking and memory protection, like other operating systems (especially those created for use on desktop computers). EPOC's approach to multitasking was inspired by VMS and is based on asynchronous server-based events.

Symbian OS was created with three systems design principles in mind:

1. the integrity and security of user data is paramount
2. user time must not be wasted
3. all resources are scarce

To best follow these principles, Symbian uses a microkernel, has a request-and-callback approach to services, and maintains separation between user interface and engine. The OS is optimised for low-power battery-based devices and for ROM-based systems (e.g. features like XIP and re-entrancy in shared libraries). Applications, and the OS itself, follow an object-oriented design: Model-view-controller (MVC).

Later OS iterations diluted this approach in response to market demands, notably with the introduction of a real-time kernel and a platform security model in versions 8 and 9.

There is a strong emphasis on conserving resources which is exemplified by Symbian-specific programming idioms like descriptors and a cleanup stack. Similar methods exist to conserve disk space, though disks on Symbian devices are usually flash memory. Further, all Symbian programming is event-based, and the central processing unit (CPU) is switched into a low power mode when applications are not directly dealing with an event. This is done via a programming idiom called active objects. Similarly the Symbian approach to threads and processes is driven by reducing overheads.

## Operating system

The All over Model contains the following layers, from top to bottom:

- UI Framework Layer
- Application Services Layer
  - Java ME
- OS Services Layer
  - generic OS services
  - communications services
  - multimedia and graphics services
  - connectivity services
- Base Services Layer
- Kernel Services & Hardware Interface Layer

The Base Services Layer is the lowest level reachable by user-side operations; it includes the File Server and User Library, a Plug-In Framework which manages all plug-ins, Store, Central Repository, DBMS and cryptographic services. It also includes the Text Window Server and the Text Shell: the two basic services from which a completely functional port can be created without the need for any higher layer services.

Symbian has a microkernel architecture, which means that the minimum necessary is within the kernel to maximise robustness, availability and responsiveness. It contains a scheduler, memory management and device drivers, but other services like networking, telephony and filesystem support are placed in the OS Services Layer or the Base Services Layer. The inclusion of device drivers means the kernel is not a *true* microkernel. The EKA2 real-time kernel, which has been termed a nanokernel, contains only the most basic primitives and requires an extended kernel to implement any other abstractions.

Symbian is designed to emphasise compatibility with other devices, especially removable media file systems. Early development of EPOC led to adopting FAT as the internal file system, and this remains, but an object-oriented persistence model was placed over the underlying FAT to provide a POSIX-style interface and a streaming model. The internal data formats rely on using the same APIs that create the data to run all file manipulations. This has resulted in data-dependence and associated difficulties with changes and data migration.

There is a large networking and communication subsystem, which has three main servers called: ETEL (EPOC telephony), ESOCK (EPOC sockets) and C32 (responsible for serial communication). Each of these has a plug-in scheme. For example, ESOCK allows different ".PRT" protocol modules to implement various networking protocol schemes. The subsystem also contains code that supports short-range communication links, such as Bluetooth, IrDA and USB.

There is also a large volume of user interface (UI) Code. Only the base classes and substructure were contained in Symbian OS, while most of the actual user interfaces were maintained by third parties. This is no longer the case. The three major UIs — S60, UIQ and MOAP — were contributed to Symbian in 2009. Symbian also contains graphics, text layout and font rendering libraries.

All native Symbian C++ applications are built up from three framework classes defined by the application architecture: an application class, a document class and an application user interface class. These classes create the fundamental application behaviour. The remaining needed functions, the application view, data model and data interface, are created independently and interact solely through their APIs with the other classes.

Many other things do not yet fit into this model — for example, SyncML, Java ME providing another set of APIs on top of most of the OS and multimedia. Many of these are frameworks, and vendors are expected to supply plug-ins to these frameworks from third parties (for example, Helix Player for multimedia codecs). This has the advantage that the APIs to such areas of functionality are the same on many phone models, and that vendors get a lot of flexibility. But it means that phone vendors needed to do a great deal of integration work to make a Symbian OS phone.

Symbian includes a reference user-interface called "TechView." It provides a basis for starting customisation and is the environment in which much Symbian test and example code runs. It is very similar to the user interface from the Psion Series 5 personal organiser and is not used for any production phone user interface.

## Devices and feature comparison

On 16 November 2006, the 100 millionth smartphone running the OS was shipped.[38] As of 21 July 2009, more than 250 million devices running Symbian OS had been shipped.[39]

- The Nokia S60 interface is used in various phones, the first being the Nokia 7650. The Nokia N-Gage and Nokia N-Gage QD gaming/smartphone combos are also S60 platform devices. It was also used on other manufacturers' phones such as the Siemens SX1 and Samsung SGH-Z600. Recently, more advanced devices using S60 include the Nokia 6xxx, the Nseries (except Nokia N8xx and N9xx), the Eseries and some models of the Nokia XpressMusic mobiles.
- Fujitsu, Mitsubishi, Sony Ericsson and Sharp developed phones for NTT DoCoMo in Japan, using an interface developed specifically for DoCoMo's FOMA "Freedom of Mobile Access" network brand. This UI platform is called MOAP "Mobile Oriented Applications Platform" and is based on the UI from earlier Fujitsu FOMA models. The user cannot install new C++ applications.

User interfaces that run on or are based on Symbian OS include:

- S60, formerly Series 60, used by Nokia and others
- Series 80, previously used by Nokia
- Series S90, previously used by Nokia
- UIQ, previously used by Sony-Ericsson
- MOAP, Mobile Oriented Applications Platform, used by NTT DoCoMo's FOMA service

Versions that are actively marketed as of April 2011 are Symbian^3, Symbian^2, Symbian^1 (previously known as Series 60 5th Edition), and Series 60 3rd Edition Feature Pack 2. For features of older versions see history of Symbian. Note that the operating system supporting a certain feature does not imply that all devices running on it have that feature available, especially if it involves expensive hardware, such as HDMI output.

| Feature | Symbian^3 | Symbian^2 | Symbian^1/Series 60 5th Edition | Series 60 3rd Edition Feature Pack 2 |
|---|---|---|---|---|
| Year released | 2010 | | 2009 | |
| Company | Symbian Foundation | Symbian Foundation | Symbian Foundation | |
| Symbian OS version | 9.5 | | 9.4 | 9.3 |
| Series 60 version | 5.2[40] | | 5th Edition | 3rd Edition Feature Pack 2 |
| Touch input support | Yes | | Yes | No |
| Multi touch input support | Yes | | No | No |
| Number of customizable home screens | Three | | One | One |
| Wi-Fi version support | B, G, N | | B, G | B, G |

| USB on the go support | Yes | | No | No |
|---|---|---|---|---|
| DVB-H support | Yes, with extra headset[41] | | Yes, with extra headset | Yes, with extra headset |
| Short range FM transmitter support | Yes | | Yes | Yes |
| FM radio support | Yes | | Yes | Yes |
| **Feature** | **Symbian^3** | **Symbian^2** | **Symbian^1/Series 60 5th Edition** | **Series 60 3rd Edition Feature Pack 2** |
| Adobe Flash support | Yes, Flash Lite version 4.0 | | Yes, Flash Lite version 3.1 | Yes, Flash Lite version 3.1 |
| Microsoft Silverlight support | | | Yes[42] | |
| OpenGL ES support | Yes, version 2.0 | | | |
| SQLite support | Yes | | Yes | Yes[43] |
| CPU architecture support | ARM | | ARM | ARM |
| Programmed in | C++ | | | |
| License | Eclipse Public License; Since March 31, 2011: Nokia Symbian License 1.0 | | | |
| Public issues list | No more | | | |
| Package manager | see .sis | | see .sis | see .sis |
| Non english languages support | Yes | | Yes | Yes |
| Underlining spell checker | Yes | | No | No |
| Keeps state on shutdown or crash | No | | No | No |
| Internal search | Yes | | Yes | Yes |
| Proxy server | Yes | | Yes | Yes |
| On-device encryption | Yes, Eseries devices, e.g., E7 | | Yes, present in no device | Yes, Eseries devices |

| Cut, copy, and paste support | Yes | | Yes | Yes |
|---|---|---|---|---|
| Undo | ? | | No | No |
| Default Web Browser for S60, WebKit engine | version 7.2, engine version 525[44] | | version 7.1.4 | |
| 3rd party software store | Ovi store | | Ovi store | Ovi store |
| Email sync protocol support | POP3, IMAP | | POP3, IMAP | POP3, IMAP |
| **Feature** | **Symbian^3** | **Symbian^2** | **Symbian^1/Series 60 5th Edition** | **Series 60 3rd Edition Feature Pack 2** |
| Push alerts | Yes | | | |
| Voice recognition | Yes | | Yes | Yes |
| Tethering | USB, Bluetooth; mobile Wi-Fi hotspot, with 3rd party software | | USB, Bluetooth; mobile Wi-Fi hotspot, with 3rd party software | USB, Bluetooth; mobile Wi-Fi hotspot, with 3rd party software |
| Text, document support | Microsoft Office Mobile, PDF, djvu | | Microsoft Office Mobile, PDF | Microsoft Office Mobile, PDF |
| Audio playback | All | | All | All |
| Video playback | H.263, H.264, WMV, MPEG4, MPEG4@ HD 720p 30fps, MKV, DivX, XviD | | H.263, H.264, WMV, MPEG4 | H.263, H.264, WMV, MPEG4 |
| Turn-by-turn GPS | 3rd party software, free global Nokia Ovi Maps, works offline | | 3rd party software, free global Nokia Ovi Maps, works offline | 3rd party software, free global Nokia Ovi Maps, works offline |
| Video out | Nokia AV, PAL, NTSC, HDMI | | Nokia AV, PAL, NTSC | Nokia AV, PAL, NTSC |
| Multitasking | Yes | | Yes | Yes |
| Desktop interactive widgets | Yes | | Yes | No |
| Integrated hardware keyboard | Yes | | Yes | Yes |
| Bluetooth keyboard | Yes | | Yes | Yes |
| Video conference front video camera | Yes | | Yes | Yes |

| Can share data via Bluetooth with all devices | Yes | | Yes | Yes |
|---|---|---|---|---|
| Skype, 3rd party software | Yes[45] | | Yes[45] | Yes[45] |
| Facebook IM chat | Yes | | Yes | |
| Secure Shell (SSH) | Yes, 3rd party software | | Yes, 3rd party software | Yes, 3rd party software |
| OpenVPN | Yes, 3rd party software | | No, Nokia VPN can be used | No, Nokia VPN can be used |
| Remote frame buffer | ? | | | |
| Screenshot | Yes, 3rd party software[46] | | Yes, 3rd party software[46] | Yes, 3rd party software[46] |
| GPU accelerated GUI | Yes | | | |
| Official SDK platform(s) | Cross-platform, Windows (preferred is Qt), Carbide.c++, Java ME, Web Runtime (WRT), Flash lite, Python for Symbian | | Cross-platform, Windows (preferred is Qt), Carbide.c++, Java ME, Web Runtime (WRT), Flash lite, Python for Symbian | Cross-platform, Windows (preferred is Qt), Carbide.c++, Java ME, Web Runtime (WRT), Flash lite, Python for Symbian |
| **Feature** | **Symbian^3** | **Symbian^2** | **Symbian^1/Series 60 5th Edition** | **Series 60 3rd Edition Feature Pack 2** |
| First device | Nokia N8 | | Nokia 5800 | |
| Devices | Nokia N8, Nokia C6-01, Nokia C7-00, Nokia E7-00, Nokia E6, Nokia X7 | NTT DoCoMo: F-06B*,[47] F-07B*,[47] F-08B*,[47] SH-07B†,[47] F-10B,[48] Raku-Raku Phone 7,[48] F-01C*,[49] F-02C*,[49] F-03C*,[49] F-04C*,[49] F-05C*,[49] SH-01C†,[49] SH-02C†,[49] SH-04C†,[49] SH-05C†,[49] SH-06C†,[49] Touch Wood SH-08C†[49] | Nokia 5228, Nokia 5230, Nokia 5233, Nokia 5235 , Nokia 5250, Nokia 5530 XpressMusic, Nokia 5800 XpressMusic, Nokia 5800 Navigation Edition, Nokia C5-03, Nokia C6-00, Nokia N97, Nokia N97 mini, Nokia X6 , Samsung i8910 Omnia HD,[50] Sony Ericsson Satio, Sony Ericsson Vivaz, Sony Ericsson Vivaz Pro | Nokia 5320 XpressMusic, Nokia 5630 XpressMusic, Nokia 5730 XpressMusic, Nokia 6210 Navigator, Nokia 6220 Classic, Nokia 6650 fold, Nokia 6710 Navigator, Nokia 6720 Classic, Nokia 6730 Classic, Nokia 6760 Slide, Nokia 6790 Surge, Nokia C5-00, Nokia E5-00, Nokia E52, Nokia E55, Nokia E71, Nokia E72, Nokia E75, Nokia N78, Nokia N79, Nokia N85, Nokia N86 8MP, Nokia N96, Nokia X5, Samsung GT-i8510 (INNOV8), Samsung GT-I7110, Samsung SGH-L870, Nokia C5-00 |
| **Feature** | **Symbian^3** | **Symbian^2** | **Symbian^1/Series 60 5th Edition** | **Series 60 3rd Edition Feature Pack 2** |

* manufactured by Fujitsu

† manufactured by Sharp

# Application development

## Qt

As of 2010, the SDK for Symbian is standard C++, using Qt. It can be used with either Qt Creator, or Carbide (the older IDE previously used for Symbian development).[30] [51] A phone simulator allows testing of Qt apps. Apps compiled for the simulator are compiled to native code for the development platform, rather than having to be emulated.[52]

## Symbian C++

It is also possible to develop using Symbian C++, although it is not a standard implementation. Before the release of the Qt SDK, this was the standard development environment. There were multiple platforms based on Symbian OS that provided software development kit (SDKs) for application developers wishing to target Symbian OS devices, the main ones being UIQ and S60. Individual phone products, or families, often had SDKs or SDK extensions downloadable from the maker's website too.

The SDKs contain documentation, the header files and library files needed to build Symbian OS software, and a Windows-based emulator ("WINS"). Up until Symbian OS version 8, the SDKs also included a version of the GNU Compiler Collection (GCC) compiler (a cross-compiler) needed to build software to work on the device.

Symbian OS 9 and the Symbian platform use a new application binary interface (ABI) and needed a different compiler. A choice of compilers is available including a newer version of GCC (see external links below).

Unfortunately, Symbian C++ programming has a steep learning curve, as Symbian C++ requires the use of special techniques such as descriptors, active objects and the cleanup stack. This can make even relatively simple programs harder to implement than in other environments. Moreover, it was questionable whether these techniques, such as the memory management paradigm, were actually beneficial. It is possible that the techniques, developed for the much more restricted mobile hardware of the 1990s, simply caused unnecessary complexity in source code because programmers are needed to concentrate on low-level routines instead of more application-specific features. As of 2010, these issues are no longer the case when using standard C++, with the Qt SDK.

Symbian C++ programming is commonly done with an integrated development environment (IDE). For earlier versions of Symbian OS, the commercial IDE CodeWarrior for Symbian OS was favoured. The CodeWarrior tools were replaced during 2006 by Carbide.c++, an Eclipse-based IDE developed by Nokia. Carbide.c++ is offered in four different versions: Express, Developer, Professional, and OEM, with increasing levels of capability. Fully featured software can be created and released with the Express edition, which is free. Features such as UI design, crash debugging etc. are available in the other, charged-for, editions. Microsoft Visual Studio 2003 and 2005 are also supported via the Carbide.vs plugin.

## Other languages

Symbian devices can also be programmed using Python, Java ME, Flash Lite, Ruby, .NET, Web Runtime (WRT) Widgets and Standard C/C++.[53]

Visual Basic programmers can use NS Basic to develop apps for S60 3rd Edition and UIQ 3 devices.

In the past, Visual Basic, Visual Basic .NET, and C# development for Symbian were possible through AppForge Crossfire, a plugin for Microsoft Visual Studio. On 13 March 2007 AppForge ceased operations; Oracle purchased the intellectual property, but announced [54] that they did not plan to sell or provide support for former AppForge products. Net60 [55], a .NET compact framework for Symbian, which is developed by redFIVElabs, is sold as a commercial product. With Net60, VB.NET and C# (and other) source code is compiled into an intermediate language (IL) which is executed within the Symbian OS using a just-in-time compiler. (As of 18/1/10 RedFiveLabs has ceased development of Net60 with this announcement on their landing page: "At this stage we are pursuing some options to sell the IP so that Net60 may continue to have a future".)

There is also a version of a Borland IDE for Symbian OS. Symbian OS development is also possible on Linux and Mac OS X using tools and methods developed by the community, partly enabled by Symbian releasing the source code for key tools. A plugin that allows development of Symbian OS applications in Apple's Xcode IDE for Mac OS X was available.[54]

Java ME applications for Symbian OS are developed using standard techniques and tools such as the Sun Java Wireless Toolkit (formerly the J2ME Wireless Toolkit). They are packaged as JAR (and possibly JAD) files. Both CLDC and CDC applications can be created with NetBeans. Other tools include SuperWaba, which can be used to build Symbian 7.0 and 7.0s programs using Java.

Nokia S60 phones can also run Python scripts when the interpreter Python for S60 is installed, with a custom made API that allows for Bluetooth support and such. There is also an interactive console to allow the user to write python scripts directly from the phone.

### Deployment

Once developed, Symbian applications need to find a route to customers' mobile phones. They are packaged in SIS files which may be installed over-the-air, via PC connect, Bluetooth or on a memory card. An alternative is to partner with a phone manufacturer and have the software included on the phone itself. Applications must be Symbian Signed [57] for Symbian OS 9.x in order to make use of certain capabilities (system capabilities, restricted capabilities and device manufacturer capabilities).[55] Applications can now be signed for free.[56]

## Competition and alternatives

In the number of "smart mobile device" sales, Symbian devices are the market leaders. Statistics published for 2010 showed that Symbian devices formed a 37.6% share of smart mobile devices sold, with Android having 22.7%, RIM having 16%, and Apple having 15.7% (via iOS).[57]

Prior reports on device shipments as published in February 2010 showed that the Symbian devices formed a 47.2% share of the smart mobile devices shipped in 2009, with RIM having 20.8%, Apple having 15.1% (via iOS), Microsoft having 8.8% (via Windows CE and Windows Mobile) and Android having 4.7%.[58] Other competitors include webOS, Qualcomm's BREW, SavaJe, Linux and MontaVista Software.

Although the share of the global smartphone market dropped from 52.4% in 2008 to 47.2% in 2009, shipments of Symbian devices grew 4.8%, from 74.9 million units to 78.5 million units.[58] From Q2 2009 to Q2 2010, shipments of Symbian devices grew 41.5%, by 8.0 million units, from 19,178,910 units to 27,129,340; compared to an increase of 9.6 million units for Android, 3.3 million units for RIM, and 3.2 million units for Apple.[59]

Symbian has lost market share in recent years; it dropped from 72.8% of the market in Q3 2006 to 36% in Q3 2010. In 2009-2010, Motorola, Samsung, LG, and Sony Ericsson announced their withdrawal from the platform, leaving only Nokia and several small Japanese-only vendors. By the end of 2010, Samsung will totally leave Symbian including the support and service and also remove all content relating to Symbian from its website, whereas Sony Ericsson will not introduce new mobile phone with Symbian.[60]

# Criticism

In November 2010, Smartphone blog *All About Symbian* criticized the performance of Symbian's default web browser and recommended the alternative browser Opera Mobile.[61]

Nokia's Senior Vice President Jo Harlow promised an updated browser in the first quarter of 2011.[62] Nokia denied any plans for switching to competitive platforms such as Android operating system, but in February 2011 announced it had signed a strategic tie up with Microsoft. Industry analysts expect Symbian's market share to decline, although it would still continue to dominate worldwide as the number two platform, after Android.[63] The announcement to switch to the "continuous development" model of Android and iPhone, where existing devices will be supported with new OS updates during their lifetime, has been welcomed by the community.

## Malware

Symbian OS was subject to a variety of viruses, the best known of which is Cabir. Usually these send themselves from phone to phone by Bluetooth. So far, none have taken advantage of any flaws in Symbian OS – instead, they have all asked the user whether they would like to install the software, with somewhat prominent warnings that it can't be trusted.

However, with a view that the average mobile phone user shouldn't have to worry about security, Symbian OS 9.x adopted a UNIX-style capability model (permissions per process, not per object). Installed software is theoretically unable to do damaging things (such as costing the user money by sending network data) without being digitally signed – thus making it traceable. Commercial developers who can afford the cost can apply to have their software signed via the Symbian Signed [57] program. Developers also have the option of self-signing their programs. However, the set of available features does not include access to Bluetooth, IrDA, GSM CellID, voice calls, GPS and few others. Some operators have opted to disable all certificates other than the Symbian Signed certificates.

Some other hostile programs are listed below, but all of them still require the input of the user to run.

- Drever.A is a malicious SIS file trojan that attempts to disable the automatic startup from Simworks and Kaspersky Symbian Anti-Virus applications.
- Locknut.B is a malicious SIS file trojan that pretends to be a patch for Symbian S60 mobile phones. When installed, it drops a binary that will crash a critical system service component. This will prevent any application from being launched in the phone.
- Mabir.A is basically Cabir with added MMS functionality. The two are written by the same author, and the code shares many similarities. It spreads using Bluetooth via the same routine as early variants of Cabir. As Mabir.A activates it will search for the first phone it finds, and starts sending copies of itself to that phone.
- Fontal.A is an SIS file trojan that installs a corrupted file which causes the phone to fail at reboot. If the user tries to reboot the infected phone, it will be permanently stick on the reboot, and cannot be used without disinfection – that is, the use of the reformat key combination which causes the phone to lose all data. Being a trojan, Frontal cannot spread by itself – the most likely way for the user to get infected would be to acquire the file from untrusted sources, and then install it to the phone, inadvertently or otherwise.

A new form of malware threat to Symbian OS in form of Cooked Firmware[64] [65] was recently demonstrated at the International Malware Conference, MalCon, December 2010, by Indian Hacker Atul Alex.[66]

### Bypassing platform security

Symbian OS 9.x devices can be hacked to remove the platform security introduced in OS 9.1 onwards, allowing users to execute unsigned code.[67] This allows altering system files, and access to previously locked areas of the OS. The hack was criticised by Nokia for potentially increasing the threat posed by mobile viruses as unsigned code can be executed.[68]

## References


[1] Lextrait, Vincent (January 2010). "The Programming Languages Beacon, v10.0" (http://www.lextrait.com/Vincent/implementations.html). . Retrieved 5 January 2010.

[2] http://symbian.nokia.com/blog/2011/04/04/not-open-source-just-open-for-business/

[3] Symbian on Intel's Atom architecture (http://blog.symbian.org/2009/04/16/symbian-on-intels-atom/)

[4] "infoSync Interviews Nokia Nseries Executive" (http://www.infosyncworld.com/news/n/11070.html). Infosyncworld.com. 2010-06-24. . Retrieved 2010-08-12.

[5] http://www.appleinsider.com/articles/11/04/29/115_growth_propels_apple_to_5_share_of_global_phone_shipments.html

[6] VisionMobile - 100 Million Club H1 2010 (http://www.visionmobile.com/blog/2010/10/smart-feature-phones-the-unbalanced-equation-100-million-club-series/)

[7] http://eu.techcrunch.com/2010/11/08/guest-post-symbian-os-one-of-the-most-successful-failures-in-tech-history/Symbian OS – one of the most successful failures in tech history

[8] (http://www.symbian.org/about-us)

[9] Symbian Foundation (2010-02-04), *Symbian Completes Biggest Open Source Migration Project Ever* (http://www.symbian.org/news-and-media/2010/02/04/symbian-completes-biggest-open-source-migration-project-ever), , retrieved 2010-02-07

[10] Symbian OS, Now Fully Open Source (http://www.watblog.com/2010/02/06/symbian-os-now-fully-open-source)

[11] "Symbian Foundation website, members section" (http://www.symbian.org/members). .

[12] http://www.engadget.com/2011/02/11/rip-symbian/

[13] http://sourceforge.net/projects/symbiandump

[14] http://code.google.com/p/symbian-incubation-projects/

[15] "Symbian^1" (http://developer.symbian.org/wiki/index.php/Symbian^1). Symbian Foundation. . Retrieved 2009-11-19.

[16] "Symbian^2" (http://developer.symbian.org/wiki/index.php/Symbian^2). Symbian Foundation. . Retrieved 2009-11-19.

[17] "Symbian^2 used in four new mobiles" (http://www.symbian.org/news-and-media/2010/06/01/symbian2-platform-used-four-new-models-ntt-docomo-foma-3g-handsets). Symbian Foundation. . Retrieved 2010-06-06.

[18] Symbian announces Symbian^3 and immediately gives it away (http://www.symbian.org/news-and-media/2010/02/15/symbian-announces-symbian3-and-immediately-gives-it-away) - Symbian press release, 15 February 2010

[19] "Symbian^3 Developer Overview - Symbian Developer Community" (http://developer.symbian.org/wiki/index.php/Symbian^3). Developer.symbian.org. . Retrieved 2010-08-12.

[20] "First look at Symbian^3 concept screenshots" (http://www.allaboutsymbian.com/news/item/10819_First_look_at_Symbian3_concept.php). All About Symbian. . Retrieved 2009-12-10.

[21] http://www.forum.nokia.com/info/sw.nokia.com/id/ec866fab-4b76-49f6-b5a5-af0631419e9c/S60_All_in_One_SDKs.html

[22] "Interview: First phone with new Symbian due from Asian vendor" (http://in.reuters.com/article/technologyNews/idINIndia-48812620100526). In.reuters.com. 2010-05-26. . Retrieved 2010-08-12.

[23] http://news.cnet.com/8301-13506_3-20053035-17.html?tag=contentMain;contentBody;1n

[24] http://news.cnet.com/8301-13506_3-20053035-17.html?tag=contentMain;contentBody;1n

[25] http://www.engadget.com/2011/04/12/nokia-announces-symbian-anna-update-for-n8-e7-c7-and-c6-01/

[26] http://conversations.nokia.com/2011/04/12/announcing-symbian-anna-aka-pr2/

[27] Nokia PR (Oct 21, 2010). "Nokia further refines development strategy to unify environments for Symbian and MeeGo" (http://www.nokia.com/press/press-releases/showpressrelease?newsid=1453894). . Retrieved 2010-11-05.

[28] AllAboutSymbian (Oct 26, 2010). "The future of the Symbian platform" (http://www.allaboutsymbian.com/features/item/12223_The_future_of_the_Symbian_plat.php). . Retrieved 2010-11-05.

[29] Nokia PR (May 24, 2006). "Nokia releases 'Web Browser for S60' engine code to open source community" (http://www.nokia.com/A4136002?newsid=1052589). *press.nokia.com*. . Retrieved 2007-03-21.

[30] "Symbian — Qt - A cross-platform application and UI framework" (http://qt.nokia.com/products/platform/symbian/). Qt.nokia.com. . Retrieved 2010-08-12.

[31] Forum Nokia (2010-06-18), *Nokia Qt SDK* (http://www.forum.nokia.com/Develop/Qt/), , retrieved 2010-06-18

[32] http://developer.symbian.org/wiki/index.php/Web_Runtime_Widgets_in_a_Nutshell

[33] http://www.forum.nokia.com/Technology_Topics/Web_Technologies/Web_Runtime/

[34] "Symbian developer community - technology domains" (http://developer.symbian.org/main/source/technology_domains/index.php). Developer.symbian.org. . Retrieved 2010-08-12.

[35] "Symbian developer community - packages" (http://developer.symbian.org/main/source/packages/index.php). Developer.symbian.org. . Retrieved 2010-08-12.
[36] "Symbian System Model - Symbian Developer Community" (http://developer.symbian.org/wiki/index.php/Symbian_System_Model). Developer.symbian.org. . Retrieved 2010-08-12.
[37] Introducing EKA2, by Jane Sales with Martin Tasker (http://media.wiley.com/product_data/excerpt/47/04700252/0470025247.pdf)
[38] Six Years of Symbian Produces 100 Models and 100 Million Shipments (http://www.thesmartpda.com/50226711/six_years_of_symbian_produces_100_models_and_100_million_shipments.php), The Smart PDA.
[39] Symbian Foundation Adds New Member, Nuance (http://news.softpedia.com/news/Symbian-Foundation-Adds-New-Member-Nuance-117209.shtml)
[40] Nokia N8 User Agent Profile (http://nds.nokia.com/uaprof/NN8-00r100-3G.xml)
[41] http://conversations.nokia.com/2010/09/09/nokia-launches-mobile-tv/
[42] http://www.silverlight.net/getstarted/devices/symbian/
[43] Inside Symbian SQL: A Mobile Developer's Guide to SQLite By Ivan Litovski, Richard Maynard, 2010, page 9
[44] http://library.forum.nokia.com/index.jsp?topic=/Web_Developers_Library/GUID-B7D6EFF3-16E6-45D5-9B74-8333BA83FC7B.html
[45] http://www.skype.com/intl/en/get-skype/on-your-mobile/?cm_mmc=m102
[46] http://www.antonypranata.com/screenshot/screenshot-symbian-os
[47] NTT DoCoMo releases S^2 devices (http://blog.symbian.org/2010/06/01/ntt-docomo-releases-s2-devices/)
[48] http://www.symbian.org/devices?manufacturer=All&platform=Symbian^2&form-factor=All&date_announced[value][year]=&date_announced[value][month] (http://www.symbian.org/devices?manufacturer=All&platform=Symbian^2&form-factor=All&date_announced[value][year]=&date_announced[value][month])
[49] "Symbian^2 platform used in eleven new models of NTT DoCoMo FOMA 3G handsets" (http://www.symbianone.com/content/view/7108/). SymbianOne. . Retrieved 2010-11-10.
[50] Samsung OMNIAHD Dazzles at Mobile World Congress with Its HD Brilliance (http://www.samsung.com/uk/news/newsPreviewRead.do?news_seq=12421)
[51] "Qt Labs Blogs » Nokia Qt SDK 1.0 released" (http://labs.trolltech.com/blogs/2010/06/23/nokia-qt-sdk-10-released/). Labs.trolltech.com. . Retrieved 2010-08-12.
[52] "Qt Labs Blogs » Qt Simulator is going public" (http://labs.trolltech.com/blogs/2010/05/31/qt-simulator-is-going-public/). Labs.trolltech.com. . Retrieved 2010-08-12.
[53] "Symbian developer community" (http://developer.symbian.org). Developer.symbian.org. 2010-01-27. . Retrieved 2010-08-12.
[54] Tom Sutcliffe and Jason Barrie Morley Xcode Symbian support (http://symbian-xcode-plugin.tigris.org/)
[55] "Capabilities (Symbian Signed) - Symbian Developer Community" (http://developer.symbian.org/wiki/index.php/Capabilities_(Symbian_Signed)). Developer.symbian.org. . Retrieved 2010-08-12.
[56] http://blogs.forum.nokia.com/blog/nokia-developer-news/2010/08/16/nokia-now-signing-symbian-apps-for-free
[57] Pettey, Christy. "Gartner Says Worldwide Mobile Device Sales to End Users Reached 1.6 Billion Units in 2010; Smartphone Sales Grew 72 Percent in 2010" (http://www.gartner.com/it/page.jsp?id=1543014). Gartner.com. . Retrieved 2011-03-10.
[58] "Majority of smart phones now have touch screens (Canalys press release: r2010021)" (http://www.canalys.com/pr/2010/r2010021.html). Canalys.com. 2010-02-08. . Retrieved 2010-08-12.
[59] "BBC News - Google Android phone shipments increase by 886%" (http://www.bbc.co.uk/news/technology-10839034). Bbc.co.uk. 2010-08-02. . Retrieved 2010-08-12.
[60] The end of Symbian http://ecellphone.net/the-end-of-symbian/
[61] http://www.allaboutsymbian.com/features/item/12323_Mobile_browser_comparison_Nove.php
[62] Meyer, David (November 9, 2010). "Nokia times first Symbian updates for 'early 2011'" (http://www.zdnet.co.uk/news/mobile-it/2010/11/09/nokia-times-first-symbian-updates-for-early-2011-40090806/). ZDNet UK. . Retrieved January 4, 2011.
[63] http://www.bmob.co.uk/2010/09/10/android-to-be-number-one-mobile-platform-by-2015/
[64] http://www.h-online.com/security/news/item/Hacker-plants-back-door-in-Symbian-firmware-1149926.html
[65] http://www.livehacking.com/2010/12/10/hacker-creates-modified-symbian-s60-firmware-with-hidden-back-door/
[66] http://en.wikipedia.org/wiki/Malcon
[67] Nokia's S60 3rd Ed security has been hacked? (http://www.symbian-freak.com/news/008/03/s60_3rd_ed_has_been_hacked.htm), Symbian Freak
[68] Symbian Freak: *S60 v3 Hacking – Mission accomplished, FP1 hacked!* (http://www.symbian-freak.com/news/008/03/s60_3rd_ed_feature_pack_1_has_been_hacked.htm)

## Bibliography


- Morris, Ben (22 June 2007). *The Symbian OS architecture sourcebook : design and evolution of a mobile phone OS* (http://eu.wiley.com/WileyCDA/WileyTitle/productCd-0470018461.html). John Wiley & Sons. p. 630. ISBN 0470018461


## External links

- Symbian foundation blog (which the homepage redirects to) (http://symbian.org/)
- Symbian (http://www.ohloh.net/p/symbian/analyses/latest) on Ohloh
- Symbian (http://www.dmoz.org/Computers/Mobile_Computing/Symbian/Symbian_OS/) at the Open Directory Project
- Symbian Developer website (http://developer.symbian.org/) – the official developer network

# webOS

**HP webOS**

HP webOS Home Screen on the Palm Pre

| | |
|---|---|
| **Company / developer** | Hewlett Packard since 2010, previously Palm |
| **OS family** | Linux |
| **Source model** | Closed Source, with some open source aspects released under GPL |
| **Latest stable release** | 1.4.5 and 2.1; see version history table |
| **Latest unstable release** | none as yet. |
| **Supported platforms** | ARM |
| **Kernel type** | Monolithic (Linux) |
| **Default user interface** | Graphical |
| **License** | Palm EULA, GPL for open source components[1] |
| **Official website** | Palm Developer Website [2] |

**webOS** is a proprietary mobile operating system running on the Linux kernel, initially developed by Palm, which was later acquired by HP.[2] Palm, HP, and most commentators have utilized "webOS" in their materials rather than "WebOS". The software was introduced by Palm in January 2009 as the successor to the legacy Palm OS, and was widely acclaimed for its ease of use, integration of Web 2.0 technologies, open architecture, and multitasking capabilities. The first device to use webOS was the original Palm Pre, which was released on Sprint in June 2009.

In 2010, HP acquired Palm; webOS was described as a key asset and motivation for the purchase.

In February 2011, HP announced a series of new devices that will use various versions of the operating system, including the HP Pre 3 and HP Veer smartphones, which will run webOS 2.2, and the HP TouchPad, a tablet computer which will run webOS 3.0, planned for release in Summer 2011. HP made the "difficult and, frankly, painful decision"[3] that the Palm Pre, Palm Pixi, and their later "Plus" revisions, would not receive over-the-air updates to webOS 2.0,[4] despite a previous announcement of an upgrade "in coming months."[5]

In March, 2011, HP announced plans for a version of webOS by the end of 2011 that would run within the Microsoft Windows operating system,[6] and which would be installed on all HP desktop and notebook computers in 2012.[7]

## Background

From 1992 to 2002, personal digital assistant maker Palm Computing (later renamed Palm, Inc.) owned and developed the Palm OS software platform. In 2002, Palm created a wholly owned subsidiary, PalmSource, which was later spun off as an independent company. Palm licensed Palm OS and Windows Mobile as it developed webOS as a new platform to replace both.[8]

webOS was demonstrated by Palm at the Consumer Electronics Show in Las Vegas in January 2009, and was first released on Sprint with the launch of the Palm Pre in June 2009. The Palm Pixi, and upgraded Plus versions of each, followed.

HP purchased Palm in April 2010, the $1.2 billion acquisition finalizing in June. HP has announced its intention to develop the webOS platform for use in multiple products, including smartphones, tablet computers and printers.

## Features

### Devices

webOS version 1.4.5 runs on the majority of webOS phones: the Palm Pre, released June 6, 2009, on the Sprint network, the Palm Pixi, released on November 15, 2009, on Sprint, as well as "Plus" versions later issued on Verizon Wireless and AT&T, and some international carriers.[9]

Pre 2 phones with webOS 2 were released to consumers in October 2010 in France by SFR,[10] 2010 December by Rogers in Canada, and 2011 February on Verizon in the U.S. Unlocked Pre 2 phones using webOS version 2 are available directly from HP.[11] [12]

Plans for additional webOS versions and devices were announced by HP in February 2011,[13] [14] including the Touchpad, the Pre 3 and the Veer.

In March 2011, HP announced that all PCs shipped by HP in 2012 will be able to run webOS in addition to Microsoft Windows.[15]

On May 5, 2011, HP announced that the Veer will be available from AT&T on May 15. The announcement also revealed that the Veer would be available in two colours.[16]

## Interface

webOS screen on a Palm Pre Plus showing the "cards"

webOS's graphical user interface design was led by Matias Duarte for use on devices with touchscreens.[17] webOS uses multi-touch gestures to navigate on the touchscreen. webOS 1.4.5 does not natively include a virtual keyboard application as the devices include slide-out keyboards, but users can obtain virtual keyboards through patching. The interface uses "cards" to manage multitasking. Applications can be launched from either the "Launcher", which displays a default of three pages of application icons in a scrollable grid, or the Quick Launch bar, which displays five icons inline horizontally. The user switches between running applications by a flicking gesture from left and right on the screen. Applications are closed by flicking a "card" up—and "off"—the screen.

## Synergy

webOS uses a feature, Synergy, to integrate information from many sources. Users can sign in to accounts on Gmail, Yahoo!, Facebook, LinkedIn, and Microsoft Outlook (via Exchange ActiveSync) and integrate all these sources into a single list. Calendars from multiple sources can be viewed together or one at a time. For messaging, Synergy combines all conversations with each contact into a single chat-style window. For example, instant messages and SMS text messages are viewed together.[18]

## Web browser

The webOS web browser, simply named "Web," uses the WebKit layout engine and accordingly renders pages in a similar way to other WebKit-based browsers such as Apple's Safari, Google's Google Chrome, and Android browsers. The screen orientation switches between landscape or portrait displays on rotating the device.

## Synchronization

By design, webOS uses a cloud-based approach rather than using a desktop sync client, but various third-party sync clients are available.

## Default Apps

In version 1.x, the webOS launcher bar and launcher pages include these default apps:

# Default applications

| Name | Usage |
|---|---|
| Phone | Telephone |
| Email | E-mail client |
| Web | Web browser |
| Music | Music player |
| Messaging | Text messaging, MMS, IM |
| Calendar | Calendar |
| Camera | Camera - to take pictures and video |
| Photos | Photo viewer |
| Video | Video app for on-device video |
| YouTube | Stream YouTube videos |
| Google Maps | Google Maps (does not feature voice-guided navigation) |
| Memos | A simple note-taking program |
| Clock | Alarm clock, digital/analog clock |
| Calculator | Calculator |
| App Catalog | To buy webOS apps or download free ones |
| Amazon MP3 | To buy music from Amazon |
| Doc View | Document viewer from DataViz |
| PDF View | PDF Viewer |
| Tasks | Used to input and be reminded of tasks |
| Contacts | Address/phone book |

Carrier specific settings and installed software are available on the Dialer screen on 1.x devices by pressing on the Title Tab and selecting "Preferences"

Despite demonstrations of potential candidate software[19] Adobe Flash cannot run on webOS version 1.

## Third-party applications

Officially vetted third-party applications are accessible from the device for wireless download by using the App Catalog.[20]

webOS was a completely new platform. To enable backward compatibility to its former Palm OS, Palm commissioned a developer, MotionApps, to code and develop an emulator, called Classic, that operates with webOS version 1. PalmOS emulation has been discontinued in webOS version 2.0.[21] MotionApps disengaged from Classic in 2010, citing HP Palm as "disruptive".[22]

Another source of applications is known as Homebrew.[23] [24] Homebrew is neither directly supported nor officially condoned by HP, and Homebrew activities could void the device warranty.[25]

# Version history

| webOS version | Release date | Notes |
|---|---|---|
| **1.0.1** | RTM[26] | The 1.0.2 OTA update was already available on the first day of sale. Some Pres required this OTA update from 1.0.1 to 1.0.2 while others already had 1.0.2 pre-loaded.[27] |
| **1.0.2** | 5 June 2009 | |
| **1.0.3** | 19 June 2009[28] | |
| **1.0.4** | 29 June 2009[29] | |
| **1.1.0** | 23 July 2009[30] | First release for Bell Canada[31] |
| **1.1.2** | RTM for Palm Pre from O2[32] | 1.2 was already available in the United States when the O2 phones were released with 1.1.2. The 1.1.3 update was already available for European OTA update when the phones were available for sale. |
| **1.1.3** | 13 October 2009 | OTA update released only in Europe for GSM Palm Pre. Available on launch day. When released, 1.2 was already available in the United States. |
| **1.2.0** | 28 September 2009[33] | This was the first release said to support paid apps from the App Catalog.[34] [35] |
| **1.2.1** | 2 October 2009 for Sprint,[36] 6 October 2009 for Bell Canada[37] | |
| **1.2.9.1** | Pixi RTM | This was a Pixi-only release. Version 1.3.1 was already available for OTA update when the Pixi was released[38] |
| **1.3.1** | 14 November 2009 for Sprint and Bell Canada[39] 22 November 2009 for O2 Europe[40] For European carriers, this was the first OTA update following 1.1.3. | |
| **1.3.2** | 2 December 2009[41] | This was a Pixi-only release |
| **1.3.3** | Not Released | Appears on the Palm Open Source Packages page as a release, but was never released on any known carrier.[42] |
| **1.3.5** | 28 December 2009[43] | Only available on Sprint. |
| **1.3.5.1** | 4 January 2010 for Sprint,[44] 5 January for Bell Canada,[45] 25 January for Verizon[46] | Only released in North America |
| **1.3.5.2** | 12 January 2010[47] | Only released in Europe |
| **1.3.8** | Pre-Release[48] | This appears to be a pre-release version used when testing the AT&T Pre and Pixi. |
| **1.4.0** | 26 February 2010 for Sprint, O2, Movistar,[49] 28 February 2010 for Verizon,[50] 4 March 2010 for Bell Cananda,[51] 5 March 2010 for Telcel Mexico[52] | This is the current version released for Telcel Mexico Pres. |
| **1.4.1** | 31 March 2010 in Europe,[53] [54] 1 April 2010 in Canada[55] | Released only in Europe and Canada |
| **1.4.1.1** | 31 March 2010 for Sprint,[56] 29 April 2010 for Verizon[57] | Released only in the United States |

| | | |
|---|---|---|
| **1.4.1.2** | Pre-Release[58] | Seen on a reviewer pre-production Vodafone Pixi Plus phone, presumed to be functionally equivalent to 1.4.1.1. |
| **1.4.1.3** | RTM for O2 Pixi Plus[59] | Released only on the O2 Pixi Plus, supposed to be functionally equivalent to 1.4.1.1. |
| **1.4.2** | RTM for AT&T Pre Plus[60] | Only on the AT&T Pre Plus, supposed to be functionally equivalent to 1.4.1.1. |
| **1.4.3** | RTM for AT&T Pixi Plus | Only on the AT&T Pixi Plus, supposed to be functionally equivalent to 1.4.1.1. |
| **1.4.5** | 14 July 2010 | The update was made available for different devices over several months starting 2010 July[61] [62] [63] with the last device to receive this update, the ATT Pixi Plus, receiving it in 2010 October.[64] Some carriers (notably Telcel Mexico) never deployed this update. This is the final update for Pre and Pixi, and so far Pixi Plus phones, with some carriers releasing further updates[65] for the Pre Plus and others not. |
| **2.0.0** | 22 October 2010 | This is an RTM release for the Pre 2.[66] Many webOS phones used by consumers currently still use 1.4.0 or 1.4.5 and may be left on those versions indefinitely. |
| **2.0.1** | 19 November 2010 | This is an RTM release, for Pre 2 phones or unlocked devices.[67] |
| **2.1.0** | 8 March 2011 | Available on the Pre 2 through an OTA update[68] and the Pre Plus for O2 Germany and Vodafone Europe through a USB-tethered "doctor" update.[69] |
| **2.2** | Summer 2011 | This is a future release, for HP Pre 3 and HP Veer phones. |
| **3.0** | Summer 2011 | This is a future release, for HP TouchPad. Despite the major version number difference, this appears to be a 2.x release that is optimized for the TouchPad hardware differences. |

# Platform

Underneath the graphical user interface the platform has much in common with mainstream Linux distributions.

The list of open source components used by the different releases of webOS, as well as the source code of and patches applied to each component, is available at the Palm Open Source web page.[70] This page also serves as a reference listing of the versions of webOS that have been publicly released.

Enyo, now in beta, is starting to replace Mojo, released in 2009 June, as the software development kit (SDK).[71]

Versions 1.0 to 2.1 are using a patched version of the Linux 2.6.24 kernel.[72]

# Development

HP provides resources for webOS developers[73] and instructions for enrolling in the HP Palm Developer Program.[74]

# References

[1] "Source code for Palm WebOS released" (http://www.h-online.com/open/news/item/Source-code-for-Palm-WebOS-released-742117.html). The H Open Source (http://www.h-online.com/). 19 June 2009. . Retrieved 2009-10-28.

[2] "Overview of webOS" (http://developer.palm.com/index.php?option=com_content&view=article&id=1761&Itemid=42). Palm, Inc.. . Retrieved 25 August 2010.

[3] "Thanks (really!) for the feedback" (http://blog.palm.com/palm/2011/02/thanks-really-for-the-feedback.html). Hewlett Packard. .

[4] "HP Breaks Promise - webOS 2.0 Upgrades for Palm Pre and Pixi Not Coming" (http://www.brighthand.com/default.asp?newsID=17498&news=hp+palm+webos+2.0+pre+pixi). Brighthand.com. . Retrieved 2011-02-13.

[5] "HP Commits to webOS 2.0 Upgrades for All Palm Smartphones" (http://www.brighthand.com/default.asp?newsID=17244&news=HP+Palm+webOS+2.0+Pre+Pixi+Upgrade). Brighthand.com. .

[6] (http://www.engadget.com/2011/03/14/hp-touchpad-coming-june-webos-for-pc-beta-by-years-end/)

[7] "Apotheker Seeks to Save HP's 'Lost Soul' With Software Growth" (http://www.businessweek.com/news/2011-03-09/apotheker-seeks-to-save-hp-s-lost-soul-with-software-growth.html). Bloomberg. . Retrieved 9 March 2011.

[8] Dieter Bohn. (precentral.net) 2009 Feb 11. Palm CEO Ed Colligan Talks Pre with Investors. (http://www.precentral.net/palm-ceo-ed-colligan-talks-pre-investors)

[9] "Palm International" (http://www.palm.com/intl/). . Retrieved 2010-07-15.

[10] por Jose Andrade (2010-10-11). "Operadora francesa SFR anuncia el Palm Pre 2 sin permiso: CPU de 1GHz y webOS 2.0" (http://es.engadget.com/2010/10/11/operadora-francesa-sfr-anuncia-el-palm-pre-2-sin-permiso-cpu-de/). . Retrieved 2010-10-19.

[11] "Pre 2 for sale in US for $449.99 direct from HP" (http://www.precentral.net/pre-2-sale-us-44999-direct-hp). PreCentral.net. 2010-11-18. . Retrieved 2010-12-23.

[12] "Unlocked Pre 2 available across Europe for 499€" (http://www.precentral.net/unlocked-pre-2-available-across-europe-499â‚¬). PreCentral.net. 2010-11-16. . Retrieved 2010-12-23.

[13] Steve Lohr. New York Times. 2011 Feb 9. Playing Catch-Up, Nokia and H.P. Try to Innovate.

[14] "HP webOS Think Beyond Event (February 9th, 2011)" (http://www.youtube.com/watch?v=VnjwG7Z8AM8). YouTube. 2011-02-09. . Retrieved 2011-02-13.

[15] "HP CEO: WebOS on all our PCs in 2012" (http://news.cnet.com/8301-31021_3-20041158-260.html). cnet. March 9, 2011. . Retrieved March 9, 2011.

[16] "HP Veer" (http://www.palm.com/us/products/phones/veer/index.html). HP. May 5, 2011. . Retrieved May 5, 2011.

[17] "How Palm Designed the Pre" (http://www.forbes.com/forbes/2009/0622/smart-phones-blackberry-how-palm-designed-pre.html). Forbes. 2009-06-22. . Retrieved 2011-02-13.

[18] Palm, Inc. (2009-01-08). "Palm Unveils All-new webOS" (http://investor.palm.com/releasedetail.cfm?ReleaseID=358392). Press release. . Retrieved 2009-05-27.

[19] Segan, Sasha (February 17, 2010), "Palm Shows Flash Running on the Palm Pre" (http://www.pcmag.com/article2/0,2817,2359899,00.asp), *PC Magazine*,

[20] http://www.palm.com/us/products/software/mobile-applications.html

[21] Derek Kessler. 2010 Oct 25. With webOS 2.0, MotionApps drops Classic PalmOS Emulator in Palm's lap. (http://www.precentral.net/webos-20-pushes-classic-palm-os-emulator-out-picture)

[22] MotionApps. 2010 Oct 25. Classic's Got a Brand New Home! MotionApps Hands Classic Over to Palm (http://www.motionapps.com/classic/)

[23] Precentral (precentral.net). Homebrew Apps (http://www.precentral.net/homebrew-apps)

[24] milominderbinder (precentral.net) 2010 Jan 22. Getting Started: Homebrew Apps, Patches, and Themes with WebOS Quick Install. (http://www.precentral.net/getting-started-homebrew-apps-patches-and-themes-webos-quick-install)

[25] Derek Kessler (precentral.net) 2010 Aug 26. UberKernel accelerates Pre to 1GHz, your life will never be the same. (http://www.precentral.net/uberkernel-accelerates-pre-1ghz-your-life-will-never-be-same)

[26] Derek Kessler (3 June 2009). "Palm Pre firmware 1.0.2, Sudoku, alarm clock" (http://www.precentral.net/palm-pre-firmware-1-0-2-sudoku-alarm-clock). *precentral.net*. . Retrieved 15 February 2011.

[27] Dieter Bohn (6 June 2009). "Palm Pre PSA: Run Update, Get 1.02" (http://www.precentral.net/palm-pre-psa-run-update-get-1-02). *precentral.net*. . Retrieved 15 February 2011.

[28] Dieter Bohn (19 June 2009). "webOS 1.03 Update Available OTA Right Now" (http://www.precentral.net/webos-103-update-available-ota-right-now). *precentral.net*. . Retrieved 16 March 2010.

[29] Dieter Bohn (29 June 2009). "webOS 1.04 Released for your OTA Downloading Pleasure" (http://www.precentral.net/webos-104-released-your-ota-downloading-pleasure). *precentral.net*. . Retrieved 16 March 2010.

[30] Dieter Bohn (23 July 2009). "webOS 1.1 for the Palm Pre Now Available, iTunes Sync is BACK!" (http://www.precentral.net/webos-11-palm-pre-exchange-many-fixes). *precentral.net*. . Retrieved 16 March 2010.

[31] Dieter Bohn (27 August 2009). "So Canada! Your Pre is Native Now!" (http://www.precentral.net/so-canada-your-pre-native-now). *precentral.net*. . Retrieved 15 February 2011.

[32] Jason Slater (23 October 2009). "Initial thoughts on the Palm Pre" (http://www.jasonslater.co.uk/2009/10/22/initial-thoughts-on-the-palm-pre/). *www.jasonslater.co.uk*. . Retrieved 25 February 2011.

[33] Derek Kessler (28 September 2009). "webOS 1.2 available for download!" (http://www.precentral.net/webos-12-available-download). *precentral.net*. . Retrieved 16 March 2010.

[34] Derek Kessler (28 September 2009). "webOS 1.2 available for download!" (http://www.precentral.net/webos-1-2-available-download). *precentral.net*. . Retrieved 15 February 2011.

[35] "webOS 1.2.0 Release Notes" (http://kb.palm.com/wps/portal/kb/na/pre/p100eww/sprint/solutions/article/50607_en.html#12). *kb.palm.com*. 28 September 2009. . Retrieved 15 February 2011.

[36] Derek Kessler (3 October 2009). "webOS 1.2.1 lands, fixes Exchange and iTunes" (http://www.precentral.net/webos-121-lands-fixes-exchange-and-itunes). *precentral.net*. . Retrieved 16 March 2010.

[37] Robert Werlinger (6 October 2009). "webOS 1.2.1 update goes online for Bell customers" (http://www.precentral.net/webos-1-2-1-update-goes-online-bell-customers). *precentral.net*. . Retrieved 15 February 2011.

[38] Dieter Bohn (15 November 2009). "Happy Pixi Day!" (http://www.precentral.net/happy-pixi-day). *precentral.net*. . Retrieved 15 February 2011.

[39] Derek Kessler (14 November 2009). "webOS 1.3.1 update available for download" (http://www.precentral.net/webos-1-3-1-update-available-download). *precentral.net*. . Retrieved 15 February 2011.

[40] Robert Werlinger (22 November 2009). "webOS 1.3.1 now available in Europe" (http://www.precentral.net/webos-1-3-1-now-available-europe). *precentral.net*. . Retrieved 16 February 2011.
[41] Dieter Bohn (2 December 2009). "webOS 1.3.2 Released for Pixi, Pre Standing By" (http://www.precentral.net/webos-1-3-2-released-pixi-pre-standing). *precentral.net*. . Retrieved 16 February 2011.
[42] "Open Source Packages" (http://opensource.palm.com/packages.html). . Retrieved 25 February 2011.
[43] Derek Kessler (28 December 2009). "webOS 1.3.5 now available for download on Sprint [UPDATED (http://www.precentral.net/webos-135-now-available-download)"]. *precentral.net*. . Retrieved 16 March 2010.
[44] Dieter Bohn (4 January 2010). "webos 1.3.5.1 Available for OTA Download on Sprint for Pre and Pixi" (http://www.precentral.net/webos-1351-available-ota-download-sprint). *precentral.net*. . Retrieved 16 March 2010.
[45] Derek Kessler (5 January 2010). "webOS 1.3.5.1 goes live for Pre users on Bell" (http://www.precentral.net/webos-1-3-5-1-goes-live-pre-users-bell). *precentral.net*. . Retrieved 16 February 2011.
[46] Dieter Bohn (25 January 2010). "Launch Day! Pre Plus, Pixi Plus on Verizon" (http://www.precentral.net/launch-day-pre-plus-pixi-plus-verizon). *precentral.net*. . Retrieved 16 February 2011.
[47] Derek Kessler (12 January 2010). "webOS 1.3.5.2 landing in Europe [UPDATE: Bluetooth tethering (!) (http://www.precentral.net/webos-1-3-5-2-landing-europe-update-bluetooth-tethering)"]. *precentral.net*. . Retrieved 16 February 2011.
[48] Dieter Bohn (18 January 2010). "AT&T Pre and Pixi Spotted in Server Logs Running webOS 1.3.8" (http://www.precentral.net/ATT-pre-and-pixi-spotted-server-logs-running-webos-1-3-8). *precentral.net*. . Retrieved 16 February 2011.
[49] Dieter Bohn (27 February 2010). "webOS 1.4 Available Now for Sprint, O2, Movistar; Verizon, Bell, Telcel Users Wait" (http://www.precentral.net/webos-14-available-now-sprint-and-verizon-users). *precentral.net*. . Retrieved 16 March 2010.
[50] Dieter Bohn (28 February 2010). "webOS 1.4 Lands on Verizon" (http://www.precentral.net/webos-1-4-lands-verizon). *precentral.net*. . Retrieved 16 February 2011.
[51] Dieter Bohn (4 March 2010). "webOS 1.4 Hits Bell Canada" (http://www.precentral.net/webos-1-4-hits-bell-canada). *precentral.net*. . Retrieved 16 February 2011.
[52] Dieter Bohn (5 March 2010). "webOS 1.4 Arrives for Telcel Mexico" (http://www.precentral.net/webos-1-4-arrives-telcel-mexico). *precentral.net*. . Retrieved 16 February 2011.
[53] Dieter Bohn (31 March 2010). "webOS 1.4.1 Brings Mobile Hotspot to O2 Users (Update: Germany and UK)" (http://www.precentral.net/webos-1-4-1-brings-mobile-hotspot-o2-users-update-germany-and-uk). *precentral.net*. . Retrieved 16 February 2011.
[54] Dieter Bohn (31 March 2010). "webOS 1.4.1 Starts Trickling Out - Updates: Netherlands, Germany, UK, Ireland, Spain, France" (http://www.precentral.net/webos-1-4-1-starts-trickling-out-updates-netherlands-germany-uk-ireland-spain-france). *precentral.net*. . Retrieved 16 February 2011.
[55] Dieter Bohn (1 April 2010). "webOS 1.4.1, paid apps to hit Bell Canada today? Update: Yep, go get it!" (http://www.precentral.net/webos-1-4-1-paid-apps-hit-bell-canada-today-update-yep-go-get-it). *precentral.net*. . Retrieved 16 February 2011.
[56] Dieter Bohn (31 March 2010). "webOS 1.4.1.1 Hits Sprint, Now Verizon Waits" (http://www.precentral.net/webos-1-4-1-1-hits-sprint-now-verizon-waits). *precentral.net*. . Retrieved 16 February 2011.
[57] Dieter Bohn (29 April 2010). "webOS 1.4.1.1 Hits Verizon" (http://www.precentral.net/webos-1-4-1-1-hits-verizon). *precentral.net*. . Retrieved 16 February 2011.
[58] Rafael Bernad (26 April 2010). "Vodafone nos enseña el Pixi Plus con webOS 1.4.1.2 y ¡Flash!" (http://www.webosmania.com/webos/vodafone-nos-ensena-el-pixi-plus-con-webos-1-4-1-2-y-flash/). *webosmania.com*. . Retrieved 16 February 2011.
[59] Ben Combee (03 June 2010). "Forums webOS - View topic - WebOS 1.4.1.3" (http://developer.palm.com/distribution/viewtopic.php?f=21&t=7435#p32069}). .
[60] Dieter Bohn (13 May 2010). "AT&T Palm Pre Plus Review" (http://www.precentral.net/att-palm-pre-plus-review). *precentral.net*. . Retrieved 22 February 2011.
[61] Albert F. (webosmania.com) 2010 July 15. Palm webOS ya está disponible. (http://www.webosmania.com/contenidos/webos-1/)
[62] Andrew Munchbach. (bgr.com) 2010 Aug 12. webOS 1.4.5 update to start hitting handsets today. (http://www.bgr.com/2010/08/10/webos-1-4-5-update-to-start-hitting-handsets-today/)
[63] Dieter Bohn (11 August 2010). "webOS 1.4.5 finally arrives for Sprint users (Update 3: working now, go get it)" (http://www.precentral.net/webos-1-4-5-finally-arrives-sprint-users-update-3-working-now-go-get-it). *precentral.net*. . Retrieved 16 February 2011.
[64] Greg Kumparak. (mobilecrunch.com) AT&T Pixi Plus finally gets WebOS 1.4.5. (http://www.mobilecrunch.com/2010/10/12/att-pixi-plus-finally-gets-webos-1-4-5/)
[65] Dieter Bohn (22 February 2011). "webOS 2.1 download posted for European Pre Plus (Updated)" (http://www.precentral.net/webos-2-1-o2-germany-s-palm-pre-plus-posted-yes-really). *precentral.net*. . Retrieved 14 March 2011.
[66] Derek Kessler (2 Nov 2010). "First webOS 2.0 Doctor hits for SFR Pre 2" (http://www.precentral.net/first-webos-2-0-doctor-hits-sfr-pre-2). *precentral.net*. . Retrieved 22 February 2011.
[67] "webOS 2.0.1 hits unlocked devices, shows how fast things happen without the carriers (Update) | PreCentral.net | The #1 Palm Pre and Pixi Community" (http://www.precentral.net/webos-2-0-1-hits-unlocked-devices-shows-how-fast-things-happen-without-carriers-update). PreCentral.net. 2010-11-19. . Retrieved 2011-02-13.
[68] Jesse Mendoza (2011-03-08). "webOS 2.1 OTA Makes Its Way to the Pre 2" (http://www.webosroundup.com/2011/03/webos-2-1-ota-makes-its-way-to-the-pre-2/). webOSroundup.com. . Retrieved 2011-03-09.

[69] "webOS 2.1 download posted for European Pre Plus" (http://www.precentral.net/webos-2-1-o2-germany-s-palm-pre-plus-posted-yes-really). PreCentral.net. 2011-02-22. . Retrieved 2011-02-22.
[70] "Open Source Packages - Palm" (http://opensource.palm.com/packages.html). opensource.palm.com. . Retrieved 2011-02-15.
[71] Jesse Mendoza. HP Rolls Out webOS 3.0 Beta with Enyo On Board. 2010 March 30. http://www.webosroundup.com/2011/03/hp-rolls-out-webos-3-0-beta-with-enyo-on-board/
[72] "Open Source Packages - Palm" (http://opensource.palm.com/packages.html). opensource.palm.com. . Retrieved 2011-02-15.
[73] "HP Palm Developer Center" (http://developer.palm.com/). Hewlett-Packard Development Company. . Retrieved 10 March 2011.
[74] "Developing and Distributing with HP: Developer Program Details" (http://developer.palm.com/index.php?option=com_content&view=article&id=1840&Itemid=34). Hewlett-Packard Development Company. . Retrieved 10 March 2011.

## External links

- Palm.com (http://www.palm.com/)
- Palm Developer Network (http://developer.palm.com/)
- WebOS Internals (http://www.webos-internals.org/wiki/Main_Page)

# Comparison of ARM tablets

This is a comparison of tablet computers which processors are ARM-based.

## Tablets

| Product | Maker | Operating system | Display size (in) | Resolution, aspect ratio | System on chip | Memory | Storage | Storage expansion | WAN available |
|---|---|---|---|---|---|---|---|---|---|
| **Adam** | Notion Ink | Android | 10.1 | 1024x600, 5:3 | Tegra 250 | 1 GB | 8 GB | microSD | yes/3G (3G is optional) |
| **Archos 101** | Archos | Android | 10.1 | 1024x600, 5:3 | OMAP 3630 | 256 MB | 8/16 GB | microSD | no |
| **BlackBerry PlayBook** | RIM | BlackBerry Tablet OS | 7 | 1024x600, 5:3 | OMAP 4430 | 1 GB | 16/32 GB | unknown | yes |
| **Galaxy Tab** | Samsung | Android | 7 | 1024x600, 5:3 | S5PC110 | 512 MB | 16/32 GB | microSD | 3G |
| **iPad** | Apple | iOS | 9.7 | 1024x768, 4:3 | Apple A4 | 256 MB | 16-64 GB | no | 3G |
| **iPad 2** | Apple | iOS | 9.7 | 1024x768, 4:3 | Apple A5 | 512 MB | 16-64 GB | no | 3G |
| **Streak** | Dell | Android | 5 | 800x480, 16:9 | QSD8250 | 512 MB | 2 GB | microSD | yes |
| **Streak 7** | Dell | Android | 7 | 800x480, 16:9 | Tegra 2 | ? | 16 GB | unknown | HSPA+ |
| **TouchPad** | HP | webOS | 9.7 | 1024x768, 4:3 | APQ8060 | 1 GB | 16/32 GB | no | 3G/4G |
| **ViewSonic G Tablet** | ViewSonic | Android | 10.1 | 1024x600, 5:3 | Tegra 2 | 512 MB | 16 GB | microSD | no |

| Xoom | Motorola | Android | 10.1 | 1280x800, 16:10 | Tegra 2 | 1 GB | 32 GB | unknown | yes |
|---|---|---|---|---|---|---|---|---|---|

## Systems on chips

This table compares the system-on-a-chip (SoC) used in the above tablets.

| Product | Maker | CPU core | Cores | Clock speed | GPU core | Production date |
|---|---|---|---|---|---|---|
| **Apple A4** | Samsung | Hummingbird, Intrinsity designed Cortex-A8 | 1 | 1 GHz | PowerVR SGX 535 | March 2010 |
| **Apple A5** | Samsung | Cortex-A9, custom designed chip | 2 | 1 GHz | PowerVR SGX 543MP2 | March 2011 |
| **APQ8060** | Qualcomm | Scorpion, Cortex-A9 based | 2 | 1.2 GHz | Adreno 220 | February 10, 2011 |
| **OMAP 3630** | Texas Instruments | Cortex-A8 | 1 | 1 GHz | PowerVR SGX 530 | February 2009 |
| **OMAP 4430** | Texas Instruments | Cortex-A9 | 2 | 1 GHz | PowerVR SGX 540 | December 2010 |
| **S5PC110** | Samsung | Hummingbird | 1 | 1 GHz | PowerVR SGX 540 | September 22, 2009[1] |
| **Snapdragon QSD8250** | Qualcomm | Scorpion, Cortex-A8 based | 1 | 1 GHz | Adreno 200 | December 2008 |
| **Tegra 2** | nVIDIA | Cortex-A9 | 2 | 1 GHz | ULP GeForce | January 7, 2010 |

## References

[1] "SAMSUNG Opens the Door to PC-Level Performance on Mobile Devices with 1GHz Low-power Application Processors" (http://www.samsung.com/global/business/semiconductor/newsView.do?news_id=1043). SAMSUNG Semiconductor. . Retrieved 7 March 2011.

# Article Sources and Contributors

**Tablet computer** *Source*: http://en.wikipedia.org/w/index.php?oldid=427783572 *Contributors*: 842U, A Quest For Knowledge, AV3000, Ahunt, Aizuku, Alvestrand, Ancheta Wis, AndrewHowse, ArtsMusicFilm, Bender235, Bigredsky, Bob bobato, Camilo Sanchez, Chuck369, Coercorash, CommonsDelinker, Crysb, Cvbommel, Cyberdiablo, DVdm, Daniel.Cardenas, Dbachmann, Dialectric, Diamondland, Diego Moya, Ecw.technoid.dweeb, Edcolins, Editor2020, Edkollin, Elizium23, Eog1916, Eraserhead1, EuTuga, Evan-Amos, Exlixe, Falcon9x5, Fishnet37222, Forresttsao, GSL-Nathan, GreenZeb, Gsarwa, Heavyrain2408, Helmuthva, Hydriz, Ionutpopa, Ipadtablet, Itsmine, IvanLanin, JaGa, Javabyte, Jerryobject, Jgera5, Jim.henderson, Jinnai, JohnSawyer, JonathanDP81, Jpod2009, Krauss, Leofranco2000, Lexischemen, LilHelpa, Lore1996, Lppa, MER-C, Macromediax, Mahjongg, Marcus Qwertyus, Materialscientist, MetaManFromTomorrow, Michael Minh, Mikitei, Mr Stephen, New Thought, Newone, OspreyPL, PeregrineAY, Pnm, Red Act, Ronz, SarekOfVulcan, Shahimbaker, Shrish, Simonrleung, Snottywong, Soundvisions1, Squids and Chips, TMV943, Taka76, Tankwan, Taxman, The Thing That Should Not Be, Tide rolls, Tony Sidaway, Toussaint, UCDS, Vanuan, Vyx, Wbrito, Weylin.piegorsch, Woohookitty, WorldBrains, Yosh3000, 92 anonymous edits

**Acer Tablet** *Source*: http://en.wikipedia.org/w/index.php?oldid=425228082 *Contributors*: AndrewHowse, Apostrophyx, Cleocri, Eg81, JLaTondre, 7 anonymous edits

**Archos 101** *Source*: http://en.wikipedia.org/w/index.php?oldid=413402399 *Contributors*: Dcxf, GreenZeb, Ludopedia, Racklever, Tlitic, 1 anonymous edits

**Archos 43** *Source*: http://en.wikipedia.org/w/index.php?oldid=421393121 *Contributors*: CaptainFalco311, Dcxf, GreenZeb, Malcolmxl5, Redsox42311, Rsocol, 3 anonymous edits

**Archos 70** *Source*: http://en.wikipedia.org/w/index.php?oldid=428481538 *Contributors*: Bearcat, Bsharitt, Chris the speller, Dcxf, GreenZeb, Jacob.flurgenn, Ludopedia, Redsox42311, Rsocol, RyanQuinlan, WereSpielChequers, 13 anonymous edits

**ASUS Eee** *Source*: http://en.wikipedia.org/w/index.php?oldid=425523081 *Contributors*: Andyvphil, ApnAEA, Dank, Daviduzzu, Emilng, Evers, Gamester17, GermanX, Helgie, Jeodesic, Julesd, Kozuch, Nakakapagpabagabag, Nopetro, Pmsyyz, Power piglet, Sandos, Scootey, SpigotMap, Toussaint, Woohookitty, Yakiv Gluck, 7 anonymous edits

**ASUS Eee Pad Transformer** *Source*: http://en.wikipedia.org/w/index.php?oldid=428588759 *Contributors*: BD2412, Beach drifter, Chris the speller, Cncxbox, Hoss789, Iamdarren, Jerryobject, Mrand, Sbmeirow, Sirclockalot, Zackaback, 15 anonymous edits

**EnTourage eDGe** *Source*: http://en.wikipedia.org/w/index.php?oldid=421601131 *Contributors*: Chowbok, Discospinster, EoGuy, Glane23, Jerryobject, Jim.henderson, Joe1997, Legitimus, 2 anonymous edits

**Pocket eDGe** *Source*: http://en.wikipedia.org/w/index.php?oldid=425011445 *Contributors*: Jerryobject, Letowskie, 3 anonymous edits

**ExoPC** *Source*: http://en.wikipedia.org/w/index.php?oldid=427751629 *Contributors*: 1mac4u, Alexandr3, Anthony Appleyard, Bearcat, CommonsDelinker, Conzorz, Dreamcat1138, GoingBatty, Green Giant, HaeB, Hervegirod, Hooperbloob, IndianGeneralist, Ionutpopa, Jim.henderson, Kevindark, Kitchj, Melab-1, Petermui, Rainabba, Rich Farmbrough, Rknelissen, Sir aaron sama girl, Stemtl, 16 anonymous edits

**History of tablet computers** *Source*: http://en.wikipedia.org/w/index.php?oldid=428212782 *Contributors*: Bearcat, Crysb, Diego Moya, Jevansen, Mahjongg, Malcolma, PenComputingPerson, Pssstdana, RHaworth, TMV943, Tengounnombre, Warpozio, Zyboris, Δ, 4 anonymous edits

**Huawei Ideos Tablet S7** *Source*: http://en.wikipedia.org/w/index.php?oldid=426006076 *Contributors*: Bearcat, CommonsDelinker, Dadu, Drmies, Etbe, Faizanalivarya, Jerome Charles Potts, 2 anonymous edits

**iPad** *Source*: http://en.wikipedia.org/w/index.php?oldid=428605841 *Contributors*: 1234r00t, 2over0, 5 albert square, 842U, A Quest For Knowledge, A5b, AFGstyla20, ANHL, AV3000, Aanhorn, Aaronmz, AbbaIkea2010, Abhishikt, Acps110, Aimoneale, Airplaneman, Aizuku, Ajfweb, Ajraddatz, Albany NY, Aldaron, Alecperkins, AlexAnnecy, AlexReynolds, AlexWelens, AlexanderMelton, Alfpooh, AlistairMcMillan, Allmightyduck, Allolex, AlphaPikachu578, Alvaro, Amason126, Amatulic, Ambobo25000, Anaxial, Ancheta Wis, Ancient Apparition, Andareed, Andreasr2d2, AndrewHowse, Andy120290, Andyjsmith, Andyzweb, Anetode, Angryapathy, AniRaptor2001, Aniket Ray, Anna Lincoln, Annoyed with fanboys, AnonyLog, Anthony Appleyard, Antivirtual, Antonov86, Anwar saadat, Apokrif, Apricot50, Arite, Arkanosis, Armor Nick, Arteyu, Arthena, Artichoker, ArtsMusicFilm, AtteL, Audin, Audiohifi, Austin512, Avatar-X, AvicAWB, Avicennasis, Aviedit, AzaToth, AznBurger, B0805444, Badman89, Banana04131, Banaticus, Barabum, Barek, Barek-public, Barts1a, Baseball Watcher, Bawwimp, Bbb2007, Bdfortin, Beao, Becritical, Beerrocks, Bejinhan, Beland, Ben b, Bencey, Bender235, Bfmv252, Bgpaulus, Bidishamukherjii, Bilby, Bility, Billare, Billy9999, BillyPreset, Billytheworld, Bjrice, BlackTerror, BlaiseFEgan, Bluerasberry, Blunt., Bo98, Bob bobato, Boing! said Zebedee, Bonusballs, Booklover7272, Bporter28, BredoteauU2, Brendanmccue, Brianreading, Brianski, Bruce1ee, Bruced1000, Bruin183, Burda001, Buyislateaccessories, C628, CWenger, Cadsuane Melaidhrin, Caiaffa, Calvinps, Canadaworker, Cartersfriendly, Catspjs01, Cdlee099, Cellmate27, Chaotic Mind, Chappy84, CharlesWoeste, Charlesbell515, Charvest, Cheong Kok Chun, Chimpflyer, Chris3037, ChrisfromHouston, Chrisperra, Christian75, ChrstphrChvz, Chzz, Clarince63, Clee7903, ClubOranje, Coasterlover1994, CommonsDelinker, CompRhetoric, ConnorJack, Connormah, Coolcaesar, Coolsonh, Corevette, Corgi5623, Countercouper, Coupin, Courcelles, CrazyDiablo, Crissov, Crisss1104, Crysb, Csigabi, Cwg25, Cwill151, Cwlq, Cybercobra, Cybertragic, CycloneGU, Cymru.lass, Cyril, DARTH SIDIOUS 2, DBAlex, DMCer, Dabomb87, Daedalus969, Dale Arnett, DalekAGB, DanWis, Daniel Hen, Daniel.Cardenas, Danielkivatinos, Danlev, Danyaddita, Darincarter, Darrell Greenwood, Darrenhusted, Darthmix, Davidhorman, Dcoetzee, Denimadept, Department of Redundancy Department, Dfsghjkgfhdg, Diamondblade2008, Diaspore, DillonLarson, Dispenser, Dmarquard, Dmartin969, Docwolf13, Doglet1, Dopefish, Dowbrandon, Dr. Blofeld, Dr.K., Drivec, Drrll, Drthatguy, DtD, Dubmill, Dv82matt, Dwayne, Dwigs, Dylanspronck, EVula, Earl CG, Eastmain, Ebe123, Ecbfilms001, Edward, Edwardyu236, Egnalebd, Ekimberly259, El3ctr0nika, Elan515, Elangsto, Eldesign87, Eleeet, Elockid, Emuroms, EnTerr, Endofskull, Engelberg, Engerim, Epeefleche, Eraserhead1, Eregli bob, Esrever, Eurovictor, Evan-Amos, Everyone Dies In the End, EvilCouch, EvilHom3r, Excirial, Exerdo666, Fainites, Falcon8765, Farleysmaster, FazilTHEone, FelixFT, Feudonym, Filmingnz, Filpaul, Finlay McWalter, Flaviohmg, Fletcher, Flodded, Florihupf, Flyguy649, Forteblast, Fourthords, Freakydisco, Frecklefoot, Fudoreaper, Funandtrvl, Fuzheado, Fygoat, G.ardaud, GDW13, GSK, GWPSP090, Ganimoth, Gari22, Gary King, GateKeeper, GaussianCopula, Gbmodern, GeneralCheese, Generalcp702, Generally Sentient, Georgewquinn, Gfoley4, Ghostrider, Glitch82, Gobbleswoggler, Gogo Dodo, Gomm, Graham87, GregA, GregorB, Groink, Gsarwa, Guy Harris, Gyrobo, HJ Mitchell, Ha us 70, Haakon, HalfShadow, HandThatFeeds, Harrigan, Haseo9999, Hcobb, Hellis, Hellsoso, Helvetica, Hengsheng120, HereToHelp, Hereforhomework2, Hermione is a dude, Hervegirod, Historic 66, Hoagie3000, Hobit, Holden15, Homyakchik, Horserice, Hpyy9yrt8j6m545b5oig5y, Hullaballoo Wolfowitz, Humble Scribe, Hurk87, Hydnjo, Hydrox, HyperCapitalist, IBoy2G, IEchuu, ISquishy, Ian Page, Iangurteen, Ianprime0509, Icairns, Iceman444k, Ieure, Ignorance is strength, Illegal Operation, Imagowan, Infrogmation, Intelati, Intgr, Islander, J1729, JForget, Jack Merridew, Jackster, Jake Wartenberg, JamesBWatson, JamesBrownJr, JamieS93, Jane wiki, Jason.Schwartz, JasonAQuest, Jatkins, Jaymo, Jbanes, Jboud, Jcrook1987, Jdcompguy, Jdtyler, Jedduff, Jedi94, Jeffpower, Jennavecia, JeremyWJ, Jeremykemp, Jerryobject, Jerrysmp, Jessamyncp, Jgera5, Jhawkbball27, Jiang, Jim10701, Jimthing, Jjaazz, Jkonrath, Jmrowland, Joako420, Jodi.a.schneider, Joe routt, Joemamagrama121, John John 216, John of Reading, JohnHWiki, JohnSawyer, Johntex, Jojhutton, Jonik, Jonjesbuzz, Joost.b, Jordyjamers, Joshua Scott, Joshualam, Jovianeye, Jpfagerback, Jtwall12, Juan M. Gonzalez, JuanC08, Judicatus, Juggle86, Julesd, Jusdafax, JustLearningWiki, Justin Ormont, Justinxtreme, K, Kalarn, Kaldar, Kansan, Karebear 1022, Karimjbacchus, Kathleen5454, Keith D, KelleyCook, Kendroche, Keyser Söze, Kflester, Kgbo, KiasuKiasiMan, Kittybrewster, Kkiller14, Klapper, Klizza, Klknoles, Koavf, Kolyma, Komitsuki, Konczewski, Korruski, Krasko, Kuru, Kuyabribri, Kwiki, Kyle1278, Kıdemli, L Kensington, LUUSAP, Lakeyboy, Lame Name, Lawl95, LeftClicker, Lemery214, Lemmypaul, Leonidas84, Lester, Letdorf, Lexischemen, Lissajous, Lo2u, Logical Cowboy, Logix16, Logwea299, Lordhighnessiii, Lousyd, Lovelovefilm, LovesMacs, Lppa, Lucien504, Luke Wattchow, Lukefinch, Lussary, MER-C, MGore24, MJBurrage, Macdude98, Macintosher, Macrakis, Madesinasia, MadnessInside, Magioladitis, Mahjongg, MammonLord, Marcus Brute, Marcus Qwertyus, Mardetanha, Mario CUSENZA, Mariordo, Markjenkinsmusic, Markles, Mathiastck, Matthieu.berthome, Mattinbgn, Mattlittlej, Mattmarks001, Mattwigway, Matěj Grabovský, Maury Markowitz, Maximz2005, Maxí, Maythammahdipour, Mcg3o, Md84419, Mdwh, Mediadatabase, Mepolypse, Mewtu, Michael Devore, Michael.poplawski, Michaeldsuarez, Michaelmas1957, Michaelmdx, Mickeys1fan, Minna Sora no Shita, MishMich, MissAlyx, Mkdw, Mlo1088, Mokakeiche, Mono, MoreNet, Mornelmornel, Mr. Erik, MrBuzz111, MrOllie, MrSoldierToBe, Mrschimpf, Mushroom, Mushroom9, Mutchy126, Muthuchakkara, Mwarren us, Myscrnnm, N3m6, NHRHS2010, NY4NY, Nakon, Nathanl1192, Naught101, NawlinWiki, NegativeIQ, Neinsun, Neitherday, NerdyScienceDude, NermalTheBunny, Neutron, Nich148 9, NickW557, Nickwaz98, Nicoli nicolivich, Night Gyr, Nightscream, Nima1024, Nmajdan, Nopetro, Northumbrian, NotAnonymous0, Notscrewinguppages, Npdoty, Nudecline, Nunquam Dormio, Nwusr123log, Nysus, Nyttend, ONEder Boy, Oahiyeel, Obsoletepower, Oclupak, Ocrasaroon, Officially Mr X, Ohnoitsjamie, Olivierjacobs, Olli, Ollycity, Oneiros, Orangemike, Orbiting234, Owain, Oxguy3, P shadoh, PRRfan, Pachang, PaleAqua, Pandar, Pardthemonster, Paul Magnussen, PaulNovitski, Paulomatsui, Pavithran, PenComputingPerson, Peter Ellis, Petershen1984, Petri Krohn, Phasma Felis, Phatom87, Phearson, Phil Sandifer, Philwiki, Phlegat, Pizarra23, Placelimit, Plau, Pmokeefe, Pnm, PolarYukon, Pragvansh, Preschooler.at.heart, Pretendo, PrincessofLlyr, Pristino, Pro66, Prolixium, Psantora, Pvt.Billinghurst, PwnedDuck, Qnonsense, Quackgrassacrez, QueryOne, Quiddity, Qviri, R'n'B, RabbleRouser, Rabhyanker, Rad vsovereign, Ral725, Random name, Reach Out to the Truth, Recipe For Hate, Reeseepup16, Reisio, Remember, RenniePet, Replysixty, Rhindle The Red, Rhyseh2007, Rich Farmbrough, Richiekim, Riffic, Rillian, Risker, Rjwilmsi, Robofish, Rockysmile11, Rod156, Roguegeek, Roguelazer, Roleplayer, Ronhjones, Ronnotel, Rorschach, RoyBoy, Rush2009, Rusty7070, Ryan Paddy, RyanLeiTaiwan, S8333631, SColombo, SHARD, Saipraneethn, Salamurai, Sam-ainsworth, Sameerb, Samibeckhhhhh, Samlikeswiki, Sandgem Addict, Sandstein, SarekOfVulcan, Schmidtja, Scjessey, Seaphoto, Seb az86556, Sfortis, Shadowjams, ShakataGaNai, ShattaAD, Shrish, Simulcra, Sjl0523, Sk8rSoda, Skiliftlover, Skim, Skizzik, Skudo900630, Sladen, Slark, Sleigh, SlimVirgin, Sman789, Smileyborg, Snappy, So God created Manchester, Sonucoolkid, Spencerk96, Spenceryoung1212, SpikeyRussia, StealthCopyEditor, StefanCT, Steinbch, Stephan Leeds, Stephen G. Brown, Stephentwest, Stifle, Stolenpotatoes, Storm Rider, Stroppolo, Stykkjet, Sumsum2010, Sundae, Suomi Finland 2009, Supreme Deliciousness, Svick, Swatjester, SwissPol, Swotboy2000, Sysrpl, TGCP, TMC1221, TMV943, TYelliot, Tabledhote, TaerkastUA, Talktrue, Tall Midget, Tammsalu, Tangoman.fr, Tarekag, Tariqabjotu, TastyCakes, Tbhotch, Teapotgeorge, Tech30, Technion, Techreation, Terrillja, Th1rt3en, The Filmaker, The High Fin Sperm Whale, The Man in Question, The Thing That Should Not Be, The Wordsmith, TheFarix, TheThomas, TheTruthiness, Themachonachoboy, Themeparkphoto, Thenoflyzone, Thepaperarmy, Therefore, Thomashoi, Thrashmetal101, Tide rolls, Tigertanghao, Tillman, Timantha102938, Timberframe, Timl2k4,

Timzor, Tiuks, Tktktk, TobiasK, Tommy2010, Tonkatsu182, Tonyr60, Tooki, Torchwoodwho, Torocmacto, Totie, Trev M, Trevor raney, Tri400, Trident13, Trieste, TrufflesTheLamb, Tweisbach, Twump, Tyrol5, Tyw7, Ukexpat, Ukimies, Ummit, Uncle Dick, UncleBubba, UncleDouggie, UnicornTapestry, Unnachamois, Unregistered.coward, Urbndude, Urdutext, Utuado, Varunpramanik, Vchimpanzee, Vegaswikian1, Vercillo, Vfx2k4, Vibodha, Villefort1790, Vsmith, W3bbo, Wackoff1000, Wanion, Warko, Waterfox, Wayne Slam, Webeffect77, Whenbongoscollide, Whisky drinker, White 720, Whitebox, Whywhenwhohow, Wiki.Tango.Foxtrot, Wikiisaac, Wikipediaman2000, Wikipeterproject, Wikiven, Will Beback Auto, William Avery, Windward1, Windyhead, Winston365, WinstonSmith147, Winstonhyypia, Wnt, Woohookitty, Worm That Turned, Wpapolis, Wtmitchell, Wuhwuzdat, Wwoods, X30ffx, Xeno, Yadiellee12, Yo yo get a life, Yodaat, Yoganate79, Yosri, Yousou, Yucan, Yug, Yworo, Zackaback, Zacman123, Zaf, ZanyRocket, Zayani, Zearin, Zeugma fr, Zhou Yu, Zinzen, Zoara, Zr40, Zwilson, Zyboris, Zzuuzz, 542 anonymous edits

**iPad 2** *Source*: http://en.wikipedia.org/w/index.php?oldid=427891449 *Contributors*: 05barbs, A Quest For Knowledge, Adterzo, Ahivarn, Alfstar1997, Almog6564, Ameliorate!, Atlana, Bility, C. A. Russell, C628, CalebJohns, Calmer Waters, Casperruegg, CecilWard, ChaosR, Cheese is a beast, Clee7903, Closedmouth, CommonsDelinker, Cookiejoey, Courcelles, Crane1995, Cybercobra, Czarbender, Dagamer34, DieSwartzPunkt, Doh5678, Dooperer, E2eamon, Ebe123, EdJohnston, Eeekster, Elangsto, Enchanter, Eraserhead1, Exavier24, Factorylad, Feezo, Fetchcomms, Flacojo32, Frecklefoot, Freemanukem, Fullstoppp, Gaius Cornelius, Gary King, Glane23, Gonfaloniere, GuacamoleEater, Hamtechperson, Hazel77, HereToHelp, Highspeedrailguy, Humphreys7, Hvn0413, Illegal Operation, Imroy, Jackster, Javier032, Jchasan, Jessemv, Jfagen5, Jgera5, Jhsounds, Jimthing, Joel181, John John 216, Justinhu8, KarmaLoop, Kevind963, Kinghusky, Kisore, Kslotte, Ktr101, Kuru, Lebowbowbowski, Lizard93, Lsimon77, MSGJ, Marcus Qwertyus, MarsRover, Materialscientist, Mc5874, Megalon, Mepolypse, Metricmike, Michaelzeng7, Mono, Mrbencooper, Msesha87, Mutchy126, Nasukaren, Nishimura335, Nster98, Ohnoitsjamie, Olivierjacobs, Oni Ookami Alfador, OspreyPL, PRRfan, Porsch1909, Portillo, Prillen, Psantora, Qantasplanes, Rajvissa, Ramdrake, Rasberry12, Reaper Eternal, RedBull2011, Redsox74, RexxS, Richiekim, Rndomuser, Roidroid, Samit Boonyaruk, Samlikeswiki, Scottama, Seaphoto, ShattaAD, Silvergoat, Slomic, Smmgeek, Snaheth, Spartaz, Spong129, Spool 26, Steve Roderick, Stinwin, Tbhotch, Terrillja, The High Fin Sperm Whale, ThegrandOya, Thomas888b, ThomasO1989, Tide rolls, Timl2k4, Tjoeb123, Vimal.ramaka, Warburton1368, Yoninah, Zollerriia, Zorxd, Σ, 维尼尔基, 221 anonymous edits

**Magic W3** *Source*: http://en.wikipedia.org/w/index.php?oldid=427464536 *Contributors*: Mw3g6, 1 anonymous edits

**Microsoft Courier** *Source*: http://en.wikipedia.org/w/index.php?oldid=417659594 *Contributors*: 0612, 10metreh, A little insignificant, Afrowildo, Blaxthos, Casablanca2000in, CommonsDelinker, ConstantineMaat, Desnish, Efficacious, HMishkoff, Jerrysmp, Jim.henderson, Karthik mut, LazDude2012, Lester, LethalReflex, Logix16, MER-C, Marek69, Placelimit, Rjwilmsi, Slavon37, SubtractM, Taabello, Tehw1k1, Templarian, Wexeb, Woohookitty, Xompanthy, Zundark, 59 anonymous edits

**Motorola Xoom** *Source*: http://en.wikipedia.org/w/index.php?oldid=427271528 *Contributors*: BCXtreme, Barek, Bender235, Brighterorange, BunnyT, Bunnyturd, C628, CPGus511, Coemgenus, Coolman13355, David N. Doorknob, DillonLarson, Dmarquard, Dylanstaley, EoGuy, FelxSoft2, Fetchcomms, FlexDo2iky, Ganeshk, Gogo Dodo, GorillaWarfare, Hakimio, Hervegirod, Ibexris, Ic7800, Isler45, Jab416171, Jalexoid, Jerryobject, JoeBikerul, LeftClicker, Lkt1126, Logan, MeLOKI2ee, Mikeribby, Mrekru, Mycomp, Myscrnnm, PaulinSaudi, Rajeh h, Rofii5, Rolandpol, SCARECROW, Sbmeirow, Seven.cardwell, Shaifaligupta, Slinky317, Soandos, Sstrader, Starcraft 2:Wings of Liberty, StewieK, Tbhotch, Tweisbach, Txaggiemichael, V2oxviesta, WaltFrench, Walterll, Yk4ever, Zouzzou, 78 anonymous edits

**Pocket computer phone** *Source*: http://en.wikipedia.org/w/index.php?oldid=425173897 *Contributors*: DragonflySixtyseven, In2thats12, Katharineamy, Mean as custard, Mw3g6

**Sakshat** *Source*: http://en.wikipedia.org/w/index.php?oldid=427459025 *Contributors*: 06baraxs, AndrewHowse, Arun K Sivanandan, Coercorash, Dialectric, Dsvyas, Error, Gdandona, Grundle2600, Infinite dreams9586, Jac16888, Jedduff, Jerryobject, Johnxxx9, K7.india, Lightmouse, Lucian303, Mahjongg, MarQ, Meco, Nareshguptaks, Neo-Jay, Prd.ban, Rajendra bn, RobertMfromLI, Rsrikanth05, Shrish, Taxman, TexMurphy, Utcursch, Virtualage, Wuffyz, 70 anonymous edits

**T-Mobile G-Slate** *Source*: http://en.wikipedia.org/w/index.php?oldid=415405295 *Contributors*: SoWhy, Zouzzou

**Toshiba Tablet** *Source*: http://en.wikipedia.org/w/index.php?oldid=426912655 *Contributors*: AndrewHowse, BuickCenturyDriver, DaneRobertStrom, Ebe123, Globular Cluster1, Hakimio, Jamietw, 5 anonymous edits

**Comparison of tablet PCs** *Source*: http://en.wikipedia.org/w/index.php?oldid=428554872 *Contributors*: 1ifes4v3r, Adammw, Ahunt, Ameliorate!, ArachanoxReal, Aronzak, Barts1a, Brian hsieh, Calmer Waters, Canthariz, Cnoizece, Colonies Chris, Crispmuncher, Davecrosby uk, Demac89, Demostene, Diamondland, Dinsintltd, Doramjan, Ebriigisto, EoGuy, Etbe, Excirial, GoingBatty, Hakimio, Hu12, Indolering, JLaTondre, Jaizovic, Jerryobject, JorgeGG, KVDP, Killy-the-frog, Kozuch, LaVieEntiere, Lancehyde, Magioladitis, Mardus, Muhandes, Nave.notnilc, Pol098, Prayerfortheworld, Pssstdana, R'n'B, Rg.smit, S3000, Shayst, Skatebiker, Ssggmm, Stephen B Streater, Sunnyquon, Templarian, UniversityofPi, Wikinaute, Woohookitty, Xjph, Yuvrajsd, 194 anonymous edits

**Microsoft Tablet PC** *Source*: http://en.wikipedia.org/w/index.php?oldid=424988017 *Contributors*: Dabomb87, Eraserhead1, Evan-Amos, Jerryobject, Jhartmann, Mahjongg, Ringbang, Steveklein, TYelliot, Tbhotch, Terrillja, UCDS, Vyx, Zyboris, 5 anonymous edits

**Encipher Inye** *Source*: http://en.wikipedia.org/w/index.php?oldid=420463196 *Contributors*: AndrewHowse, Bearcat, CommonsDelinker, Malcolma, Tomalexander, Wazobianaija

**EO Personal Communicator** *Source*: http://en.wikipedia.org/w/index.php?oldid=422269457 *Contributors*: A Generic User, DNewhall, Dawynn, GregorB, Jusdafax, Maury Markowitz, Nihonjoe, PDAgeek, PenComputingPerson, Plr4ever, Saforrest, Skierpage, Thumperward, Vegaswikian, Wbvanrij, Woz2, 12 anonymous edits

**Fujitsu Lifebook T900** *Source*: http://en.wikipedia.org/w/index.php?oldid=425441528 *Contributors*: Bearcat, Brianmay27, Bubba73, Cwbh10, GoingBatty, Rich Farmbrough, Tabletop, Zyboris, 1 anonymous edits

**Gateway C-Series** *Source*: http://en.wikipedia.org/w/index.php?oldid=375370990 *Contributors*: AniRaptor2001, KathrynLybarger, Lester, Rjwilmsi

**HP Compaq TC1100** *Source*: http://en.wikipedia.org/w/index.php?oldid=414458078 *Contributors*: Adavidw, AeonicOmega, Agent Fog, Akamarshall, AndrooUK, Astrotoy7, Beetstra, CharlesC, Dangerous-Boy, Dorien.herremans, Fethroesforia, GoldDragon, IndianGeneralist, Jfowler27, Jmundo, Kaplanmyrth, Kylu, MeekMark, Mrwojo, Muhandes, NFAN3, NeoChaosX, ObfuscatePenguin, Otterfan, Pearle, Perivision, Salamurai, SimsHsia, Thiseye, Tweenk, WNewquay, Y2kcrazyjoker4, Ytrottier, 60 anonymous edits

**HP Compaq TC4200** *Source*: http://en.wikipedia.org/w/index.php?oldid=414446412 *Contributors*: Dawynn, IndianGeneralist, Jfowler27, John of Reading, MeekMark, R'n'B, 2 anonymous edits

**HP Compaq TC4400** *Source*: http://en.wikipedia.org/w/index.php?oldid=414458181 *Contributors*: A. S. Castanza, Dawynn, IndianGeneralist, Jfowler27, MeekMark, Obaidz96, Orthografer, R'n'B, 4 anonymous edits

**HP Pavilion TX1000 Series Tablet PC** *Source*: http://en.wikipedia.org/w/index.php?oldid=418555651 *Contributors*: 22curious, Alvin Seville, AvicAWB, CLW, Cander0000, Dvroegop, Formula350, Harmeetsg, Jeremymilligan, Jim.henderson, Julekmen, Kathleen.wright5, Kevinzhengli, MER-C, MeekMark, Mikemoral, Mild Bill Hiccup, SF007, Shanusmarty, Starkiez, Sumsum2010, Swotboy2000, TisGrimUpNorth, WasAPasserBy, 15 anonymous edits

**HP Slate 500** *Source*: http://en.wikipedia.org/w/index.php?oldid=422449075 *Contributors*: 5 albert square, A Quest For Knowledge, Abhishikt, Alansohn, Alex.muller, Andries, Bender235, C628, E=MC2orisit, ENeville, Editor2020, Eeekster, EoGuy, Foremi11, GC29180, Gary King, Garysu, Harej, Ilikebike, JLaTondre, Jebus989, Jedduff, JonForst6, Josephtd, JuanC08, Kmanthatscool, Logix16, MER-C, Magioladitis, ManosGR, Mattius92, Mephiston999, Michaelkourlas, Mizon, Myscrnnm, Nwusr123log, Phosgram, Placelimit, Qwyrxian, Rfraleigh, Riittaajo, Samwaltz, Shrish, Talktrue, The wub, UCDS, Wjemather, Wuffyz, Xomm, Zyboris, Милан Јелисавчић, 143 anonymous edits

**HP TouchSmart** *Source*: http://en.wikipedia.org/w/index.php?oldid=418263428 *Contributors*: 4meter4, Abc1234567891011 1, Andrewrp, Btilm, Cherryguy93, Danigro456, Debresser, Editor2020, Edward, HPTouchsmart, Ionutpopa, Julekmen, Kozuch, Lituus, Lkt1126, Myscrnnm, NatureA16, Nightscream, Nopetro, Nwusr123log, Pineapple fez, Pointillist, SF007, Tomy9510, Travis.Thurston, WasAPasserBy, Yowuza, 29 anonymous edits

**HTC Flyer** *Source*: http://en.wikipedia.org/w/index.php?oldid=428515227 *Contributors*: AvicAWB, FamilyGuy1998, Horizonsperson, IGEL, JoeBikerul, Mr Sheep Measham, Sin-man, SoWhy, Zackkatz, 29 anonymous edits

**Ink Serialized Format** *Source*: http://en.wikipedia.org/w/index.php?oldid=389916901 *Contributors*: Dawynn, EoGuy, Giraffedata, Ground Zero, HAl, KathrynLybarger, Lester, Rjwilmsi, 3 anonymous edits

**MobileDemand** *Source*: http://en.wikipedia.org/w/index.php?oldid=420965477 *Contributors*: Diego Moya, Eraserhead1, Pssstdana, Racklever, 1 anonymous edits

**OLPC XO-3** *Source*: http://en.wikipedia.org/w/index.php?oldid=399658492 *Contributors*: Dvaer, Excelsoft, Stepho-wrs

**Pepper Pad** *Source*: http://en.wikipedia.org/w/index.php?oldid=415730658 *Contributors*: Apotheon, Asterion, Avhell, CSWarren, Eptin, Hasek is the best, Ionek, JLaTondre, Kozuch, Myscrnnm, NeopetsWiki, Nintendude, Quadell, Silver hr, Someoneinmyheadbutit'snotme, Stepho-wrs, Tomhannen, Tomhormby, Trunkmonkey, WegianWarrior, White 720, Ww, 14 anonymous edits

**Soft Input Panel** *Source*: http://en.wikipedia.org/w/index.php?oldid=425136907 *Contributors*: Jerryobject, LilHelpa, Malloth, Mild Bill Hiccup, Quokly, Warren, 1 anonymous edits

**Tablet personal computer** *Source*: http://en.wikipedia.org/w/index.php?oldid=427795289 *Contributors*: (jarbarf), 0612, A.k.a., AIMSzpc, AUBIH- Boky, AV3000, Abhishikt, Abtin, Acdx, Adam zappul, Aelman, Airodyssey, Aizuku, Alan Liefting, Alanse, Alansohn, Aldebaran66, Aldie, Alessgrimal, Alexius08, Alexpmuller, Algont, AlistairMcMillan, Alphachimp, Ancheta Wis, Andre Engels, Andrew Werdna, Andrewrutherford, AndyCook, Anonymous Cow, Anonywiki, Apavlo, Arancı, Arctosouros, Arrenlex, Ashbas, AstareGod, Atlant, Atlanta800, Aude, Austinite, BD2412, Back ache, Badgernet, Bakkster Man, Bart133, Beland, Bemus, Bender235, Biancasimone, Bikepunk2, BlaiseFEgan, Blathering1, Blaxthos, Bluetulip, BorgHunter, Brian hsieh, Brontide, Bschreib, Btwied, Bungalowbill, Bushytails, Bvisual, Bzbert, C628, Calabraxthis, CameoAppearance, Camilo Sanchez, Can't sleep, clown will eat me, CanadianLinuxUser, Canterbury Tail, Capricorn42, Catgut, Cenigma13, Cessna315, ChaChaFut, CharlesC, CharlieZeb, Choster, Chris G, Chris Ssk, Chris the speller, Chrisch, Cisum.ili.dilm, CledusQ, Closedmouth, Colemanyee, CommonsDelinker, Connormah, Coolhawks88, Crispmuncher, Crysb, Css2002, Cumbiagermen, Cyberviolin, DBombardier, DKqwerty, Da monster under your bed, Dan Fuhry, Daniel.Cardenas, Darkfight, David Edgar, Demostene, Dennispangcg, Deviator13, Diego Moya, Dinsintltd, Discospinster, Diza, Doja8437, Donbert, Doramjan, Downes, Dpark, DrPretto, Dreaded Walrus, Drewboy64, DropDeadGorgias, Dsg 430, Editor at Large, Editor2020, Edwin456, Eirik, Emma23 K, Encsoft, Eraserhead1, Escape Orbit, Espoo, Exe, Fairhursta, Fastguy397, FeldBum, Fermion, Fishnet37222, Flamingo2, FleetCommand, Flowanda, Forever Anonymous, Forresttsao, Fury, GOR42, GSL-Nathan, Gaius Cornelius, Galloglass, Garrett750, Gary King, GaryDunn808, GeneMosher, GeneralAntilles, Geologyguy, Georgehm3, Giftlite, Gogo Dodo, Golgofrinchian, Grant M, Gsarwa, Gyrferret, HAl, Hadal, HaeB, Haleron, Hanslicht, Harryboyles, Hatman22, Hdantman, Heat fan1, Heatlesssun, Hebrides, Hecticb, Helmuthva, Hemidemisemiquaver, Henryhartley, Hop77, Hu12, Iamthebob, Ike9898, Illuminatedwax, IlyaHaykinson, Imediacorporation, Imroy, Ionutpopa, Itharu, Itohacs, JFreeman, JaGa, Jacotto, Jaksmata, Jamesfed, Janto, Jason C.K., JasonAQuest, JayBaxter, JeffBurdges, Jeffrey Mall, Jehochman, Jerome Charles Potts, Jerryobject, JessieTurner, Jfowler27, Jgera5, Jhartmann, Jim.henderson, Jinnai, Jkanner, Jklsc, Jncraton, JohnSawyer, Johnsonbben, Jointless, JonHarder, JorgeGG, Josh the Nerd, Jriihi, Julesd, Jusdafax, KGasso, Kcomstock, KeloGitiM2, Kevin Beckman, Khflottorp, Kiand, Knipping, KnowledgeOfSelf, Knubbi, Koopa turtle, Kozuch, Kvdveer, Lanjoe9, Lankiveil, Launchpad 72, Laurinmail, Lester, Likelife, Linkspamremover, Litenghuan, Little Professor, Lord Pistachio, Lornova, Lovalle, Lupin, Lurker, Lynbarn, MER-C, Mac, Magiccarpetrider100000, Magog the Ogre, Mahjongg, Malibukai, Marcus Qwertyus, Mario CUSENZA, Markdl58, Marla 89, Martarius, Martinp23, Mastercampbell, Materialscientist, Maythammahdipour, Mcg3o, Merctio, Merusso, Mfolozi, MiGGim, Michael Hardy, Michael english, Michaelbusch, Micke, Midknightr, Mikael Häggström, Mike876, Minesweeper, Mini me, Minna Sora no Shita, Miranda, Mirek2, MirekDve, Mjflory, Mlshoe, MoChan, Mohammad7410, MrChupon, MrWhipple, Mrwojo, Mrzaius, Mulad, Myscrnnm, Mzajac, N1RK4UDSK714, Nabeth, Nagle, Nahferrari66, NeonMerlin, Newone, Nhirji, Nick, Ninjagecko, Nixdorf, Njan, Nneonneo, Nono64, Nopetro, NuclearWarfare, Nwusr123log, OlavN, Olecwiki, Olz06, Omegatron, PPGMD, PRRfan, Pak21, Pamlovely, PanSorKit3, PaperConfessional, Park70, Pat Yost, Paulkramer, Paxsimius, PenComputingPerson, Pennywisdom2099, Pentalis, Peteyuen, Petiatil, Pgk1, Phantomt, Phatom87, Philip Trueman, Pianohacker, Pinethicket, Pitalia, Pnm, Pol098, Porty, Powderfreak80, Prasannavigneshr, PseudoSudo, Psssstdana, Qsecofr, RW Marloe, Radon210, Raysonho, Reconsider the static, Redguard101, Rg.smit, Rgrof, Rhobite, Rich Farmbrough, Richard0612, Rjwilmsi, RobertG, Rockfang, Rockysmile11, RoyalWitCheese, Rpalmquist, Rwwww, S.K., SF007, SQ Minion, Salam32, Sandgem Addict, Saran456, Savvy47, ScooterSES, Searchme, Sen amitava, Seth Ilys, Sfmusicfan1, Shane Lawrence, Shawnc, Sheepunderscore, Shopfujitsu, SimonLyall, Simonrleung, SimsHsia, Sir Nicholas de Mimsy-Porpington, Skierpage, Skura Corporation, Slurslee, Snori, Snottywong, Societyalum, Spudtater, SpuriousQ, Ssggmm, Staus, Stellakatherine, Stephenb, Stephenchou0722, Steveoph, Stevevance, Succendo, Summitpark, Sunderland06, Sunnydigit, Sunnyquon, Sunroof, Superway25, TMV943, TabletKiosk Gail, Tabletpcccccccccc, Tankwan, Tarun2701, TastyPoutine, Tbonge, Tcncv, Techmdrn, Technobadger, Tellyaddict, TerriersFan, Terrillja, Tewdrig, Thatguyflint, TheTablet, Thealok, Thecurran91, Thejoshwolfe, Themfromspace, Thenature, Thumperward, Tide rolls, Timsdad, Tjhowse, Tntnnbltn, Tobych, TomTheHand, Totalwise, Toussaint, Tovarish, Toytoy, Travis.Thurston, Tyrol5, Uriber, Veryfaststuff, Victorpardosi, Vistafreak, Vivacissamamente, Vizion, Vorratt, Vyx, WNewquay, Waqas1987, Warren, WasAPasserBy, Wayiran, Whaa?, White 720, Whitebox, WikiSpector, Wikimachine, WikipedianYknOK, Wikitumnus, Wmahan, Woodsstock, WookieInHeat, Wumpus3000, Wwoods, Xep, Xpclient, Zachpw, Zepppep34, Zevemiel, Zigger, Zollerriia, Zouzzou, Zzuuzz, आशीष भटनागर, 1001 anonymous edits

**Tablet PC Input Panel** *Source*: http://en.wikipedia.org/w/index.php?oldid=406314216 *Contributors*: Gogo Dodo, RobertHelm, Umar1996, VernoWhitney, Xpclient

**TabletKiosk** *Source*: http://en.wikipedia.org/w/index.php?oldid=379090305 *Contributors*: Chowbok, CledusQ, Closedmouth, Eastmain, Findepi, Habanero-tan, Johnmanoahs, Kozuch, Protonk, Rjwilmsi, TabletKiosk Gail, Tabletpccccccccc, 3 anonymous edits

**Ultra-mobile PC** *Source*: http://en.wikipedia.org/w/index.php?oldid=428524372 *Contributors*: 3alowi99, A-Ge0, Agentguy, Ahoerstemeier, Alerante, AlistairMcMillan, Allentownpa, Altenmann, Amjoe, Anthony Appleyard, Aradit, Archerman2000, Aronzak, Arthena, Back ache, Barsoom79, Baumi, BenFrantzDale, Bjornstar, Borgx, Callidior, Ceccccccc, Chowbok, Chris the speller, Corevette, Cumbiagermen, Cynical, Dbmoore, Deathawk, Dekonega, DeluxNate, Diego Moya, DireWolf, Drange net, DropDeadGorgias, Ebreier, Electron9, Eptin, Error -128, Esperant, Espoo, FIGATT, Favonian, Flamingo2, Fleminra, Freedom to share, GeneralAntilles, Ghettoblaster, Giftlite, Goosnarrggh, Grafen, Grayshi, Haakon, Habanero-tan, Hankwang, Hemidemisemiquaver, Hightonumpc.cn, Jabencarsey, Jackwoodby, Jamesfed, Jared, JasePow1968, Jasonbrinks, Jchurch, Jeff G., JeffGr, JefferyTo, Jeremy Visser, Jerryobject, JohnnyUltra, Jopo, Jrleighton, KVDP, KimmyMarie, Kittyg, Kleinheero, Kozuch, Ksyrie, Lester, LightSpeed3, Ligulem, LilHelpa, Ling.Nut, Lusheeta, MER-C, MMuzammils, MN, Mac, Mahjongg, Martarius, Matt.Hoy, Mazin07, Modster, Moxfyre, Mr Beige, MySchizoBuddy, Nealmcb, Nicklinn, Nil0lab, Nzeemin, Of, On the other side, Original1, Overlord11001001, Parhamr, PenComputingPerson, Pendulumfan, PeteMuller, Petersam, Pgan002, Plier, Pol098, Poweroid, Programmerman, Psssstdana, Quadell, R'n'B, Ramu50, Randalllin, Retodon8, Rg.smit, Rich Farmbrough, Rick Browser, Rightofcenter, Rivkid007, Rodrigue, Rogerd, Ronz, RufusThorne, Russau, Ryan Norton, SagaciousAWB, SamJohnston, Shadow demon, Signalhead, Sjkim11, Skipahead, Slatedorg, Slickrick8, Sockatume, Soumyasch, Ssggmm, Stephenchou0722, Stepho-wrs, Steppres, Summitpark, TabletKiosk Gail, Tabletop, TerriersFan, Thatedeguy, TheCoffee, Thebrid, Themindset, Thorn van dee, Thoughtfix, Thrane, Thumperward, Tokek, Toussaint, Toytoy, Tradlos, Transisto, Traut, Treekids, Trescomplex, Truerock2, Ultraexactzz, Uncle Milty, VMlemon, Vandermude, Veinor, Visualclue, Waderockett, Wafulz, WazzaMan, Whatswith, Wiki fanatic, Wmahan, Woohookitty, Xquietlydyingx, Ykhwong, Zhuravskij, Zyboris, 387 anonymous edits

**Windows Journal** *Source*: http://en.wikipedia.org/w/index.php?oldid=425411508 *Contributors*: 54ggg, Android272, Bebo2good1, Dadu, Eastlaw, Edward, GoddersUK, J.delanoy, Plau, Rayloman, Steffen2, Stephenchou0722, Techmdrn, Tuanese, Uriel222, Warren, Xpclient, 16 anonymous edits

**Mobile operating system** *Source*: http://en.wikipedia.org/w/index.php?oldid=428544297 *Contributors*: A tumiwa, Adileader, Aleph Infinity, Alunphillips, Andries, Anna Lincoln, Aravindan Shanmugasundaram, Aurora317, Bender235, Bgkwtnyqhzor, Bongwarrior, Bounce1337, Cab88, CalumCook234, Caulde, Cdw1952, Cenora, Chmyr, Colonies Chris, DKqwerty, Darkguy, DaveChild, Diego Moya, DominiqueHazaelMassieux, Drench, Efa, Egil, Enterprise12, Eried, Erimaxbau, Evan-Amos, Ferritecore, Fiftyquid, Frap, Gabriel2008, Ghettoblaster, GoingBatty, Ham1000, Hopbit, Hypon888, IBoy2G, Illegal Operation, Immunmotbluescreen, Interframe, InternetMeme, Jack007, Jaz246, Jerryobject, John of Reading, Keith139, Kiore, Kotiyanimr, Kozuch, Lester, Lightmouse, MA LópezMolina, MER-C, Macungie, Mancini, Mc nacho, Mdwh, Megarhythm, Mike Restivo, N2e, Nekohan, Nemesis of Reason, NerdyScienceDude, Nono64, Oicur0t, Oscaroe, Over shown badn, PXUmais, Paraplegicemu, PieterDeBruijn, Rogernightman, Rothgar, Rwwww, Rzęsor, SF007, Sam4others, Shankarnikhil88, Solanki.3108, Solphusion, Spidermario, Stekse, Stichbury, The Anome, The RedBurn, TheWikiAuthor, Themfromspace, Thumperward, Ukexpat, VoluntarySlave, Wamp wamp, Wave4, Woohookitty, Wysprgr2005, Zarinfam, Zayani, 340 anonymous edits

**Linaro** *Source*: http://en.wikipedia.org/w/index.php?oldid=428445549 *Contributors*: Bearcat, Daemonic Kangaroo, Frap, FredCote, Hydriz, Jencastelino, JustAGal, Mortense, Nikai, 5 anonymous edits

**Maemo** *Source*: http://en.wikipedia.org/w/index.php?oldid=426537714 *Contributors*: 21655, Ahunt, Aisujin, AlexeySmirnov, Andypham3000, Animist, Apalsola, Are you ready for IPv6?, Azimout, Baron1984, Bdushaw, Bender235, Bgkwtnyqhzor, Biktora, Bluesubaru, Bobbed, Bounce1337, Brontide, Brtkrbzhnv, Bunnyhop11, C. A. Russell, CMBJ, Cameron Scott, Centrepull, Chealer, Chris Caven, Chris Ssk, Cshay, Cyclonenim, DJE, Davewho2, Debresser, Drpickem, Dumol, Durval, Ecobun, Efa, Elgaard, Emj, EnTerr, Erki der Loony, Erud, Faerloev, Fale, Fetchcomms, Frap, Fudoreaper, Gaborgulya, Gagravarr, GeneralAntilles, Gnulinux, Gomcoite, Grafen, GreenReaper, Gronky, Guyjohnston, Haakon, Hardaker, Herakleitoszefesu, IByte, Int21h, InternetMeme, Intgr, IvanLanin, JLaTondre, JaGa, Jake Wartenberg, Jamesmorrison, JasonWoof, Jeff3000, Jeremyb, Kedadi, Kesla, Khalid hassani, Kosebamse, Kozuch, Kwamikagami, LMB, Lester, Lkt1126, Llamabr, Lproven, Lrothc, Luke-Jr, MMuzammils, Mac, Mahjongg, Mandor, Mazin07, Medovina, Michapma, MishMich, Mohammad7410, Momet, Monkbel, Morte, Mortense, NealePickett, Neustradamus, Pacini409, Palosirkka, PanagosTheOther, Pawpawyoung, Pelago, Pete.Hurd, Petr Kopač, Piotrus, Ppavan1, Prashanthns, Predakanga, ProbablyX, Qgil, QwertyFP, R'n'B, Ramedar, Raul654, RaviC, Rchandra, Rebroad, Rich Farmbrough, Rjwilmsi, Rodhullandemu, Rosenbluh, Runtime, SEWilco, SF007, SRG275, Samwaltz, ShakataGaNai, Shelnutt2, Sigmundur, Silpol, Silver hr, Sjgadsby, Slon02, Somercet, Speculatrix, Spoon!, Squash Racket, SugarKane, Swadallal, TA-t3, The Anome, The Wednesday Island, TheParanoidOne, Thejapanesegeek, Thumperward, Tommy2010, Toniher, Torrg, Toussaint, Trbdavies, Trevor Marron, Twaelti, Typ932, UKER, Umptious, UnDeRTaKeR, Vadmium, Verdatum, WakiMiko, Wavelength, WegianWarrior, Wiktoryn, Woohookitty, Xeno, Xomm, YUL89YYZ, Yellowdesk, Yworo, Zyboris, 234 anonymous edits

**MeeGo** *Source*: http://en.wikipedia.org/w/index.php?oldid=427557665 *Contributors*: Ahunt, Alanthehat, Alisha.4m, Andrea09falco, Andries, Arielco, Astralbat, Avicennasis, AxelBoldt, Bender235, Boing! said Zebedee, Bzhb, C1010, Cameron Scott, ClamDip, Cliboub, Crysb, Cyberdiablo, Darxus, David Levy, Deineka, EagleEye96, Eeekster, Efa, Erkan Yilmaz, Firechris, Fishnet37222, Frap, Gamester17, Ganryuu, Gary King, Heroicrelics, Icaro, Jankratochvil, Jason24589, JenniferHeartsU, Jephir, Jhattara, Justin545, KAMiKAZOW, KDesk, Kinema, Kkm010, Kluebunny, LavrenovNN, Lester, Ltilve, MER-C, Maggu, Mamanel, Mcld, MesiLoKdiw2, Michi.bo, MishMich, Mlogic, Mudd1, Mugunth, Nameless23, Nisavid, NoisyMe, Ojdon, Palosirkka, Panscient, Ph.eyes, PieterDeBruijn, Propeng, R0m23, Reisio, Reonic, Rhe br, Rpyle731, Runtime, Sf5xeplus, Shimi.chen, Simon-in-sagamihara (usurped), Suwa, Tabletop, The Anome, Thrapper, Thumperward, Tmoll, Tohma, Tranter, Trbdavies, Tuxcantfly, Typ932, Ulric1313, Vacatalada, WakiMiko, Wikante, Wubuntu, Xomm, Yosh3000, 109 anonymous edits

**MotoMagx** *Source*: http://en.wikipedia.org/w/index.php?oldid=422880060 *Contributors*: AnchoDotto, CoolingGibbon, DEW3yl, Dangherous, DeltaSPARTAN003, IamPortuguese, InternetMeme, Kb, LilHelpa, Lucky 6.9, Mathiastck, Miss Saff, Mysdaao, Welsh, 22 anonymous edits

**Palm OS** *Source*: http://en.wikipedia.org/w/index.php?oldid=427422639 *Contributors*: 5ko, A Man In Black, A-giau, Ablivio, Adrianf, Ahoerstemeier, Alansohn, AlexPlank, AlistairMcMillan, Alunphillips, Amolkumar, Ancheta Wis, Andrewferrier, Armando, Baksanir, Bdesham, Bdr9, Bearda, Bobo192, Bonsai8, Breno, Bruce89, Buhlerh, C. A. Russell, C777, Caerwine, Cameron Scott, Can't sleep, clown will eat me, CaribDigita, Cdmarcus, Cellindo, Chadparker, Chmyr, Chowbok, Chris Roy, Computerjoe, CoolFox, Cooldudefx, CopperSquare, Corti, CraigTheBrit, Cwitty, CyberSkull, Cybercobra, D'Agosta, DARTH SIDIOUS 2, DJPiZaNt, Damian Yerrick, Dan100, David Hoeffer, DavidCary, Declark, Dcreemer, Deviceapps, Diadya vova, Djmutex, Dod1, Domiriel, Dougmerritt, Dukat74, Dysprosia, Eball, Ed Poor, Edcolins, Edward, Enchanter, Enfors, Enochlau, Eptin, Eric Jack Nash, Erik Zachte, Erkan Yilmaz, Erud, Eyetoeye, F-402, Faithlessthewonderboy, FlashSheridan, Frankdrebin, Frap, Friviere, Gaius Cornelius, Ghettoblaster, Gklka, Grafen, Greatwall98, Gurch, HDCase, Haakon, Hdante, Heron, Hgnsd, Hoshie, Hotmop, Hu12, Huji, Hydrofuran, Hydrox, Ilaiho, Illyria05, Imran22, Interiot, InternetMeme, Iridescent, Ishi Gustaedr, J00tel, J7, Jake6535, Jdlyall, Jerryobject, Joe Sewell, Joffeloff, John of Reading, Jordan Brown, Jparenti, Jshiell, Jtuttle, Jwdietrich2, Kaszeta, Kazvorpal, KelleyCook, Kim Moser, Kimiko, Kirkjerk, Kpr00, Krich, KrysKool, Kuru, KyraVixen, LC, Lafraia, Lambtron, Lawyer2b, Lbecque, Lcaa9, LeaveSleaves, Lester, Letdorf, Lochaber, Logan shaw, Lord Hawk, LorenzoB, LostLeviathan, LrdChaos, Luminus69, Luna Santin, MER-C, MSTCrow, Maba6803, Makaristos, Malik Shabazz, Mangoman88, Marcelo Huerta, Marknew, Martin451, Matt Keleher, MattTM, Maximus Rex, Mboverload, Meaningless, Michael B. Trausch, Mikeroodeus, Miracle Pen, Mordka, Mr. Mackie Mmkay, Mschlindwein, NHRHS2010, Nathanww, Natl1, Ngoodman, Nickcerda, Notbyworks, Oknazevad, Olivier, Orderud, Ozzieboy, Palmhandy, Pfc432, Pomakis, Psantora, Quickliger, Qyd, R'n'B, RProgrammer, Rchamberlain, RemitMan, Rettetast, Riadlem, Rich Farmbrough, Rick Block, Rjwilmsi, Rl, Robertre, Robofish, Rodneybf, Runtime, Sam Hocevar, Sanjuuro, Sdfisher, SearedIce, Shrish, SilasM, Simonfraser, Solipsist, Sprocket79, Squid tamer, Streamcipher, StyleTap, Surv1v4l1st, Syrthiss, TPK, Tabletop, Tamhanna, Taras, The Anome, The machine512, Themfromspace, Thumperward, Tobias Bergemann, Toby Bartels, Tomlouie, Tony Sidaway, Tonyho, Torritorri, Toytoy, Traroth, Trevalyx, Tuju, Urod, Uucp, Vaganyik, Veinor, Vespristiano, Wackymacs, Warren, Weevil, Wiki-do, Wikiborg, Wikiborg4711, Wmahan, Wysprgr2005, XtinaS, Yacht, Yamla, Yannick56, Yaronf, Ysangkok, Yuhong, Yworo, Zingus, Zipflash, Zundark, Zytsef, 376 anonymous edits

**Pilot-link** *Source*: http://en.wikipedia.org/w/index.php?oldid=407467064 *Contributors*: Baryonic Being, Bearcat, Diego Moya, Gioto, Santryl, Sdfisher, Xezbeth, 5 anonymous edits

**PlayStation Portable system software** *Source*: http://en.wikipedia.org/w/index.php?oldid=428094664 *Contributors*: 1wolfblake, A1a2s, ADR14N, ARC Gritt, Adam2893, Addict 2006, Aericanwizard, Ahmadzzz1, Akadewboy, Alex mayorga, Americanfreedom, Antimatter31, Awesomeness95, BasicXP, Bender235, Benlisquare, Blacksabbath990, Brady4mvp, BurstDragon, Calvin 1998, CaptnDan, Casper10, Catgut, Chocobogamer, Chowbok, Chris the speller, Chrsorlando, Daigaku2051, Damien2014, Dar-zero, Darren23, Dingyv03, EliasAlucard, Errorlines, Fantasydragon, Ffgamera, Fireblaster lyz, FoFiX 999, Fratrep, FredStrauss, GSK, Haseo9999, Hda3ku, Hounder4, Hyde101, Iamcool234, Illnab1024, Isidore, J.delanoy, Jack Masamune, Jckenny, Jhdroque, Jheinz, John-joe123, Joriel1995, Junkcops, Karlhendrikse, Katoh, KeN JaX, KiasuKiasiMan, Konradek, Kozmefulanito, Kyrios320, Locke Cole, LordOfPuppets, MOBIUS 876, Mad lion, Mark260591, Megamanfan3, Mozzy92, Mrinck, Musicomputer, Myscrnnm, Nascar360, Nnickn, O keyes, Oni Lukos, Oscarthecat, OutRider2003, Pavel.nps, Polaralex, Psantora, Roadstaa, SchfiftyThree, ShinraiTS4, Silver Edge, Simeon24601, T-borg, THEemu, Tails0600, Terebigemuwan, Thingg, Tilen Lesjak, Tobz1000, Toehead2001, Toxicroak, TravKoolBreeze, Uaqboost, Vereux0, Vitz-RS, W Tanoto, WikiCats, Wysprgr2005, Yafai jordan, Yousou, 467 anonymous edits

**Series 30 (software platform)** *Source*: http://en.wikipedia.org/w/index.php?oldid=415938305 *Contributors*: Blakegripling ph, Jeff Song, Lkt1126, 2 anonymous edits

**Series 40** *Source*: http://en.wikipedia.org/w/index.php?oldid=428542251 *Contributors*: Agreimann, Alex Perry, Aniac, Ashrutisingh, Azuya, Bjelleklang, Blakegripling ph, Calltech, Canaima, Centrx, Chapzboy, Charivari, Cnj, Daverocks, Diwas, Djlarz, Djr xi, Dktz, Dublinclontarf, Elspif, Ettrig, Evilboy, Flod logic, Florin92, Gaius Cornelius, Hjorten, Imroy, JLaTondre, Jasonon, Jesjimher, LordBen5000, MMuzammils, Milan292208, Monkeyhousetim, Msulik, Petri Krohn, Rich Farmbrough, Rlobkovsky, Roleplayer, Rudiedude, Rwwww, SimonMenashy, The Seventh Taylor, TheParanoidOne, Tirkfl, UKER, Vegaswikian, We hope, Xkury, ZeroOne, Zhernovoi, 90 anonymous edits

**Smarterphone** *Source*: http://en.wikipedia.org/w/index.php?oldid=420469924 *Contributors*: Ben Ben, Guppie, Rjwilmsi, Suborbital, 1 anonymous edits

**Smeegol Linux** *Source*: http://en.wikipedia.org/w/index.php?oldid=414908089 *Contributors*: Gamester17, 5 anonymous edits

**Symbian Foundation** *Source*: http://en.wikipedia.org/w/index.php?oldid=427557287 *Contributors*: Armando, Bambinetta, Cameron Scott, CapitalLetterBeginning, CaribDigita, Chowbok, Cybercobra, Cynical, DenisKrivosheev, DmitryKo, Dopetimes, Drbreznjev, EdH, Exonie, Ghettoblaster, Ianweston, Imcdnzl, J.H. McAleely, JonForst6, Jontintinjordan, Karan.102, Kozuch, Lester, Liftarn, LindfK, MMuzammils, Mabdul, Maju wiki, Mathiastck, Nature4567a, Pgan002, Rangoon11, SPKirsch, Sanremofilo, Stichbury, Tedats, The real cirrus, VMlemon, Woohookitty, Yosh3000, Yworo, ZirconiumTwice, 83 anonymous edits

**Symbian** *Source*: http://en.wikipedia.org/w/index.php?oldid=427164040 *Contributors*: AJ-India, Ahmadadam96, Airplaneman, Andries, Apdevries, Arbitrarily0, Armando, Arnaud92, Aymen ka, B0o-supermario, BD2412, Belastro, Bpringlemeir, Brianreading, BrideOfKripkenstein, Capdor, CapitalLetterBeginning, Ceancata, Clsin, Cyberdiablo, Daniel.Cardenas, DarwinPeacock, Davidjcole, Digitalsurgeon, DmitryKo, Edward, Elephant in a tornado, Empty Buffer, Erianna, Fences and windows, Ferrero777, Fetchcomms, FireyFly, Florin92, Freddiegjertsen, Fru1tbat, Gene91, Gmihaylo, Gryllida, Gsarwa, Haakon, Hersfold, Hoshie, Hu12, IJK Principle, Imcdnzl, Intractable, JaGa, Jaizovic, Jayantanth, Jeffrey04, Jerryobject, Jfourgeaud, Jfromcanada, Jondoelocksmith, Jwoodger, Kinema, Krashlandon, Krischik, LemChops, Lester, Ligertail, Ltomuta, Magister Mathematicae, Martarius, Mdwh, Micahblitz, Minikola, Mnia786, Muhandes, Myscrnnm, Narasimhanator, Nate1481, Notedgrant, OlEnglish, Parthibls, Pnm, Pol098, Polluks, Ponydepression, R'n'B, Rabit gti, Reboot, Sainath468, Seth Nimbosa, Sharcho, Shrish, SoWhy, Soulxlight, Soumilj, Stichbury, Surya Prakash.S.A., Thumperward, Timotheus Canens, Tirim4, Tomjenkins52, Truth Lover80, UKER, VMlemon, Vervamon, Vishnunj, Wattyirl, Weeder 001, Yavoh, Zagothal, ZeroOne, ZirconiumTwice, Zvrkljati, 170 anonymous edits

**webOS** *Source*: http://en.wikipedia.org/w/index.php?oldid=428234108 *Contributors*: ACupOfCoffee, Addihockey10, Agent2x0r, Aguy likeme, Ahunt, Akitayo, Akral, Amikael, Andrewrp, Andries, AniRaptor2001, Anilo, AshwiniKalantri, Astral highway, Avicennasis, B64, BD2412, Barsoomian, Beao, Ben Ben, Bender235, Blastoboy1000, Bshedwick, ByteMaster0, Calimo, Cameron Scott, Cap'n Refsmmat, Charles Matthews, Choster, Chowbok, Chris the speller, CommonsDelinker, CopperSquare, Cupy 52040, Cwhii, CyberSkull, Cybercobra, Cyrus Grisham, Daggerbox, Decora, DennisIsMe, Diadya vova, Dndk82, Doramjan, Drmies, Droll, Drunauthorized, Drybones5, Dukat74, Eddiekuns, Enigmaticland, Enquire, EoGuy, Ercrt, Erebus555, Escape Orbit, Eugenian, FeatherPluma, Forteblast, Fragglet, Gazpacho, Ghettoblaster, Gilo1969, Golftheman, Heat fan1, Hedge777, Hombrelobo, Hroðulf, Husond, Ian Dalziel, Ixfd64, J, JLRedperson, JLaTondre, JW1805, Jeff Wheeler, Jeff3000, Jhessela, Joe Sewell, Joffeloff, Johann Wolfgang, John of Reading, John85, JohnLBurger, JohnPritchard, Johnio25, Jæs, KAMiKAZOW, Kareshka, Kenny goo, Kkm010, Kozuch, Kragnerac, Kranux, Ktotam, Kyro, Lambiam, Le Enfente Orange, Legacysho, Lester, Lookatmygrlyfont, M6ixty2wo, MER-C, Magnesium, Mangoman88, Mathmo, MichaelAaronson, Midgetman433, Milominderbinder2, Mohanbharath, Moocha, Nblschool, NeaNita, Newsboy85, Nnh, Nyco, OlavN, PLA y Grande Covián, PS2pcGAMER, Patcat88, Phyburn, PizzaMan, Psantora, Rat2, Ringbang, Robertholf, Rrob13, S1312, Shawalli, Shervin, Silas S. Brown, Sinistrum, Skierpage, SoWhy, Solbu, Sunborn, Taka76, Tedpersson, The godfaza, TheParanoidOne, Thecurran91, Thumperward, Toehead2001, Trigatch4, TunaSushi, Typhoon, Uncle Dick, Waltonkbbl, Warren, Whaledad, William.stryker.08, Woohookitty, Wysprgr2005, Yannick56, Yrithinnd, Zweinstein, 小莠特立, 283 anonymous edits

**Comparison of ARM tablets** *Source*: http://en.wikipedia.org/w/index.php?oldid=425229063 *Contributors*: Adammw, BD2412, Dellagustin, GoingBatty, Hakimio, Jeroesch, Jerryobject, Kozuch, Mesfin, TMV943, Tabletop, TheIguana, TomorrowsDream, Tony Sidaway, Zyboris, 25 anonymous edits

# Image Sources, Licenses and Contributors

**File:IFA 2010 Internationale Funkausstellung Berlin 03.JPG** *Source*: http://en.wikipedia.org/w/index.php?title=File:IFA_2010_Internationale_Funkausstellung_Berlin_03.JPG *License*: Creative Commons Attribution-Sharealike 3.0 *Contributors*: User:Bin im Garten

**File:IFA 2010 Internationale Funkausstellung Berlin 18.JPG** *Source*: http://en.wikipedia.org/w/index.php?title=File:IFA_2010_Internationale_Funkausstellung_Berlin_18.JPG *License*: Creative Commons Attribution-Sharealike 3.0 *Contributors*: User:Bin im Garten

**Image:人-order.gif** *Source*: http://en.wikipedia.org/w/index.php?title=File:人-order.gif *License*: unknown *Contributors*: Aotake, Sarang, Swift, Wikic

**Image:人-red.png** *Source*: http://en.wikipedia.org/w/index.php?title=File:人-red.png *License*: unknown *Contributors*: Sarang, Ymursal, Yug

**File:Lenovo-X61-Tablet-Mode.jpg** *Source*: http://en.wikipedia.org/w/index.php?title=File:Lenovo-X61-Tablet-Mode.jpg *License*: Public Domain *Contributors*: Ahmed Musa

**File:N800 frontside2.jpg** *Source*: http://en.wikipedia.org/w/index.php?title=File:N800_frontside2.jpg *License*: Public Domain *Contributors*: Zxc

**File:IPad in Case.jpg** *Source*: http://en.wikipedia.org/w/index.php?title=File:IPad_in_Case.jpg *License*: Creative Commons Attribution 2.0 *Contributors*: Yutaka Tsutano

**File:Xo3-fuse-2.jpg** *Source*: http://en.wikipedia.org/w/index.php?title=File:Xo3-fuse-2.jpg *License*: Creative Commons Attribution 2.5 *Contributors*: laptop.org

**File:ARCHOS 43 it front.jpg** *Source*: http://en.wikipedia.org/w/index.php?title=File:ARCHOS_43_it_front.jpg *License*: unknown *Contributors*: GreenZeb, We hope

**File:Archos 70.jpg** *Source*: http://en.wikipedia.org/w/index.php?title=File:Archos_70.jpg *License*: unknown *Contributors*: GreenZeb, Redsox42311, We hope

**File:2008Computex ASUS Eee Box white with customized skin.jpg** *Source*: http://en.wikipedia.org/w/index.php?title=File:2008Computex_ASUS_Eee_Box_white_with_customized_skin.jpg *License*: unknown *Contributors*: User:BrockF5

**File:ASUS Eee White Alt.jpg** *Source*: http://en.wikipedia.org/w/index.php?title=File:ASUS_Eee_White_Alt.jpg *License*: Creative Commons Attribution 3.0 *Contributors*: Original uploader was Red at en.wikipedia

**File:2008 Taichung IT Month Day2 ASUS Eee Top.jpg** *Source*: http://en.wikipedia.org/w/index.php?title=File:2008_Taichung_IT_Month_Day2_ASUS_Eee_Top.jpg *License*: unknown *Contributors*: User:BrockF5

**File:2008Computex ASUS Eee Stick red.jpg** *Source*: http://en.wikipedia.org/w/index.php?title=File:2008Computex_ASUS_Eee_Stick_red.jpg *License*: unknown *Contributors*: User:BrockF5

**File:Entourage eDGe pinch jeh.jpg** *Source*: http://en.wikipedia.org/w/index.php?title=File:Entourage_eDGe_pinch_jeh.jpg *License*: Creative Commons Zero *Contributors*: User:Jim.henderson

**Image:ExoPC-Color-Logo.png** *Source*: http://en.wikipedia.org/w/index.php?title=File:ExoPC-Color-Logo.png *License*: unknown *Contributors*: Jacques Desplant

**Image:2001interview.jpg** *Source*: http://en.wikipedia.org/w/index.php?title=File:2001interview.jpg *License*: unknown *Contributors*: Cholmes75, Diego Moya, Jason Palpatine, Luigibob, Melesse, Nehrams2020, NuclearWarfare, Skier Dude

**File:iPad wordmark.svg** *Source*: http://en.wikipedia.org/w/index.php?title=File:IPad_wordmark.svg *License*: Public Domain *Contributors*: Apple

**File:1stGen-iPad-HomeScreen.jpg** *Source*: http://en.wikipedia.org/w/index.php?title=File:1stGen-iPad-HomeScreen.jpg *License*: unknown *Contributors*: User:Evan-Amos

**File:Steve Jobs with the Apple iPad no logo (cropped).jpg** *Source*: http://en.wikipedia.org/w/index.php?title=File:Steve_Jobs_with_the_Apple_iPad_no_logo_(cropped).jpg *License*: Creative Commons Attribution 2.0 *Contributors*: matt buchanan

**File:IPad 2 White Front.jpg** *Source*: http://en.wikipedia.org/w/index.php?title=File:IPad_2_White_Front.jpg *License*: unknown *Contributors*: User:Mono

**File:64 GB iPad underside 1.JPG** *Source*: http://en.wikipedia.org/w/index.php?title=File:64_GB_iPad_underside_1.JPG *License*: Creative Commons Attribution-Sharealike 3.0 *Contributors*: User:BrokenSphere

**File:IPad 2 Smart Cover at unveiling crop.jpg** *Source*: http://en.wikipedia.org/w/index.php?title=File:IPad_2_Smart_Cover_at_unveiling_crop.jpg *License*: Creative Commons Attribution 2.0 *Contributors*: Robert Scoble

**File:1st-Gen-iPad-WiFi-iBooks.jpg** *Source*: http://en.wikipedia.org/w/index.php?title=File:1st-Gen-iPad-WiFi-iBooks.jpg *License*: Public Domain *Contributors*: User:Evan-Amos

**File:iPad 2.svg** *Source*: http://en.wikipedia.org/w/index.php?title=File:IPad_2.svg *License*: unknown *Contributors*: Apple Inc.. Original uploader was Humphreys7 at en.wikipedia

**File:IPad 2 speaker.jpg** *Source*: http://en.wikipedia.org/w/index.php?title=File:IPad_2_speaker.jpg *License*: Creative Commons Attribution 2.0 *Contributors*: Robert Scoble

**File:IPad 2 Smart Cover at unveiling.jpg** *Source*: http://en.wikipedia.org/w/index.php?title=File:IPad_2_Smart_Cover_at_unveiling.jpg *License*: Creative Commons Attribution 2.0 *Contributors*: Robert Scoble

**File:Motorola Xoom.jpg** *Source*: http://en.wikipedia.org/w/index.php?title=File:Motorola_Xoom.jpg *License*: Creative Commons Attribution 2.0 *Contributors*: Ben Miller

**Image:India-35-dollar-tablet.png** *Source*: http://en.wikipedia.org/w/index.php?title=File:India-35-dollar-tablet.png *License*: Creative Commons Attribution-Sharealike 3.0 *Contributors*: User:Virtualage

**Image:Indian Rupee symbol.svg** *Source*: http://en.wikipedia.org/w/index.php?title=File:Indian_Rupee_symbol.svg *License*: unknown *Contributors*: User:Orionist

**File:Toshiba tablet 1.JPG** *Source*: http://en.wikipedia.org/w/index.php?title=File:Toshiba_tablet_1.JPG *License*: unknown *Contributors*: cnet

**File:Green check.svg** *Source*: http://en.wikipedia.org/w/index.php?title=File:Green_check.svg *License*: Public Domain *Contributors*: User:gmaxwell

**File:Red x.svg** *Source*: http://en.wikipedia.org/w/index.php?title=File:Red_x.svg *License*: Public Domain *Contributors*: User:David Levy, User:Gmaxwell

**Image:Tablet.jpg** *Source*: http://en.wikipedia.org/w/index.php?title=File:Tablet.jpg *License*: Public Domain *Contributors*: Janto Dreijer

**Image:EO Communicator 440-880.jpg** *Source*: http://en.wikipedia.org/w/index.php?title=File:EO_Communicator_440-880.jpg *License*: Public Domain *Contributors*: Original uploader was Wbvanrij at en.wikipedia

**Image:Eo-kindle.jpg** *Source*: http://en.wikipedia.org/w/index.php?title=File:Eo-kindle.jpg *License*: Creative Commons Attribution-Sharealike 3.0 *Contributors*: Colin Warwick aka Woz2

**Image:TC1100-1.JPG** *Source*: http://en.wikipedia.org/w/index.php?title=File:TC1100-1.JPG *License*: Public Domain *Contributors*: Original uploader was Jfowler27 at en.wikipedia

**Image:Tc1100-2.JPG** *Source*: http://en.wikipedia.org/w/index.php?title=File:Tc1100-2.JPG *License*: Public Domain *Contributors*: Original uploader was Jfowler27 at en.wikipedia

**Image:Hp touchsmart.jpg** *Source*: http://en.wikipedia.org/w/index.php?title=File:Hp_touchsmart.jpg *License*: Creative Commons Attribution 2.0 *Contributors*: DBegley (Flickr user)

**Image:Touchsmart pc.jpg** *Source*: http://en.wikipedia.org/w/index.php?title=File:Touchsmart_pc.jpg *License*: Creative Commons Attribution 2.0 *Contributors*: DBegley (Flickr user)

**File:HP TouchSmart trade.jpg** *Source*: http://en.wikipedia.org/w/index.php?title=File:HP_TouchSmart_trade.jpg *License*: Creative Commons Attribution-Sharealike 2.0 *Contributors*: mgminthu

**File:HP tm2 laptop.jpg** *Source*: http://en.wikipedia.org/w/index.php?title=File:HP_tm2_laptop.jpg *License*: unknown *Contributors*: SF007, Skier Dude2, We hope

**File: HTC Flyer Front View.png** *Source*: http://en.wikipedia.org/w/index.php?title=File:HTC_Flyer_Front_View.png *License*: unknown *Contributors*: Horizonsperson, Sfan00 IMG

**File:Xo3-fuse-4.jpg** *Source*: http://en.wikipedia.org/w/index.php?title=File:Xo3-fuse-4.jpg *License*: Creative Commons Attribution 2.5 *Contributors*: laptop.org

**Image:Pepperpad2.jpg** *Source*: http://en.wikipedia.org/w/index.php?title=File:Pepperpad2.jpg *License*: Creative Commons Attribution-Sharealike 2.0 *Contributors*: Original uploader was Tomhannen at en.wikipedia

**Image:SIP.PNG** *Source*: http://en.wikipedia.org/w/index.php?title=File:SIP.PNG *License*: unknown *Contributors*: User:Malloth

**Image:SIP2.PNG** *Source*: http://en.wikipedia.org/w/index.php?title=File:SIP2.PNG *License*: unknown *Contributors*: Malloth

**Image:SIP3.PNG** *Source*: http://en.wikipedia.org/w/index.php?title=File:SIP3.PNG *License*: unknown *Contributors*: Malloth

**File:Tablet.jpg** *Source*: http://en.wikipedia.org/w/index.php?title=File:Tablet.jpg *License*: Public Domain *Contributors*: Janto Dreijer

**Image:Tablet PC Input Panel handwriting.png** *Source*: http://en.wikipedia.org/w/index.php?title=File:Tablet_PC_Input_Panel_handwriting.png *License*: unknown *Contributors*: Umar1996

**Image:Tablet PC Input Panel ocr.png** *Source*: http://en.wikipedia.org/w/index.php?title=File:Tablet_PC_Input_Panel_ocr.png *License*: unknown *Contributors*: Umar1996

**Image:MathInputPanel win7.png** *Source*: http://en.wikipedia.org/w/index.php?title=File:MathInputPanel_win7.png *License*: unknown *Contributors*: Umar1996

**File:Wibrain B1 UMPC.jpg** *Source*: http://en.wikipedia.org/w/index.php?title=File:Wibrain_B1_UMPC.jpg *License*: Creative Commons Attribution 2.0 *Contributors*: VIA Gallery from Hsintien, Taiwan

**Image:UMPC Samsung-Q1-Ultra.JPG** *Source*: http://en.wikipedia.org/w/index.php?title=File:UMPC_Samsung-Q1-Ultra.JPG *License*: Creative Commons Attribution-Sharealike 2.5 *Contributors*: User:Coaster J

**Image:Windows Journal Viewer Icon.png** *Source*: http://en.wikipedia.org/w/index.php?title=File:Windows_Journal_Viewer_Icon.png *License*: unknown *Contributors*: GoddersUK, Postdlf, The coast holds, Tuanese

**Image:Windows Journal.png** *Source*: http://en.wikipedia.org/w/index.php?title=File:Windows_Journal.png *License*: unknown *Contributors*: User:stephenchou0722

**Image:Mobile os.png** *Source*: http://en.wikipedia.org/w/index.php?title=File:Mobile_os.png *License*: Creative Commons Attribution-Sharealike 3.0 *Contributors*: Darkguy

**File:Smartphone_share_current.png** *Source*: http://en.wikipedia.org/w/index.php?title=File:Smartphone_share_current.png *License*: GNU Free Documentation License *Contributors*: --Eraserhead1 <talk> 12:49, 3 March 2010 (UTC) Graph created by myself. Original uploader was Eraserhead1 at en.wikipedia

**File:IPad-WiFi-1stGen.jpg** *Source*: http://en.wikipedia.org/w/index.php?title=File:IPad-WiFi-1stGen.jpg *License*: Public Domain *Contributors*: User:Evan-Amos

**File:Palm-pre-webos-lg.png** *Source*: http://en.wikipedia.org/w/index.php?title=File:Palm-pre-webos-lg.png *License*: unknown *Contributors*: Beao, Meand, We hope

**File:Maemo logo color.svg** *Source*: http://en.wikipedia.org/w/index.php?title=File:Maemo_logo_color.svg *License*: unknown *Contributors*: maemo.org-Projekt

**File:Maemo5-screenshot.png** *Source*: http://en.wikipedia.org/w/index.php?title=File:Maemo5-screenshot.png *License*: unknown *Contributors*: Slon02

**Image:OpenOffice Writer in Maemo 5.jpg** *Source*: http://en.wikipedia.org/w/index.php?title=File:OpenOffice_Writer_in_Maemo_5.jpg *License*: Attribution *Contributors*: Closedmouth, Mandor

**Image:Maemo desktop.jpg** *Source*: http://en.wikipedia.org/w/index.php?title=File:Maemo_desktop.jpg *License*: GNU General Public License *Contributors*: User:RaviC

**Image:Itos 2006 dates.jpg** *Source*: http://en.wikipedia.org/w/index.php?title=File:Itos_2006_dates.jpg *License*: GNU General Public License *Contributors*: Original uploader was GeneralAntilles at en.wikipedia

**Image:Itos 2007 desktop.jpg** *Source*: http://en.wikipedia.org/w/index.php?title=File:Itos_2007_desktop.jpg *License*: GNU General Public License *Contributors*: Original uploader was GeneralAntilles at en.wikipedia

**Image:Itos 2008 desktop.jpg** *Source*: http://en.wikipedia.org/w/index.php?title=File:Itos_2008_desktop.jpg *License*: GNU General Public License *Contributors*: Original uploader was GeneralAntilles at en.wikipedia

**Image:Maemo5-screenshot.png** *Source*: http://en.wikipedia.org/w/index.php?title=File:Maemo5-screenshot.png *License*: unknown *Contributors*: Slon02

**File:MeeGo logo.svg** *Source*: http://en.wikipedia.org/w/index.php?title=File:MeeGo_logo.svg *License*: GNU Lesser General Public License *Contributors*: This is a logo owned by the Linux Foundation for representing the MeeGo operating system.

**File:Meego netbook ui.jpg** *Source*: http://en.wikipedia.org/w/index.php?title=File:Meego_netbook_ui.jpg *License*: GNU Free Documentation License *Contributors*: Intel Nokia Meego

**Image:meego-handset-launcher.png** *Source*: http://en.wikipedia.org/w/index.php?title=File:Meego-handset-launcher.png *License*: Apache *Contributors*: Nokia and Intel

**File:MeeGo Tablet Computex 2010.png** *Source*: http://en.wikipedia.org/w/index.php?title=File:MeeGo_Tablet_Computex_2010.png *License*: GNU General Public License *Contributors*: MeeGo developers (software) / Blender Institute ("Big Buck Bunny" trailer)

**File:Meego-ivi-1.1-home.png** *Source*: http://en.wikipedia.org/w/index.php?title=File:Meego-ivi-1.1-home.png *License*: GNU Lesser General Public License *Contributors*: Intel

**File:Meego_Architecture.jpg** *Source*: http://en.wikipedia.org/w/index.php?title=File:Meego_Architecture.jpg *License*: GNU Free Documentation License *Contributors*: Intel

**File:MeeGo_Roadmap.jpg** *Source*: http://en.wikipedia.org/w/index.php?title=File:MeeGo_Roadmap.jpg *License*: GNU Free Documentation License *Contributors*: Intel

**Image:Palm-m505.jpg** *Source*: http://en.wikipedia.org/w/index.php?title=File:Palm-m505.jpg *License*: Public Domain *Contributors*: Original uploader was Coplan at en.wikipedia

**Image:Palmaddybook41.png** *Source*: http://en.wikipedia.org/w/index.php?title=File:Palmaddybook41.png *License*: unknown *Contributors*: Hoshie, 1 anonymous edits

**Image:Palmcalc41.png** *Source*: http://en.wikipedia.org/w/index.php?title=File:Palmcalc41.png *License*: unknown *Contributors*: Hoshie, 1 anonymous edits

**Image:Palmdatebook41.png** *Source*: http://en.wikipedia.org/w/index.php?title=File:Palmdatebook41.png *License*: unknown *Contributors*: Hoshie, 1 anonymous edits

**Image:Palm hotsync.png** *Source*: http://en.wikipedia.org/w/index.php?title=File:Palm_hotsync.png *License*: unknown *Contributors*: EagleOne, Sdfisher, Wackymacs, 1 anonymous edits

**Image:Palmmemopad53.png** *Source*: http://en.wikipedia.org/w/index.php?title=File:Palmmemopad53.png *License*: unknown *Contributors*: Taras

**Image:Palmtodo41.png** *Source*: http://en.wikipedia.org/w/index.php?title=File:Palmtodo41.png *License*: unknown *Contributors*: Hoshie, 1 anonymous edits

**Image:Palmnotes41.png** *Source*: http://en.wikipedia.org/w/index.php?title=File:Palmnotes41.png *License*: unknown *Contributors*: Hoshie, 1 anonymous edits

**Image:PSPSLIMMODELNUMBER.gif** *Source*: http://en.wikipedia.org/w/index.php?title=File:PSPSLIMMODELNUMBER.gif *License*: unknown *Contributors*: Sony

**Image:PSPBRITEMODELNUMBER.gif** *Source*: http://en.wikipedia.org/w/index.php?title=File:PSPBRITEMODELNUMBER.gif *License*: unknown *Contributors*: Sony

**Image:PSPGOMODELNUMBER.gif** *Source*: http://en.wikipedia.org/w/index.php?title=File:PSPGOMODELNUMBER.gif *License*: unknown *Contributors*: Sony

**File:Nokia1600 01.jpg** *Source*: http://en.wikipedia.org/w/index.php?title=File:Nokia1600_01.jpg *License*: Creative Commons Attribution-Sharealike 2.5 *Contributors*: User:Dzoker

**Image:Nokia 6300.jpg** *Source*: http://en.wikipedia.org/w/index.php?title=File:Nokia_6300.jpg *License*: Public Domain *Contributors*: Original uploader was Racklever at en.wikipedia

**File:Vibo 2.jpg** *Source*: http://en.wikipedia.org/w/index.php?title=File:Vibo_2.jpg *License*: Creative Commons Attribution-Sharealike 3.0 *Contributors*: User:Suborbital

**File:Symbian logo 4.svg** *Source*: http://en.wikipedia.org/w/index.php?title=File:Symbian_logo_4.svg *License*: unknown *Contributors*: Fetchcomms, Lester

**Image:Nokia C6-01.jpg** *Source*: http://en.wikipedia.org/w/index.php?title=File:Nokia_C6-01.jpg *License*: unknown *Contributors*: Pboy2k5, We hope

**File:webOS logo.svg** *Source*: http://en.wikipedia.org/w/index.php?title=File:WebOS_logo.svg *License*: unknown *Contributors*: AshwiniKalantri, JohnnyMrNinja, Sfan00 IMG

**File:Palmcards 2010-12-07 101125.png** *Source*: http://en.wikipedia.org/w/index.php?title=File:Palmcards_2010-12-07_101125.png *License*: unknown *Contributors*: Melesse, S1312, Wysprgr2005

# License

CPSIA information can be obtained at www.ICGtesting.com
Printed in the USA
LVOW131852090112

263061LV00003BA/5/P